Quiché Rebelde:
Religious Conversion, Politics, and Ethnic Identity
in Guatemala

LLILAS Translations from Latin America Series

Quiché Rebelde:

Religious Conversion, Politics, and Ethnic Identity in Guatemala

By Ricardo Falla

Translated by Phillip Berryman

With a new foreword by Richard N. Adams
and a new epilogue by the author

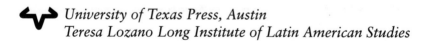
University of Texas Press, Austin
Teresa Lozano Long Institute of Latin American Studies

This book was originally published in 1978 as *Quiché Rebelde: Estudio de un movimiento de conversión religiosa, rebelde a las creencias tradicionales, en San Antonio Ilotenango, Quiché (1948–1970)*. Copyright © 1978, Editorial Universitaria de Guatemala.

Translation copyright © 2001 by the University of Texas Press
All rights reserved
Printed in the United States of America

First University of Texas Press Edition, 2001

Requests for permission to reproduce material from this work should be sent to Permissions, University of Texas Press, P.O. Box 7819, Austin, Texas 78713-7819

∞ The paper used in this publication meets the minimum requirements of American National Standard for Information Sciences—Permanence of Paper for Printed Library Materials, ANSI Z39.48–1984.

Library of Congress Cataloging-in-Publication Data

Falla, Ricardo.
    [Quiché rebelde. English]
    Quiché rebelde : religious conversion, politics, and ethnic identity in Guatemala / by Ricardo Falla ; translated by Phillip Berryman ; with a new foreword by Richard N. Adams and a new epilogue by the author.— 1ˢᵗ University of Texas Press ed.
        p. cm. — (LLILAS Translations from Latin America series)
    Includes bibliographical references (p.) and index.
    ISBN 0-292-72531-0 (alk. paper) — ISBN 0-292-72532-9 (pbk. : alk. paper)
    1. Quiché Indians—Religion. 2. Catholic action—Guatemala—Quiché. 3. Conversion. 4. Catholic Church—Guatemala—Quiché. I. Title. II. Series.

F1465.2Q5 F3513 2001
200'.97281'72—dc21
            2001049136

Contents

Foreword

The author of this book is remarkable in many respects. He is one of the most prolific Guatemalan social anthropologists at work today.[1] His work as a Catholic priest combined with scholarly research has yielded much new knowledge on Central America and neighboring Mexico. It also produced one of the most telling and important works in Guatemalan anthropology, *Masacres de la selva*, a detailed account of civilians under attack in a revolutionary context. It necessarily earned him the deep enmity of Guatemalan military authorities, who accused him of being a *guerrillero*—they dubbed him Comandante Marcos—as well as, subsequently, the Martin Diskin Award granted by Oxfam and the Latin American Studies Association.

From the outset, Ricardo Falla's anthropological interests were an adjunct to his work as a priest. He pursued graduate training as part of a group of Central American Jesuits who wanted to bring a higher level of scholarly competence to their work and to build a stronger capacity for social research in the region. In the late 1960s, Falla and his colleagues were active in the development of a social research program in the new Universidad Rafael Landívar in Guatemala City. After finishing his dissertation in the early 1970s, Falla, along with his Jesuit colleagues, was dedicated to consciousness raising in Central Guatemala and investigated political participation and election fraud. During the next two decades he carried out and directed research in Guatemala on the south coast, in the Ixcán, in the northwest Mexican border region, in the entire Franja Transversal, as well as in El Salvador, Nicaragua, Panama, and Honduras.

Since the arrival of the Spaniards in the sixteenth century, the Maya population of Guatemala—a community of which is the central subject of this study— has adapted to extraordinary challenges. Having survived the biological holocaust that followed the Spanish conquest, reducing their population by perhaps 90 percent, the Maya society has now surpassed its preconquest numbers, while contributing to the generation of the so-called ladino society of Guatemala. They adapted to the imposition of the Catholic religion, a colonial exercise requiring indigenous peoples to change what they were doing but denying them critical choices in that change. The Spanish colonial policy was to maintain control for purposes of tribute, production, and labor. For the Indians, the problem was to change enough to satisfy the more vital demands of the Spaniards while resisting those not absolutely necessary for their survival under the colonial regime. For four centuries the Maya Indians adapted and re-adapted, applying their understanding of the world to the realities they confronted daily. Although the centuries of submission to Spanish colonial and republican authorities destroyed much of their pre-Columbian culture and wrought major changes in their way of life, the Maya have rigorously regenerated their self-identity and reworked their culture to cope with the new realities that are constantly challenging them.

Falla studied a recent phase in this long evolution, focusing on how one Maya community, San Antonio Ilotenango, used religion as a major tool of adaptation to the changing world. He picks up the story early in the nineteenth century, but concentrates on what happened between the 1930s and the early 1970s. He shows how the process that has become known as "globalization" required that the people of San Antonio change not only their way of dealing with the generally hostile political world of the non-Indians and the Guatemalan state but also their plan for living and their vision of themselves.

Although the history was not smooth, the Catholic Church still worked in some harmony with the Guatemalan state until the reforms of the 1870s. These reforms ended the growth of the Catholic clergy, eliminated the land-based power of the church, and promoted Protestant missions. In subsequent years, the directing of religious activity fell to Maya religious leaders and laymen. Although the state-church alliance of the colonial era was broken by the liberal government in the 1870s, it found a way of continuing in Maya communities with the *cargo* system, which assigned and carried out political and religious duties by retaining a close interdependence of religious and political-administrative posts and responsibilities. As San Antonio Ilotenango had very few non-Maya, this organization was almost entirely in the hands of the Maya throughout most of this history. The Catholic Church itself had essentially lost control over the flock not only in San Antonio, but in all of Guatemala.

After the 1870s the clergy appeared, at most, annually to baptize and marry people. Thus, from the point of view of the Catholic Church, the problem became how to separate the Maya from their now traditional religious practices, how to bring them back to an orthodox church as defined in Rome. At the same time, the church was deeply concerned about the growth of international communism and saw the Maya as being vulnerable to the proselytizing of this secular ideology. The church chose to evangelize through a new orthodoxy, the Acción Católica (Catholic Action) movement, whose members became known as *catequistas* (catechists). As Falla relates, *catequistas* challenged not only the traditional community religious practices but the entire existing local power structure. This was complicated in the mid-twentieth century as the state itself underwent revolutionary changes, opening up political alternatives that would not have appeared under a mere religious-conversion process.

The focus of Falla's study is on the conversion of traditional Catholic Maya to the newly promoted Catholic Action. He argues that the conversion process was stimulated and affected by economic and demographic changes: not only did conversions appear in a new opening of commerce, but the gradual success of a social class based on these economic and occupational differences led to the decline of the conversion process itself. The commerce grew because of the relaxation of forced labor under the administration of Jorge Ubico (1931–1944), and then its ultimate eradication with the revolution of 1944. Not only did the increase in trading activities stimulate growth in the rural and provincial economy, but contact with other areas also increased the knowledge and sophistication about events at the provincial, national, and international levels.

When Ricardo Falla wrote this study in 1974, few beyond the Maya themselves knew that they could adapt to globalization without suffering crippling losses in their culture. A hundred years of Liberal governments had pressed for the assimilation of the Indian, sometimes expressed as "civilizing," while simultaneously excluding them from the benefits of capitalist development and political participation. In order to avoid the government-mandated forced labor, many Indians simply fled the system. Some anthropologists, including the present writer, misread the demographics that showed declining percentages of Indians to indicate a real decline in the number of Indians. The reverse was actually the case. Although the Indian population was increasing, the non-Indian population apparently entered the demographic transition earlier than did the Indians. Their numbers increased more rapidly during the middle half of the twentieth century than did those of the Indians. In the second half of the century this process slowed and reversed, so that today the Indian population is reproducing itself more rapidly than the rest of the population.

The larger picture that Falla describes here is that of the breakdown of what Eric Wolf, after Weber, identified as a "corporate community." These Maya communities were organized around a ranking of kin organizations under the control of a system of elders and religious leaders. Falla has chosen to describe this in terms of the change in the structure of social power in San Antonio Ilotenango within the larger Guatemalan scene. The increased wealth of community members as well as the contacts with Catholic Action and with the church hierarchy added power to these local agents of change. To this he adds an analysis of the process by which belief in a system can be rejected and replaced through a transition that often involves personal crisis.

Finally, Falla's work is the first major empirical study to demonstrate how changes of this kind could occur with no serious loss of Maya identity. Indeed, his study made clear that conversion was a device that could strengthen ethnic identity.

Ricardo Falla offers a seminal study of some dynamics behind the vigor of contemporary Maya society and culture and shows how religious conversion is related to more general processes of political and social change. His perspective as an anthropologist and a priest allows a stereoscopic vision unavailable to most people.

—Richard N. Adams
June 2000

Acknowledgments

With the publication of the translation of this book, which in Spanish has gone through several printings in Guatemala, I would again like to thank all those who made it possible. First, my deceased father, who always encouraged me to finish what had been begun. Then the dear friends in my Jesuit community, who gave me broader perspectives, especially César Jerez, who as a political scientist and with a good deal of common sense used to kid us anthropologists for our up-close magnifying-glass view of things. César is now dead, but his inseparable companion, Juan Hernández Pico, is still with us, and for years I have passed anything I write for publication through his hands. People used to jokingly call us the Blessed Trinity: César was the Father, Pico the organizing Logos, and yours truly the Spirit who is continually getting out of line.

I owe a debt of gratitude to the people of San Antonio Ilotenango, to so many who helped me as informants and companions with complete trust. Don Gabriel Yat was my closest companion; since he lived near the town and was the sacristan, he saw me every day and answered my questions both about what to do and what I needed to know. One day I was deeply moved, because he said he was willing to give his life for me, in connection with conflicts that could arise in the municipality. I would like to thank him and many of the members of Catholic Action, some of whom are now dead, either from illness or as victims of the repression. I especially want to mention the Guch family in the canton of Chichó, four of whose members were abducted and murdered by the army, no doubt because Don José was a powerful and assertive merchant, and the military must have decided that he was providing help to the guerrillas. I also thank Lorenzo Xanté Xic, a young man whose eyes glowed with yearning to get to know the outside world, who served as my secretary in getting information on the municipality, and likewise Matías Osorio Cor, who was mayor during my fieldwork and a friend and very close co-worker in disentangling the kinship ties and events in his canton, Canamixtoj. His name also appears among the thousands of victims listed by the Historical Clarification Commission. When I was awarded the Golden Quetzal prize by the Association of Guatemalan Journalists in 1979, I left it with the people of San Antonio, and I am taking advantage of this occasion to once more thank all those people.

The staff of the Teresa Lozano Long Institute of Latin American Studies at the University of Texas at Austin deserves special mention for daring to publish a book translated from Spanish, one written thirty years ago and now out of fashion. I am very grateful for their confidence in the value of this book. I am also grateful for their great patience and respect when we had to negotiate over what to cut out and what to leave. (As a writer, you feel that they are cutting away at your newborn child, but they have a more objective view.) I especially want to thank Virginia Hagerty, who has been in charge of the publication, and Heather Teague, who worked so hard on the illustrations and layout.

I should also mention the diligent work of the translator, Phillip Berryman, a dear friend and very knowledgeable about Guatemala in the 1970s and 1980s, for seeking what I wanted to say in the Spanish text, and the copyeditor, Nancy Warrington, who has gone over every line of the translation with an eagle eye. I can say that after this laborious process the translation and the original are complementary and shed light on one another. Some parts of the translation are elaborated more fully in the original, as is to be expected, but the translation sheds light on the original, inasmuch as there are obscure lines that were very clear for me, but which I now realize were not understandable even in Spanish.

I thank Richard N. Adams, not only for overseeing this book when it was a doctoral thesis, but for helping me in my analysis of his theory of power. That theory has apparently now gone out of fashion, but I think it is still a useful tool for understanding processes and for making decisions in the midst of those processes. I also thank him for his help in revising the translation.

Finally, I acknowledge the recent assistance I received from those who helped me write the epilogue by providing information on San Antonio Ilotenango in the year 2000. Among them I want to thank Alvaro Colom, an engineer and a mystic, one who loves the town, and at the same time is a politician who ran for president; my Irish friend Domhnall Maccionaith, who now works in Santa Cruz del Quiché in an ecumenical association; Father Rigoberto Pérez, coordinator of the REMHI (Recovery of Historic Memory) Project, likewise in the department capital, Santa Cruz; and Manolo García of SERJUS (Legal and Social Services), who is very familiar with many communities in the highlands; Clara Arenas of AVANSCO (Association for the Advance of Social Sciences) for effective guidance in finding sources; and Matilde González, who has done a study like mine in the municipality of San Bartolo Jocotenango, El Quiché, which suffered tremendously under the repression and remains under paramilitary control.

In acknowledging the AVANCSO team, I cannot fail to mention Myrna Mack, who undeservedly saw me as her second mentor, after the Guatemalan anthropologist Joaquín Noval, now likewise deceased. Myrna continues to be the butterfly, fluttering at the edge of our vision—Myrna, the martyred anthropologist, who with her blood is pressing young people to love anthropology like a mother and to use it for the benefit of the people most in need, even when that means facing the danger of death.

As always, the responsibility for the work is mine. In this case, that goes for the translation as well, inasmuch as I have been so involved in deciding key points on it. Let us hope that it will serve to bring the reality that I have lived close to English-speaking readers. Many thanks.

Note to Reader

The original Spanish edition of this book, *Quiché Rebelde: Estudio de un movimiento de conversión religiosa, rebelde a las creencias tradicionales, en San Antonio Ilotenango, Quiché (1948–1970)*, was published in 1978. This first English translation keeps the author's original wording with regard to time references. Therefore, the reader should be aware that the time frame pertains to a period some twenty-five years prior to the date of this publication.

The theoretical framework that appeared in Chapter 1 in the original edition, and included a discussion of the theories of power and liminality, has been consolidated into an appendix in this edition (p. 253).

Translations of Spanish terms are provided in the text in parentheses following the first occurrence of a term.

List of Abbreviations

ADISA (Asociación de Desarrollo Integral de Servicios Comunitarios / Association for Integral Development of San Antonio Ilotenango)

ASODESPT (Asociación Desarrollo para Todos / Association for Development for Everyone)

CACIF (Comité Coordinador de Asociaciones Agrícolas, Comerciales, Industriales y Financieras / Chamber of Agricultural, Commercial, Industrial, and Financial Associations)

CADISOGUA (Coordinadora de Asociaciones de Desarrollo Integral de Sur Oriente de Guatemala / Coordinating Body for Integrated Development Associations of Southeastern Guatemala)

CDRO (Cooperación para el Desarrollo Rural de Occidente / Cooperation for Rural Development)

CEH (Comisión para el Esclarecimiento Histórico / Historical Clarification Commission)

CEPAL (Comisión Económica para América Latina y el Caribe / Economic Commision for Latin America and the Caribbean)

COPMAGUA (Coordinación de Organizaciones del Pueblo Maya de Guatemala / Coordinating Body of Organizations of the Maya People of Guatemala)

CUC (Comité de Unidad Campesina / Peasant Unity Committee)

DC (Democracia Cristiana / Christian Democrats)

EGP (Ejército Guerrillero de los Pobres / Guerrilla Army of the Poor)

ESA (Ejército Secreto Anti-comunista / Secret Anticommunist Army)

FIS (Fondo Inversión Social / Social Investment Fund)

FONAPAZ (Fondo Nacional para la Paz / National Fund for Peace)

FRG (Frente Republicano Guatemalteco / Guatemalan Republican Front)

FUNCEDE (Fundación Centroamericana de Desarrollo / Foundation for Central American Development)

INTECAP (Instituto Técnico de Capacitación y Productividad / Technical Institute for Training and Production)

MAS (Movimiento de Acción Solidaria / Solidarity Action Movement)

MDN (Movimiento Democrático Nacionalista / National Democratic Movement)

ODHAG (Oficina de Derechos Humanos del Arzobispado de Guatemala / Office of Human Rights of the Archbishop of Guatemala)

ORPA (Organización del Pueblo en Armas / Organization of the People in Arms)

PADEL (Proyecto de Apoyo al Desarrollo Local / Project for the Support of Local Government)

PAIN (Proyecto de Atención Integral / Project for Integral Attention)

PAN (Partido Acción Nacional / National Action Party)

PR (Partido Revolucionario / Revolutionary Party)

PROYECTO KICHE (Quiché Project)

REHMI (Proyecto Interdiocesano, Recuperación de la Memoria Histórica / Interdiocesan Project for the Recovery of Historic Memory)

RN (Renovación Nacional / National Restoration)

SERJUS (Servicios Jurídicos y Sociales / Justice and Social Services)

SODIFAG (Sociedad para el Desarrollo Integral de la Familia Guatemalteca / Society for the Integral Development of the Guatemalan Family)

CHAPTER 1

The Study

Origins of the Project

A different tree ought to have grown out of the seed of this study. When I went to the countryside of the western Maya area of Guatemala in July of 1969, I took with me the design for research into the consequences of population pressures on the social structure and culture of a community. I had chosen a number of municipalities in the western highlands of Guatemala, which I then visited to choose the one that displayed, through certain indicators, the greatest population pressure in terms of its resources. All of those under consideration were municipalities in the Quiché or nearby Cakchikel area. I had been studying the Quiché language for a couple of years; hence, I did not go looking for an appropriate research site in the Mam- or Kekchi-speaking areas. In order to work with a manageable population, I sought out only municipalities with fewer than 10,000 inhabitants. While traveling, moreover, I ruled out some small municipalities, such as those along Lake Atitlán that Stanford University was then planning to include in its genetics project and were then being "occupied" by students from both Berkeley and Stanford. The municipalities visited were Santa Cruz Balanyá, Santa Apolonia, San José Poaquil, and San Antonio Nejapa (administratively a village of Acatenango that resembled a municipality) in the department of Chimaltenango; Patzité, San Antonio Ilotenango, San Pedro Jocopilas, and San Bartolomé Jocotenango in the department of El Quiché; Santa Lucía la Reforma, San Andrés Xecul, and San Bartolo in the department of Totonicapán; Concepción in Sololá; and Zunil and San Francisco la Unión in Quetzaltenango.

After taking into account the number of people, the territorial extension, the quality of the land, the resources made possible by being near a major town with some economic activity, migrations to the coast, and other factors proper to each municipality, I chose San Antonio Ilotenango and San Andrés Xecul, intending to live in the former, whose lands were drier than those of

Xecul, which had greater migration to the coast and was more isolated from sources of work in the capital city of the department, Santa Cruz. Two university students who wanted to help me would live in Xecul, which would provide me with a point of comparison. However, it turned out to be impossible to place the students in Xecul, so one moved to Patzité and the other to San Pedro Jocopilas. As a result of our contact with Patzité, the students and I published two articles on some of the processes that led to the religious conversion of two-thirds of the population, but I do not include those data in this book because they do not contrast sharply with those from San Antonio, the next municipality over (Baltodano, de la Cerda, and Falla 1970).

After I had begun to live in San Antonio, I became increasingly convinced of an idea that had occurred to me while I was doing the preparatory travel, namely, that although the communities visited had clearly reacted to population increase, it was not a topic that concerned them nor something people talked about, as they did about other recent phenomena. I was in danger of imposing my own issue. If research into population pressure was to be fruitful, the people in the area themselves would have to be aware of the problem. Such awareness existed, but it was not then, nor is it even now, so pressing that the people of the area were often dealing with the issue and discussing it.

Yet, two recent developments were far more striking, as determined by the frequency and interest with which people were talking about them: the adoption of chemical fertilizer and religious conversion. Almost everyone was by then using chemical fertilizer, after having held back for a few years. That change took place in the 1960s and was already a fait accompli (Falla 1972b). Conversion, on the other hand, which had begun in 1948, was still taking place in certain cantons in a process that divided groups on the municipal level and created divisions between neighbors and relatives, and sometimes between parents and children.

This rebellion in beliefs had been stirring the indigenous western highlands of Guatemala since the mid-1930s (Baltodano, de la Cerda, and Falla 1970), and after 1945 it had spread throughout the department of El Quiché. All the municipalities that I had visited on my rounds had been thrown into turmoil over it. According to calculations I made in 1970 with the help of men who were familiar with the various municipalities in El Quiché, in that department alone (which, according to the 1964 census, had 249,704 inhabitants) around 70,000 people had joined "Acción," or Catholic Action (CA), as the movement in opposition to the Tradition[1] is known. This number does not include the various groups of evangelical Protestants, who have followed a course similar to that of Catholic Action members.

Thus, when I went to the western highlands and began to live in a town there, I myself was affected by this religious phenomenon and was personally involved in it. Indeed, the focus of my study gradually changed: because of its power to reshape society and the thinking of the people in the town, religious conversion became the new topic.

MAP 1.1. *Republic of Guatemala*

Thus, I did not choose the site in terms of the research topic, but rather, choosing the site led me to the topic, which does not rule out the possibility that another site might have turned out to be even more revealing.

Constraints and Advantages

What I did among the people of San Antonio and my position in that society have to be explained in order to clarify both the limitations and the strengths of this study. I presented myself to the town as a Catholic priest; I said nothing about being an anthropologist. I could have said nothing about my identity as a priest and passed as someone who wanted to study the customs and problems of the town, as I did on another occasion in Venezuela with the Yaruros, who had no idea what it meant to be a priest or a Catholic. But that was impossible in Guatemala because my identity was public knowledge, and Guatemala is a small country.

The upshot of my position was that contacts, information, and, as I have already said, the focus of the study were automatically selected. I arrived in the town after being briefed by the priests in Santa Cruz del Quiché, the administrative capital of the department. There had been no resident priest in San Antonio for several centuries. I sought out the mayor, who was a convert[2] and a past president of Catholic Action in his district, and the sacristan, who also held the position of fifth *regidor* (town councilman). Both were very pleased at my arrival, because even though they did not say so, it would bolster the prestige of their organization, Catholic Action, in its struggle against the Traditionalists (*Costumbristas*), those who stand by their tradition, and to a lesser extent against the evangelical Protestants. They were also pleased that I would serve them with my ministry. After a mass in one of the cantons where the bishop officially introduced me to three hundred persons, some participants in Catholic Action began to request that San Antonio become independent of Santa Cruz by becoming a parish, and that the times for weekly Saturday and Sunday masses be changed.

As a result of these requests, my functions were restricted. Since I would be there only one year, I would not have to take on any of the weekly activities of the priest who came in from Santa Cruz (classes, Sunday mass, baptisms, and marriages), nor would I have any jurisdictional function. All decisions proper to the pastor or his representative would remain with him. My services as a priest were reduced to celebrating private masses, ordinarily on weekdays; giving last rites to those who were dying, when they or their relatives requested it; and helping with confessions. All these services were requested by the parishioners themselves, either in general or in particular cases. I took practically no initiatives of my own along these lines and devoted most of my time to talking with the people.

The first time I was asked to help with confessions, a few days after my arrival, I was reluctant for a moment, but I gave in when I noticed the reaction on the face of a Catholic Action leader; I therefore decided to wait until later before making an overall decision. I did not want any reader of this book to think that the information had come from confessions, because a priest must hold such information in absolute secrecy. I heard many confessions, generally following a standard formula; those that were more detailed and personal, and which I did not understand well at first, I could filter out and forget, simply by not recording them in my journal. I have not used this specific information for this study. Nor did I ask other people in the town about things that I had heard from particular people in confession, and acted instead as though I knew nothing.

At mass it was assumed that I had to preach. Thus I could not fail to do so, and I had to deliver my message with conviction, which brings up a problem regarding the scientific method: was I changing the object under study, or could I know to what extent I distorted it? The answer—perhaps disappointing for a priest—is that my influence was practically nil. What I said was that they should not drink, not be unfaithful to their wives and vice versa, not fight among themselves, that they should try to rise up to improve their lives and that they should strive for mutual respect and to bring people together, even those who believed differently. This last message perhaps took some of the edge off the radicalism of conversion. They hoped rather that I would fan the flames so that they would convert more followers, but for personal reasons, I could not make my message favor proselytizing, even though at that time it would have been very welcome to them.

Another problem was the customary mass stipend, Q 4.00 for low mass and Q 10.00 for high mass. (The Quetzal was on a par with the dollar.) The stipend for low mass was Q 3.00, but they added Q 1.00 for the gas of the priest who came from Santa Cruz. I was to charge 4.00, just as he did, so as not to stir up differences and protest. The going rate for a day's work was Q 0.60; thus a mass was equivalent to six days of a man's work plus a little more. Without consulting anyone, I decided not to charge for saying mass. I did not need this money because I had a fellowship from the National Science Foundation, granted to the University of Texas at Austin for a study on genetics and behavior. (My study would provide information on behavior.) But when I had said a few masses for free, the Catholic Action leaders came to tell me that I had to charge because otherwise the people were going to become used to it, and when I left a year later, they would not want to pay another priest. I gave in, and we set aside this money for buying medicine, but the people did not act as though they were aware of this "act of self-sacrifice" when the sacristan and I tried to explain it upon accepting the money. Some Traditionalists who, despite the conflict, continued to have masses said sought to bargain over prices.

Because I was accepted in the Catholic Action group, its members took me into their confidence almost absolutely, and they had the patience to provide me with very systematic information on almost everything they knew. Therefore, from the outset I was considered an enemy of the Traditionalists. By simply strolling along the paths or going out into the square I could tell who was in Catholic Action and who was not, because they either greeted me or averted their gaze. As someone who, in my anthropological training, had more or less internalized certain perhaps inherently questionable attitudes of neutrality, this was painful to me. I saw that I needed this (quite self-interested) neutrality for my study to be objective and in order to obtain information, but I felt myself being pulled in a particular direction in the community by my identity as a priest. Either I agreed to be in that position, or I would have no place in the community.

Yet I still tried to resist. When by my own choice I went to my first funeral wake for a Traditionalist, where relatives of the deceased from both Catholic Action and the Tradition were in attendance, I was almost attacked by a member of Catholic Action because I was listening to a Traditionalist who had been drinking tell a joke, and my laughter was misinterpreted. On other occasions, I went to celebrations of the *cofradía* (religious brotherhood), which is the Traditionalists' organization, and they were happy to see me accept a "little drink" from them. However, Catholic Action members found out and could not comprehend how I could be taking part in something that was off-limits for them. I felt like someone who has a wife and gets involved with another woman and would like to have both, but the wife finds out and kicks him out of the house. I gradually realized that it would be better for me to establish roots in my own group because, otherwise, should the Traditionalists want to kick me out of the town, no one would come to my support. A Traditionalist had asked me why I did not go back to Guatemala City, where there were seventy priests without work, rather than coming to take away the people's money. They saw me as being there to make money. A rumor was already circulating that they were drawing up a legal petition against me to take to the Ministry of Governance. It was the first time in their lives that these people were experiencing a priest living in the religious order's residence in the town; in 1955, a priest had tried to start working there but they threw him out, accompanied by shouting, insults, and threats.

Although I later managed to get along better with the Traditionalists, when they realized that I was not fiercely against them, I was never able to obtain systematic and patient informants among their leaders (*principales*). This is the most significant limitation of this work. It presents only one side, that of those who belonged to Catholic Action. However, I have tried to reconstruct the other side through the Catholic Action members who were at one time Traditionalists.

To this limitation must be added another, which is only partly rooted in the division of the people, and that is that the study is little concerned with women. Women normally do not talk with men outside their household, particularly when their husband is not present, and in San Antonio almost all speak only their own Mayan language, not Spanish. I did not become very fluent in Quiché because I did not practice it enough with monolingual women or male Traditionalists to hold long conversations.

Gathering Data

Within these limitations, information was gathered in various ways. The primary method was systematic conversation on topics that seemed meaningful to the people and to the question under investigation. Some men, ordinarily Catholic Action leaders from various districts, came to speak with me at the parish house for six, seven, and even eight hours a day. I let them speak almost without interrupting them, unless something came up that I did not understand. I realized that if I tried to say nothing at all so as to let them take the lead entirely, the conversation became listless. The more interest I showed in what they were saying, the more fruitful was the conversation for a deep understanding of their society and culture. I took down all their responses in writing. At first the speakers were disconcerted because they did not know whether I was listening to them while I wrote. I tried to register their expressions and manners, although not in shorthand. My own questions I wrote down only on special occasions, because it was hard to ask questions and write at the same time. Nor did I usually tape the conversations, because unless I had had time to transcribe them exactly, I would not have gained anything. Most of the few recordings were made in Quiché, and afterward they were translated for me with the aid of the speaker himself or of a "secretary." Otherwise, the conversations were held in Spanish.

Another method was that of systematically gathering information on people in the cantons. The informants were the same as those mentioned above: Catholic Action leaders familiar with their canton. In all cases, I tested the accuracy of the information with a second informant from the same district. This was how we drew up the list of the houses of all the inhabitants of the municipality. The informants determined the order of the list, sometimes very insistently, in keeping with the local geography, because the houses and the lands are lined up according to certain principles. Next we checked the approximate ages of the men in each household, if they were married, or of the woman head of the household if they were not; where their wives/husbands were from and to whom they were related; the number of wives/husbands they had had; the age of the house; the religious group to which they belonged; their work; their degree of literacy; their knowledge of Spanish; whether they had a radio; whether they worked on the coast or in the salt fields. We also gradually drew up the family relationships of people in the area with the same last name. We then situated each house over enlarged aerial photos, which all the informants except one were able to understand. Their faces lit up when they recognized the different places. Ordinarily I note that these men are very proud of their intelligence; they took reading the photograph as a kind of test to resolve a doubt over whether they were going to be able to "handle it." They showed a great deal of pride in their district, they were happy to be able to correct someone else, and they were sometimes disappointed when they were unable to provide responses to specific questions, such as Who is that woman a daughter of? and the like.

Another method was the preparation of a census solely of Catholic Action members, since we knew in advance that the Traditionalists would not agree to answer and that if we tried to include them, the only result would be a futile protest. To begin the census we met with a group of seven men, generally the secretaries of the Catholic Action centers. We went over the written questionnaire in Spanish, as they were not trained to read Quiché, we ran tests to see how they filled it out, and then they went out to their districts to carry it out. I monitored them closely, visiting them and settling their doubts when they did not know how to record situations that were not envisioned in the questionnaire or that we had not explained. With the exception of one center, which closed down entirely, the census proceeded with no problems. We particularly looked for demographic data that we could not obtain from other people, such as the number of children, living and dead. The reason for compiling this information was set forth in the original focus of the study. But we also included questions on conversion, which was presented as an effect of demographic growth. For all systematic work that required a significant amount of time and in cases where my assistants missed a full work day or half a day, I paid them Q 1 for eight hours.

Finally, information was also gathered through direct observation and participation in celebrations such as weddings, meals, burials, and so forth. In view of the vast array of activities carried out in a community, observation was limited, and that was even more true of participation, since one cannot do everything at once and a year is a short time. Moreover, the functions I performed as a priest prevented me from participating in certain celebrations or rites of the opposition group.

Data gathering was conditioned by the origins of the study, and that in turn affected the content. As I began to pursue the social and cultural consequences of population pressure, I devoted myself to gathering population data. In addition to the census, archival work in the municipal registry was utilized for this purpose. The lists of people in the municipality provided overall information and also served to show the layout of houses on the map. But as the research focus gradually changed, I found myself left with no theoretical framework and no methodical plan for gathering data. Hence, the procedure became one of first obtaining as much information as possible to shed light on the two extremes of the process of change, and, second, focusing on some processes within this change that seemed to be significant for explaining conversion. The first approach entailed preparing two monographs on the site, one dealing with the present and the other dealing with information from people's memory or from documents of the recent past before the change, which in this case meant conversion.

The second approach (seeking explanatory factors for conversion) meant gradually engaging in the research with no theoretical framework. In the censuses and lists made prior to refocusing the study, some questions had been included on conversion and on the characteristics that might be related to it, such as age, work, and number of spouses. However, conversion was there being viewed as a possible effect of population growth. When the study was redirected, I completed the lists for some other cantons, but now my pursuit was moving in another direction. Through accounts of converts about their own conversion and that of others, or about resistance of others to being converted, I began to note some characteristics that seemed to be constants in the process, such as whether the convert lived with his parents at the time of conversion; whether another relative had been converted before him; whether the occasion of conversion had been an illness, a "temptation" (suffering), or his own decision; whether the conversion had had an effect on drunkenness, on attendance at a weekly class, or on going to the *zahorín* (shaman, or indigenous religious leader).[3] I gathered the same information on nonconverts, in order to discover the reasons why they had not converted.

As I had done before the project's intent changed, I continued to gather information on resources, because there seemed to be a connection between conversion and certain ways of earning a living, such as being engaged in trade. Adopting the use of chemical fertilizer resembled a conversion in the realm of technology that had been affected by the other conversion. Moreover, the increase in the number of well-off people in the municipality seemed to be quite connected to the strength of proselytizing and the change of belief, so we looked into these matters.

Conversion was more and more proving to be a process with ties outside the community, to the church, to the government, and to political parties. One way of disentangling these connections was to narrate all the conflicts at the municipal level from the time when the division had begun. In this account, made from inside the community, the outside agents are necessarily seen from outside.

Hence, it is obvious that the theoretical framework for the study was not laid out prior to the gathering of data, but that it was subsequently applied when the data were analyzed. Some information turned out to be superfluous, while other material fit because theory was applied to the intuition with which it was gathered, and still other information was missing or in short supply.

Earlier Studies

Religious conversion as such had not been a research topic in the literature on indigenous people in Guatemala prior to 1974, but political and religious division, which in many instances was the product of such conversion, *had* been studied. Community division had been studied by a number of authors for twenty years. Elsewhere (Falla 1972a) I published an article on political and religious developments among indigenous farmers in Guatemala during the previous twenty-five years, using data from monographs and articles on the issue in eight communities: San Luis Jilotepeque, in the department of Jalapa (Gillin 1957, 1958); Chinautla, in the department of Guatemala (Reina 1960, 1966); Alotenango (Moore 1966) and Magdalena Milpas Altas (Adams 1957) in Sacatepéquez; Panajachel (Tax 1964; Hinshaw 1968; Tax and Hinshaw 1970), San Pedro la Laguna (Paul 1968), and Santiago Atitlán (Mendelson 1965; Douglas 1968) in Sololá; and Cantel, in the department of Quetzaltenango (Nash 1957, 1958).

Here I simply report the general conclusions of that study on how religious groups form alliances, to serve as a background against which I can outline what is new in this study within anthropological literature about Guatemala, up to 1974 when I finished writing this book. The conclusions were organized into three main sections: one on the Traditionalists, that is, the *cofrades* and *principales*, who had been carrying on the traditional religious organization that I found operating in San Antonio Ilotenango at that time; Protestants, including a variety of churches and groups, all of which were then a recent development in indigenous municipalities; and, finally, new Catholics, including all those who had broken away from the traditional organizations, especially the *cofradías*, to form new associations linked to the Catholic Church. The present work will focus specifically on this latter category, although I am also interested in comparing the process of the Protestant movements in other communities to determine which elements of their process have been repeated in San Antonio Ilotenango among new Catholics, inasmuch as Protestants were a small and weak group in San Antonio at the time.

In order to understand certain references to the nation's political development in these conclusions, the time may be divided into three periods: (a) pre-1945; (b) 1945 to 1954; and (c) 1954 to 1969. According to the principles of the October 1944 Revolution, which were ratified in the Constitution of 1945, municipal mayors had to be elected by popular vote and political parties began to operate with explicit recognition in the law. With this legislation, the windows of the community were opened to the winds of politics, and religious groups took advantage of this impulse. The second period (starting in 1945), which over time moved toward the left (agrarian reform was passed in 1952), ended abruptly in 1954 when Colonel Castillo Armas staged a coup with the support of the United States and encouragement from the Catholic Church. All kinds of organizations of the lower sectors, such as labor unions, peasant leagues, and agrarian committees, were suppressed. To this day, no government has provided political support to the less well off, and repression has become systematic, with periods of greater or lesser violence and bloodshed.

As I began my research, my survey of the literature on religious groups in Guatemala could be summarized along the following lines.

Traditionalists

The traditional type of organization had not remained utterly static, because to protect itself from the innovating groups, the *principales* or *cofrades* often had to set up a legally recognized committee, either to rebuild churches destroyed by earthquakes in the most central area of Guatemala or simply to organize the *cofradías* with legal department-level recognition.

The *principales* generally still held their positions for life, although in one or another municipality closer to Guatemala City, such as Alotenango, a new modality whereby *principales* served three-year terms was becoming visible. However, even in this modality, the *principales*, regardless of whether they were organized into committees, were part of the "old folks" who, even if not organized formally, were lifelong *principales* by definition and kept a certain generational identity that made itself felt in important community decisions.

The *principales* or their equivalents generally still appointed all the *cofrades*, although in some cases this was because the new Catholics, or Catholic Action members, had taken over the *cofradías* or had been absorbed into them. Such a relationship never occurs with Protestants, who are, as it were, in another world, since they meet elsewhere than the Catholic church building and have broken away from devotion to the saints. The Traditionalists and the reform Catholics have always shared this common space—namely, the Catholic church building, which has been a bond of union but also a point of contention.

The main reason for the reaction of the innovators, Catholic or Protestant, against the *cofradías* always had to do with the imposition of the *cargos* (responsibilities for patron-saint celebrations) and the large financial contributions these entailed. During the twenty-five years covered by the studies listed above, Traditionalists were still being pressured to serve in the *cofradías*, but the *principales* no longer enjoyed the same power to impose their will as they had before, inasmuch as the towns were no longer unified around one form of organization; in addition to *cofradías*, there were Protestants, *hermandades* (voluntary religious brotherhoods), Catholic Action groups, Third Orders (branches of a religious order whose members are laypeople), and so forth.

Another factor in the loss of the Traditionalists' power was that the strict connection between serving the saints through the *cofradía* and the municipality had been lost. A de facto relationship had always been maintained between the mayor and the religious group, Traditionalist or otherwise, to which the mayor belonged, but this did not enable him to support the appointment of even a fellow religious believer, let alone of someone who was not. After 1945, the birth of *hermandades* in those towns with greater non-Indian influence and greater proximity to the large cities was even then shaping this new idea of free service, to which the *cofradía* was gradually adjusting.

Where the *principales* or their equivalents, through their control over the *cofradías*, still exercised control over the municipal system, they profited from the 1945 elections, because they could choose the candidate for mayor. In some municipalities, the *cofrades* at this time began to envision how the *cofradías* might be revitalized and how the civic and ritual wings might be merged, but they were soon disappointed. As political parties moved in, Traditionalists lost control over events and they had to become the opposition to the innovators, who were more skilled than they in dealing with the new political machinery. In some municipalities where the *principales* formed the bulk of small landholders, the 1952 agrarian reform accentuated the clash. Because they were smallholders, they had not fled from the town and so they could support *cofrade* ritual activity.

Protestants

Protestants were generally the pioneers of change in the communities in the pre-1954 period. In some communities, they split away from traditional observance ten years before 1945 or even earlier, as in some towns on Lake Atitlán (Panajachel, San Pedro, and Santiago). The reason is plain: Protestants were social outcasts. Sometimes this marginal status was due to the "foreign" status of Protestant indigenous persons who had come into the community from elsewhere looking for work, such as in the tourism trade in Panajachel. In other instances, such marginalization was due to the poverty of the indigenous people in the community who were no longer leaving it in search of work and were connected to the outside world through Protestant groups, as in Chinautla. Hence the Protestants made religious or political-party alliances with ladinos within the community, especially with those hungry for land.

In some places during the 1945–1954 period, the alliance, whether explicit or not, between the left-leaning Protestant Maya and the radicalized ladinos prompted a mirror-image alliance between better-off ladinos and Traditionalist Indians. This alliance need not be understood as long-lasting but rather as a temporary agreement in opposition to the radicals. It did not necessarily entail belonging to the same party. On the other hand, among radicals, a greater merging of the two ethnic groups into a single party or within a single Protestant religious group did occur. As a result, the degree of Indian-ladino tension, which was quite sharp before 1945, generally tended to decline with the incipient class struggle brought about by the changes unleashed by the October 1944 Revolution.

After the fall of Jacobo Arbenz in 1954, "communist" Protestants were persecuted. As a result, they became frightened and disillusioned, tended to become depoliticized, and felt there was no longer any point to interethnic alliances. As it became impossible to engage directly in politics, bureaucratic methods for gaining power became widespread (e.g., drawing up legal accusations designed to unseat mayors and prove electoral fraud), and Protestants became more otherworldly, that is, they became more oriented to holding worship, preaching that politics is dirty and that God's Kingdom alone is to be sought.

New Catholics

No single religious organization represented the Catholics. On one side stood the *hermandades*, which had been less divisive with regard to traditional belief. On the other side were more aggressive organizations such as the Third Order and Catholic Action, which had better connections to the Catholic clergy. The Third Order received orders directly from Franciscans in the cities, beyond the reach of the parishes in the communities; Catholic Action, with which this book is concerned, had support from bishops. Catholic Action was especially active in the western departments of the country, which were in the diocese of Quetzaltenango. As we will see below, this movement, which began in Totonicapán in the 1930s, was systematically encouraged by the auxiliary bishop of the diocese and was known to be aggressive.

After 1954, with the triumph of the anticommunist movement known as the Movement for National Liberation, and with the arrival of young, foreign clergy with energy, resources, and money, Catholic Action grew stronger, especially in the more remote rural areas.

Catholic priests began to experience the more or less covert opposition of the *zahorines*, as they were then called, those who understood and followed the 260-day Maya calendar. The *zahorines* tended to become concentrated in some municipalities, while elsewhere they declined until they almost disappeared. Catholic priests as a rule attacked them as agents of the devil, especially if the *zahorines* were soothsayers and prayer reciters who healed with prayer and charged money for their ceremonies.

I focus my study against this background literature survey in order to highlight what is new about it. All the works cited in one way or another touched on the political and religious changes summarized in the three categories of Traditionalists, Protestants, and new Catholics noted above. But in only two of these works do the changes in religious beliefs constitute the core of the work: in Mendelson's book (1965) and in the article by Tax and Hinshaw (1970). Mendelson studies a conflict between already established groups and their worldviews. By contrast, in this book I look at the very process of the formation of these groups: religious conversion, that is, the change of beliefs and its causes and consequences, one of which is conflict.

Tax and Hinshaw study the change from the worldview of the inhabitants of Panajachel in 1930, contrasting it to that of today's more forward-looking Indians. They compare the two extremes of the process but do not carefully study the process itself, which the authors call the "erosion" of beliefs. This is not the same thing as a conversion, because here a belief, rather than being painfully replaced by an opposing one, is simply gradually lost during the socialization process, through the informal contact of the indigenous child with ladinos in the later years of school. There arises a new generation now deprived of certain nonladino ideas, or perhaps ready to drop them, but having nothing with which to replace them. Emphasis is placed on comparing the two distinct generations.

By contrast, although I also assume that the socialization of the converts did not sow the beliefs so deeply into them as in the nonconverts, I focus on the more dramatic cases where the change has meant the uprooting of one idea, not a mere erosion after which the previous belief does not disappear but is simply reversed. In these cases, the innovating group, though it attracts an outer circle of uncommitted opportunists, is sustained by a core of people who have given their complete assent to a belief that runs counter to their former belief. Such people, I assume, would be willing to surrender their lives (hence the totality) to sustain that assent, which in turn is life-giving for them. In the course of the book, I will come to dramatic cases. By contrast with the other two studies, which have not focused on the process of people in their immediate sociological context, the household, I will move down to that level in this work.

Thus the original feature of this study within anthropological literature on Guatemala is that it studied the religious conversion process itself within a sociological framework that, starting at the household level, connects individuals to the political and religious forces of the community and the nation.*

---

*For a full discussion of the theoretical framework, including the theories of power and liminality, see the Appendix, p. 253.

CHAPTER 2

San Antonio Ilotenango

In this chapter I provide a physical, demographic, economic, and sociological description of San Antonio Ilotenango, the community under study, to give a frame of reference for the phenomenon of conversion. Because conversion is just one of many changes that have occurred in the past twenty-five-years (1945–1970), I also describe other important changes that the community has undergone. The frame of reference itself is changing.

Physical Description

The municipality of San Antonio Ilotenango covers 178 *caballerías* (almost 20,000 acres) and is located in the southern part of the department of Quiché (see Map 1.1). It sits on the northern slopes of the Totonicapán ridge with height variations of no more than 350 meters over the fourteen kilometers of the municipality's south-to-north expanse. Hence any differences in temperature, rain, soils, and types of crops at opposite ends of the municipality are barely noticeable. This is in sharp contrast to the municipalities on the border with Totonicapán to the south, where the mountains reach heights of 3,500 meters, whereas the highest points in San Antonio are 2,200 meters above sea level.

Because San Antonio sits below the high mountains of Totonicapán, the creeks that come rushing down from those sharp peaks, upon reaching the flatlands, become rivers that cross the municipality. Erosion has carved out large canyons from 100 to 150 meters deep that serve as natural boundaries for the administrative divisions of the cantons. These rivers, whose names can be seen on Map 2.1, augment the flow of the Negro or Chixoy Rivers beyond the municipality, then run into the Usumacinta River, which empties into the Atlantic Ocean.

Between these sharply cut canyons are gentle valleys with small lakes at the bottom. Next to one of these small lakes stands the town of San Antonio, with

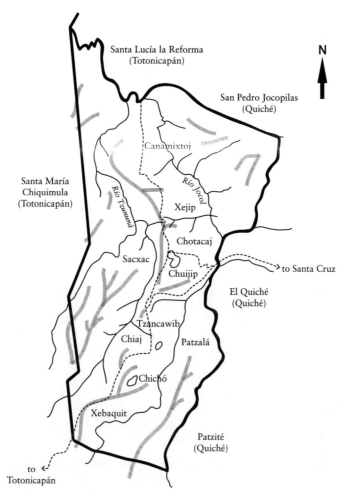

Santa Lucía la Reforma
(Totonicapán)

N

San Pedro Jocopilas
(Quiché)

Canamixtoj

Santa María
Chiquimula
(Totonicapán)

Río Tzununá

Río Jocol

Xejip

Chotacaj

Sacxac

Chuijip

to Santa Cruz

El Quiché
(Quiché)

Tzancawib

Chiaj

Patzalá

Chichó

Xebaquit

Patzité
(Quiché)

to
Totonicapán

MAP 2.1. *San Antonio Ilotenango*

its church, municipal building, shops, *cofradía* houses, and some residences. Throughout these valleys or sometimes around the lakes rise small hills, which are the foothills of the Totonicapán ridge that come to an end in the valleys. These hills also serve as markers for the divisions into cantons.

Average annual rainfall for the municipality is 1,000 mm (39 inches) a year. The rainy season begins in May and ends in October, and planting follows this cycle. In recent years, however, the people have noticed a change in the rain pattern: not only is it raining less, but it is raining wildly out of season. These changes are probably partly due to deforestation, which, as crops were planted, occurred first in the valleys, and as wood was taken to build houses, has gradually risen up the slopes. A local carpenter says that in one of the cantons where the hillsides are richest in pine, only around 1,500 large trees are still standing. A house measuring 10 by 15 yards uses six of these trees. The need for firewood has also taken its toll on small pines and oaks.

The prevailing winds are from the east and begin to blow at around 2:00 P.M. and last until 5:00 P.M. Average temperature varies from 15° to 20° C (59° to 68° F) all year long. Because it is a little warmer in the north of the municipality, some families can grow sugarcane and oranges. The pine forest is also thinner in the north. By contrast, wheat is grown in the south.

Soils range, from best to worst quality, as follows: black (*k'ek*), red (*qu'iak*), yellow (*k'an*), clay (*xk'ol*), gray powder (*rex poklaj*), and white powder (*sak poklaj*). Soil classification is very complicated: some types are dirt (*ulew*), while others, such as powder (*poklaj*), are not. In general, however, the blacker the richer. Soil types tend to go along with the particular nature of a place. In the deeper parts of the valleys, where water gathers, clay (*xk'ol*) is found. When it dries out, it is very hard to cultivate. Black soil is found outside the basins, and red and yellow on the slopes. When erosion is powerful, it uncovers under the soil a very hard layer of volcanic ash (*xák*). The hills on the western and eastern borders of the northern part of the municipality have a rather whitish dust. White dust is also found in the canyons, where crops cannot be grown. The population has concentrated in the valleys because water is available in the lakes and the soils are fertile, but gradually the pursuit of land has driven people up the hills into the areas on the outskirts of the municipality where the land is almost sterile.

Population

San Antonio and Nearby Communities

Before I give population figures for the last few years, a look at those for previous centuries will help make comprehensible the process that led to the increase of witchcraft and that paved the way for conversion. Table 2.1 presents the figures for four other communities along with those for San Antonio Ilotenango. A comparison of Santa Cruz del Quiché, San Pedro Jocopilas, and San Antonio Ilotenango with Santa María Chiquimula and Momostenango indicates that the first three, which used to belong to the district (*corregimiento*) of Sololá, lost population and reached their lowest point in the eighteenth century, while the other two, which belonged to the district of Totonicapán, began to recover in the late sixteenth century or early seventeenth. This demographic imbalance among the communities led to conflicts and invasions of the people of Chiquimula into Santa Cruz, Jocopilas, and Ilotenango in the late nineteenth century (Falla 1971a). In light of these events, the rise of witchcraft must have occurred in the late nineteenth century, when the municipal limits of San Antonio had already been set and the enemy from outside the community had disappeared (see Chap. 4). Thus, as the population increased,

TABLE 2.1. *Combined Indian and ladino population totals for San Antonio Ilotenango and four nearby communities, 1524–1964*

Communities	Year							
	1524	1570	1675	1732	1770	1893	1950	1964
San Antonio Ilotenango	3,700*	1,280	640	350	380	2,061	4,156	6,048
San Pedro Jocopilas	4,100	1,420	568	437	479	3,305	6,196	8,419
Santa Cruz Quiché	5,800	1,769	440	420	526	11,914	19,888	30,584
Santa María Chiquimula	1,920	960	1,640	—	1,500	12,374	10,015	14,716
Momostenango	4,500	2,250	2,400	—	3,550	18,632	26,050	32,974

Sources: (a) For 1570–1770 data: Velasco (1952); Vásquez (1937); Gómez de Parada (1732); Cortés y Larraz (1771); AGG: A.1.11.13; 48-802.-5794; AGG: A.3.16.1; A 1.3g; 1752, fol. 15. (b) For 1893–1964 data: Censuses of the Dirección General de Estadística.
* Underlined figures are reconstructions.

the "enemy" came to be seen as within the community rather than being external to it.

Population by Ethnicity

The municipality of San Antonio is almost entirely indigenous. In 1893 there were no ladinos; according to the 1950 census, ladinos accounted for only 0.7 percent; in 1964 they made up 2.2 percent (numbering 133). According to my 1969 count, there were only 106, which indicates that the count for the 1964 census was somewhat inflated. Because the percentage of ladinos is so small, I will treat the total population as though it were entirely indigenous.

Population Growth

The average annual population growth rate between 1893 and 1950 was 1.2 percent and between 1950 and 1964 it was 2.7 percent, according to the census figures. I cannot calculate an exact rate for the two decades, 1950–1959 and 1960–1969, for which I have figures for births and deaths from the municipal records, because I do not have a precise figure for the number of those who moved away. However, the lowering of the ratio of deaths to births (0.462 vs. 0.449) indicates a higher growth rate for the 1960–1969 decade, which is all the more likely since the number of deaths for the first decade has not been fully recorded.

Mortality

The gross death rate for 1950–1964 is 2.6 percent, according to the census figures, and for 1960–1969 is 2.38 percent, according to the municipal records. The rate likewise declines from 2.45 to 2.35 percent between 1960–1964 and 1965–1969, according to the same municipal records. Mortality has steadily declined. If we analyze this change more closely, we see that the proportion of deaths for the 0–4 year age group declined from 55 percent of all deaths in 1960–1964 to 52.8 percent in 1965–1969.

If we examine the 0–4 age group, we find that the overall rate for infant (less than one year of age) mortality has declined from 11.1 to 7.6 percent from the period 1960–1964 to the period 1965–1969, while the rate for the second and third year has not decreased. This contrast may be due to the betterment of the diet since chemical fertilizer was adopted. The better diet of the mother seems to affect the children who are less than one year old more than those who are two or three years old.

Mortality is highest in February, when measles often attack, possibly spreading through crowds at the town celebration in mid-January. The disease may be brought from the coast that month, when the workers return from the cotton farms. Mortality is lowest in December.

Fertility

The raw birth rate for 1950–1964 is 5.33 percent, and for 1960–1969 it is 5.32 percent. The 1960–1964 and 1965–1969 periods have rates of 5.51 percent and 5.16 percent, respectively. At least during the decade of the sixties fertility has declined, perhaps because the age at which a woman has her first child has gradually been rising, from approximately 16.3 years in 1950 to 18.7 years in 1969, according to a survey of mothers in Catholic Action.

The difference between the raw birth and death rates for the 1960–1964 and 1965–1969 periods yields a growth rate of 3.06 and 2.81, respectively. The declining fertility rate has lowered the growth rate, which is confirmed with the rise in the ratio of deaths to births in the two periods from .444 to .454. These growth rates should be compared with the 2.7 percent increase in the annual average growth rate for 1950–1964 presented above.

Migration

Currently there is not much definitive outmigration, that is, people who leave to go live in other municipalities and do not return. I do not have figures for making comparisons between decades. Those who have left are primarily single men who at age 16 or 17 go looking for work on the coast and remain there for good, or some women on the outskirts of the municipality who are sought in marriage by men nearby. Their number may be canceled out by that of indigenous women from outside the municipality who are sought in marriage in outlying regions or farther away.

Economy

Means of Subsistence

The people of San Antonio Ilotenango live primarily from the soil, planting a combination of corn, beans, squash, and *chilacayotes* (a type of squash). In the cool lands of the south, they plant wheat. Lemon and orange trees grow in the warm areas to the north, as do avocado trees here and there, especially in the central cantons.

Corn is grown in two ways. One method, called *jumba*, is employed in the valleys where water gathers and where black soil holds moisture from harvest time (November and December) to the planting season in March. The corn is planted before the rains begin. The rows are prepared starting in December, and they are piled high so as to retain moisture until March. In the second, rainy-season method, *rech jab*, planting is done after the first two or three rains, ordinarily in June. This latter system is more widespread, and corn grown by this method is harvested in November and December, whereas that of the *jumba'* is ready by the end of September. Even though the *jumba* provides corn early, it has the disadvantage of being more expensive, because it requires from 6 to 8 days of work per *cuerda* (a unit equivalent to 25 by 25 meters), whereas the *rech jab* only requires from 4 to 5 days of work for a 30-meter *cuerda*. Wages have been steadily increasing—from Q 0.10 per day in 1940 to Q 0.50–0.60 now, and up to Q 0.75 during times of harvest and weeding—and with the adoption of chemical fertilizer, there is no longer any corn shortage before November, so the *jumba* is gradually being abandoned. Currently around 400 *cuerdas* (43 acres) are planted in *jumba* out of the 31,580 *cuerdas* (4,854 acres), according to our approximate calculations of what is being planted in the municipality (a 25-yard *cuerda* is roughly one-ninth of an acre; a 30-yard *cuerda* is about one-sixth of an acre).

Each head of a household plants an average of 20 *cuerdas*. Some plant over 100, while among the poorest there are some who plant only 2 or 3 *cuerdas*. With chemical fertilizer, each *cuerda* produces an average of 1.85 quintals of corn, 30 pounds of beans, 2 or 3 squash plants, and 2 or 3 *chilacayote* plants. Without chemical fertilizer, one *cuerda* only produces 70 pounds of corn, 12 pounds of beans, and no squash or *chilacayotes*. If the corn sells for Q 3.50 a quintal, beans for Q 9.00 a quintal, and squash and *chilacayotes* at Q 0.02 and Q 0.10 per unit, respectively, the average of 20 *cuerdas* was providing a harvest worth Q 67.00 without chemical fertilizer and Q 146.50 or Q 131.98 with chemicals, depending on whether the fertilizer was bought at Q 5.00 cash or Q 7.20 on credit. The amount of chemical fertilizer used per *cuerda* averages 33 pounds. Adopting chemical fertilizer makes the land yield 1.97 to

2.2 times more than it would produce without it. Chemical fertilizer entered the community in 1959, but its use was not accepted by many people until after 1965. (For a more complete study of its adoption, see Falla 1972b.)

The wheat grown in the mountains in the south, where there used to be scattered five-*cuerda* plots, has almost disappeared because of the adoption of chemical fertilizer; those who used to plant wheat now tend to think that it makes more economic sense to plant corn, because between the rows of corn they can also grow beans—which bring a good price—squash, *chilacayotes*, peas, and lima beans, all of which could barely be grown or not at all, without chemical fertilizer. Wheat, on the other hand, cannot be combined with any other crop.

Fifty years ago the municipality produced wool, and over half the male population was involved in spinning wool. There was ample pasture land, and most people had at least a small flock of sheep, while others had flocks as large as 100 or 150. Today population growth has made pasture lands increasingly scarce, and the number of sheep has dropped. Only 20 percent of heads of family have flocks, averaging between 15 and 25 sheep. This scarcity of sheep has led to the almost total disappearance of wool spinners (there are only 24, or just 2 percent of the adult male population). Another result of the decrease in the number of sheep is the lack of organic fertilizer, an unavailability that made chemical fertilizer even more welcome and sheep herding in turn lost further utility.

Finally, people raise and fatten pigs, of which there are around three thousand in the municipality. The increased supply of corn has meant that more chickens and turkeys are raised than before; and these are taken to market like pigs. The only butcher-prepared meat eaten is pork—and chicken at holiday celebrations. Turkeys are sent to Guatemala City in December.

A high percentage of workers goes down to the cotton-growing areas on the coast. Around 700 of them are men over 15, 150 are younger than 15, and around 75 are women over 15. They go for at least one month a year, and some spend as much as three or four months there. Most go down for the harvest between the months of December and February. December is when the largest number go, because the town feast day celebration is in January and harvests are best in December. Another small group goes down for the weeding period from July to October. According to informants, the adoption of chemical fertilizer has led to a notable decline in the number of workers who go down for weeding.

According to farm payrolls, the average pay for workers in a crew on a cotton farm in Retalhuleu in December 1968 was Q 0.72 a day per person. The worker who earned the most simply for harvesting (i.e., not as a foreman) earned Q 1.25. In February, by contrast, pay is lower. The second and third harvests are less productive. As one worker commented, "If I make 10 pounds at 3 cents I earn 30 cents. I'm better off staying here in the municipality where I have something to eat. And if I get two days of work here, I earn a peso. You go to the market to buy and you have nothing in your pocket. . . . Six or seven years ago, because we have nothing to eat . . . because there was no chemical fertilizer, that's why we go to the coast."

Starting in 1945 a few people began to find work in the Santa Rosa salt fields near the port of San José, and currently 115 men, a few with their wives, spend half a year there during the dry season gathering salt in the yards. The work is very hard, because one has to continue day after day, with no rest for feast days or Sundays. If the salt were not gathered in the yards every day, the salt water would dry and then the salt would have to be gathered with hoes. There are also two shifts, one from 3 A.M. to 6 A.M. to pile the salt with rakes and shovel it onto tables, and another from 2:00 P.M. to 4:30 P.M. to take it in wheelbarrows to the warehouses. But when compared to wages in the municipality, the pay is very good. The workers get paid for a seventh day and Sunday (double), so they keep Q 13.57 cash a week. But because they get worn out from the fast pace and rough work, and because of the boredom and the hours (at midday in the sun and in the middle of the night), the workers spend almost a third of their earnings on soft drinks and liquor. Those who go there intending to save to build a house are able to save around Q 125 in six months. Most are young people, under 30 years old. If there were more jobs, more would go. However, because the job is so rough and monotonous, and has disruptive effects (drinking, women), it is given up after a few years.

Trade is another source of income. Besides the 170 merchants in the region, there are over 200 merchants whose work is buying and selling outside the municipality, in the capital or in other major cities on the coast like Mazatenango, Escuintla, and Retalhuleu. There have always been regional merchants with rotating markets, but the other type began to appear when the debts that held the coastal workers enslaved were abolished (1934). Being a merchant is the type of work that offers the greatest mobility. Of the 200 merchants selling outside the municipality, there are now twelve who have operating capital of from Q 500 to Q 1,000; fourteen with capital between Q 1,000 and Q 5,000; and twelve with capital of over Q 5,000. The latter include the truck and bus owners. These merchants sell clothes, small wares, grains, fish, pigs, chickens, and beans. Among the most prosperous are traders in clothing, fertilizer, raw sugar, and hoes.

Those engaged in other types of work (in 1970) include 57 barbers, 42 weavers of sashes and blankets, 24 spinners of wool thread, 35 tailors who make shirts and pants, 5 jewelers, 25 lumber mill workers, 25 masons, 20 roof-tile makers, 22 carpenters, 25 manufacturers of clandestine liquor, 14 makers of fruit drinks, 11 owners of mills for making tortilla mix, 12 butchers (most of whom are ladinos), 6 fishermen, 8 breadmakers, 4 healers, 18 marimba players, 11 candlemakers, 6 contractors, and 8 drivers. To these should also be added the 58 *zahorines*, or shamans. Many of these lines of work are practiced for a certain period of time or a certain number of days a year in combination with agricultural work. Among the new lines of work that did not exist twenty-five years ago are those of butcher, mill operator, liquor maker, tailor, barber, jeweler, healer, driver, and driver's assistant. Lines of work have become more diversified. Likewise, there are kinds of work in which proportionally more people are now working. That is true of masons, roof-tile manufacturers, saw operators, and carpenters. This increase is due to the growth in the number of houses being built, which are in turn a reflection of higher income. On the other hand, fewer people are now working as fishermen, wool spinners, *zahorines*, and candle makers. The number of fishermen is limited by the municipality's resources. The shortage of sheep, as noted, has led to the declining number of wool spinners. Religious conversion has reduced the number of *zahorines* and candle makers.

Consumption

Table 2.2, which shows the average adult food consumption and its cost for 1940 and 1970, indicates changing trends as a result of the changing income described above.

The increase in both quantity and cost is noteworthy. In the 1940s, scarcity was widespread and people endured hunger, "like a twisting pain inside that calmed down when you ate." One individual said that "as a child I ate stubble grass with salt. The corn didn't come up. I suffered a lot." Lack of corn caused people to eat more salt. They made use of tips of squash and cooked *xilote* points, which now are given to pigs. Today, by contrast, "life is easy . . . children today don't even come in to eat because they're out playing."

In the difficult months from June to August, however, people still experience hunger, because corn becomes scarce. During months of scarcity, people tend to prioritize foods according to how essential they are, in the following order:

1. Corn and salt
2. Greens
3. Chile
4. Beans and onions
5. Coffee, raw sugar, meat, and some fruit
6. Bread.

Hunger during these months has declined, and the number of people enduring it has dropped since chemical fertilizer began to be used. Of the 134 surveyed in 1969, 20 said they had never experienced hunger, 85 responded that they stopped experiencing it between 1959 and 1969, when chemicals came in, and 29 said they still experience it.

The amount spent on food has risen 4.5 times. Prices have tripled, paralleling rising pay on the coast (from Q 0.20 to 0.60). The index of improvement is thus a rise of 1.5 (4.5 ÷ 3).

In recent years more money is being spent on clothes than in the past, primarily by women. In 1940, a man was spending around Q 2.50 a year on clothes and a woman, Q 2.80. Currently a poor man is spending Q 6.50, and a well-off man up to Q 28.00, while women are spending Q 11.00 to Q 38.00, respectively.

TABLE 2.2. *Approximate adult food consumption and cost per month in 1940 and 1970 (by most important foods)*

Food	Quantity		Cost (in *quetzales*)	
	1940	1970	1940	1970
Corn	40 lbs.	60 lbs.	0.50	2.10
Beans	2 lbs.	4.5 lbs.	0.06	0.45
Salt	1 lb.	12 ounces	0.04	0.03
Chile	2 ounces	4 ounces	0.05	0.10
Meat	6 ounces	1 lb.	0.05	0.35
Squash	10	30	0.02	0.30
Avocado	2	2	0.005	0.02
Bananas	1	4	0.005	0.04
Oranges	2	2	0.01	0.02
Coffee	8 ounces	12 ounces	0.05	0.21
Sugar	8 ounces	2 lbs.	0.03	0.16
Bread	0	4	0	0.10
TOTAL	—	—	Q 0.82	Q 3.88

Note: The 1940 data are from memory.

Thirty years ago a man would wear a colored scarf around the neck, a shirt and pants of white cloth, a belt (*pe'r*) around the waist, a red sash, a black wool coat, and sandals. Now he wears a cloth or nylon shirt, with a T-shirt and underwear, sometimes the red sash under the pants to pull in his stomach, pants, belt, sweater, and, unless he is very poor, sandals or shoes, often without socks. Some of the better off have a complete suit (*tacuche*) but never wear a tie. Changing dress has been partly influenced by the fact that merchants who travel to the cities—who are regarded in the town as the best dressed—have had to adjust to city customs.

Women's clothing is more expensive than that of men and has changed little, but has improved in quality. A woman remains at home while her husband seeks his living outside the municipality. A man's prestige comes from his wife's elegance. "He has her looking good," they say. The ribbon (*xk'ab*) used to tie up a woman's tresses on her head, which formerly was a woolen band, is now a ribbon embroidered in silk with many colors, with two pompoms colored red, yellow, and blue on the ends, held in place over the forehead. This ribbon is one of the clearest distinguishing marks denoting a woman from San Antonio. They use gold wire earrings with pendants of stones, flowers, and other decorations. The necklace is made of strings with golden balls; one with twelve strings is considered elegant; the poor have only two or three strings. The *huipil* used to be made out of plain cloth; now it is sometimes embroidered in silk in fine cloth with pleats and embroidery. Brassieres are not used. A wrap-around cloth is the skirt, and it goes down to the feet. The price depends on the cloth. They do not use underpants of any kind. The skirt is held up with a sash. Over that is an apron with machine-made decorations. On top, they wear a many-colored woolen shawl with tassels at either end. Towels with colored flowers are also being used as shawls. A colored cloth (*ek'bal*) and a woolen belt serve for carrying a child on the back.

Very few women have changed traditional items of clothing for ladino ones, even though ladino clothing is cheaper than indigenous clothes. At most, it would be a colored cloth blouse instead of a *huipil*. I do not recall a single instance of a woman regarded as an Indian by the Indians and married to an Indian who did not use the wraparound skirt (*corte*). If she gives up wearing the wraparound skirt for a ladina skirt, she has to wear underpants. Before deciding to put aside the traditional skirt, she will spend a few months testing underpants to become used to them. The traditional skirt seems to be the last bulwark of her femininity as an Indian. Men, on the other hand, do not experience such limitations.

Men are also tending to spend more on personal embellishments, including the clothing, combs, hair grease, hand soap, razors, and such that are sold as "dry goods." That is why barbers are so busy on market days; no one is going to go without a haircut just to save 10 cents. Clothing is washed every week or two in the river. Although these forms of personal embellishment would appear to have made men more ladino, this is not really the case because more and more money is spent on what sets women apart as indigenous, and that has indirectly helped strengthen men's ethnic identity.

A whole range of tools have recently been adopted: electric razors, ice raspers (for snow cones), syringes for injections, jewelers' pliers, screwdrivers, watchmakers' magnifying glasses, and so forth, making it possible to create new lines of work. Other machines are even more expensive, such as sewing machines (Q 159), power-driven mills (Q 79), and especially trucks (Q 8,000) and buses. When the people of San Antonio began to see trucks and buses for the first time forty years ago, they thought they ate people and used to go hide. Today they are considered one of the highest ideals, and children constantly draw them in their school notebooks.

Other objects are useful and also bring prestige. The radio "came out" (onto the market) around 1955, and the first person to buy one paid Q 200. Since 1964, it has spread among the people. The cheapest ones cost Q 18, and 25–30 percent of homes have radios. They play music and lists of greetings sent to the stations by people, including those from San Antonio: "It's like having a marimba band in your house . . . it's fun." There are around thirty bicycles (Q 20–112) in the cantons that are not separated from the town by canyons. Merchants wear wristwatches (Q 15).

The adobe and tile-roof houses with wooden beams generally cost from Q 150–500, depending on the size. There has been a great deal of construction in recent years, and the number of houses has grown more rapidly than the population has.

Finally, many Traditionalists spend Q 50 a year on liquor—more than they spend on food. Members of Catholic Action, who shortly after conversion were quite abstemious, perhaps spend between Q 10 and 15 a year on alcohol. The purchase of liquor is a major drain on community resources.

Market Activity

Before 1947 there was no market or market day in San Antonio. People only got together in the town every three months on feast days. So when their own corn ran out, they had to earn additional corn by working with ladinos or Indians in the cantons of Estancia and Panajxit in Quiché; or they packed it in on animals from Cotzal and Chajul, where it cost Q 1–1.50 per quintal (100 lbs.), because there was no road that far; or they brought it from Joyabaj and Uspantán. Those who spent half the year on the plantations received it with their daily food ration. Others bought it at the home of neighbors in San Antonio who had sheep.

Beans and greens (*ichaj*) were generally bought from neighbors. Salt, raw sugar, chile, coffee, and matches came from nearby markets, such as those in Quiché and Totonicapán, where San Antonio residents went to sell pigs, chickens, lambs and wool, woolen twine, and corn husks. They drank almost no coffee because they were so poor. Tobacco, to be wrapped in corn husks, came from Chiché. Some people used to have a neighbor bring all these things, while others used to set up tiny stores at trail crossings.

Woolen items, such as women's sashes, men's *rodilleras* (knee-length apronlike garments), jackets, and blankets, were woven in the town. Cotton cloth that was bought in Quiché was used to make shirts and underpants for men and *huipiles* for women in San Antonio: "Shirts would be mended over and over until you could no longer see the original shirt." Colored ribbon was brought from Totonicapán to braid in the hair of the better-off women. Poor women used a woolen tie. A merchant used to bring the skirt material from Totonicapán to be resold out of his house. For the January 15 feast day, merchants came from other places to sell clothes in the square.

A market was set up in Santa Lucía la Reforma in 1935, in San Pedro Jocopilas around 1940, and in San Antonio on March 18, 1947. The community was thus brought into a rotating market system: Tuesday, San Antonio; Wednesday, Santa Lucía; Thursday, Quiché, Chiquimula, and Patzité; Friday, San Pedro Jocopilas and a minor market in San Antonio; Saturday, Chiché and Santa Lucía; Sunday, Quiché, Chiquimula, and Patzité; and Monday, nowhere, as Monday is the day when merchants return from the major markets.

The municipality urged the merchants of San Antonio to come to the town square on Tuesday. People came from Panajxit, Santa Cruz Quiché, with their beasts of burden to sell corn. Then the old road was fixed so trucks could transport corn for the many people of San Antonio who had begun to plant this crop on fresh plots of ground on the coast. Two merchants replaced their pack animals with a truck and another bought a bus.

Currently (1970), on a market day there were twenty-two merchants selling food and household items (rice, refined sugar, salt, soap, spices, raw sugar, coffee, chile, fish, shrimp, ropes); twenty-five selling clothing (belts, sashes, skirt material, aprons, shawls, *huipiles*, ribbons, sheets, shirts, pants, T-shirts, underpants, bathing suits); nine offering dry goods (combs, soap, razors, hair oil, matches, locks, pencils, hooks, nails, needles, thread, rubber for sandals, toothbrushes and toothpaste, pot scrapers, plastic toys, and sweet bread for eating); ten with kitchenware (porcelain jars, pots, and pans; clay jugs and large pots; *comales* [flat dish for baking]); eleven selling fruit (bananas, oranges, onions, cabbages, tomatoes, *jocotes*, lemons); three selling candles; nine butchers (offering pork, lamb, beef, tripe, heads, feet, blood for *moronga* [a kind of sausage]); six selling beverages (*atol*, cool drinks, milk-rice drinks, coffee, and *xecas*); five with bread for sale, twelve tortilla and *chuchito* (small *tamal* without filling) makers; three fish sellers (with side items like tomatoes, coffee, plantains, and fruits); two sandal makers; one jeweler (earrings, chains, rings); two selling incense (*copal*, salt, grains, ties); three selling grains (corn) from a truck and twenty selling out of bags; forty women selling poultry (turkey, chicken); thirty selling pigs; ten selling sheep; six selling wool; and eight selling lime. Fifteen food stands were in operation. This picturesque list gives us an idea of what kinds of things are bought in San Antonio.

Before chemical fertilizer was adopted, around 8,000 quintals of corn a year were imported from the coast or Uspantán. Today, by contrast, the municipality sells corn, but it purchases around 8,400 quintals of chemical fertilizers. By our calculations, in 1969, corn production stood at 58,400 quintals, and the people of San Antonio ate around 37,300 quintals themselves, fed over 12,000 quintals to large pigs, and another 4,000 to piglets, roosters, chickens, and turkeys. The amount of surplus corn that is sold is about 5,000 quintals.

Chemical fertilizer is purchased with the proceeds from the sale of beans. Hence people say, "I'm selling three quintals of beans to buy fertilizer." Around 4,000 quintals of beans at Q 10 pays for the municipality's fertilizer, and something is left over for consumption. These beans go to towns on the coast. No intermediaries in the municipality monopolize such sales.

The town's weekly consumption of meat costs approximately Q 600 for three head of beef (Q 300), seven pigs (Q 245), and four sheep (Q 56). In other words, around Q 31,000 a year is spent on meat. Part of this money goes to Chiché and to the coast, from which the beef cattle are brought. Part of it stays in the municipality where the pigs and sheep come from. Indeed, the sale of pigs comes to about Q 37,000 a year; more than a third of the pigs are sold to butchers in the town and the rest to ladino butchers in Quiché and to buyers of small pigs at markets in Totonicapán, Momostenango, and San Francisco el Alto. Chemical fertilizer has also made it possible to raise more pigs.

Finally, clothing is what takes the largest amount of money out of the community, around Q 60,000 a year. Agricultural workers earn this money from the cotton farms, from the salt flats, from small surpluses from various lines of work, and from trade. Money earned on the coast also goes to liquor. Each year between 350 and 400 boxes of liquor (each containing 96 liters) are sold, all of them registered with the Revenue Administration. It is also calculated that a similar or larger amount (Q 6,000) is made from liquor produced clandestinely in the canyons, which is sold at half the price—legal liquor costs

Q 0.30 per 1/8 liter bottle and the clandestine type, Q 0.15. The clandestine business is excellent: almost half the price goes to the bar owner and the rest to the liquor maker. If it were to be legalized, that would no longer be true; without the danger of being caught by the Treasury Police, anyone could engage in it, so prices would fall. The ladino cantina owners would not be able to send their children to school, and the Treasury Police would be deprived of the hen that lays the golden eggs; it is in the latter's interest to appear to be stamping it out, in order to get bribes, but not to ever stamp it out.

Economic Summary

The trend of the changes that have taken place in the economy of the community in the past twenty-five years is toward an ever greater penetration of the world from outside the community and an ever stronger integration of the community into the nation and even beyond. Because of the land shortage caused by the increasing pace of population growth, sheep herding declined and with it the possibility of fertilizing the land organically. Ever larger numbers of people were forced to go out looking for other sources of income in the piedmont area (coffee), on the coast (cotton), in the salt flats, in trade in the ladino administrative towns of the departments, and in the capital city. Because of this economic connection through labor, the daily wage in the community steadily changed in accordance with what was paid on large farms; as it rose there, it also had to rise in the community. Likewise, the lack of organic fertilizer made people more willing to accept imported fertilizer (by about 1965), thanks to which land productivity doubled, pig and poultry breeding increased, and it became possible to "export" corn. At the same time, some kinds of crops were being eliminated, such as dry-season corn, which became expensive as wages rose, and wheat, which yielded less than the combination of corn, beans, squash, and *chilacayotes*.

Thanks to increased productivity, after 1965 fewer work crews went to the coast seeking employment because it began to yield less than doing agricultural work in the municipality, especially during certain months of the year. When the pay elsewhere, such as at the salt deposits, was considerably higher, the number of workers did not drop. Nor in this case did wages increase, because of limits on salt production, which was at a comparative disadvantage vis-à-vis El Salvador. Thus, growing dependence on imported technology had a debilitating effect on lower-paying work. One bond was replaced by another, although the cotton plantation owners did not notice because they still had vast supplies of labor in work crews from the highlands. In the country as a whole, no competition between large commercial farmers and fertilizer dealers has been noted.

A corresponding rise in living standards has been noted, although there are still reports of people going hungry in the months of scarcity, June to August, when the corn in storage runs out. A particularly noteworthy item has been the outflow of money for the purchase of clothing, especially for women, which used to be largely made in the municipality. The clearly symbolic character of clothing is reinforced by the accent on small luxury spending by the men, who, albeit gradually, have gone over almost completely to wearing ladino clothes. Even so, they maintain an indigenous pattern in the way the pieces of clothing are combined, which is unmistakable for indigenous people themselves. The upshot of this relatively comfortable situation has been that few people have left for good, and the ethnic identity of the people of San Antonio has been reinforced.

Many tools manufactured outside the country have entered into use in Guatemala. Some have opened the way for new kinds of work. Others, like the radio, have proliferated and have broadened the contact of people in the community with events in the rest of the country. Finally, some of these tools, such as heavy vehicles, which were brought into the community after new roads were built, have integrated the municipality into a wider market area, have concentrated certain kinds of things in the hands of some merchants (fertilizers, hoes), and have been the clearest and most powerful force for a noticeable class stratification.

Regional trade has intensified because of population increase, and it is to be assumed that there are more merchants from San Antonio in nearby markets in the rotating system into which the municipality has been integrated since 1947. Trade outside the region—made possible by the extension of roads and communication around the country, the existence of rapid transportation, and the gradual freeing of indigenous labor after 1934, when debts were forgiven— has been a source of revenue for merchants with varying amounts of investment, as well as an avenue for new ideas. It is curious to note, for example, that the pace of new house construction is higher than that of population growth. All of this indicates that the prosperity of recent years must be regarded as an improvement in comparison to the years of the world depression and the following decade, though perhaps not to periods before that crisis (e.g., the 1920s), when the population increase was slower and people had not been forced by that situation (as opposed to legal requirements) to go elsewhere to earn money.

In conclusion, then, we may note that although for now the community's enhanced connection to productive technology and transportation, in terms of prices and the purchasing power on a national market, has led to higher incomes, improved living standards, and an affirmation of ethnic identity, this connection nevertheless bears the mark of dependence, and hence adverse developments outside the community will affect the community's life more profoundly than used to be the case. It is against the background of these processes that in the chapters to come we will study conversion from traditional beliefs to beliefs entering from the outside world.

Social Organization

The Domestic Unit

The most immediate framework for the conversion process is the household, where tensions are established between its various members, particularly between father and son. Hence it is useful to give a detailed description of the domestic unit.

A domestic unit is defined by shared residency in a house (*ja*). Approximately 62 percent of the houses in San Antonio are inhabited by just one couple, 31 percent are inhabited by two or more couples, and 6 percent have a single occupant (usually a widow). Of the 31 percent containing two or more couples, in 70 percent of the cases it is a father and son and their partners, or the sons and their partners without the father or the grandchildren. As might be expected, the composition of the domestic unit varies. However, underlying these variations is a discernible basic model for San Antonio, which is that unit composed of two or more couples in which the men are related as father and son(s). From this model derives the unit of only one couple, which occurs when the father or the mother (or both) of the husband of that couple is (or are) deceased. In most (89%) of the houses with only one couple, the husband has lost his father, who would probably be living with him had he not died. When the father dies, if several sons are left, each married, they continue to live together for a time until the younger ones start building their own houses and go away to live as one-couple units, and the eldest remains in what was formerly his deceased father's house. Therefore, if people lived longer, there would be more grandfathers and more units made up of couples in which the males are father and son.

The fundamental model assumes that descent is patrilinear and residence is patrilocal. A small number of matrilocal units do occur, generally because the father and head of the house has only daughters, and the husband of one of them therefore ends up living in his father-in-law's house.

I next offer an example of a domestic unit composed of three couples: the father and his wife and his two sons and their wives. Only one of the latter has children. The house measures 20 by 7 yards, and hence it is larger than the more usual 7 x 5 size. It is made up of two rooms (many have only one). The fire is in the smaller one, which is the kitchen. There is only one fire, thereby indicating that the household economy of the couples is not divided, and that the two sons hand over what they earn to their father. In some instances, however, when a dispute breaks out between couples and they cannot afford to build a new house, they have more than one fire and each room constitutes something of a separate house.

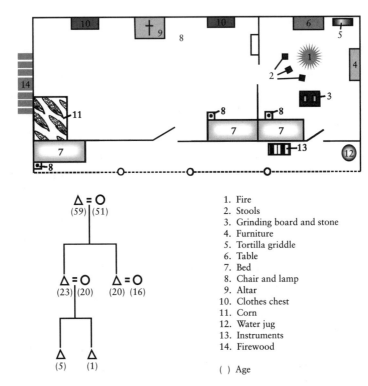

DRAWING 2.1. *Drawing of one home in the canton of San Antonio, showing the kinship relationship of its members*

1. Fire
2. Stools
3. Grinding board and stone
4. Furniture
5. Tortilla griddle
6. Table
7. Bed
8. Chair and lamp
9. Altar
10. Clothes chest
11. Corn
12. Water jug
13. Instruments
14. Firewood

( ) Age

It is the men's role to earn money. One of them is a merchant in Guatemala City, using capital from his father; the other handles the farming on his father's land (they plant 75 *cuerdas*). The father, who is unquestionably the head of the house, runs a motorized tortilla mill. The women handle the animals: the father's wife looks after the cows, and the younger, still childless daughter-in-law manages the sheep, which she takes out to graze on the hillsides from morning until evening. The other daughter-in-law is nursing her son, who is a year and a half old; nursing lasts for two years. She also helps her mother-in-law to move the tortilla dough through the mill and to cook. There is no cooperation in washing clothes: that is the primary thing a wife does for her husband after marrying him.

For sleeping, they occupy both rooms and the covered area in front of the house: the parents sleep in the kitchen so the mother can light the fire very early. The older son, when he is home, sleeps in the large room with his wife and their two children, all on the same wooden boards. The adults sleep on the edges of the rustic bed so that the children are between them and the wall and will not fall off. The nursing child is with the mother. Finally, the younger son and his wife sleep out under the overhang, protected from the wind by curtains sewn out of flour sacks. They sleep outside to be alert for when the dog barks and to be ready to defend the penned-up sheep from coyotes.

It is customary for one of the grandsons to bear the name of his grandfather or that of one of his great-uncles. The grandfather then says that this grandchild is his *c'axel*, or replacement. This idea suggests that the domestic unit is divided into three major periods, or generations. This division is replicated in the social world of the *cofradías*: those who do not yet participate in them ("grandsons") and those who have already served ("grandparents"). The outer groups take it easy, while those in the middle ("sons") bear the burden of serving the *cofradías*.

Inheritance

By the rules of inheritance, only male children inherit land. Hence a woman neither owns property nor can she leave an inheritance. But if the father has no sons and has only daughters, then they do receive an inheritance and pass it on to their sons. If the father has no children of either sex, he does not pass his inheritance on to his wife or to the male children that she may have had from another man before becoming a widow; instead, it is divided among the brothers of the deceased, or his sisters, if he has no brothers. If he has no siblings of either sex, it goes to the male descendants of his father's brothers. In these cases, the *chuchkajaw* becomes involved; he is one of the oldest male relatives in the lineage segment (see below), and it may happen that he keeps half the inheritance to divide among his descendants when he dies, and distributes the other half to another older relative.

The eldest son receives the father's house. The other sons, with the help of the eldest or of the father if he is still alive, build their own homes on a piece of land normally next to that of the oldest house. As generations go on, more and more houses are built, but people know which is the oldest, the one they came from as branches from a trunk. I call this group of relatives related by the patrilinear line the *lineage segment*. There is no term for it in the Quiché language. It is not difficult to manage these inheritance rules because family ties are remarkably imprinted on the division of the land.

Inheritance rules are also reflected in certain kinship terms, such as, for example, those defining the relationship between parents and children. The children, male and female, call their parents *tat* (father) and *nan* (mother), but while the father distinguishes the sex of his children, calling them *c'ojol* (son) and *mi'al* (daughter), the mother does not make a distinction and calls them both *al* (son, daughter). From the father's standpoint as testator, the son is different from the daughter. From the mother's standpoint, both are equal because she cannot pass any inheritance on to them. This correspondence between these terms of relationship and inheritance rules is confirmed by other terms that we cannot pause to examine here.

Alliance

Another very important term, already mentioned in another context, is that of *chuchkajaw*. When a boy and girl unite in marriage, their mothers and fathers become *chuchkajaw* among themselves (something like joint fathers-in-law and mothers-in-law), and by extension the parents' parents become *chuchkajaw* among themselves. This relationship entails a great deal of respect. The fact that it extends to all the forebears in a straight line from the parents of the spouses shows how marriage is an alliance not only between two houses, but between two lineage segments. The persons who have the most *chuchkajaw* relationships are therefore the oldest. They are the *chuchkajaw* par excellence, and that term reflects a guiding position in the lineage segment. It also therefore comes to mean the function of *zahorín* that such an older person tends to perform. It must be pointed out, finally, that *chuchkajaw* is composed of *chuch* and *kajaw*, terms that mean "mother" and "father," respectively. As one informant stated, "Saying 'my *chuchkajaw*' is somewhat like saying 'my mother-father,' bearing in mind that I am also his or her 'mother-father.'"

Marriage

The traditional form of choosing a wife was for a boy's parents to arrange the marriage, selecting a mate for their son while he was still very young and the girl often even younger. Today, however, although some still practice this traditional form, it is the groom himself who chooses his future wife, and she is consulted. In another chapter, we will examine in greater detail this process, which has been part of a broader rebellion by children against their parents. Further on, we will also study the change in the pattern of marriages between cantons, which has led to a reorganization of the municipality and has paved the way for conversion.

The traditional marriage rite (*c'ulnem*) is one of the most marvelous things about this culture. In its general structure, it is still observed by members of Catholic Action and by Protestants. After the groom's parents have chosen the girl and have consulted over the choice, especially with the mother's relatives, since parents tend to look for a wife for their child from the area where the mother came from, the *zahorín* is consulted, and if he grants approval, a traditional rite (*costumbre*) is performed in the forest in order to "tame the girl's father." The whole ritual process, which sometimes lasts over a year, then begins. It is made up of four parts: (1) the petitions; (2) the *tz'onoj*, or gifts; (3) the marriage itself, or *c'ulnem*; (4) the *ji'ixic*, or process by which the boy becomes a son-in-law.

1. *The petitions*. Two petitions are generally made. In the first one, the boy's father and mother go alone in the early morning to the house of their future joint in-laws, offering liquor and asking them for their daughter's hand. The second time they go, again bearing liquor, they are accompanied by other

witnesses, older relatives of the boy's father, to receive the official answer to the first petition. During the period between the two petitions, the parents of the girl learn about the boy and consult with the *zahorín*. If they belong to Catholic Action, liquor is not used but only bread and sugar will be served with the coffee that the girl's parents will offer those making the petition. If there is any doubt about the prospective husband, the Catholic Action members consult with the president of the center.

2. *The gifts.* Once the petitions have been made, by mutual agreement a date is set for the boy's parents to come with the gifts. These visits with gifts are the *tz'onoj*. There are usually four combined *tz'onoj* or eight simple ones. If there are eight, on the first one, *atol* (a thick, corn-based drink) and bread are brought; and on the second one, meat and tamales; on the third, *atol* and bread; on the fourth, beef and tamales; and so forth. If there are four, the four types of gifts are combined in one visit. The *tz'onoj* are spread out over a three- to twelve-month period and cost around Q 50. They are more expensive if the girl's parents are well off. Today the fiancé is generally allowed to visit and talk with his fiancée, something that was once prohibited.

If the parents of the young people belong to Catholic Action, they generally make only six simple *tz'onoj*. The prospective bride and groom then present their birth certificates to the Catholic priest in the sacristy and attend eight classes that deal with marriage, given by a catechist appointed by the Catholic Action board members from the entire municipality, before whom they must appear for an examination. They then go through a civil marriage ceremony at the local courthouse. The groom's relatives first head to the bride's communal house. This is the house in town that belongs to the lineage segment, but no one lives there; it is used only for celebrations. Both groups of relatives file out of this house on their way to the courthouse. There, in the presence of the mayor, the couple are married. Then the groom's parents pass out sodas or juices. When the civil ceremony is over, they all head to the communal house of the groom's segment, where a meal is provided, which equals the seventh and eighth *tz'onoj*. After the meal, the groom's relatives leave with the bride for their communal house. At each entry and departure a locally made firecracker is set off.

The next day the church marriage is performed. Again the groom's relatives head to the communal house on the bride's side. The best man and bridesmaid (a married couple) help the bride and groom get ready and give advice. The best man places a golden chain on the groom, and the bridesmaid combs the bride's hair while she is on her knees, and perhaps weeping. When her hair is ready, the bridesmaid places a white veil on her head and a crown of paper flowers. The line then proceeds to the church, where the church wedding takes place, and afterward a meal is provided at the groom's house.

3. *The wedding itself.* Now comes the *c'ulnem*, or traditional wedding. If the bride and groom are Catholic Action members and have married civilly and ecclesiastically, they leave the groom's communal house and proceed in

line to the bride's communal house. The groom's relatives bring gifts equaling a ninth and tenth *tz'onoj*. At the bride's communal house, the witnesses for both the bride and groom (*c'ulel*) come together to offer advice to the couple.

If they do not belong to Catholic Action and there has been no civil or church ceremony in which the witnesses offer their advice, this takes place at the bride's house in the canton. The groom's relatives arrive in a line, with him leading and carrying a load of firewood. When they reach the bride's house, the witnesses are ushered into the large room where the bride's witnesses are waiting while the groom is fed in the kitchen. Sitting there among the women, the bride has her hair combed and her clothes arranged. The young man is embarrassed and does not speak. The witnesses meanwhile are seated in two opposing rows, the bride's to the left of the small home altar and the groom's to the right, and have begun to smoke and then to drink the hard liquor that the groom's witnesses have brought to serve. They then warm up, calling to the bride and groom and making them get down on their knees and pass before the witnesses, each of whom offers them a long series of counsels. This is when new family ties are established, because in receiving the advice, the newlyweds greet their in-laws for the first time with the proper term of father-in-law (*ji'*) or mother-in-law (*ulib'*). The witnesses then drink, and sometimes the newlyweds are allowed to drink, each taking half from the same glass.

It should be noted that among the Traditionalists, whose *c'ulnem* is celebrated with liquor, there are no sponsors (*padrinos*, or best man and bridesmaid). Everything is done by the witnesses, who are seated and ranked by age. First comes the oldest man in the father's segment; second is the oldest man in the mother's segment; third is the next in age in the father's segment, and if there is a closer relative, such as the father's father or older brother, some of these; fourth, same in the mother's line; fifth, the father. There may be one more if there are other close relatives of the father. In that case, the number of witnesses is six. The father of the groom or the bride, however, always occupies the last position, which in this case would be number six. Each witness is accompanied by his wife, or if she is not there, by someone representing her. But though the men are seated on benches with their backs against the wall, the women are on the floor. "Holy liquor" is placed in the middle.

After having offered advice to the bride and groom, the witnesses give advice to the groom's parents, because the newlyweds are going to live with them. The witnesses are given a glass of liquor. Finally, the wife of the bride's first witness gives her a blanket. The groom's witnesses say good-bye, and the young man stays in the house of his new wife and sleeps with her for the first time.

4. *Becoming a son-in-law.* As an addendum to the whole process comes the *ji'ixic*, or becoming a son-in-law. For two or three months, the groom sleeps in the house of his in-laws, and he brings them firewood and water as signs of service, but during the day he works with his own father. One or two weeks after this begins, he asks his in-laws to allow their daughter to go wash his clothing at his parents' house. The young woman then stays there and sleeps a

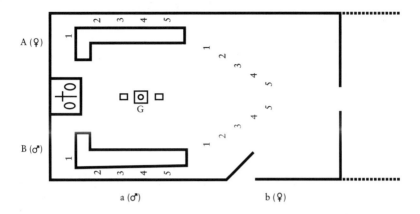

A: Bride's segment   a: Male witnesses
B: Groom's segment   b: Female witnesses
G: Holy liquor (*guaro*)

DRAWING 2.2. *Placement of witnesses in traditional wedding* (c'ulnem)

couple of nights in her future house, and each time she goes to wash her husband's clothes she stays more days. Things continue in this manner until the young man's parents carry out a final ritual (*costumbre*), taking their joint in-laws an offering of *atol*, bread, meat, and tamales so that the girl may come to stay for good in her husband's home, that is, his parents' home.

Lineage Segment and Lineage

I use the term *lineage segment* to define a group of patrilinearly related relatives who are likewise neighbors. A *lineage*, by contrast, is made up of various segments and is known because, like members of the same segment, they bear the same surname, but unlike members of a segment, they are not neighbors, but live in various hamlets in the same canton or in different cantons. Lineage members are considered descendants of the same ancestor, and within the segments there are generally some older people who know the oldest house from which people went to live in other settlements. The segment is exogamous, as is the lineage, although not quite as strictly.

I am not familiar with any term in the Quiché language for either lineage or lineage segment. Although the idea of lineage exists, it is almost never invoked. That is not so for the lineage segment. A clear example is that of the witnesses of the traditional wedding, as presented in the previous section. Moreover, it is recognized by the canton inhabitants themselves as a unit in a place when they refer in the plural to the "Ajpop," the "Tzampop," or the "Sion" (plural forms of family names) when listing groups who live in the canton. One informant drew me a map of a part of his canton with the legend "Here are (1) the Cortes; (2) the Lobos; here (3) the Velásquez; here (4) the

Ajpop; here (5) the Chajon; etc.," indicating each with an oval, making it clear that the canton is made up of these discrete units. Names like Ajpop, Tzampop, and so forth are surnames that are passed on from father to son. As we will see in the main part of this study and as I have already written (Falla 1970), the lineage segment lends its specific form to the conversion process.

The authority of older people in the segment has weakened considerably today. Their position in it is almost exclusively a ritual remnant. From these ritual remnants, such as that of the ranking of the witnesses at a traditional wedding, one can detect how the segment was organized some years back and what kind of authority older people enjoyed. They must have been judges in matrimonial conflicts and probably also judges in conflicts over inheritance. Even today, when the father is old, the land is still divided up in the presence of the witnesses from the father's segment. In some instances, one of the elders (*ancianos*) is even called in from another segment of the same lineage in a nearby canton. But now the authority of the elders has shifted to the town mayor, who is the common arbiter in matrimonial disputes, and to the regional judge in Santa Cruz del Quiché, who resolves inheritance conflicts. The strengthening of these authorities has paralleled the weakening of the segment authorities.

Another factor that has probably contributed to this weakening of authority is the disappearance of segment or lineage communal lands. All that is left of these lands are some pieces of canyon from which the members of some segment or other have the right to get firewood. The value of these areas and their wood resources are very low, because the white powder soil (*poklaj*) is of poor quality.

I have already explained how the oldest man in the lineage is the *chuchkajaw* par excellence and how he tends to also be a *zahorín*. In the central part of this study, I show how even though the lineage and its segments have been relegated to serving as a ritual organization, these old men retain great power over their people in terms of beliefs. That is why they present an obstacle to conversions.

Each lineage or group of segments—if it is one of the latter it is not very large—has a communal house in the town, as already mentioned in the discussion about the wedding. These houses, of which there are about sixty, are used for celebrations like feast days of the *cofradías*, wakes, and weddings. They tend to have one large room and two or three other rooms at right angles. The *cofradía's* dance (sarabande) is held in the large room. Two hundred or more can squeeze in to dance. One of the other rooms serves as the *cofradía's* kitchen, and the other as the kitchen for the relatives of the *alcalde* of the *cofradía*. Each room has a wooden key and there are generally three copies of each key, held by three different segments.

The communal houses in the town are the sign of unity of all the lineages in the municipality. Around the center of the town stand the oldest houses of the oldest lineages. As the lineage grew, other houses were built alongside the first, and then each of them was assigned to a segment or segment groups. The visibility of the closeness of the segment houses in the cantons is then replicated in the town. The lineages formed by people who are recently arrived (three or four generations ago) have fewer houses and are located on the outskirts of the town.

When one of these houses over a hundred years old needs to be repaired, the heads of each house of the lineage hold a session. They also meet to assign rooms for the exclusive use of different segments or to put up a new communal house for an entire segment.

There are forty-eight surnames in the municipality, which may correspond to forty-eight lineages and over one hundred segments. Some lineages have up to six segments, while others that are recent arrivals or have almost disappeared over time have only one.

Cantons

There are ten cantons in the municipality of San Antonio Ilotenango, and they are generally listed from north to south: Canamixtoj, Xejip (under the hill), Chotacaj (on the flat), Sacxac (white *talpetate*), Chuijip (over the hill), Tzancawuib, Chiaj (next to the sugarcane), Chichó (facing the lake), Xebaquit (under the oak), and Patzalá (in *tzalá*).

The cantons are territorial divisions. Their limits are clearly defined when a river or ravine comes between them. Otherwise, the boundaries are known only to the owners of bordering lands. They know on which canton's list they appear. Apart from some exceptions that occurred after 1945 for the more densely populated central cantons, all members of a canton live in it.

In each canton, some places are given special names, which are of two types, one indicating where a lineage segment lives, for example, Chi Sionib, or "at the Sion," and another whose etymology is ordinarily topographical. This latter type of place I will call a *hamlet* (*paraje*), a term not used by the local people. Each canton contains many hamlets. By way of example, the hamlets in the Canamixtoj canton are: "Canamixtoj itself," which is like the center of the canton, and the place that has been populated longest; Xotzirimak (where there is pumice rock); Chuitzununá (over the Tzununá River); Pacbaltem (where beams are cut); Patzám; and so forth. Some of the larger hamlets are separated from neighboring ones by rivers and tend to become cantons, as we will see by the geographical patterns of marriage alliances in the conversion part of the study. This tendency has also had an influence on conversion.

The ten cantons are divided into four groups. Each group is represented in the municipality by one *mayor*, one *auxiliar*, and a certain fixed number of *alguaciles*. In the entire municipality, there are twenty-four *alguaciles*, four *auxiliares*, and four *mayores*. The appointment of *mayores* and *auxiliares* is by turns around the cantons of the same group. Their order is indicated in Figure 2.1.

FIGURE 2.1. *Order of* mayor *and* auxiliar *appointment by canton*

	1st	2nd	3rd	4th
Mayor	Canamixtoj	Sacxac	Tzancawib	Chuijoj
	Xejip		Chichó	Patzalá
			Chiaj	
			Xebaquit	
Auxiliar	Xejip	Sacxac	Chiaj	Patzalá
	Canamixtoj		Xebaquit	Chuijoj
			Tzancawib	
			Chichó	

This means that the first *mayor* always comes from Canamixtoj or Xejip. "The first *mayor* goes from one canton to another," they say. One year he is from one and the next he is from the other. When the *mayor* comes from one, the *auxiliar* comes from another. The second *mayor* and the second *auxiliar* are always from Sacxac. The third *mayor* is by rotation from Tzancawuib, Chichó, Chiaj, and Xbaquit, and the third *auxiliar* likewise rotates from Chiaj, Xebaquit, Tzancawuib, and Chichó. The fourth *mayor* and *auxiliar* change off between the two divisions of the Patzalá canton: Patzalá itself and Chuijoj. The two central cantons, Chuijip and Chotacaj, never have the right to appoint either a *mayor* or an *auxiliar*. They can appoint only the first and second *alguaciles*, who switch back and forth between the two cantons. These two *alguaciles*, like the *mayores* and *auxiliares*, have a staff of office with a silver top and they are appointed by the *cruncipales* (see below) at the suggestion of those leaving office on November 1 each year. By contrast, the other twenty-two *alguaciles* have neither a staff nor are they appointed by the *cruncipales*. They look for their replacements by themselves. There are two from each canton, plus two from Chuijoj.

Every week, one *mayor* and one *auxiliar* has to serve in the municipality with their group of six *alguaciles*. The service rotates weekly through the first, second, third, and fourth *mayor*. This rotation matches the geographical rotation from north through west, south, and east. The *mayor* receives orders from the mayor and passes them on to his *auxiliar*, who with his *alguaciles* goes out to implement the order. The elder stays in the municipality while those under him leave to do their assignments. The *alguaciles* also perform the functions of messengers and a kind of police that jails drunks. This whole system is still operating today as it is described.

Moreover, each canton has a clerk and a treasurer. The former handles the lists of men who can work, which ordinarily includes those who are married and those who are over 60. They are obliged to work on fixing the roads in the cantons, and they are charged a fee to pay for feast-day masses throughout the municipality. The treasurer keeps the extra money. The terms of both positions are for several years.

Each canton also has its group of *principales* (the older men used the word *cruncipales*, probably because some of them crucified Christ during Holy Week). Currently, I have not been able to check how many there are, which indicates how fuzzy the notion of this position is. In 1943, according to a list of participants in a November 13 municipal session held to discuss repairing the church— which had been damaged in the August 1942 earthquake—and completing a section of road, there were thirty-seven *principales*. From some cantons four show up, and from one as many as eleven. It has to be noted, however, that they were probably *principales*, according to the judgment of the municipal clerk, a ladino who drew up the minutes.

It seems that, strictly speaking, there were only two *principales* in each canton. If one died, then when the time came for the annual meeting to organize the repair of local roads, at the end of the work the old men and all the people by common agreement named a replacement. It was the *principal's* task to watch over road conditions in his canton.

Municipal Organization

President Jorge Ubico enacted the Law of Municipalities on August 9, 1935, by which mayors popularly elected according to the 1921 Constitution (Art. 5.96) were replaced by an intendant appointed by the political chief of the department. In indigenous communities, this intendant was almost always a ladino from outside the community. The other council members, however, continued to be popularly elected.

Until 1935 there were two mayors in San Antonio who took turns week by week, one *síndico*, and six *regidores*. When the ladino intendant came on the scene, the *síndico* seems to have replaced the mayor for ritual matters, such as appointing *cofradía* members. When the intendancy remained unoccupied, sometimes for one or two months, one of the higher-ranking council members was chosen by the municipal council and other residents, probably elders (*principales*), to replace the intendant. The *síndico* and the *regidores*, as was also the case with the mayors before 1935, were appointed by the *principales* of all the cantons on November 1 each year. In San Antonio, there has never been an indigenous mayor's position as distinct from the ladino mayor, as is the case in San Pedro Jocopilas, Santa Cruz del Quiché, Chichicastenango, and elsewhere, probably because there were almost no ladinos.

Thus it is clear that other than the ritual contributions for feast days and the work on roads and bridges, no other common purpose links the people of one canton and separates them from members of other cantons, either now or in the recent past. Although the officials (*mayor*, *auxiliar*, and *alguacil*) represent the cantons, they are part of a municipal organization with municipality-wide functions. Likewise there are no *cofradías* from just one canton. Neither before the entry of Catholic Action nor afterward were there canton places of worship. Further on it will become clear that in terms of organization, it is here that a change takes place, because when Catholic Action centers with their chapels (*oratorios*) and small Protestant churches are set up, these organizations include several cantons, or just one, or part of one. Later I show how the need to organize such centers arose, as neither the canton-level organization nor the municipal-level *cofradías* met the challenges imposed by population growth. That reorganization further contributed to conversion.

With the 1945 Constitution, the position of intendant was abolished and the mayor was now popularly elected. The *principales* included the mayor in their election on November 1, as had been the case before 1935. I will deal separately with how the political parties became involved and developed, when I take up the growth of Catholic Action.

Contrary to the *mayores*, *auxiliares*, and *alguaciles*, who have a separate room in the municipal building, the *regidores* even today are involved in helping the mayor to judge. They sit alongside him by rank along the wall, behind the mayor's desk, and form a judicial body together with him.

Besides the administrative positions (*cargos*), there are those of the *cofradías*, whose functions have to do with celebrations. Until 1970 there were eight *cofradías*, four to celebrate major feasts ("they have more rank") and four for minor feasts. The major feasts are San Antonio (St. Anthony), San Sebastián (St. Sebastian), Sacramento (Blessed Sacrament), and San Juan (St. John). San José (St. Joseph), María (Mary), Santa Cruz (Holy Cross), and Santa Ana (St. Anne) are the minor ones. Their feasts were and are celebrated on January 17 (San Antonio and San Sebastián); the day of Corpus Christi in May or June (Sacramento and San Juan); and on March 19, September 8, September 14, and November 1 for the other four, respectively (in 1970, after I left the town, these four were dropped). In order of importance—and matching the placement of the *cofradía alcaldes* (from left to right) in church, in processions, or at banquets—they are San Antonio, Sacramento, San Sebastián, San Juan, San José, Santa Cruz, María, and Santa Ana. However, when they list them verbally, they do so in chronological order by their feast days.

Each *cofradía* is made up of six men (*achí*), or *cofrades*, and six women (*ixok* or *chuchuxel*), ranked in order from first to sixth. The first man is also called *alcalde* (*ajcalté*) and the woman with him is called *ixokajaw* (the master's wife). Men and women of the same *cofradía* do not intermarry nor do they belong to the same lineage segment, especially *alcaldes*, who have to make the largest expenditures. Each *cofrade*, man or woman, seeks an assistant from among his or her relatives to carry water, carry the saint (if a man), or cook or wash dishes (if a woman). But the *alcalde* looks for around ten men from his segment, with their wives, to be his *mucumab*, or assistants. The *alcalde* of the *cofradía* has to feed all his assistants while the celebration of the feast is going on. The *cofrades* eat separately in another room. That is why *cofradía* celebrations entail a double celebration, that of the lineage segment and that of the *cofradía* as such.

A person born in San Antonio must serve the community, rising from less important to more important *cargos* over his or her lifetime. Naturally, not everyone can become mayor of the municipality or *alcalde* of one of the more important *cofradías*. Such service entails time and dedication for the less important *cargos*, and money for those of greater importance, especially the *cargo* of *alcaldes* of the *cofradía* or their wives (*ixokajaw*).

The path of ascent by grades (*ek'elen*) from lesser to more important *cargos* is not clear. Some persons begin their service as a *chajal*, the one who takes care of the church. Every man has an obligation to serve as *alguacil*. He then rises to the grade of sixth male *cofrade* and later (through his wife) to that of sixth female *cofrade*. This means that although the woman appeared in the ceremony, in the procession, for example, her husband helped with the necessary expenses; likewise, when the man had his *cargo*, his wife helped him. This was the order of progression, rising first by the man's *cargo*, and then by the woman's, until it went past the third *cofrade*. It could be from any *cofradía*. Out of the group that had reached that point, the *principales* appointed the *auxiliares*. Next came the grade of second *cofrade*, and out of the group that had gone through this *cargo* they chose the *mayores*. One who had served as *auxiliar*, however, might not have to serve as second *cofrade*, and because of his time and experience in the municipality, he would move up to being *mayor* without having had to be a second *cofrade*. The next step would be the office of *regidor* or *alcalde* of one of the lesser *cofradías*, followed by that of *ixokajaw* of any of the same four lesser *cofradías*. The next step was that of *alcalde* of San Sebastián or San Juan if the individual had money. Some seem to have risen instead to being mayor of the municipality or *síndico*. Then the mayor of the municipality and the *síndico* took the position of the *alcalde* of the *cofradía* of San Antonio and Sacramento respectively. This step is still preserved today. If no one was found to serve as *alcalde* of the lesser *cofradías*, someone who had already taken that position volunteered once more. The one who had been *alcalde* of the *cofradía* of San Antonio seems to have had to still be *ixokajaw* of San Antonio. He was then seen to be free from commitments and was given a special rank: he was now a *principal*. It is not clear to me whether others who had served as *alcaldes* in other *cofradías* became *principales*. Nor is the relationship between these *principales* and those in each canton clear. Perhaps those for the canton were chosen from these *principales*.

Although the mayor of the municipality, *síndico*, *regidores*, *auxiliares*, and first two *alguaciles* used to be appointed by the *principales* meeting on November 1, the *cofrades* were chosen by the municipal mayor. With the exception of the mayor, the *síndico*, and the *regidores*, who are now chosen by popular vote, the other appointments, including the *cofrades*, are still made by the *principales* and the mayor. Nominations for *cofrades* are suggested by the *mayores*, *auxiliares*, and *alguaciles*, who keep track of the services performed by the people in their cantons in their memory. The mayor calls to his office those who have to serve. He used to force those appointed to accept under pain of imprisonment, unless they presented a convincing excuse. People from different cantons entered each *cofradía*. The *cofradías* are not spontaneous groups; they are formed by the authorities. Today there is resistance to serving, and so the *alguaciles* spend a lot of time summoning the people and the mayor, trying to convince them to serve.

No remuneration was given for *cargos* in the municipality, nor are they remunerated today, with the exception of the town mayor, who in 1956 began to earn Q 12 a month. Before 1945, the ladino intendant earned Q 20 a month. The municipal clerk, a position that has existed in the department of Quiché since 1885 (Leyes de Guatemala, vol. 4, p. 561), was appointed by the political chief until 1945, and subsequently was hired by the municipal corporation. In 1970, the mayor of the municipality was earning Q 20, the clerk received Q 60 for work as clerk plus Q 25 for work in the treasury, and the *oficial* (a ladino, like the clerk) earned Q 20 for Civil Registry work and Q 35 for handling mail.

The yearly expenses incurred by the *cofrades* of a minor *cofradía* are currently (1970) Q 150 for the *alcalde* and Q 30 for each of the other eleven *cofrades*. The *alcalde* of the San Antonio *cofradía*, by contrast, spends Q 250 or more, because he has to pay for more sarabande dances and has to pay for higher-priced marimba bands. The other *cofrades* of the San Antonio *cofradía* have to pay Q 60 apiece. It is more expensive for the *alcalde* because besides the shared expenses, such as the marimba band and meals for the *cofrades*, he has to provide food for the people in his own segment. He has to set up two cooking operations and pay two separate sets of expenses.

The sacristan takes orders from the six *chajales*, who are responsible for caring for the church and are appointed by the *principales* at the request of those finishing each year. The sacristan, whose position is permanent, prepares the ceremonial items used by the priest, and at one time would have been appointed by the priest together with the *principales*. Currently, the latter also make him responsible for caring for the church building and obeying the *chajales*.

The *fiscal* was also appointed by the priest when the latter used to visit the municipality frequently. Today, however, the *principales* choose him while he is young so that he can learn alongside the *fiscal* whom he will eventually replace. It is a lifetime position whose purpose used to be to replace the priest in certain actions, such as processions, burials, and in the *cofradías* themselves. He has remained as a figure who directs some ceremonies in which the *cofrades* participate and as a literate prayer leader who can read prayer books or rituals in Latin.

Zahorines divine people's fate and the nonempirical reasons for misfortunes using the 260-day Maya calendar, and they "carry out traditions" (rituals) of burning incense and candles on the hillsides, in the church, in the cemetery, and in private homes. They pray for all kinds of people and take part in celebrations of the *cofradías* and the *alcalde*'s office. Hence, they have influence on all levels. One becomes a *zahorín* by training with another, more experienced *zahorín*, but in addition, one needs certain innate qualities, such as a more delicate sensitivity to the signs of one's own blood and body, and the signs of fate or unexpected callings or promptings (dreams). (See the explanation of the Maya calendar in note 2 of Chapter 3.)

Catholic Action Organization

Today, the way Catholic Action is organized in the municipality parallels how the *cofradías* are organized. There are seven *centers* located in the following cantons: Chiaj, Canamixtoj, Chuijoj, Chotacaj (where the town is located), Chichó, Patzalá, and Sacxac. These are ranked by age. Chiaj was the first one founded, then Canamixtoj, and so forth. The succeeding ones split from one already founded, just as a segment splits from its lineage.

Each center is run by a board composed of a president, vice-president, secretary, and treasurer, appointed every two years by the catechists, from among catechists at a center meeting held at the center chapel or, if there is none, at the president's house. Catechists are appointed by the president from among those men who are already married by the church. There are also many members who are not married by the church but are married by the traditional wedding ceremony and have converted. Hence, members are ranked in ascending order as follows: (1) unmarried members of Catholic Action (they have not "gone through the church"); (2) those who are married; (3) catechists; (4) those on the board. The person who becomes president tends to be someone who has previously occupied one of the other three positions on the board, so that this position (*cargo*) is regarded as another level (5). One who finishes his service as president is a *principal* of Catholic Action of that center. At a meeting of all Catholic Action members of the municipality, one of them is chosen to be president of the headquarters (*central*), which is equivalent to the board of each center, but at the municipal level. This headquarters board is composed of a president, vice-president, secretary, and treasurer. The other three on this board are generally appointed from among those who have held these positions (*cargos*) on a center's board. When the president of the headquarters board finishes his term, he is regarded as a *principal* of all municipal-level Catholic Action.

The council members (*síndico, regidores*) tend to be chosen from those who have been center board members, and the alcalde, from among those who have been presidents of some center or headquarters presidents.

Members of Catholic Action do not serve in the *cofradías* just as Traditionalists do not serve in Catholic Action. Thus, they are two parallel organizations competing to have control over municipal positions and over people. Even so, Catholic Action people do serve as *alguaciles, auxiliares,* and *mayores,* appointed by the *cofradía principales.* Even if the municipal *alcalde* belongs to Catholic Action, he is pressured by the *cofradía principales* to appoint *cofradía* members and he in turn pressures them to serve. Thus, although the two organizations parallel one another, they have points of contact and of friction. Approximately one-third of the houses in the municipality (326) belong to Catholic Action.

Besides these two organizations, there are those of pentecostal Protestants, who account for sixty-four houses grouped around two chapels, both of which are under the New Jerusalem Church of God from the nearby municipality of Santa María Chiquimula, where the president of the pastors lives. One of these chapels is in the canton of Chuijip, near San Antonio, and the other is in the town itself. Each has a pastor appointed by the members of the chapel, four elders (*ancianos*), and several deacons, who are ordained by the pastor and the elders.

Outside of these three organizations of a religious nature, there have been efforts to organize the Catholic Action people into "circles" under the cooperative in Santa Cruz del Quiché, in a peasant league, and in a farmers association. Later discussions examine their relationship to Catholic Action. Committees have also been set up around the schools that have been built. Finally, the number of youth soccer teams in the cantons has grown recently. Ladinos play on some of these teams from more centrally located cantons.

Ladinos

In 1970, the ladino population in San Antonio was about one hundred persons, living in seventeen houses, almost all of them located in the town or nearby (Chotacaj and Xejip). This number does not include the municipal clerk or the teachers who come to work six days a week but return to their families in Santa Cruz every week.

Although the figure of 133 ladino individuals in the 1964 census turns out to be a little inflated, it can be concluded that from 1950 to 1964 the number of ladinos increased by a higher percentage than the population of the municipality. Conversely, from 1964 to 1970, possibly because of people leaving and the incipient use of contraception by ladinos, there was a decline in the number of ladinos.

The roots of the ladino presence in San Antonio can be traced to the beginning of the twentieth century. The first to arrive was a municipal clerk who brought his family and bought land in the town. Others then came from Chajbal (municipality of Santa Cruz) seeking land. The indigenous people did not want them to become established because they believed them to be in cahoots with the ladino authorities who forced them to go to the coast and to work without pay on roads in the area. They were also a threat to the availability of land. Ladinos were also unwilling to accept *cargos* in *cofradías*, and though at first they might have tried to learn the indigenous language, they would go on to set up a community of their own, separate from the indigenous community.

Hostility between the groups seems to have declined with the rise of Catholic Action. The hostility of Catholic Action members against the Traditionalists, both of them indigenous groups, reduced interethnic hostility.

Today the ladinos live off the land they possess, which is usually not very much. They own small stores and bars, and they are butchers, truck drivers, notaries, teachers, policemen, and nurses. For some of these jobs, such as teacher and policeman, they leave the municipality. They tend to go elsewhere to make a living and then to stay there. Hence there are fewer ladino men than women in the town.

The children of the six main families (i.e., surnames) are linked by marriage. Many of those in the third generation are first cousins. This forces them to think about marrying someone outside the community, and the men either remain elsewhere or return with their wives. Since the women do not go elsewhere to work, almost none go out to study, and there is no work for men who might come to the town and marry them, the surplus of women has the effect that they remain single or they have children whose father is unknown or they enter an interethnic marriage.

Among the few interethnic marriages, the most common involves an Indian man who marries a ladino woman. Even during the years of hostility, some marriages of this type took place, thereby enabling the man to rise in status, and the woman's family to take hold in the community. This type of marriage is easier today, especially if she (as a ladina) is the daughter of an indigenous father and a ladina mother, or if he (as an Indian) is the son of a ladino man, even if he has not been legally acknowledged by his father.

Unions between a ladino man and an indigenous woman are, as a rule, neither stable nor openly acknowledged. The Indians say that such a woman is the ladino's "mistress" (*casera* = "housemate"); they do not say she is his "wife." Sometimes the ladino does not give her money, even though he visits his mistress regularly.

Children of interethnic unions in the town are invariably considered ladinos. This is the case even if the father is an Indian, and the ladina mother is the daughter of an Indian and a ladina. Only if the ladino father has not acknowledged his son is the son regarded as Indian.

In the case of the male children of the few interethnic unions in the cantons where the majority of the people are Indian, if the mother is a ladina, they tend to grow up as Indian, their parents obtain for them Indian wives, and their children will be Indian. Thus a drop of ladino dissolves in an indigenous sea. If, however, a family is inclined to treat a daughter of such a union as a ladina, like her mother, she is given ladino clothing. Her identity is then in constant tension: with the ladinos in the town she feels ashamed, and among the Indians she is rejected. She runs the risk of becoming the mistress of one or more of her indigenous neighbors.

Even though a few years ago there was more interethnic hostility, there were proportionally more stable interethnic marriages than there are now. The ladinos who first arrived with their wives and children set up their households among the Indians. Giving their daughters in marriage to those Indians who had more experience of the world and who knew Spanish was a way to overcome hostility. Their situation was similar to that of the tiny ladino islands in

TABLE 2.3. *Intra- and interethnic marriages of ladinos, by decade contracted (relative to 1970)*

Period	Marriages of Ladinos	
	Intraethnic	Interethnic
More than 20 years ago	3	5
Less than 10 years ago	15	2

the indigenous cantons today: they did not have the pressure of a ladino society preventing them from choosing a wife from among the opposite ethnic group. But as the number of ladinos grew and it became possible to unite the children of ladino families among themselves, the number of interethnic marriages declined in proportion, as can be seen in Table 2.3.

No religious organization binds the ladino community together. It once had a *cofradía* of the Child (Jesus), but it disappeared. In contrast to the indigenous community, it is characterized by its lack of local religious organization, its external marriage ties, its openness to the wider ladino community of the country, and its position in the socioeconomic structure.

Summary

The social organization of the indigenous people of the municipality of San Antonio Ilotenango can be summed up by indicating the power base and domain of the various units described, before and after Catholic Action appeared. (See Appendix for a discussion of social power.)

Before Catholic Action

We can order the different domains by distinguishing the lines of power that connect the units at different levels within the community.

First, there are the *kinship* relationships. Children, parents, and grandparents (if there are any) make up three levels of articulation, normally within the domestic unit, the basis of superordination being house and land. Kinship, in this instance patrilinear, is a way of dividing land and designating who occupies the house. At the level of the parents or grandparents can be found the head of the segment (*chuchkajaw*) with his group of witnesses and heads of segment, who form a tribunal before which the marriage alliance takes place. At an even higher level, with control over distinct segments of the same lineage living in various cantons, is the lineage chief surrounded by the segment heads, who some time ago used to make up a tribunal before which the land occupied by the lineage in several places was divided up. Now they make up a body that meets only on rare occasions for common matters, such as, for example, dealing with a common house belonging to the lineage in the town. Finally, at an even higher level is the body of the *principales* of the lineages and of the most important segments, on whom ultimately fall decisions having to do with the governance of the municipality. It should be noted that this is an idealized description.

Second, there is the *ceremonial* activity of the *cofradías*. The *cofradías* are jointly responsible for celebrations of feasts throughout the year. Their 96 members are hierarchically ordered within each of the eight *cofradías*, and the *cofradías* are also ranked by their importance. The *alcaldes* of the *cofradías* occupy the municipal level, and each *alcalde* stands over just eleven couples, usually chosen from different cantons. The *cofradías* are a channel for distributing prestige and power, because after an individual has accomplished particular ceremonial responsibilities, he can occupy positions in the municipality, up to *alcalde*, and once he has fulfilled that role, he joins the *principales*.

The third organizational structure is *governance*. At the upper level are the *principales* who appoint the municipal mayor and delegate him to govern the municipality for one or two years. They also demand that he fulfill his responsibilities. Along with the *síndico* and the *regidores*, the mayor forms a true governing and judicial body. Together they discuss decisions that will be binding on the entire population, such as taxes, and together they judge conflicts that have not been able to be settled in the segments and lineages. The mayor passes his orders to the people through the *mayores*, *auxiliares*, and *alguaciles*. The latter operate as a police force, imprisoning those who disturb order and disobey orders from higher authorities. In addition, the mayor draws power from the department governor and from the regional judge, either through the municipal clerk or directly.

Finally, there is what we could call *charismatic* activity by the *zahorines*, whose power lies in their divining and propitiatory quality, which is recognized by the people once they have passed through a training process with other *zahorines*. The *zahorines* are advisors who have an influence at every level, from the mayor's governing circle and his council to parents and grandparents. Due to their age, *zahorines* also tend to be *principales*, heads of segment or lineage, and men who have performed the primary functions in the *cofradías* and the municipal government. I am not aware of any body made up solely of *zahorines* comparable to those of the mayor and his council, the eight *alcaldes* of the *cofradías*, or *principales* on various levels.

Since the Emergence of Catholic Action

Catholic Action did not seek to suppress the line of derivation through kinship or that of the municipal government; it competed only in the areas of ceremony and charisma. The same can be said of the Protestants.

Just as performing *cargos* in the *cofradías* constitutes the ladder for assigning prestige and recruiting members into the body of the *principales*, so also performing duties within the Catholic Action structure leads to a gradual progression toward the role of *principales* of Catholic Action, replacements for the traditional *principales* who in some instances have tried to impose in a more or less coordinated way their decisions on the mayor. Lower down are board members of the central headquarters, with municipal domain; the boards of centers, with canton domain; and catechists, with domain over a number of houses where it is their duty to pray. From position to position *(cargo)* the individual tends to become prepared to function in some responsibility in the municipality to the point of being mayor. In the charismatic line, the *zahorines* have been replaced by some center board members and by the priest from outside.

CHAPTER 3

Trade as a New Source of Social Power

This chapter delineates how trade by San Antonio merchants outside the municipality gave rise to a new power base within it, which many merchants then went on to use as support for breaking with the traditional beliefs firmly sustained and defended by the *principales* and *zahorines*. Trade, which requires dealings with the ladino world outside of the municipality, also made merchants more open to reassessing beliefs from outside, thereby paving the way for their reception.

"Outside" Merchants

Definition

Informants make a distinction between merchants "around here" and "outside" merchants. The former are those who sell in San Antonio or in one of the markets within the rotating system already described for the towns of Momostenango, San Francisco el Alto, Totonicapán, Chichicastenango, and Quezaltenango. They "stay just around here (San Antonio)" and do not spend weeks outside the town doing business. The "outside" merchant is one who goes beyond this local area.

The local merchants are those who, before 1947, when the marketplace was first set up in San Antonio, generally took their products, such as pigs, beans, red sashes, wool, and so forth, only to nearby markets. Some of them also used to come back with merchandise to sell in San Antonio, as described in the previous chapter. They also included those who used to go out to bring in some specific product like corn. But they did not buy outside the community to also sell outside it. *Outside merchants are those who primarily buy outside to sell outside*, and most operate in ladino areas. Thus, whenever merchants are referred to in this chapter, outside merchants are meant unless explicitly stated otherwise.

There are merchants who now work in Santa Cruz del Quiché (the capital of the department of Quiché), for example, and yet they have been classified as "outside" because some years ago they worked outside, they retain all the style of those outside, and they are familiar with their way of doing business.

Origin

A little historical background can show how doors to other regions opened up for the merchants. The information indicates that even though before 1934 a few merchants used to serve the plantation labor gangs, it was around 1934, when the debts of plantation workers were canceled, that a larger number could go into business.[1]

One of the first merchants observes:

> I owed 3,000 pesos and my mother owed 3,100 at Soledad [plantation]. It was because my brother drank a lot. He went to borrow money and he went deeper into debt. They took us [because of him we had to go] to the Zapote plantation; it was because of my brother that we went. I paid my brother's whole debt at Zapote. "Either you pay for your brother, or you're going to jail," they told me. Through Don Casimiro [the labor contractor], I switched the debt to Soledad. That's because El Zapote was very far away. We used to [travel] with the *cacaxte* [frame for carrying a load]. No truck. Just in shorts. No pants. Rubber-tire shoes. It was a six-day walk. Soledad was just three days. We went there because of my brother.
>
> If the debt hadn't been forgiven, I might still be there. Nothing but sorrow. Poor. No clothes, nothing. Every two weeks they give an allowance of 25 cents apiece. I have sixty days' work and my mother thirty [to do]. And we don't meet the daily workload. When is this going to end? My God. Okay, there's food [corn to eat]. But your clothes wear out and where's the money to pay for it?
>
> Then they set us free: we could work there or in the town. But we stayed there for six months as contract labor and I went into business selling cold drinks. I'm free.

This man, who was then 24 years old, continued working a few months, and after getting together the money needed, he bought an ice scraper, glasses, syrup, and ice. He began to serve the workers who continued to work on the Pacific Coast, no longer because of debt but out of economic need. He sold vegetables as well as cool drinks.

Spreading Out

Many people from San Antonio continued to work on the coast because corn production in San Antonio did not cover their own consumption needs. But others ventured into trade as a way of making a living. Like the juice vendor, they bought food items, such as potatoes, shrimp, chewing gum, onions, and green vegetables, or woven mats and hats for the labor crew workers. They then extended their radius of activity by visiting towns on the coast and in the foothills (through which they had passed as members of work crews) on their feast days. They also went to towns near San Antonio on their feast days, and some went on foot up to the northern part of the department of Quiché, to Nebaj, Chajul, and Cotzal, which could not be reached by bus.

By 1940, some were earning more in the area of Cobán, the capital of Alta Verapaz. With the money earned on the coast, they would buy a burro (Q 4.00) that they could load up with 100–130 pounds of goods on the twenty-day journeys on foot that they used to make to Cobán. They took bowls, beaters, and apples from Totonicapán, and came back with chile. On the way out they earned around Q 5.00 in profit from the combined load on the burro and on the merchant (100 pounds), and on the way back, around Q 25.00 if they brought 200 pounds of chile to sell in the markets of Santa María Chiquimula, San Francisco el Alto, and Totonicapán. They rested a few days at home, and then began another round. Some invested, bought more animals, and covered a larger area or simply increased their sales volume.

Around 1950 trucks began to travel between Guatemala City and Cobán. The merchants gradually stopped using animals for these long trips, but they kept using them for trips to Totonicapán, where they would go to buy things like bananas. It was still cheaper along these stretches to use an animal than to pay a fare. In 1951, one of the first merchants doing business in Cobán bought the first bus for the town. This same man later (in 1969) had a monopoly on passenger transportation from San Antonio to Santa Cruz del Quiché with three buses. Also in 1951, one of the few ladinos in San Antonio bought the first truck from a dealer. By 1954 two more Indians who had sales in Cobán bought a truck. One of them now has a business with more than Q 10,000.00 invested in Cobán. They used the truck to trade in corn, which they brought from the coast to the town and to the cool highlands. Sometimes the truck owner himself had corn planted in lands rented on the coast, and his harvest revenue was combined with that from freight to even out possible losses. At that time there were merchants with Q 1,000.00 invested, but with no truck so they paid freight costs. Some of them went broke selling corn, but truck owners who both had businesses and grew crops kept getting richer.

As has been shown, the growing number of merchants has paralleled transportation facilities. In 1935, the bus from Guatemala City did not go as far as Santa Cruz del Quiché but only to Tecpán (department of Chimaltenango). The trucks that in 1945 were beginning to take labor crews to the coast were picking them up in Totonicapán, because larger vehicles could not get over the road between Totonicapán and Santa Cruz del Quiché (which goes through San Antonio). When buses began to go to Totonicapán in 1950, the fare from San Antonio to Totonicapán was Q 0.60, that is, about three times as much as a day's wage in San Antonio. People say that before 1945 or 1950, motor vehicle transportation generally did not exist or was too expensive.

Particularly important has been the increasing ease of transportation to Guatemala City in the past ten years. Between 1950 and 1960, the fare from Santa Cruz del Quiché to Guatemala City varied from Q 1.25 to Q 1.50. In the early 1960s, it dropped to Q 1.00, by 1968 it stood at Q 0.75, and in 1969 it sometimes even dropped to Q 0.50. Competition between the two groups of bus drivers from Santa Cruz del Quiché has been fierce, thereby allowing the fare to become four or five times cheaper in real terms over the past ten years.

Guatemala City, which in the early 1950s was only a transit point for merchants from Cobán and those who went to the salt operations in Puerto San José (on the Pacific), gradually became a purchasing center that opened possibilities for new kinds of trade, such as buying spices to be sold in Cobán; clothes to sell in the department capital of Escuintla, in Puerto San José, in Iztapa (near the port) or on plantations; or boots, magazines, and chewing gum to be sold in Joyabaj (department of Quiché).

In the 1960s, some merchants still traveled on foot. San Andrés Sajcabajá, isolated by the clay muds of the terrible roads in the department of Quiché, the small settlements in Masagua, Escuintla, on the coast, and the cotton plantations are some of the places to which small merchants still had to go on foot, carrying their merchandise wrapped up in a multicolored large cloth.

By 1965, the trend was for merchants to have established a booth in the regional markets of the department of Quiché, and in Sacapulas, and especially in Santa Cruz del Quiché, where there are now around thirty merchants from San Antonio who sell primarily food and clothing. Their warehouse is in Santa Cruz, but during the week they go out to other markets such as Chiché or to San Antonio itself, and when there is a feast day in some nearby town, such as Joyabaj, Sacapulas, Aguacatán, Nebaj, or elsewhere, they visit it. Some of them used to be merchants in Cobán and Guatemala City, but because they did not have much capital (Q 500), they have withdrawn from these places where the competition has forced them out, in order to sell where the advent of chemical fertilizer has caused more money to circulate. The fourth truck in San Antonio was purchased in 1965. At that time, some truckers began to sell fertilizer. The number of small dealers in beans who sell in Quetzaltenango and those who sell pigs in Totonicapán also began to grow.

Since around 1967 the market is filling up more and more with merchants from many towns who go around the markets of Guatemala City and Escuintla with only Q 40 or Q 50 or even less invested. Handling small retail sales demands that there be many potential buyers rather than large sales; hence, merchants head for the larger cities. But in Guatemala City and Escuintla there are "established" merchants with large sales who pay for their reserved spots. They tend to complain about those who wander about the streets paying no fees and avoiding the police who might pursue them. Because the market is full of merchants and because chemically fertilized land offers more security than trade, some from San Antonio have sold their businesses and returned to the town. In addition, in recent years, some merchants have reached as far as Mariscos, in the department of Izabal.

San Antonio merchants generally do not go to the eastern part of Guatemala because fares and business taxes are higher. They are afraid of the east—and increasingly of the coast—after some assaults and robberies that merchants from San Antonio and from other parts of the highlands have suffered at the hands of "Salvadorans," as they say. Likewise, they do not often go to towns in Huehuetenango, where people do not have much money.

Number and Location

Currently (1970) there are around 60–70 clothing and grain merchants in Guatemala City; around 40 in Escuintla, especially of clothing; around 30 set up in Santa Cruz del Quiché; about 20 in Cobán; some 20–25 scattered through Mariscos, Retalhuleu, Cuyotenango (La Máquina), Mazatenango (capital), Santo Tomás la Unión (the latter three towns are in Suchitepéquez); another 15–20 who specialize in Aguacatán and Huehuetenango (both in Huehuetenango) or in Sacapulas, San Pedro Jocopilas, and Joyabaj (these three in El Quiché). The number in Guatemala City and Escuintla rises in December (Christmas) and for Lent (Holy Week, fish). There are generally more merchants in the dry season than in the rainy season.

According to lists drawn up with informants from various cantons, there are 194 outside merchants from the entire municipality. This figure is consistent with the 201 valid licenses for merchants in 1970 (issued from 1965 to 1970). The number rises starting in 1965, when chemical fertilizer was providing peasants with greater purchasing power and when fares dropped sharply. The declining trend that I have mentioned begins around 1969.

Summary

In conclusion, new trade alternatives opened up when the control of plantation owners, contractors, and money lenders over a broad sector of highland Indians, and accordingly of people from San Antonio, was broken starting in 1934. Because of their knowledge of the region, San Antonio people were able to go into business in the squares of the towns with which they were familiar and on plantations on the coast and in the foothills above the Pacific coastal plain. They also began to visit markets near San Antonio and to make their way on foot into the area in the northern part of El Quiché.

A second wave, probably mixed with merchants from other municipalities, then went into Cobán and nearby regions. A third wave, which involved purchasing buses and trucks, had the effect of bringing some merchants back to San Antonio at a higher level of business activity. Underlying the purchase of vehicles was the building of roads and the import of technology from outside the country after World War II. A fourth wave headed to Guatemala City, which previously served only as a transit area, and to Escuintla. A fifth wave, possibly caused by rising productivity resulting from chemical fertilizer, came back to Santa Cruz del Quiché. Finally, as a result of additional highway construction, some inroads have been made into Mariscos and recently to the Petén.

Gradually, a broader area of the country has opened to merchants who, in pursuit of greater earnings, go out to distant plazas and who in some instances use trucks and have gone into business inside the municipality or elsewhere while specializing in a particular kind of merchandise.

Strata of Merchants by Capital and Religious Affiliation

In order to account for the capital-buildup processes that are the foundation of the increased power of some units in the community, I next provide a classification of merchants according to the amount of their capital. This classification, whose cutoff points were decided on the basis of my impressions, will nevertheless point out some elements crucial to capital buildup and for the subsequent determination of religious affiliation.

Below merchants are divided into four levels: A, numbering 12, whose capital is over Q 5,000; B, of whom there are 14, whose capital ranges from Q 1,000 to Q 5,000; C, numbering 12, whose capital ranges between Q 500 and Q 1,000; and D, numbering 156, whose holdings are Q 500. Table 3.1 shows some of the average characteristics of each of these levels.

Stratum with Capital over Q 5,000

The average capital of the twelve merchants who make up this category is Q 8,600. Some have as much as Q 15,000 invested in their businesses, according to the most conservative calculations. All except two, one with a store in San Antonio and another who sells clothing and shoes in Sacapulas, have one or more vehicles. The one with the largest number of vehicles has three trucks, which he uses to deal in corn (sometimes bringing it from the Petén), fertilizer, fish, and beans. He also has an outlet in Río Dulce (Izabal). Working under him are two of his sons, each of whom goes along with the trucks, and a brother, who handles sales in Río Dulce, working as his employee. I have not counted among the vehicles the two tractors owned by a man from San Antonio who has land in La Máquina and who also has a pair of pickups to deliver

TABLE 3.1. *Merchant profile by level of capital*

| | Strata | | | |
| | A | B | C | D |
	N = 12	N = 14	N = 12	N = 156
Classifiers				
Average capital (*quetzales*)	8,600	2,100	690	130
Vehicles per merchant	1.5	0.14	0	0
Land bought (*cuerdas*)	460	32	0	6
Individual Factors				
Literate (%)	59	78	54	50
Workers on coast (%)	47	21	63	64
Workers in salt flats (%)	0	42	0	7
Merchants < age 15 (%)	33	38	50	30
Merchant father (%)	50	43	60	33
Average age began in trade	20.4	20.5	18.6	32
Average age at present	46	41	36	41
Economic Factors				
Land inherited (av. *cuerdas*/person)	29	42	55	45
Trade in San Antonio (%)	42	29	8	6
Trade in Guatemala City (%)	0	36	25	44
Wife from outside San Antonio (%)	42	14	0	0
With store (%)	75	35	8	0
Work with relatives (%)	78	35	17	20
Related to co-owner (%)	41	35	17	20
Social Factors				
Father dead < age 15 (%)	30	21	40	28
Shown trade by relative (%)	63	41	77	54
Were in *cofradía* (%)	25	28	16	35
Converts (%)	58	78	75	66

the bread that he makes for the stores, nor another tractor owned by another landowner, who also has a truck in La Máquina, Cuyotenango (department of Suchitepéquez).

These merchants have bought a remarkable amount of land (460 *cuerdas* each on average), especially in comparison to the average number of *cuerdas* inherited by each of them (29 *cuerdas*). This indicates—particularly when compared with the figures for the other levels—that the amount of land they inherited has not influenced the rise of powerful businessmen. Indeed, it seems that their average is less than that of other strata and not very different from the average amount of land held by a San Antonio man today (around 20 *cuerdas*). It should be noted that this means that when these merchants received their inheritance, perhaps about twenty years ago (since their average age is 46), the average amount of land owned per man in San Antonio was over 20 *cuerdas*. Their average land inherited (29 *cuerdas*) was approximately equal to or perhaps less than the average land owned by a man in San Antonio at that time (over 20 *cuerdas*).

Not all the land has been bought in the municipality. Two merchants, those owning lands in La Máquina, each bought around 800 *cuerdas*. But the other merchants who have bought land did so in San Antonio. The one with the most has 2,400 *cuerdas*, another around 600, another has 300, and others have 50, 40, and 15 *cuerdas*. The only ones who are said not to have bought any land are two brothers who now live in Amatitlán (Guatemala), where each has a store.

With regard to the place of business of these merchants, five sell in San Antonio and other places as well. Three of them have retail stores in San Antonio dealing in corn, fertilizer, soap, hoes, clothing, food, and hats. They sell at lower prices because they buy wholesale. Two more merchants have their stores in Cobán and Carchá (Alta Verapaz), where they sell cuts of cloth made in Totonicapán for women's skirts. Two more have their stores in Amatitlán, and two are in La Máquina, while another is in Sacapulas. No one sells in Guatemala City, except during a particular season such as Holy Week (fish).

Those who work in Amatitlán and La Máquina have taken their wives from San Antonio to be with them there. Even though they have employees from San Antonio working for them in their store, especially those in Amatitlán, they never speak the Indian language now. One of them has a car. They are not completely disconnected from the town, since they visit it for feast days. Some, particularly those from La Máquina, also visit their relatives on special occasions, such as weddings or the building of a new house, and one has even given his daughter in marriage to a San Antonio man who lives in the municipality. Of all these merchants, the ones in Amatitlán are the only ones who show signs of becoming ladino.

Most (78%) work with a relative, although in almost half the cases the relative is not a co-owner of the business but simply an employee. In almost all instances, co-owners are sons of the merchant, who could now live by themselves because they have a wife. In all cases, the employees are either brothers or cousins (sons of their father's brother).

Religiously, most (58%) are converts to Catholic Action; none of them is Protestant. Among the five who have not converted, only two have served in *cofradías*. The other three are either away from the community and its opinions, as are the two in Amatitlán, or are ambiguous. Those who have participated in *cofradías* help to finance their political struggles; likewise, two of those who converted have invested a great deal of money in building a chapel and pay for lawyers when conflict occurs, such as when a Catholic Action member is jailed for innovations in the church.

Stratum with Capital from Q 1,000 to Q 5,000

The average amount of capital invested by the merchants in this category is Q 2,100, though amounts range from Q 1,000 to Q 4,000. Only two of these fourteen merchants have a vehicle; one uses his for distributing soft drinks, sugar, soap, and cigarettes from a store that he has in Guatemala City, and the other to deal in clothing and fish from Mariscos to Guatemala City. This latter man is a Protestant and shares ownership of the truck with another "brother" from the small church in his canton in San Antonio. They also have dugout canoes for supplying people who live along the shore of Lake Izabal.

The average amount of land purchased by each of these merchants is 32 *cuerdas*. One has bought 200, followed by three with 50, another with 40, one with 25, two with 15, one with 1 *cuerda* (which cost him Q 800), while the other five have not bought anything. The one who has 200 *cuerdas* has no vehicles, does not work the land himself, and works full-time dealing in food, especially chile. He inherited no more than 10 *cuerdas*.

In terms of their place of business only four (29%) sell both in San Antonio and elsewhere. Three are in Guatemala City and Mariscos, dealing in clothing, fish, chile, and other foods. Three operate only in Guatemala City, selling grains and fish and running the store mentioned above that distributes merchandise. Two are in Escuintla selling clothing. Hence, it is clear that as capital goes down, the percentage of those selling in San Antonio drops and the percentage of those selling in Guatemala City rises.

Fewer in this group have their own store—35 percent as opposed to 75 percent in the stratum above. Two of the stores are in Guatemala City, one in Mariscos, another in Escuintla, and another in San Antonio.

Practically no one is becoming ladino (i.e., not wanting to be regarded as "Indian") in this stratum, because the two who have their wives outside, one in Mariscos and the other in Guatemala City, are evangelicals. The one in Mariscos is pastor of his little church in San Antonio. This religious bond ties them to the way their community is organized, and, in the places where they have their business, they make up a core group that provides support when things are difficult and arouses enthusiasm in their faith.

In this category, only 35 percent work with a relative, either older sons or brothers. Some have Protestant "brothers" as employees or servants.

The proportion of those who have converted in this stratum is the highest of all four strata. Three are Protestants and seven are Catholic Action, although some are merely opportunistic, not attending meetings or classes. Another was counted as converted (or not a Traditionalist), even though he has participated in *cofradías*, because I am told that he is not a member of any community religious organization. Of the remaining three who are Traditionalists—all of whom do business in San Antonio—only two have been active in *cofradías*.

It is clear that in San Antonio, unlike other towns such as perhaps Santa María Chiquimula, Protestants are not found in the stratum with the highest capital. Even so, the richest Protestants, like the two in this category, are also pastors of churches in San Antonio.

With regard to Traditionalists, especially if we compare this group to stratum A, there seems to be a certain correlation between selling outside of San Antonio and being converted to Catholic Action, or between selling in San Antonio and being a Traditionalist. It should be kept in mind, however, that only "outside" merchants are being considered here, and that the informants included in this term even those who were selling in San Antonio but who at other times had sold outside the region. I have not been concerned with merchants "from around here" because their amounts of capital are so small.

Stratum with Capital from Q 500 to Q 1,000

The twelve merchants at this stratum have an average capital of Q 690. Individual amounts mostly range from Q 500 to Q 800, and merchants at the top of this stratum are scarcely different from those who have a capital of Q 1,000 or a little more in the previous stratum. The largest amount of land purchased by any of these merchants is 50 *cuerdas*, and it was bought by a man who was not recognized by his father (i.e., is seen as illegitimate), and who received only 5 *cuerdas* from his mother's inheritance. Six have not bought any land, including one man who received an inheritance of around 100 *cuerdas* and has capital of around Q 700 invested in clothing. Another, who has an inheritance of about 100 *cuerdas*, once had a truck because his now-deceased father was one of the first merchants, and fifteen years ago one of the richest. This man is now selling off land, because he is heavily in debt. He is the only merchant who has owned a truck and still failed in business. He has lost the volume of business that having a truck once enabled him to have.

In starting their businesses, they have had a stronger foundation of inherited land (55 *cuerdas* average) than the previous strata, and when the numbers of those who began to sell at age 15 or younger (50%) is examined, it is clear that those in this stratum began earlier than others who are now nevertheless richer. They are also now on average younger. In this group, two types can be observed: those who are now over 40 and have probably reached their limit, and those who are not even 35, some not even 30, and who are still on the rise.

Only one has his place of business in San Antonio. The others are out in La Máquina, Escuintla, Guatemala City, Mariscos, and La Tinta (Alta Verapaz). One sells hats in Huehuetenango. Except for those in Mariscos, who also sell vegetables, they all deal exclusively in clothing. The only one with his own store is the one in Huehuetenango.

None of them has his wife living with him outside San Antonio. Merchants return to San Antonio as a rule every twenty days, and rest at home for four or five days.

Only two work with their sons, but just as this is the stratum in which the largest portion lost their fathers while still children, it is also the stratum in which there are more merchants who have learned from their relatives, such as an uncle or even their father before he died.

The number of converts is almost as high as in the previous stratum, and the proportion of Protestants is higher.

On this level we find two ladino brothers who have stores in San Antonio, but I have not counted them in the percentages in Table 3.1. There are other stores owned by ladinos in the town, but these two, with estimated investments of Q 500 or Q 600, are the strongest. Their father owns a truck and has some 60 *cuerdas* of land.

Stratum with Capital of Less than Q 500

I have only incomplete information for some of the 16 in the random sample of this group, which numbers 156. I have taken the percentages for those on whom I had information. Hence, we cannot place too much confidence in the results. Even so, because this stratum as a group stands in contrast to the other strata, and based on the opinion of my informants, the data I do have are more trustworthy.

Average capital in this group is Q 130; none has a vehicle; and the largest amount of land purchased is 28 *cuerdas*. Two are in debt, and one has lost almost 100 *cuerdas*. Seven of the sixteen have bought no land. A high percentage (44%) do business in Guatemala City. Five of them are in Escuintla, another in Retalhuleu, another in Mariscos, and another goes from one celebration to another in ladino and indigenous towns. Half of them deal in clothing. More of them are Traditionalists and former *cofradía* members than those in other strata. The average ages, when compared to those in stratum C, indicate that there is one group of those who are over 50 who are at a standstill (five in the sample), and another group of those who are under 30 (also five) who conceivably have a more open future.

Comparison of Strata

By comparing the strata we can identify certain factors that have been crucial in the merchants' differing amounts of capital and in their religious affiliation.

The first and foremost factor is transportation, especially trucks. This technological innovation, made possible through the building of highways and the import of technology after World War II, clearly distinguishes various kinds of merchants in ascending order. First are those who do not have access to it. Second are those whom it enables to reach a broader area and deal in a larger volume of merchandise, and who establish a direct relationship with the main distribution points (soap factory, dealership for hoes and fertilizers, salt deposits), which are normally located near the capital city. They can thus ignore the intermediary at the department level (the wholesaler).

The latter can be subdivided by their relationship to the consumer into those who continue to sell—as they did before buying the truck—at retail in a store set up in the main town in the municipality or in certain department capitals and large towns; and those who sell products (for example, salt, soap) wholesale to other local business people, who then resell the merchandise in the town square. In this last subtype, not only have the merchants dispensed with the department intermediary but they themselves have become intermediaries. Merchants who have a truck normally do retail sales from their store and deal wholesale in only some articles.

There is yet a third type that for other reasons is connected to a motor vehicle, namely, fertilizer merchants. They sell both retail and wholesale, and they buy their product directly from the dealerships. Furthermore, they are able to obtain the merchandise on consignment to be paid without interest for a certain number of months. In this case, the vehicle serves them as collateral with the main dealership for taking out the merchandise. In some cases, depending on the consignment deadlines, this arrangement works out quite profitably for the merchant who sells on credit at high interest, as is customary in the region, or on time. Although he is not paying interest, he is charging it, even though the consignment time period is shorter than that of the credit.

These three types, but especially the second, include merchants who cover one place or several, depending on the number of trucks. If they have two or three trucks, they can become intermediaries in several places, one of them being the municipality, for example, and the others being Río Dulce or La Máquina. The latter places of business are usually overseen by their relatives.

Hence, transportation enables merchants not only to increase the amount of their business by investing in a power base of their own, but also to derive economic power from outside the community in the form of consignment. The power base (their enlarged capital) and the derivation of power (consignment) give them the means, through other processes that will be examined in the next chapter, to place themselves on a level of power that hitherto did not exist in the community and to break away from traditional redistribution-based values. One of the points of conflict of the conversion movement has been precisely the break with the *cofradías*, which impose this redistribution ideal.

The second factor is the place of business. The community itself can only accommodate a certain number of merchants from within the community who operate at the level of business made possible by a vehicle. Just as merchants from other municipalities are hindered in setting up businesses in San Antonio, those from San Antonio cannot set up shop in other indigenous towns with small populations.

Some truck-owning merchants operate outside the community. As a rule, they go into business in distant department capitals or in large towns (Cobán, Carchá, La Máquina, Mariscos) or faraway places where merchants have not yet opened wholesale stores. Such places have opened to trade only in the recent past. That is not true of the ladino department capitals, such as Escuintla, Mazatenango, or Guatemala City. Truck-owning merchants set up their stores in towns that are somewhere between small municipal communities and ladino cities. No truck-owning merchant has yet succeeded in becoming established on the level proper to the wholesale dealers from a department capital, so as to supply all the municipalities that constitute its hinterland.

Merchants who do not own trucks but who, because of how much capital they hold, are approaching being able to buy a vehicle and move up a level in trade would have to move out of the ladino department towns and the capital where they operate and go into the areas recently opened by roads to accomplish that end. Alternatively, they would have to wait until either the opportunity for a new type of business opens in the town or the one they have can expand as a result of population increase. Merchants without trucks who have a foothold in the town or do business near the new frontiers will probably be the ones to move up a level by buying a truck.

The third factor, conversion, is intimately connected to the two previous ones. When the matter is considered from the standpoint of reorganization in the next chapter, how the process of stratification led to internal division in the community will become clearer. Here I will only note that conversion contributed to the economic expansion of merchants for two reasons: first, because it withdrew them from *cofradía*-related expenses, and second, because it enabled them to spend more time traveling outside the municipality without being bound by their community service on certain dates and celebrations.

It is assumed that one who converts stops serving in *cofradías* and that one who does not convert would have to serve in them. However, this does not preclude that some who converted may not have previously served in *cofradías* and that some who did not convert had necessarily served in *cofradías*. Hence, in Table 3.1 the percentage of *cofradía* members and the percentage of those converted does not add up to 100. Not all the converted were non-*cofradía* members, nor have all the nonconverted been *cofradía* members.

With regard to nonconverted merchants, a few conclusions can be drawn to shed light on the relationship between conversion and building up capital: (1) Some who are in the top category have not served on *cofradías* because they have been disconnected from the municipality. Their nonconversion is due to the fact that they situated themselves outside the shared terrain of the clash between Traditionalists and Catholic Action (or Protestants), which is the identity of indigenous people from San Antonio.

(2) Others on the same level who have served in *cofradías* are merchants whose place of business is the town itself. Serving in *cofradías* has not entailed being less devoted to business. In addition, the connection with Traditionalists in the town or its surrounding areas, as we will see in the next chapter, forced them into the redistribution characteristic of the *cofradías*. The high average age (46) of those in stratum A indicates that these merchants began to do business when the Catholic Action movement was just beginning (1950),

and the requirement to serve in *cofradías* may have been stricter than it is now. Similar to these wealthy merchants are those in the average of strata B and C, who do business in the town.

(3) In the bottom stratum, D, many have served in *cofradías*, and that may be the reason that they are not getting ahead. They tend to do business far from the municipality, and the *cofradías* have undermined them in the two ways noted above: expenses and time spent carrying out *cofradía* duties. This assumption tends to be confirmed by the fact that at this level are found more *cofradía* members and unconverted people than at the upper two levels, and that the age of the nonconverted tends to be higher than that of the converted in this stratum (49 as opposed to 39). Such data suggest that these merchants are at a standstill in terms of financial growth, and that it is because of the *cofradías* that they are not advancing.

(4) Finally, on all strata there are some nonconverted merchants who have not served in *cofradías*. I am assuming that they are younger than those who have served because they have had to devote themselves to business, when the demand from the Traditionalists to serve in the *cofradías* has been adapting to the rise of the merchants and has gradually declined. One sign of this decline is the greater proportion of Traditionalist merchants today (1970) than twenty years ago, as will be explained further on. Moreover, this decline coincides with a process of technological and economic adaptation of groups with contrary beliefs that has taken place elsewhere in this community. When a technological innovation with seemingly positive economic effects has appeared on the scene, groups opposed to it and unsure of its success have taken it as a symbol of their opposition, but later when the innovation proves to be clearly advantageous, it ceases being a symbol of contrary beliefs and is gradually accepted by the group that had rejected it, even though the belief itself has not been accepted. That happened in San Antonio with chemical fertilizer, which is now used by Traditionalists and Catholic Action members alike, even though that was not the case when it first arrived in the municipality. I assume that something similar would happen with the relaxing of the demands from *cofradías* vis-à-vis success in trade.

By contrast, with regard to the *converted merchants*, who are the largest proportion, as will be shown further on, it can be concluded that (1) the wealthier converts (truck owners) have implicitly claimed the terrain of conflict, ethnic identity, and even though they do business outside the municipality, they take part in Catholic Action celebrations; and (2) these converts tend to do business or to have done business after they converted outside the municipality. The same can be said of the merchants in the intermediate B and C strata, who are building up capital outside the municipality; if they do business in frontier regions, they will probably increase their wealth. (3) At the bottom in D are some merchants who, judging by the few years that they have been doing business, have not yet reached the stagnation point.

With regard to stagnation, it must be pointed out that with the growth of Catholic Action and the institutionalization of its centers, especially since 1965, one of the factors that is causing economic stagnation within the *cofradías* is coming back into the new organization: that of requiring dedication and commitment from those in leadership positions in the centers. These positions do not demand expenditures, as they do in the *cofradías*, but they do require that the board member be in the municipality, so he cannot easily go away to do business. Thus one either devotes oneself to farming or, more usually, becomes a regional merchant based in San Antonio. In this way the very growth of the conversion movement, which benefited from the existence of many merchants, has been slowed by the organizing required by such growth and by the limitations that such organizing has placed on merchants.

Wealthy merchants customarily pay expenses to Catholic Action that are considerably higher than those paid by the Traditionalists to the *cofradías*, for example, to build a chapel, but because they enjoy a higher level of trade, the demand for redistribution by other Catholic Action members (small farmers or medium-level merchants who have suffered because of their *cargos* in Catholic Action or merchants who are stuck for other reasons) does not weaken their economic position. Among them, as among those merchants who have been less successful, there are also those who pay for lawsuits to defend Catholic Action against the Traditionalists. Merchants in category A who are Traditionalists lend money or spend it directly to support the accusations against Catholic Action.

The demands of many *cargos* in Catholic Action (thirty-two with two-year terms each), on the one hand, and the loosening of the *cofradías* (in 1971 four of the eight were suppressed), on the other, means that the conditions for capital buildup, which initially were different for Catholic Action members and Traditionalists, have been evening out over time, and hence the conversion movement is also likely to have declined.

Merchants and Conversions

I now indicate briefly how merchants have played an important and sometimes decisive role in the birth, development, and continuity of Catholic Action.

Catholic Action Pioneers

Since the early years of Catholic Action, merchants have played a decisive role in the development of the movement as catalysts for more conversions. The three pioneers who introduced Catholic Action in different cantons were merchants. It was brought to Chiaj by a merchant from the coast and Cobán, who "received the seed" of Catholic Action from another merchant from Santa María Chiquimula in 1948. It reached Patzalá through a merchant who sold goods in Chichicastenango, where he first heard the news from another merchant from the municipality of Totonicapán in 1949. It was started in Canamixtoj by a merchant from Cobán who in 1949 or 1950 first attended

Catholic Action meetings in Santa Lucía la Reforma, a nearby municipality with many merchants who traveled widely. Each of these three converted neighbors and relatives from his own canton, some of whom were likewise merchants. The pioneers later were in contact with one another, and they set up a common board for the whole municipality in a very dramatic process that we will study in another chapter.

Development of Catholic Action

I have a 1952 class attendance list with the names of the members and their board. There are fifty persons, seven of whom are under 13 but are already active. Of the forty-three remaining, I have information on only thirty-three, of whom eighteen (42%) were merchants. Many of them knew each other because they had sold in the same plazas outside their town and had made long journeys together, often on foot. The board on the list is made up of four merchants, two of whom were among the pioneers.

I do not have precise information on the number of merchants among the Traditionalists from that period. An approximation based on the number of Traditionalists in San Antonio at that time (around one thousand) and the number of Traditionalist merchants, who could not have numbered more than fifty, indicates 5 percent as a maximum.

In 1955 a clash broke out in the municipality between Traditionalists and Catholic Action because a priest had tried to come to live in the town; it even reached the point of beating and kicking. The most active Catholic Action members were merchants, who, because of their knowledge of the world outside the community, went to authorities outside the municipality, such as the regional judge. Additionally, because they had enough money, they paid expenses for the legal procedures. This conflict served to multiply the number of converts to Catholic Action.

In 1964, when another conflict broke out over repairs to the church, again it was a group of merchants, some of whom had been converted after 1955, who paid for the legal defense vis-à-vis regional authorities. The movement expanded further and three more centers emerged, in addition to the four already existing. In two of the new centers, the main promoters of conversions were merchants. Especially notable was the activity of a powerful merchant from the fifth center (Chicó–Xebaquit), who after a revelatory dream in which he was covered in flowers (his future *compadres*) went forth day and night to convince his neighbors, using arguments, arm-twisting, help, and threats.

Today's Converts

In 1970, I prepared Table 3.2 comparing a count of the number of merchants with the number of converts. The table includes all adult men, that is, those who are married or, if not, "ought" to have a wife, because they are over 20.

TABLE 3.2. *Adult men from entire municipality, showing total outside merchants and total converts*

| | | Is he an outside merchant? | | |
		Yes	No	Total
Is he a convert?	Yes	114	436	550
	No	80	1,054	1,134
	Total	194	1,490	1,684

These are normally the ones counted as converts. Among converts I include those in Catholic Action and Protestants. The contrast is sharp and shows the relationship between being a merchant and having converted.

The percentage of merchants among the converts is less in 1970 than the estimate for 1952 (22% vs. 42%), while, on the other hand, the percentage of merchants among nonconverts is now greater (8% vs. 5%). This indicates that in the subsequent growth of conversions other factors besides being merchants came into play and that the fact of being a merchant has gradually ceased being a characteristic leading to conversion.

Values of Merchants and Converts

I have examined the processes by which merchants build up capital and are predisposed to conversion, according to where they sell and when they went into business, and have shown the correlation between trade and religious conversion. I must now trace some values proper to merchants to which they attribute their success, albeit partially, so as to compare them with certain ways of acting and attitudes of converts and understand in what fashion they are propitious for the reception of new beliefs.

Qualities of Merchants and Converts

From my field journal I can glean some qualities that various informants attribute to merchants that are also shared by converts.

A good merchant has a series of qualities that are expressed as follows: *he is sharp* [*tiene chispa*, lit., "he has spark"] (he is imaginative); he *uses his head* (he plans); he *understands* (he understands the reasoning of the outside world); he *is tough* [*aguanta*, lit., "puts up with," "holds out"] (he dares to struggle); and he possesses an intuition that sometimes translates into *revelatory dreams*.

Being *sharp* means one has the imagination to draw in customers, setting up music with loudspeakers, kidding around if necessary, or calling out in rhyme. A merchant who is homesick or stands with his arms crossed, quietly waiting for customers, is no good. Proselytizing for conversion likewise entails looking for ways to engage one's neighbor, to refute his objections, and to bring him to accept the new belief. Drawing in customers and attracting new converts go hand in hand.

Using one's head is characteristic of merchants who have to handle several businesses and plan their travels in an organized way to save time and locate markets with the best prices. They are like board members of centers who organize the work of their catechists in accordance with demands from their members and have established a well-organized set of regulations along the lines of a traditional organization of responsibilities, particularly like those of the local court system (*alguaciles, auxiliares, mayores*).

A merchant *understands*. He is not "stupid" or "just plain dumb" or "foolish" (*tonto, directamente bruto, baboso*), as people are who do not realize the absurdity or narrow-mindedness of how they act. He understands explanations given by ladinos and grants them credibility. Because he is "in the know," he judges himself to be more open to new ideas:

> A merchant is a little more able to take things in than someone who isn't, like a sheepherder. When I was a kid, we used to go into a church in Guatemala City. I was really astounded. We didn't see a single *costumbrero* area (a place to burn candles and incense). Where have you seen a ladino burning incense? But someone who's never gone anywhere . . . doesn't understand.
>
> It's easier to convert a merchant, because a merchant always understands things. But for a peasant laborer it's hard. Merchants can hear the preaching of the gospel or the church. At the salt fields, however, there's a lot of drinking. On a cotton plantation they're gambling all day and saying bad things.

In other words, in comparison to a worker in the countryside, such as a sheepherder, a laborer on the cotton plantation, or a worker at the salt flats, a merchant is more serene and better disposed to accept messages from outside.

A good merchant is *tough*, that is, he takes risks, struggles, and is willing to lose big sums in order to win. One has to be prepared to lose—even Q 1,000—says a chile merchant, if one wants to get out of being a farm worker and not always be "swinging a hoe." The first converts in the movement have displayed this quality of struggle, sometimes by risking being disinherited, being beaten and jailed, and even more, at the time of conversion, by taking the step toward possible death entailed in breaking with the traditional beliefs of their ancestors and the guardian of those beliefs, the *zahorín*.

Finally, in some special instances, merchants have had *revelatory dreams* in which they perceive the parallel between the intuition of big decisions, like the option to buy chile when everyone is selling, risking the entire business, and the decision to be converted, risking their life. The revelations, both of economic success and of conversion, come from a realm that is "infinitely" nameless, as the following account puts it:

It came time for the chile harvest, and chile dropped to Q 10–12. Good chile. It's stupid I said, I'm going to buy chile. I know where I'm going to buy it . . . I had another revelation. A man gave me a heap of little green birds, and I gave him chile. And boy, did he give me a lot of little green birds! Some green, all parrots, some like parakeets, little birds, parrots . . . "It's a good deal, guys," I told them, "it's stupid." I'm going to buy chile, so I'm thinking to myself. I was going to deal in merchandise, all kinds of things: clothes, watches, bowls, dishes, cacao, pepper, even gunpowder. So I have Q 1,200–1,300 in San Pedro Carchá. Already set up in a market booth. I started thinking.

We began to prepare sacks. "And what are you going to do?" "I'm going to buy my hundred-pound sacks for my home consumption." Ridiculous! I'm not going to bring in sales except by building up, building up, and buying chile. I bought myself 150 bags. I borrowed a bit of money. And it went up to Q 40. I bought at Q 12, 13, 14, 15, and even 18. Ruined. Down to Q 7–8. It has to go up. I bought around Q 1,600 of chile. I was left with only around Q 80 of things for sale . . . a bit of cinnamon, a bit of pepper, a bit of cloves . . . My merchandise is all spread around. And there's nowhere . . . (Laughter) "What happened?" they ask me. "I brought in my money, because I've got it loaned out." (Laughter) "Ridiculous—you have it for chile." "No, the chile I was taking is a friend's," I told him.

It rose from December to March. I began to sell. I made Q 2,000 clear profit. That was a revelation by parrots of a mountain of chile. I believe in that revelation. Some revelations are infinitely . . . (He sighs, and does not say what they are.)

I cannot resist presenting another "revelation" from this same merchant that was the sign of his conversion. Like the previous one, carefully transcribed from the recorder, it shows the intuition that, through a dream, reorganizes the mental map of someone who is troubled by doubt.

One of my children died. He was five. Healthy and sound. The one after J. I'm feeling somewhat sorry. I'm pondering lots of things. I have two *zahorines*. Then came two would-be *zahorines*. They began to do crazy things, traditional practices. Six days later my son died. When my child died, my uncle P. said we had done enough of traditional practice. For two months we started drinking out of sadness for the kid. Then P. (says to me): "The Tradition has to be completed. Today we're going to do the Tradition." They didn't come. He goes to wait. "Ridiculous. Let's eat." So we go to sleep. No way I'm going to wait up. Then, . . . "O my God, might it be true, real, what they're (*zahorines*) doing? It's all lies." I want to know what is most important here on earth. It's either Religion (Catholic) or it's Protestant. I was just going round and round like that. Just a little while like that, and I went off to sleep.

There comes news, a revelation . . . So I went to sleep. And my wife is sitting there. How she calls out to me. I went to sleep. The message came. An old man appeared in the dream. He said to me:

"You, what are you thinking?"

"Nothing. Just thinking."

"Well, why are you sad?"

"I'm not sad."

"Yes, you're sad that Tin died, you told me, your little boy? Why didn't you tell me you're happy? I know why you're sad. Because your little child died," he told me.

"That's true, "I said to him.

"Do you know why your boy died? You don't know why?"

"Well, no . . . ," I said to him. "Because I wanted to know why," I said to him.

"Ah, you remembered. Remember you were told there when you were in San Pedro Carchá (in another dream) you were asked for a sacrifice . . . ?"

"Yes," I told him.

"And who performed the sacrifice?" he asked me.

"Well, us," I said to him, "Pedro . . . he performed it."

"Okay . . ." he said to me. "Ha, ha," he said to me. "So you weren't laughing at these men that could make this sacrifice? Cursed before my Father be those who are engaged in this evil Tradition. They will be cast into hell, separated by my Father; he orders that these miserable people end their life in hell. Do you want to be condemned with them?" he said to me.

"No, sir, no." [I laughed, and he said to me]: "Yes, the dream is sad." [And he went on with his story.]

"Do you want to be condemned with them?"

"Since I didn't do it . . ."

"But you're paying with your money."

"Yes, Lord, because I don't know which is more important . . . for the law of man. But since I don't know," I said to him, "why don't you tell me what is more important here on earth for the law of man?"

"You don't know? Cursed because you don't know. Get up," he said to me, "I'm going to show you, because you don't know." He grabbed me here. We went into the church here in San Antonio. "I feel as though . . . like this, like this . . . how can I put it? . . ." he is saying. The Lord took me. We went inside. He offered a Rosary. He began to sing. But what a song they were singing, so beautiful. Like a whole bunch of children, I'm telling you.

"Fine. Today I'm going to teach you what my Father wanted," he said. "Today, or tomorrow, or the next day if you don't do what my Father wants, then you will be condemned," he told me.

So I repented there. I was ashamed. So I got up. Then I went down on my knees to ask God for forgiveness. What is the Tradition . . . ? Then I began to tell my wife.

O my God, what a dream I'm having; a dream seems like something sad. "Why?"

"I dreamed some things . . . Now I'm screwed," I told her.

I made arrangements to go . . . I went to Esquipulas. I went on pilgrimage. I went back to pilgrimage, I came back from pilgrimage to convert to the [true Catholic] Religion.

I was sick for seven years. I've dreamed a lot of things. I'm forgetting some of them, there are some things that . . . Yes, yes, that's why I converted to Religion.

We began to battle the Traditionalists. We began to battle. "That's not right! [What you do] is ridiculous!"

Without discussing these wonderful stories for now, we see how a merchant's major decisions when he decides to build up stock and that of the convert when he converts are similar and are settled in an act of intuition, which is sometimes expressed in dreams. Later, we will determine what it means that both processes, capital buildup and conversion, are attributed to the same source that is beyond experience.

Knowing Customers and the Outside World

The merchant is a traveler who is familiar with the customs, tastes, and intentions of the most diverse buyers from different regions, such as Cobán, Guatemala City, La Máquina, and Santa Cruz del Quiché. When new ideas enter the municipality from outside, a merchant can recognize with whom he is dealing and can accept them, if he is convinced by them, certain that he is not going to be deceived.

A merchant recognizes when someone does not know how to buy, such as engineers and tractor drivers from the plantations who quickly pay whatever is asked or others who "seem not to realize that some things are more expensive" and make offers that are ridiculously low. He recognizes those who are not in a buying mood and are only going to handle the merchandise without taking it away; good customers who are familiar with the unit price but not the price for a dozen; merchants who deal in dozens; and, finally, thieves, who try to snatch things, gesturing with one hand and grabbing with the other, asking for several things at once and confusing a merchant.

Because they know customers, who are often ladinos, merchants take note of those they can trust. They are the part of the municipality that has opened up to the outside and are confident enough to establish ties and discuss with its representatives without fear of being deceived. This confidence, which is not simply based on the understanding described above, has paved the way for accepting new ideas from outside.

This economic opening has then made possible the derivation of power from other levels and is found repeated in the opening to religiosity, as expressed in certain religious gestures. For example, instead of looking toward the earth in his prayer to the Sacred World, as Traditionalists who burn incense in the hills normally do, a convert raises his eyes up to the God in heaven. For him, the center of his nonempirical power, like that which is empirical, is not within the community, but outside it.

Nonempirical Explanations of Success

In the previous discussion, I explored some explanations for capital buildup that transcend what can be experienced, and I indicated some assessments given by merchants in the capitalization process as contrasted with small farmers and with a certain type of merchant who resembles a small farmer in his experience of constraint because he is at a standstill. Inasmuch as I assume that, in starting their business, most merchants experienced a breach in the constraints on small farmers, and that this experience paralleled the conversion movement, I tried to make both experiences, that of capital buildup and that of conversion, meet. At this point, we seem to run up against—as strange as it may seem to state this at this moment—the liberation brought by capitalism's first impact, which is propitious for capital buildup.

Merchants tend to explain success by invoking the notion of luck (*la suerte*), which is one more of those qualities mentioned above of imagination, drive, understanding, and so forth, and yet it is not what luck is ordinarily understood to mean, in the sense of randomness. Let us see what it is.

> Some sell more. People buy more. That's luck, it's not being sharp, because some are sharp and still don't sell. It's something else. Everyone has their luck . . . Sometimes an older merchant who is no longer enthusiastic hasn't got luck. Some just go into business, and they sell. It's luck. Our Lord can't give everyone the very same food. Just a little bit to each one. Luck passes from one to another according to the days. Some get angry. Not me, I know that luck came to someone who sold a lot. You get sad. I'm far away from the town, and I don't have anything to pay for a meal. All the worse if it's that way tomorrow, or the day after, or if you're in debt . . .

This passage introduces us to two meanings of what is understood as luck. The first is that it is an influence that starts with oneself and comes from another source that distributes it in an orderly way. According to Tradition, that source is the Sacred World (Heart of the Earth), and according to Catholic Action, it is God (in Heaven).

As seen in Tradition, which is best represented by the *zahorines* and whose most well elaborated reflection is the 260-day calendar (*cholaj k'ij*), each of the days has its Lord, which is like the heart of the day, and people born on that day are necessarily influenced by that heart. Thus the Lord of the day marks their luck.

Some of the twenty Lords of the day are favorable, some are practically neutral, and others are malevolent. Their distribution is preset and organized in such a way that although on each passing day some luck is leaving an undefined time (probably the Sacred World) and this Origin can be regarded as unlimitedly pregnant with luck, nevertheless the manner in which luck comes out is predetermined and could probably be found inscribed in the Origin from which it emerges. Time keeps doubling back in a spiral (not circular) manner, but always according to hidden rules.[2]

This model of time seems to reflect a society growing at a steady pace, where new communities break off as replicas of the original one in a process similar to the transformation of settlements into villages or cantons, and of cantons and villages into municipalities, as described in Chapter 4. Since the preconquest stratification would be reflected in the range of four supreme days out of twenty, stratification must have been foreseen, and its growth could not exceed certain inscribed calculable rules through which any change is foreseeable, if one knows how to read the deep current of luck.

Catholic Action converts ridiculed the *zahorín* calendar, comparing the names of the days with their animal meanings in order to make them contemptible, but they maintained a degree of belief in the secret influence of the days on human beings and their activities, which tends to come out indirectly in conversations on other matters. It is God who attributes one or another influence to days, but He apparently does not assign them directly, but rather has an inherent relationship with them through the saints whose feasts are celebrated on particular days. Hence, ultimately, God is not different from the Origin of luck conceived as the Sacred World.

The difference may lie in the fact that the order with which time and luck flow is not inescapably inscribed in God, as it is in the Origin of the days and of luck, but He determines it at his free choice, distributing people's luck without being subject to constraint himself. I propose that this vision of a free God is proper to some converts who are likewise merchants, as I explain further on.

A second meaning is similar to the previous one, namely, that in addition to this innate predisposition, there is an influence that is not fixed, but rather comes and goes according to the *zahorín* calendar or as distributed by God. Hence, someone is lucky one day, but not the next, and so forth. That is why luck is referred to above with the words "Luck passes from one to another, depending on the days." This is similar to the first meaning because ordinary men (those who are not *zahorines*) are not aware of how it is determined, likewise in accordance with days, and because it is assumed that the flow of luck dispensed is limited, so one day it goes to one, and another day to someone else.

Sometimes getting rich is explained in other ambiguous, dangerous, or reprehensible ways that seem to have nothing to do with luck, but yet, when properly observed, are related to it, such as by magnetic rocks that draw customers, by special prayers that may even harm other sellers, or by contracts with the Lord of the Hill to serve him as a slave in exchange for multiplication of goods (Falla 1971b). These ways are reprehensible because they are efforts to disturb the balance of luck set up in an orderly way, and assuming that the flow of luck is limited, because they secretly take from others what is rightfully theirs, inexplicably destroying the order by which luck is dispensed.

However, a merchant, for example, who has risen in wealth will deny that his capital comes from the Hill or from the magnet, as claimed by someone who is unable to explain such a disorder in the distribution of luck without intervention from beyond the empirical. According to one who is experiencing an increase of capital previously inconceivable to him and unprecedented in the community, there is a source of luck that operates unexpectedly in a way that is not pre-established. Here it is well to recall the merchant with amazing revelations. The image he has of the Lord who makes him wealthy (let us call him God) is that of a free person who is not subject to certain standards of conduct imposed by society, like those of traditional redistribution. By contrast, a small farmer or a merchant who is at a standstill has the image of God or a source of luck as an origin that is orderly, predictable, and to some degree handicapped by the laws of time, which are a reflection of the traditional norms of redistribution. For one who has gone beyond previous levels of enrichment, the traditional norms are broken. For one who is suffering the limits of being a small farmer[3] or who is at a standstill, those norms, which may once have appeared to be shattered, have now been reinstated. The images that people hold of God or of the Origin of luck are images of the experiences they have had with such norms.

These two visions also seem to correspond to two periods in the Catholic Action movement. The newer vision corresponds to the rays of hope from the early years of conversions and of trade, when a new order seemed to have been set up ("everything has changed"). The traditional vision is that of a period when routine has set in, when many merchants have gone as far as they can go and have been disillusioned. The converts, for their part, have begun to set up regulations for the society that they created, similar to those of the previous one. The traditional vision, which is not the exclusive property of Traditionalists, has reemerged among Catholic Action members. For the majority who remain stuck in the traditional constraints of the peasant community, neither trade nor conversion has proven to be the threshold of a new age.

Thus, a series of values common to merchants and converts suggests that the two processes are mutually self-reinforcing. Such values include not only those qualities of imagination, struggle, and planning that they have acquired or honed so as to bring in more customers/members, but also those that entail an opening to the world outside the community, both in order to understand how it thinks and to trust in its people, and to create a favorable predisposition for accepting new beliefs. Moreover, capital buildup and conversion are two facets of the same experience of breaking with a community's norms of redistribution, even though as the years go by and some of the merchants who converted begin to experience their own economic stagnation, they have given voice to a demand for redistribution that the original religious movement now institutionalizes.

Conclusion

As we have seen, merchant capital buildup went hand in hand with conversion and was prompted by events outside the community: the elimination of debts and forced labor, the extension of the road network, and the introduction of motor vehicles. We also saw that owning trucks placed merchants on a higher level of trading activity than was previously available in the community, and that their situation was enhanced when they not only sold wholesale but also began to obtain merchandise on consignment and multiplied their places of business, thereby covering several power domains, even if they were scattered. The next chapter takes up the detailed analysis of the organization of power within the community, with all the relationships (debtors, laborers, *compadres*, and so forth) resulting from capital buildup, and the analysis of the stratification process as a determinant of the division between Traditionalists and Catholic Action. Here we have focused more on the mutual determination between conversion and capital buildup, both of them at odds with service in the *cofradías*, which because of the expenditures and time entailed used to level out capital.

Merchants doing business out in frontier areas, where there were no middlemen to block them and where they were far from the municipality and from serving in *cofradías*, built up capital and converted. Meanwhile, merchants doing business in the town, even though they did not convert and did serve the *cofradías* by devoting some of their money to them (but not their time, since they were in town), built up capital because they had a monopoly on certain articles or services.

The growth of Catholic Action, driven by the merchants with their qualities of imagination and aggressiveness, nevertheless produced a multitude of positions (*cargos*) and commitments, similar in terms of time requirements to those of the *cofradías*, so that as it grew, the movement gradually became limited to itself. Moreover, the Traditionalists became used to doing business outside the municipality, and the demands of the *cofradías* gradually diminished.

In addition to the higher category of merchants, others have done business at a level similar to that of truck drivers, judging by the amount of their capital. Some of them have not only taken part in running Catholic Action, but together with Catholic Action truck owners, they have helped defend it. This group of merchants constitutes the major source of the division within the municipality, because without their power it is unlikely that it would have been possible to draw on (additional) power from outside to formally confirm the division. On the Traditionalist side, the division is also backed by powerful merchants.

Finally, we have shown how these processes of capitalization and conversion came together in the discovery of new values of imagination, creativity, planning, and struggle, but also of being open to the world from which merchants derived their wealth. The intrusion of capital for a few years enabled some to glimpse a new world apart from the norms of redistribution, with a God who was more free, less handicapped, and to some degree more erratic, but always marvelous. However, the experience of some who converted and later came to a standstill in business has once more closed the horizon and brought them to demand redistribution in the form of participation in *cargos* and symbolic expenses.

CHAPTER 4

Social Reorganization

Because conversion entails not only changing beliefs but joining a different social unit, I am assuming that this adherence must be rooted in a social reorganization. In this chapter, I examine how this reorganization, motivated by rather disparate causes, has influenced conversion.

I will first focus on the change that has taken place in the choosing of a bride. Then, I will consider how that has given rise to a new marriage pattern in which the canton becomes highly endogamous, and what that change has meant for setting up Catholic Action centers. Third, I will study "confessional" endogamy (within each religious group), resulting from the reorganization wrought by conversion, and the energy that this reorganization has injected into the conversion movement. Fourth, I will analyze how the divisive forces that social stratification has aroused in the community, among subordinates and superiors as well as among equals, has also given rise to Catholic Action, in opposition to the Traditionalists (*cofradías*). Fifth, I will study the evolution of community authority as a prerequisite for understanding the surge of witchcraft and the explosion of the rebellion against the *zahorines* (conversion) in the late 1940s. This fifth section will complete the analysis of the undermining of community power, begun in the previous section. I will have covered social reorganization in the household, canton, municipality, and, to some extent, in the nation itself, and its influence on conversion.

Choosing a Bride

A change has taken place with regard to who chooses a bride: the decision has shifted from parents choosing a future bride for their son to the son himself making the choice. At the outset of my research I did not realize what connection this change had with conversion; I only understood that there was a relationship. My informants made it clear that the Catholic Action movement had promoted this change and had taken it as one of a number of symbols of what was new about the movement, inasmuch as it somehow replicated the rebellion of children against their parents or that of innovating young people against the beliefs of the older people that was entailed in conversion. After making my analysis, however, I realized that this change is the decision-making aspect of the reorganization of marriage alliances, because that reorganization has been carried out in keeping with the tastes and informal associations of young people, and not, it would seem, of their elders.

I will describe in greater detail how a wife used to be chosen traditionally and how it happens now, and I will offer an illustration. Then I will show that the change has been widespread, and I will try to trace some of the reasons for that change. Finally, I will connect the change more explicitly to conversion.

Traditional and New Ways of Choosing a Bride

In the traditional manner of choosing a bride (which has not completely disappeared), the boy's parents chose their son's mate when the boy was still a very young child and the girl even younger. Without consulting the boy, they would go to see the prospective bride's parents a couple of times to ask the parents for their daughter's hand, and they, likewise without consulting her, either accepted the request or did not. It was an alliance between two households. This alliance was so firm and so clear in some cases that the bride for the second or even third son came from the same household. Today there are still some instances among adults of two or three brothers married to women who are siblings.

It was ordinarily the boy's mother who checked on the availability of girls in the canton from which the mother herself had come (it should be kept in mind that this society is patrilocal), and sometimes from her own lineage segment or from segments near her own. When the bride was sought from the same segment as the mother, the alliance extended from segment to segment.

In the new procedure, however, the son chooses his bride himself. Conflict with the parents' choice has occurred not so much because the son has taken the initiative first, but because the son has refused to accept the woman that they have chosen for him, or because after living with her for a couple of years, he has rejected her and has chosen another woman in tune with "his blood." To avoid such a separation or divorce (never legally), many parents have anticipated the disadvantages of a divorce caused by their own imposed choice and have refrained from marrying off their son before he can decide for himself.

Parents and son usually have an implicit understanding. The tastes of son and parents are usually not poles apart. The son may refuse to accept a particular girl as his wife, but he generally does not rebel against the custom of his father going to ask for the hand of his future wife, because such a rebellion would thereby entail abducting the girl or paying for the bride's gifts out of his own funds (not those of his father). Since that is not normal, the father can veto a girl chosen by his son simply by not asking for her hand. The son, therefore, while holding on to the initiative of the choice, adjusts to the tacit or explicit rejections of his father.

The son may have channels for selecting other than those of his mother or stepmother. He can directly choose a girl who stands out from others because of the economic position of her parents. He can get information from his group of friends in the canton, from his fellow soccer players, from those with whom he does business, or from those with whom he converses at the Catholic Action center. If his mother is dead or separated from his father, he can get information from his other relatives and use that information as an alternative to that presented by his stepmother. Many of these types of associations through which the young man receives information are new; others, like that of the mother's relatives, are old, but new factors are enabling the son to use them as real alternatives.

Illustration

This is the story of Simón, son of Don Eulalio (names are fictitious). In 1946, when this happened, Simón was 14, and Eulalio 35.

Don Eulalio had gone into business when President Ubico canceled people's debts in 1934. As a child, Don Eulalio had suffered a great deal on the coast. He did not have much luck with his wives either, because the first one, Simón's mother, died very young. The second died of fever, and the third was unfaithful to him. Finally, however, in his travels as a merchant, he met an Indian woman from outside the municipality, won her over, and brought her to live in San Antonio.

After his mother's death, Simón was placed in the care of one of his mother's brothers. He began to accompany his father on his business travels when he was 8 years old. Until then he could not speak Spanish and was afraid of ladinos, but because he had to help his father with sales, he gradually learned Spanish. He also learned to go work on the coast with his uncles on his mother's side and their sons.

In 1946 Simón was living with his father and stepmother, and that year his stepmother had her first child. Although the future perhaps could not be foreseen, and there was no intention of manipulating him, this new son and the stepmother's other two sons were going to be the sole heirs of Don Eulalio's land and Simón would not receive anything, contrary to all the usual norms.

The year Simón's half-brother was born, his parents sought a wife for Simón. Somewhat because of Don Eulalio's taste for things ladino (Don Eulalio was a merchant and dealt with ladinos, and the stepmother was familiar with ladino cooking), they found him a daughter of an indigenous man and a ladina woman, who was from the same canton. This girl was unusual in the municipality because even though a small percentage of ladinos lived in the municipality, they always married among themselves.

Don Eulalio asked her parents for her hand and they accepted. Simón says he was embarrassed to speak to her because she was a ladina and he did not like her because she did not have money. He says that he laid down the condition that she dress as an indigenous woman, something she would not accept. The father and stepmother became angry and remarked "how he wants to order them around." Furthermore, they had already asked for her hand and if they did not return with the gifts, it would bring them shame. But Simón refused and threatened to go to the coast, which they knew he could certainly do.

Simón then began looking for himself. He also seems to have been drawn by ladino ways, because without first talking with her, he chose a woman who was the child of indigenous parents, but who dressed like a ladina. Her father was well-off.

Don Eulalio did not want to ask for her hand because she was the daughter of rich people and was "used to eating well." By contrast, the ladina's parents were poor, so Don Eulalio said that it was better to ask for her hand because "it's not going to cost us," meaning the price of the customary gifts.

A friend of Simón's, a 22-year-old merchant who lived nearby, told him that his older brother had a daughter suited for him. At this time, Simón was barely 15. An aunt, the sister of his now deceased second stepmother, gave him encouragement, and she herself went to tell the prospective father-in-law that Simón was coming to ask for his daughter's hand. Simón still did not know her, and he asked a merchant friend to point her out to him on market day in the town square. There he saw her seated beside the church. He was embarrassed to speak to her and asked his aunt to ask her if she were willing; she said she was.

But Don Eulalio was unwilling to ask for her hand, because "she lives in the town, goes to school, and is lazy." The girl's father did not want to grant her hand either because he had money. Don Eulalio wanted to asked for the ladina again, because she was cheaper, but at the same time, he probably was not displeased with the idea that, because times were changing, his son might perhaps receive an inheritance from the girl's father. Thus he gave in, and he asked for her hand three times, until her parents finally granted her for his son. Simón was then 16, as was his wife. Three years later they had their first son.

This account illustrates the son's power base, which enables him to stand up to his father and stepmother: he is familiar with the coast and can go there to work; he has relatives on his mother's side to whom he can turn; and he has other sources of information for choosing on his own, independently of his father and his stepmother. He can resist the choice they impose on him, but he cannot conclude his choice by making the proposal and reaching an arrangement. We also see opposing tastes: that of the stepmother, which seems to adjust to the father's because she seeks to make an alliance with a household

TABLE 4.1. *Wife selection by men from different Catholic Action centers, by year of marriage*

| Year of marriage | Did you choose your first wife? | | |
	Yes	No	Total
Before 1924	0 (0%)	5 (100%)	5
1925–1929	0 (0%)	4 (100%)	4
1930–1934	1 (8%)	11 (92%)	12
1935–1939	4 (20%)	15 (80%)	19
1940–1944	7 (26%)	20 (74%)	27
1945–1949	17 (38%)	28 (62%)	45
1950–1954	17 (57%)	13 (43%)	30
1955–1959	13 (45%)	16 (55%)	29
1960–1964	27 (47%)	31 (53%)	58
1965–1969	40 (73%)	15 (27%)	55
Total	126	158	284

Source: Survey of Catholic Action members by centers.

that, like her own, is an exception in the municipality, and that of the son, who inclines toward merchant values in which wealth is prized and lets himself be guided by the advice of his merchant friend.

General Observations on the Change

Table 4.1 shows this change in bridal selection with statistics. It presents the 284 Catholic Action men from different centers, constituting 19 percent of all men in the municipality who have, or have had, a wife. Prior to 1945, three-quarters (74%) or more of them were not involved in choosing their first wife, while in the most recent five-year period (1965–1969), almost three-quarters (73%) had chosen their first wife.

The partial nature of my information has prevented me from making a direct comparison between Catholic Action men and Traditionalists with regard to their role in choosing their wives. Later I will utilize indirect data (i.e., entailing a reconstruction) to show to what extent this change has spread to Traditionalists and what sets them apart from Catholic Action members.

Causes of Change in Bride Selection

Possible causes of this change must now be considered. The first such cause I will call *reorganizational*; it includes everything that has tended to bring about a reorganization in marriage patterns or that may have affected the opposition between choice by parents and choice by sons, such as population increase, conversion itself, and stratification. In the following sections, I will consider how population increase has helped make cantons become more endogamous, how conversion has produced "confessional" endogamy, and, finally, how the appearance of merchants and their buildup of capital has given rise to another kind of incipient endogamy between well-off merchants or their children. The subsequent sections will study these factors' relationship to conversion.

The second cause has to do with the *son's power* vis-à-vis his father. In order to oppose his father, a son must have more power than was his traditionally. One way that a son can have more power than his father is if the father's situation weakens. The father's traditional power base has been land, and that is what enables him to threaten to take away the son's inheritance, his future means of livelihood. However, the average landholding has had to be divided in half during the past twenty-five years as the population has doubled. If the average amount of land worked is now 20 *cuerdas* per landowner (according to surveys made in one canton), twenty-five years ago it was 40 *cuerdas* and thus a father had a greater power base then than he does now. Moreover, as a result of growing stratification of the population, some are considerably below this average and some are higher. According to data from 75 heads of household in this canton, we may distinguish three strata of people in terms of land and production: the first group comprises 22 people who have enough land to sell corn; the second, 34 who neither buy nor sell corn; and the third, 19 who buy corn. Among these last are some who have only 2, 3, or 5 *cuerdas*. They are in a weak position vis-à-vis their sons, particularly if the sons have other sources of income, such as trade. When conflict arises, as for example over the choice of a bride or in matters of belief, they have no base from which to impose their authority.

The third cause is the *rising age* of the son when he marries his first wife. This began to happen even before sons started choosing their own wife. When a son, for reasons beyond his parents' intentions or his own—such as time spent outside the municipality on the coast—has been growing up and does not yet have a wife, and he reaches an age considerably above the age at which most other young men get married, he has greater leeway for refusing to accept the woman that his parents impose and to seek one himself. He is more awakened to sex and sometimes even dares to speak to the girl and to woo her, a practice still frowned upon by most people in the municipality. The average age of men when they marry has been rising, from 17.65 years old in 1924 to 18.64 years of age in 1969.

The age of women upon their first marriage has also been rising, and even more quickly: from 14.51 to 17.57 years (1924 to 1969); their age when they first give birth has likewise risen from 15.8 to 18.46 years. This last information on the relationship of the rising age of the woman when she first gives birth to the rise in the ages of first marriage for both women and men, and hence with the change in who chooses the bride, will later enable me to demonstrate that the change of who chooses the bride has been greater within members of Catholic Action than among Traditionalists, by noting the higher average age of Catholic Action women than Traditionalist women when they first give birth.

The fourth cause must have been the rise in the number of *divorces* taking place in recent years. Here, divorce is regarded as the separation of husbands who were united in matrimony according to Tradition, that is, through the traditional rite (*c'ulnem*), and have since formed unions with other women. Divorce has an effect on who makes the choice in the following respects. First, in households where divorce occurs, the sources of power available to the children doubles. Children in a household where their father and mother live together have no relatives who are not also relatives of one parent or the other. By contrast, the children of a home where their father is living with their stepmother can go to their mother's relatives seeking support against the intention of their father or stepmother. In this first aspect, their parents' divorce has the effect of increasing the children's power, and therefore making them more likely to rebel against their parents in handling their own life, such as in choosing a future wife and accepting that decision or in changing their beliefs. Second, the *perception* (ever clearer as more and more divorces took place) of the relationship between divorce and imposed choice of the bride must have made parents stop to think, and therefore not to impose their choice on their sons so as not to lose the price that they themselves would pay for the gifts to their son's bride, when the son abandons his wife after living with her for a couple of years.

Relationship of the Change to Conversion

The change in who it is who chooses the bride is related to conversion in the following ways. First, according to information provided by Catholic Action members, more of them began the custom of allowing the son to choose the bride than did the Traditionalists, and it was the procedure that they urged on their followers in conscious opposition to the traditions of their ancestors. This new way became one of a number of *symbols* of the new dissident attitude of Catholic Action members.

To check statistically this relationship expressed by my informants, I could only make use of indirect data, given my scarce information on the Traditionalists. I said earlier that there was a relationship between the average age of the woman at her first childbirth and the average age of the woman and the man when they marry for the first time, and that likewise there was a relationship between these two data and the fact that the man himself had chosen his wife. I then reasoned that if I found that Catholic Action women were older than Traditionalist women when their first child was born, the relationship between Catholic Action and the change in the choice of a bride would be confirmed. The difference indeed exists, although it is small: 18.87 years versus 19.5 years for Traditionalist and Catholic Action women, respectively. Among Traditionalist women, 86.3 percent first gave birth at age 20 or before, while only 79.1 percent of Catholic Action women did so. These differences therefore confirm the impressions of my informants.

Second, in taking this innovative stance toward choosing marriage partners, Catholic Action was assimilating a way of adapting to the times, particularly in dealing with the reasons for the growing number of *divorces*. Encouraging greater freedom in choosing the bride would slow the number of divorces, because, as we have seen, divorce is a way of opting against one's parents' choice by rejecting the woman they imposed, even after one has lived with her.

Those most likely to adopt this new custom by joining Catholic Action were those who had had the experience of divorce in their home and were perhaps seeking to remedy it for future generations. Side A of Table 4.2 indicates that in a group of fifty-three men over 30 from two hamlets in the same canton who were married before 1958, there is a higher proportion of divorces among those who subsequently converted to Catholic Action than among those who continued to be Traditionalists. I conclude that Catholic Action must have *been more attractive to those who were divorced* than to those who were not.

The group of thirty-one men under 30 from the same hamlets (side B of Table 4.2) does not display any differences between Catholic Action members and Traditionalists. In this group, the proportion of divorces is lower than in the previous group (A), and it indicates that the number of divorces slowed after 1958. If such a slowing has occurred, it would appear to have been where there was a greater propensity to divorce, namely within Catholic Action, and thus it is perhaps for that reason that there does not appear to be a correlation between divorce and Catholic Action in Group A. On the other hand, we could say that applying the remedy of allowing children to choose has had positive effects in reducing divorce.

The determination to reduce divorce is confirmed by the policy established by Catholic Action to legalize marriages before a judge and in the church (they speak of "getting married" [*casarse*] as opposed to simply "living together" [*juntarse*]). Formal marriage had fallen into disuse in the municipality after the persecution of the church in 1871 and the resulting drop in the number of priests. Catholic Action resurrected this custom, with positive results for the stability of marriage, inasmuch as of the forty who married both civilly and in the church in the past ten years, only four have separated from their wives and only one of these has begun to live with another. Acceptance by the authority beyond the municipality, with its power derived from the law, has compensated for the weakness of the authority of parents *and the witnesses* (relatives) in the segments.

It is noteworthy that the factor of *divorce is influential* in conversion *independent* of the factor of engaging in trade (previous chapter). In the total of 84 men in the forgoing table there are only six merchants, two of whom have left their wives. This means that, first, because the table presents an almost en-

TABLE 4.2. *Men from two hamlets of one canton, grouped by age (A and B) and according to the variables of conversion (Catholic Action) and divorce (leaving wife)*

| | | A) More than 30 years old Are you Catholic Action? | | | B) Between 20 and 30 Are you Catholic Action? | | |
		Yes	No	Total	Yes	No	Total
Did you leave	Yes	11	11	22	4	3	7
your wife?	No	10	21	31	12	12	24
	Total	21	32	53	16	15	31

Source: Informant from one of the hamlets (1970).
Note: The correlation between conversion and divorces obtains only for Group A.

tirely non-merchant population, the variable "trade" has remained outside my testing; and second, that in this small number (6) of merchants, the proportion of divorces is practically equal to what it is among non-merchants (6/2 versus 78/27, i.e., 3 versus 2.9).

Hence, with regard to divorce and conversion, I conclude that Catholic Action has been a movement that has offered formulas more suitable for achieving stable marriages, for example, freedom to choose the bride, and civil and ecclesiastical marriage. It also seems that the individuals whom we can assume to have been attracted to these ways are those who had experienced divorce in their homes and were destined to impose new customs on the next generations; and that the correlation between divorce and conversion is independent of that between trade and conversion.

Finally, the changes in bride selection and its counterpart, divorce, are related to conversion in a third way that has been hinted at throughout this section. That change has to be considered as the process of choice that reflects the rapid movement to reorganize marriage patterns, to which I devote the next three sections.

Endogamy within the Canton

Description of Canamixtoj Canton

Local patterns of marriage alliances have been changing over the years and have contributed to social reorganization within the municipality. In analyzing this change I will focus on one canton, Canamixtoj, for which I have the most detailed information in this regard.

Canamixtoj Canton (see Map 4.1) borders on four municipalities: Santa María Chiquimula, Santa Lucía la Reforma, San Pedro Jocopilas, and Santa Cruz del Quiché. It is located in the far north of San Antonio Ilotenango and borders only two other cantons of San Antonio: Sacxac and Xejip. Although there are trails connecting Canamixtoj to Sacxac, movement between these two cantons does not compare with that between Canamixtoj and Xejip, which

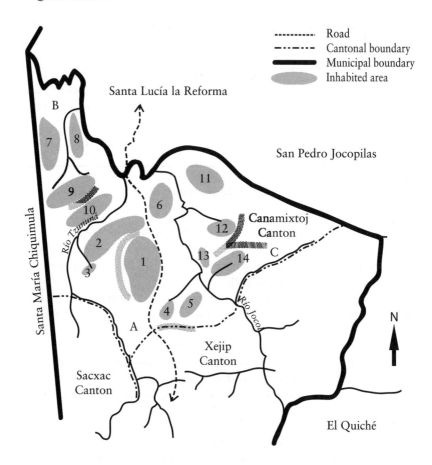

MAP 4.1. *Canamixtoj Canton and surrounding area*

are linked by the road that runs north to Santa María and south to the town of San Antonio.

Crossing Canamixtoj are the Tzununá and Jocol Rivers, which divide the canton into three sections (A, B, and C). The people do not give these sections a name, but there are indications that they regard them as units larger than the hamlets in the canton. One indication is the existence of soccer teams for each of these sections and only for them in the canton.

The canton is made up of fourteen hamlets, each of which is separated from the others by a geographical feature such as a river, a creek, or a small mountain, or by a road. Houses are spread apart in the small valleys of the hamlets.

Marriage Patterns

Table 4.3 shows the percentages of unions made between partners from within the canton, from this canton and other cantons, and from this canton and other municipalities. The age of the man at the time of marriage provides us with an indication of the time when the alliance took place. Those who are between 15 and 29 years of age were married from approximately 1958 to 1970; those who are between 30 and 39, between 1948 and 1958; those between 40 and 49, between 1938 and 1948; and those over 50, before 1938. Using the age of the men in those unions we can establish dates for the marriages and therefore which direction the change has gone, if any.

There has not been any significant change in unions with mates from other municipalities, as the percentages in column C show. The fact that the municipality is flanked by four other municipalities has not raised these percentages, which by themselves are quite low.

On the other hand, the decline in the percentage of marriages between inhabitants of Canamixtoj and those of other cantons has been quite striking. People in the canton have turned inward, reduced the number of alliances with other cantons, and become increasingly endogamous and self-sufficient in terms of the search for their wives. From the canton of Sacxac I have been able to check on the origins of 82 percent of the parents of those over 40 who are still living, and it turns out that 28 percent were from that canton and 82 percent from another. These data confirm those of Canamixtoj and indicate that the process has not been restricted to a single canton, because, as might logically be supposed, if alliances of one canton change with respect to the others, those of the other cantons are also going to change with respect to that one. Thus the local patterns of one canton have the effect of reorganizing those of all, provided there is no barrier to communication that would isolate one (as there has not been in this case).

To go back further in time, I investigated the surnames (of father and mother) of those over age 50 in Canamixtoj, of whom there are thirty-five. Of these thirty-five, I studied only twenty-two cases, because I did not have information on some, and in other instances where there were siblings I eliminated all

TABLE 4.3. *Marriage unions within the canton (A), between cantons (B), and between municipalities (C) of men living in the canton of Canamixtoj, by age*

Age of man when married	Marriages within canton (A)	Marriages between cantons (B)	Marriages between municipalities (C)	Totals
15–29	44 (70%)	17 (27%)	2 (3%)	63
30–39	32 (59%)	19 (35%)	3 (6%)	54
40–49	24 (53%)	20 (44%)	1 (2%)	45
50 and over	12 (34%)	23 (66%)	0 (0%)	35
Totals	112	79	6	197

Source: Informants in Canamixtoj. Out of a total of 219 marriages, I obtained information on only 197 (90%).

but one. Seventeen of these twenty-two (77%) have surnames of a father and mother from different cantons, while five (23%) have surnames from the same canton. If we compare these data with those in Table 4.3 (66% of unions between cantons for those over 50), we note a tendency toward intercanton unions further back in time. My rather summary inspection of the baptism registries from the middle of the last century suggests that the number of unions between municipalities was much greater at that time than it is today. I therefore find that whereas alliances used to take place between partners from great distances, now they more often occur between people of the same canton or nearby cantons; some years ago, it was between widely separated cantons; and in the last century, between persons from different municipalities.

What has caused this shift toward greater endogamy within the canton? I believe it is primarily expansion of the population—it grew at an annual rate of 2.7 percent from 1950 to 1970. This increase has had two consequences: (1) more young people can now meet and form couples; and (2) due to the scarcity of centrally located land in cantons, more people have spread toward their outer edges and the municipal boundaries, thereby moving physically farther away from other cantons.

Consequences for Conversions

The main consequence of this trend has been that as the formal organization of the municipality has lost the substratum of municipal-level marriage alliances, that organization has inevitably faltered. The backbone of the organization has been the system of eight *cofradías* with their twelve *cargos*, each of them designed to relate men and women from different cantons in a single *cofradía*, and hence to represent in a ceremonial manner the unity of the municipality. But as fewer marriages across cantons have taken place, the *cofradías* have accordingly faltered.

People have been recruited for these positions impersonally, through the *alguaciles* who have summoned them, the canton secretaries who have chosen them, and the mayor of the municipality who has appointed them. In *cofradías* in San Antonio, friends have not gathered around the *alcalde* of the *cofradía*, sought out by him, as happens in other places. Moreover, those responsible for making the choice have striven to assure that people from different cantons are serving in each *cofradía*. Since there are twelve positions, six for men and six for women, and the women cannot be wives of the men who are serving, it is possible for a single *cofradía* to have people from the ten cantons. This has happened in one *cofradía* every year, and it has also happened in the other seven. Hence in the eight *cofradías* and in their ninety-six positions, there has been a continual mixing of people from different cantons year after year (the positions are not for life).

However, when marriage alliances are no longer occurring between cantons, the likelihood of being in a *cofradía* with people one is related to by marriage declines considerably, even to the point of disappearing if the canton becomes completely endogamous. Fellow *cofradía* members in the same service do not know one another, and it naturally becomes difficult to share a celebration. One sign that the members are concerned about who their fellow members will be is that when summoned before the mayor of the municipality to receive their *cofradía* assignment, they immediately ask who the people are with whom they will be celebrating. Hence, these changing marriage patterns had to weaken the *cofradía* structures, and it then became easier for converts to rebel against them.

Other factors contributing to the weakening of the *cofradías* have been resistance to the expenses demanded by the Tradition, the geographical isolation of individuals who left the municipality and dropped out of this hierarchy of prestige, and the gradual stratification of those who began to build up capital through trade and were unwilling to submit to redistributing their earnings. I have sought to elaborate this latter factor here because I am not aware of it having been mentioned in the literature on Central America analyzing the decline of the *cofradías*.

In the past, changing marriage patterns must have constantly affected social organization, but because the demographic increase was not so rapid then as now (annual growth rate of 1.2% from 1893 to 1950 as opposed to 2.7% from 1950 to 1964), the adaptation must inevitably have been smoother and more gradual than it is now. I sense that the municipalities near San Antonio (Patzité and Santa Lucía la Reforma), which were originally settled by people from Santa María Chiquimula, were formed by later breaking off from those municipalities as independent and relatively endogamous entities, which entailed the existence of an organization independent from their earlier one, although identical to it. Thus was born the village (*aldea*) and then the municipality, with *cofradías* independent from those of the mother municipality.

In San Antonio, however, reorganization did not lead to the formation of a kind of village with its *cofradías* independent from those of the town. The need for reorganization was latent and was becoming increasingly urgent, especially because endogamy was almost complete, if the cantons are not considered individually but as a group close to one another. This was the time when the Catholic Action movement entered, and it took advantage of the push toward division to set up a center, not a *cofradía*, with people from two or three neighboring cantons, to which its members would owe allegiance and service. By setting up this new organization, power was thereby denied to the municipal organization of the *cofradías* and to the *cofradía* as such.

It is nonetheless curious that the need for a municipal organization was not denied, as happened in the towns mentioned. The municipal tie was necessary because when the conversions began, the dissidents needed mutual support against the municipal organization that was defending the *cofradías* and upholding the beliefs on which they were based.

It was at the point when each group of cantons had enough converts that the centers were formed, with a basis of operation and point of reference in the house set up by the person serving as center president, who was usually the first to have converted. The center in Canamixtoj, for example, which also included Xejip, was set up in 1955. Then, as enthusiasm and the number of converts grew, they collected money to build a chapel. This chapel did not break away from worshiping at the main church in the municipality, because the priest used to come almost solely to celebrate mass. The organization of the center, with its four elected leaders and group of catechists, was formed under the authority of the board members for Catholic Action for the entire municipality, thus making it clear that the reorganization involved creating a submunicipal level of organization.

These centers arose with a combative spirit, quite different from the way the *cofradías* were organized. The *cofradías* have operated under the assumption that all inhabitants of the area are potential *cofrades*. A center operates under the assumption that not everyone belongs to Catholic Action, that those who do not are struggling against them in one fashion or another, and that they have to defend themselves, the best defense being to gain as many followers into their ranks as possible. *Cofradía* meetings have consisted of meals, drinking, dancing, processions, and prayers, but those attending are not exhorted to do anything that goes beyond the ceremonial. In Catholic Action meetings, which take place in the chapels or in homes, in addition to a hefty portion of prayers, there is preaching in which members are exhorted to remain steadfast and to convert others. Over a loudspeaker outside the church, the gospel or the catechism is explained, with very direct references aimed not at those inside but at those in the canton who have not come or do not want to come. Finally, in the *cofradías* and in the rites of the *zahorines*, there is almost never a person leading prayers to which the others respond as a group, whereas in Catholic Action, the center community prays and sings together in response to the catechist or board member and so experiences the "power of prayer" as opposed to the power of the *zahorín*'s traditional ways. This praying and singing in the centers, which is bolstered at the church in the town, takes away recent converts' fears of possible witchcraft directed at them by the *zahorines*, who have made death threats involving incense and burying bones against some converts. According to Catholic Action members, the prayers and rituals of the *zahorines* have power because they communicate with the devil, but praying together in Catholic Action centers is more powerful.

Before finishing this discussion, let us examine the marriage unions between the hamlets of Canamixtoj to guess at the future a little. People in section A (see Map 4.1) surpass the others in the unions they have with partners from the nearby canton of Xejip because of the road, but in marriages with other cantons, they are almost equal. Section B is the most endogamous, because it is closed in by the Tzununá River at one corner of the municipality. Section C is the least endogamous of the three, perhaps because it is less populated than A and therefore needs more women from outside. Also, because it is closer to Xejip than B, it can extend alliances in that direction. These three strongly interrelated canton sections point toward a future in which the relationship that Canamixtoj has had with the other cantons will be imitated, and the three will become small cantons of Canamixtoj. At the time of writing (1974), the tiny section C has now become another Catholic Action center, while B remains impenetrable by Catholic Action, bolstered by its marriage alliances with the Traditionalists in A and other cantons and by its own endogamy.

"Confessional Endogamy"

As Catholic Action came into the municipality of San Antonio, a limitation in marriage patterns was established, consisting in what I call "confessional endogamy," that is, the tendency and ideal of seeking a bride from the group professing one's own beliefs. Before Catholic Action came on the scene, the entire population of the municipality professed the same faith and that profession could not be the basis for making any distinction between wives. However, when Catholic Action entered, followed by the "Gospel" (evangelical Protestants), three groups emerged in the municipality, each with a well-defined set of opposing beliefs. When the first cases of having to choose a wife arose, efforts were made to seek for their sons women who were children of Catholic Action parents, or the sons themselves did so in accordance with their parents' wishes. Likewise, daughters of Catholic Action members were not allowed to marry young men from the Traditionalist side whose parents came asking for their hand on behalf of their sons. Moreover, because of the need to obtain wives for their sons or husbands for their daughters, a drive for conversions arose, one of whose purposes must have been to obtain potential wives or husbands. I do not mean that this was a conscious motivation, but certainly analysis reveals this as one of the factors driving the movement.

Origin of the Ideal of Endogamy

Where did this ideal of endogamy come from? Did it come from outside, as part of the message preached by the Catholic Church? Or did it rather come built into the conversion movement, apart from the church's message?

It seems to me that it did not come from the Catholic Church's precept to be married before its own minister nor from the church's preference for a spouse professing the same religious belief. I came to this conclusion, first, because the church makes provision for mixed marriages, and even though it does not recommend them, if such endogamy were due solely to the church's recommendation, there would still be some mixed marriages. But in San Antonio there has never been a mixed marriage, nor are Catholic Action members and Traditionalists aware that such a possibility exists. Second, the church's preference for a spouse of one's own confession assumes that it has recognized the existence of the other confession. Such a recognition has not taken place with regard to the Traditionalists, who because they are baptized by a minister of the Catholic Church are Catholics. Even though today Traditionalists generally do not have church weddings, they do remember that their grandparents or great-grandparents were married in the church. Hence it is plain that endogamy as a guideline did not come from the church, although its priests, after being influenced by the grass roots, have recommended it.

Rather, the ideal of confessional endogamy is rooted in something else: the break that has come with conversion. This break has rejected a set of values and symbols, one of which is that which makes possible and brings about, as a mediating symbol, marriage alliances. This symbol, which is the centerpiece of the traditional marriage ritual (*c'ulnem*), is liquor (Chapter 2). If liquor's unifying force has been rejected, then the entire meaning of the marriage rite has also been rejected, and the possibility of alliance with all those who confer such a unifying value has also been rejected, for they cannot conceive of a marriage union taking place without that symbol being present.

But why has Catholic Action rejected that symbol? Could it have declined to reject it, as it did not reject the saints (which evangelical Protestants do reject), or as it did not reject other ritual items in the *c'ulnem*? Apparently it could not; I think it had to reject it. Ethical reasons alone—such as that liquor results in vice, failure in business, fights, and so forth, which are the reasons for converting given by those who overcame drunkenness through conversion—do not seem sufficient to us.

Something else is needed to link these ethical reasons with belief and complete adherence, as will be seen more clearly in the next chapter. This reason lies in the fact that conversion entails a rejection of the value of the life and "salvation" (i.e., healing) in the social group from which the convert turns away, in which one seemingly felt oneself to be dying, through drunkenness, illness, meaninglessness, and so forth. If that social group is lacking in meaning for the convert, and hence communicates death to him, the convert rejects union with it and negates the symbol of that union. The symbol is therefore rejected because the possibility of union with the social group is being rejected and not the other way around, that such a possibility is rejected because the symbol is rejected. Hence any symbol of the marriage union would be rejected, and the rejection of liquor as symbol has to be distinguished from the rejection of liquor as an element of failure.

Drive of Endogamy toward Conversions

Table 4.4 shows us various things about the drive that endogamy transmits to the conversion movement. First, there is the fact that the ideal of endogamy does translate into facts, because out of a total of 143 unions from four cantons (1965–1970), 118 (96 + 22), or 83%, are endogamous unions. If endogamy translates into reality, it means a threat to Catholic Action members, especially when the group is small, as it was in the early days of the movement, and there is a fear of being left without a wife. This threat drives the movement to make converts.

The endogamy index, defined as the ratio of endogamous to nonendogamous unions, is considerably higher for Traditionalists ($96/25 = 3.84$) than for Catholic Action members ($22/25 = 0.88$). This means that Traditionalists are pro-

TABLE **4.4.** *Marriages between Traditionalists (A), between Catholic Action members (B), and interconfessional (C) of men living in four cantons, broken down by whether the woman changed her religious profession upon marrying or not*

(A) Marriages between Traditionalists					96
(B) Marriages between Catholic Action members					22
(C) Unions between Traditionalists and Catholic Action members	Women accepted by Traditionalists	Lost to Catholic Action	1		
		Not lost to Catholic Action	6	7	
	Women accepted by Catholic Action	Lost to the Tradition	18		
		Not lost to the Tradition	0	18	25
Total					143

Source: Canton informants (1970).

Notes: a. These marriages were all celebrated in the 1965–1970 period. b. For one of the cantons, marriages from 1960–1965 are also included because Catholic Action was introduced five years earlier there.

portionately more endogamous than Catholic Action members. The reason for this is that Traditionalists are more numerous and are not forced to break the rule, as are Catholic Action members, of whom there are fewer. It may be assumed that at the beginning of the movement the Traditionalist bloc was proportionally more endogamous and Catholic Action less so than at present. Hence the movement must have tried to resolve its shortage of wives by proselytizing in connection with marriage itself, that is, marrying Traditionalist women with the intention of converting them at marriage or thereafter.

Many interconfessional unions have been made with the anticipation of converting the spouse. Violation of the rule by Catholic Action members does not mean ignoring endogamy. In such cases, the Catholic Action member accedes to the Traditionalist parents and goes through the traditional wedding with liquor, trying not to get drunk. Sometimes the father of the groom, or the future husband himself, if he is of age, tells the bride's father that he hopes he will allow his daughter to be converted. Sometimes they celebrate the traditional wedding without liquor, although they still do not marry civilly or ecclesiastically, and they assume that the woman who marries the young man is converted by the very act of joining him.

The forgoing table shows the relative strength of Catholic Action as a proselytizing group through its interconfessional marriages, as compared with the strength of the Traditionalists. In these twenty-five interconfessional unions, before marrying, seven women were part of Catholic Action and eighteen were Traditionalists, but after the marriage, twenty-four belonged to Catholic Action and only one was a Traditionalist. In other words, the Tradition not only lost these eighteen Traditionalist women, who upon marrying Catholic Action husbands converted to Catholic Action, but it also lost six Traditionalist men, since of the seven Catholic Action women only one became a Traditionalist with her husband, while in the other six cases it was the husband who went over to Catholic Action. It is obvious that Catholic Action as a group is stronger in its proselytizing than the Tradition. We cannot say at this point to what extent this strength is due to its minority status as compared to other factors, such as its organization.

These figures also indicate that it is easier to convert a woman than a man through marriage (18 women as opposed to 6 men). The reason lies in this society's norm of patrilocal residence. The woman goes to live in the home of the groom's father and is taken away from her parents' home and the neighborhood of her relatives (segment). The young man, however, stays in his own surroundings. Converting him is like driving a wedge of division into his parents' household and into the segment. By contrast, when the woman converts, she is adapting to the way of life of the household to which she has been brought to live.

Social Stratification

In the previous chapter, we saw that in the entire municipality of San Antonio there are 12 merchants with an average capital of Q 8,600; 14 with Q 2,100; 12 with Q 690, and 156 whose capital averages around Q 130. I noted that the stratification process has occurred recently, and I indicated that the existence of people who are relatively powerful as a result of the money they manage (e.g., to pay for a court case) entails a restructuring of power in the municipality, which until recently was concentrated in the prestigious elders known as *principales*.

At this point I intend to describe how this restructuring has come about, how relations of subordination and confrontation that previously did not exist have emerged, and how these relationships are at the root of the conflicts between the two main organized groups, the Traditionalists, through their *cofradías*, and Catholic Action, through its centers.

A New Level of Hierarchy

The process of restructuring power took place as follows. Some of the individuals who were affected by the shortage of land in the community took advantage of the opportunities for trade described in the previous chapter.

Those who had enough land generally did not have to leave the municipality to make a living. Gradually, a first significant division occurred between those who went on to become merchants and the small farmers who continued to depend primarily on the land and on other work related to it. As proof of the correlation between being merchants and scarcity of land before becoming merchants, it should be recalled that the average number of *cuerdas* inherited by these now wealthy men was the same or less than the average held by men of San Antonio at that time.

There then arises a network in which, over time, the more powerful units become employers, money lenders, godfathers, and so forth, while the more subordinate become their laborers, debtors, relatives by baptism, and so on. Had the latter not needed money because of sickness, economic failures, the death of some member of the household, or ceremonial expenses, they would not have sold a portion of their land; and had the former not earned money from trade to buy this land, that land would have gone into the hands of a money lender from outside the municipality.

Because they had more money, some department-level money lenders were able to make loans at lower interest rates, attract more creditors, and set up a system of collection and seizure of land with lawyers that smaller money lenders in the municipality could not afford. The merchants did not arouse resentment among those who lost their land, because it was not they who seized the land.

These town merchants who are also money lenders generally do not operate in the same manner as those at the department level. Their small loans tend to gradually trap borrowers who cannot pay, but they are usually not brought to court, especially when it is a *compadre*, relative, neighbor, or fellow member of Catholic Action. Those who do not pay and who nevertheless continue to receive favors and loans, although increasingly fewer, become "separate" laborers for such a merchant. He has them work on his ever-growing lands during the usual labor periods. If he happens to sell fertilizer, he supplies them with fertilizer, but at a lower price, and in a time of scarcity he gives them some of the corn that he produces in larger amounts and sells in the municipality or elsewhere by transporting it in his truck.

Around these employer/money lender/merchant/landowners there forms a constellation of *compadres* from baptism (both Traditionalists and Catholic Action) and marriage (only for Catholic Action). Before the emergence of stratification, the godfather relationship linked all households in the municipality on the same level. If household A, for example, had the head of household B as the sole baptism sponsor for all their children, this godfather had the head of C as his children's sponsor, C had the one from D, and then D back to A. Although the pattern was not completely circular, no one accumulated many sponsorship relationships with other households. With the emergence of Catholic Action, the sponsorship alliance by which all the children of one household ought to have the same godfather was broken, and a new godfather was sought within Catholic Action, one different from the one of the first children. When choosing a godfather, many chose the same one, who combined in himself the characteristics of merchant-employer, plus often the position of Catholic Action board member. By means of this relationship, a *compadre* would seek out the protection of his child's godfather in times of illness, death, or some unanticipated need for money. This relationship also softens tensions between employer and laborer and gives the wealthy *compadre* power, through the number of persons who support him, even if for the moment it is only by not attacking him, not speaking ill of him, or by favoring him with their vote.

Something similar happened among Catholic Action members with the marriage sponsor. Imitating a ladino custom for all weddings before a priest in church, they began to name a godfather and godmother, who were not the same people as the witnesses required by the church or the traditional witnesses. This couple was then given an important role in the traditional wedding ceremony, being placed closer to the home altar than the most elderly members of the lineage of both groom and bride. The introduction of this element had the effect of accentuating stratification (signified by the sponsor) over kinship. The Traditionalists still do not generally include the sponsor because they do not celebrate marriage in the church.

As a final observation on this phenomenon, individuals may find themselves hierarchically superior in various relationships. Each of these relationships includes roles that vary from case to case. For example, sometimes it can be one of being a *compadre* but not an employer; it can be of *compadre* and employer, but not money lender, and so forth. Godfather relationships are generally more concentrated (i.e., an individual has more *compadres* than laborers), precisely because they do not require the money-lender relationship, although they imply that a poor man seeking a *compadre* relationship will view his *compadre* as a potential money lender. Those with the most *compadres* have fifty or more, while the one who has the most land can give work to no more than twenty laborers and some ten women, not all of whom are debtors.[1] It must also be borne in mind that not all wealthy merchants who bind themselves with some of these relationships have exclusive power over those below them, because the latter may be laborers for one but seek someone else as a *compadre*; nevertheless, power becomes increasingly unified as debt rises. On the other hand, a clear separation by religious confession is taking place, to the point where in everything having to do with stable relationships a Catholic Action member no longer seeks a baptism or marriage sponsor outside Catholic Action. Instead, Catholic Action members now tend to work for, sponsor, or borrow from fellow Catholic Action members.

Emergence of Division

How has the birth of this new level of hierarchy influenced the emergence of conflict between those who set up Catholic Action as a formal organization and the Traditionalists, whose formal organization coincides with that of the municipality, in which the mayor and the *principales* occupy the upper levels of power?

Along with the growth in the number of "outside" merchants, as described in the last chapter, a relationship of mutual aid developed among them, especially among those who had become established in the same market far from their home town. They loaned one another money, they watched over one another's sales booths, they joined together to rent a room for sleeping and storing merchandise, and so forth. In this still informal group whose members came and went, relationships with blurred boundaries developed in which each one mutually granted and accepted the support of others, with no one really having a great deal more power than another. In a single place, for example in Cobán, where all the merchants from San Antonio knew one another, were identified as from there, and shared orientations and interests despite the competition proper to merchants, smaller coordinated units emerged of two or three or perhaps more merchants who traveled together and jointly decided on the time when they should be together. Then they divided and formed other similar coordinated units. Thus several collaborated on a number of occasions with several others, not just in one place, for example, not only in Cobán but in Guatemala City and Escuintla, to which they were drawn in the search for better customers.

New Ways of Valuing

As some accumulated capital to the point of being able to employ others from other places (not their own children, for example), a stable bond and a new kind of unit was formed, one in which one member, such as a merchant, had independent power (his wealth) and yet needed the labor of a small farmer.

Among these units, which at the same time formed an identity unit, a new value system emerged, one proper to the outside merchant and favorable to conversion, as explained in the closing sections of the previous chapter. Some of its elements included trust in the world beyond the community as a source of wealth and, by projection, as a source of nonverifiable power; the experience of breaking through the limitations of the poverty of a peasant whose surpluses are taken away from him;[2] and the possibility of building up capital and the hope for a previously unimagined situation of wealth. Such ways of valuing inevitably clashed with the practice of redistribution inherent to the *cofradías*, in which prestige was tied to giving rather than to having, an ideal of equality imposed on the community by the lack of ways to invest productively and get ahead.

These new values were reinforced as "outside" merchants became marginalized from the *cofradía* system. Because they were geographically absent from the municipality for most of the year, albeit sporadically, and because population growth provided enough people to serve in the *cofradías*, these merchants, initially few in number, stopped serving in the *cofradías* and hence ceased to be imbued with the principles of the traditional values as a result of such services, which have effects similar to initiation rites. Thus they not only acquired a new set of values through their own experience of business success or that of others, but they did not undergo the experience previously shared and suffered together of the older values of redistribution resulting from *cargos* in the *cofradías*.

To this merchant population must be added the non-merchant population that had to leave the municipality for other work, such as planting corn on the coast, ongoing work that some had as sharecroppers on the coast, and work in the salt flats at Puerto San José. Although these generally poor non-merchants differed from the merchants in not sharing in the experience of building up capital, they resembled them in not serving in the *cofradías* and not sharing in their characteristic redistribution experience. Some of these non-merchants would also become followers of the new Catholic Action way of life, but the merchants were its spearhead.

Traditionalist Merchants

How are we to explain the existence of the recent level of articulation among Traditionalists, in view of the fact that they must have had to come into conflict with the values of redistribution in order to accumulate capital? Before answering this question, it must be noted that we are leaving out of this problem the successful merchants, such as those in Amatitlán who, because they took their wives and moved out of the municipality (even though they still employ some people from San Antonio), have built up their capital outside the municipality without encountering any resistance. They tend to take on ladino ways and to abandon the shared basis of identity for the conflict, namely, the fact of being indigenous people from San Antonio. It should also be noted that the problem is centered on a small number of "outside" merchants who have not converted, because, as we have seen, there is a high correlation between being a merchant and belonging to Catholic Action. The problem remains, however, even though it is centered in this small number, because these Traditionalist merchants are largely the source of the economic power that pays for the legal battles against the Catholic Action adherents, and it is they who have propped up the formal structure of the *cofradías* and who keep the division going. There are three of them in stratum A, three in B, and two in C.

Although these Traditionalist merchants have had the experience of being "outside" and so they have been included in this category, they later found their main place of business in the municipality and its surroundings. There, especially when they are strong (A), they have achieved a monopoly on some service, like the bus line, or some item, like soap or hoes. They usually leave their house out in the cornfields of the canton and move into the town itself to watch over the goods they store at a site they either own or rent. Centered around their work sites—the storage space, a store or bar that they set up, or their truck—arise work relationships with people who know how to sell but who do not need the experience of an outside merchant. Here they also do better in incorporating the women in their household (wife, daughters), who would not be able to watch over the business if it were far from the municipality but who can do so if it is in the town. Because they are serving a primarily Traditionalist clientele, they do not open up to the ladinos or "outside" customers who provide a livelihood for the other merchants, nor are they interested in clashing with Traditionalist customers. Their general tendency is to appreciate the traditional values of the community, although because they are experiencing capital accumulation, they are finding worth in something contrary to those values. Hence, their position is ambiguous, but in the end they lean toward the *cofradías*, especially if their employees are Traditionalists, if they have been acquiring more and more ties through baptism sponsorships among Traditionalists, and if they have served on some *cofradías*. They tend to have built up enough money so that those *cargos* that they fulfill, albeit without much enthusiasm, do not entail a great deal of loss. Indeed, their very connections with the Traditionalist group sustain that capital.

Some merchants sell in both the town and in Santa Cruz del Quiché and yet belong to Catholic Action. Their situation can be explained by the fact that they converted before going into business in Santa Cruz or San Antonio, and through conversion they had already established a set of relationships that they would now find it difficult to break. Among them can sometimes be noted the same ambiguity as that existing among the Traditionalists. For example, some powerful men sell not only in the town but in a number of places far from the region where they need the connections of the converts. In San Antonio, they also establish ties with Traditionalist merchants, with whom they sometimes get drunk. Their binges seem to be the sign of this ambiguity.

The small number of Traditionalist merchants in the higher strata can also be explained by their monopoly over some goods in the town market or somewhere else in the region: they face greater market limitations than those in more populated department capitals, like Escuintla, Cobán, some places in Suchitepéquez, and so forth. Hence there are fewer of them.

The Crystallization of Hierarchy

When those merchants who have converted to Catholic Action begin to split off, very soon those cells of coordinated units that had been becoming units with a superordinate unit, or were on their way to becoming them, become a new formal unit of a corporative type, whose authorities are on the same level as the *principales* (Adams 1973: 132). They then become connected to a department-level organization from which they derive power and formal recognition of their delegated authority: department-level Catholic Action and the church. In Chapter 6, we take up the power derived from the church. Here we need only note that without the divisive drive of merchants who created another level of articulation within the community, there would have been no attempt to derive power and approval from the church to struggle against the traditional community power structure. The presence of the church, which now has more priests than in previous years, would not necessarily have been divisive.

However, the *cofradías* and the system of *principales* as a formal structure traditionally linked to the state through the mayor, who is selected by the *principales* but appointed by the government, seek to remain attached to this derivation of power, because they have nothing to replace it, such as perhaps some sort of department-level confederation of *cofradías*. However, they do not achieve it, except through the more powerful Traditionalist merchants who finance the apparatus (lawyers, judges, etc.) that authenticates the delegation of authority and, therefore, the derivation of power from the government. This takes place through the political parties, which began to operate in 1945, and which are sought out by Catholic Action members. The political struggle is described in another chapter.

Stabilization of Division: Marriages

The internal split of the community, sustained by merchants from both religious groups, takes firmer hold through endogamous marriages within Catholic Action and among Traditionalists as well, albeit to a lesser extent. This is a particular case of endogamy by confession, which nevertheless is in keeping with what was said above about labor relations made possible by accumulated wealth. An examination of a total of 46 marriages of wealthy merchants—that is, of merchants who both employ day laborers and have a truck or have had one—or of their sons and daughters from 1950 to 1970 shows that the 31 marriages of Catholic Action merchants (or of their children) have been with Catholic Action people (100% endogamous), and of the marriages of the 15 remaining Traditionalist merchants (or their children), 11 have been with Traditionalists (73% endogamous).

A work relationship has been part of 17 of the 31 endogamous Catholic Action marriages in one manner or another. It may not have been very close (e.g., the parents of the bride and groom worked in the same place), or it may have been closer (the son-in-law was the powerful merchant's driver or employee before or after becoming his son-in-law). Likewise, behind almost half of the Traditionalist marriages there was a work relationship.

Thus, while all of the 31 Catholic Action marriages were entirely endogamous, 4 of the 15 Traditionalist marriages were not, for they were undertaken between daughters of Traditionalist merchants and Catholic Action or Protestant men. Another factor seems to be at work here, namely, the standard of living. The son of a well-off merchant can bring a poor woman into his home, and she, as she rises up, becomes used to it. On the other hand, a daughter of a well-off merchant does not become used to coming down to the level of the home of her husband who is beneath her. Among the daughters of these merchants, however, it is more common for them to marry well-off merchants, who are usually converts. These husbands are generally attracted by their father-in-law's business, if it is bigger than their own or that of their father, so their identification with Catholic Action becomes questionable. They are "infected," as it were, by the ambiguity that some of the daughters of those merchants show toward the situation of their father, who is close to the people and the Traditionalist majority and yet is experiencing capital buildup. *This ambiguity may offer the bridge that can stanch religious division in the future.*

Stabilization of Stratification and Suppression of Division

Now we move into another aspect of the conversion dynamic. Stratification has created a vertical split, but there are signs that this split is likely to be temporary. One such sign is that a not-yet-described kind of endogamy has emerged among the more powerful merchants (stratum A). This is particularly evident in the Catholic Action group of merchants in this stratum, where, of the 31 marriages, 10 are between merchants or children of this level. The already described tendency of some daughters of wealthy Traditionalist merchants to cross the religious line to find marriage partners also tends to occur between well-off people. However, if we consider marriages of merchants or their children, ignoring the level to which they belong, the percentage is even higher. Of the 31 Catholic Action marriages, 22 are marriages with merchants or their children. This indicates that a sector of the population that is identified by its line of work is growing, and that this line of work distances it economically and socially from non-merchants in the community.

Another sign of the growing stratification is the formation of groups of small farmers, most of whom are not merchants, who come together to get a loan for chemical fertilizer offered by a foundation from Guatemala City at lower interest rates than those of the local fertilizer dealer. Although sometimes one or another of these merchants, especially if he is not powerful, offers his name to obtain fertilizer at a lower interest rate and then resell it, this fact shows that there is a growing gap between those who are being left with less and less land who are farmers, and those who are accumulating it who are merchants, even if that gap is mitigated by baptism sponsorship ties.

The accent on the horizontal split seems to be bringing quite serious consequences for Catholic Action: the number of converts is now at a standstill. No one says that the reason is the horizontal split, but that seems to be the underlying reason why the movement has come to a halt. In brief, the stratification that gave rise to the division will now, as it becomes sharper, be what will bring about a fusion once more—although how many years will pass before that happens is uncertain.

Ladinos

Finally, we come to the ladinos, of whom there are not many nor have they been economically strong in San Antonio. The businesses in the market have more capital than the ladino shops. Ladinos have not monopolized labor contracting for themselves, nor do they own small farms with hired workers and land desired by their neighbors. Hence, although their entry into the municipality in the first half of the century was viewed with suspicion because they bought some pieces of land and were exempt from services in the community and from doing road work, with the emergence of religious division among the Indians, their relationships with both groups became more evenhanded, and they even occasionally served as arbiters between the two contending indigenous sides.

Summary

To summarize, then, initially some of those without lands went away and sought to make a living through trade. They thereby built up capital, then bought land in the municipality, sold corn, employed laborers, loaned out money, and acquired a large number of baptism ties. Thus a new level of articulation took shape.

This process contained the seeds of the division of the community into two religious sectors. Merchants formed groups that I have called "coordinated units" of two or three merchants who traveled together, and so forth. These units were then dissolved and others were formed. At each market site outside the municipality, San Antonio merchants were identified as merchants and as native to San Antonio. As they became well off, some established stable ties among merchants, replicating the new level of articulation within the municipality. This bond was then reinforced in many instances where there was a marriage between merchants or their sons or daughters, especially at the top level. This new relationship then paradoxically in some cases served to suppress that bond of subordination, because with the aid of marriage, the subordinate became independent and rose to the level of the superordinate (e.g., of his father-in-law).

Thus there took shape among merchants a "society" whose limits were imprecise but whose organization was quite solid. This society entailed a way of assessing value that arose with the process of accumulating wealth and becoming independent from farming, albeit incompletely. Such assessment and accumulation were at odds with the traditional *cofradía's* redistribution system. The inevitable upshot was division.

This division has been maintained by these Catholic Action and Traditionalist superordinate units. The Traditionalists have been able to remain within the Tradition, albeit in a state of ambiguity and despite the experience of accumulating capital because (1) they have become established merchants in the town center, usually by monopolizing some service or merchandise; (2) they have had working relationships with people in the town or its environs; and (3) the Traditionalists themselves have needed them to keep their *cofradía* system from falling apart for lack of economic support.

The two sides have higher-level outside connections with formal units: Catholic Action to the church and to its own department-level organization, and Traditionalists to the government, because their political and religious organization has traditionally been connected, albeit tenuously, to civil authorities through the mayors. The division and struggle is sharpened when both parties

pursue the mayor's office, because Catholic Action needs more than derivation of power from the church.

Marriages, especially those between less and more wealthy merchants, indicate that the division will probably disappear gradually—conversions are already at a standstill—and that a stronger opposition between the two levels
(or two "social classes," set apart by their relationship to the means of production) will emerge as the number of people with little money needing credit,
working as hired laborers, and so forth rises, and the accumulation of the land
in a few hands increases. As stratification, which brought about the vertical
division, increases, it will probably do away with that division.

Finally, it should be noted that ladinos have been practically absent from
these processes.

Historical Background to the Expansion of Witchcraft

Here I intend to show what brought about the real or assumed increase in
witchcraft that preceded the birth of Catholic Action, against whose supposed
practitioners, the *zahorines* (*aj k'ijab*, in plural), Catholic Action adherents
rebelled. To do so I will go back to the last century to trace the evolution of
the power of the community authorities, because I am assuming that as their
power declined, the use of nonempirical means to settle conflicts between
members of the community must have risen. I will divide the period being
reviewed (often by hypothesizing and projecting from the present to the past)
into two eras: 1821–1871 and 1871–1945.

From Independence to the Liberal Reform: 1821–1871
Community Authorities

As is clear from the court records of conflicts over land with the neighboring
community of Santa María Chiquimula from 1813 to 1820, the authority
over the community (*común* in colonial terminology) of San Antonio Ilotenango
during this time was constituted by two *alcaldes*, or justices (*justicias*), the
principales, and the *cofradías* (probably meaning the *alcaldes* of the *cofradías*)
(AGG: A45.7; 8184.392). Judging by traditional customs, which were still
observed up to 1945, the *principales* appointed the *alcaldes*, who subsequently
went on to act as *cofrades* in the two most important *cofradías*, San Antonio
and Corpus. Along with the *alcaldes*, and also appointed by the *principales*,
there must have been *regidores*, for whom there is provision in the Laws of the
Indies (1.VI, titl. III, law XV), *mayores*, *auxiliares*, and *alguaciles*—in short, a
whole administrative body connecting people spread throughout the cantons
of the community to their authority, who derived their power almost solely
from the community. There was, in addition, an indigenous scribe who—unlike the *alcaldes*, who rotated each year and who were not even able to speak
Spanish (they needed interpreters when dealing with authorities in Sololá)—
had a permanent position and who knew and could write Spanish, although

not easily. The scribe had probably gone to the school in San Pedro Jocopilas, to which some children at that time, due to the lack of a school in San Antonio, had traveled to attend class.

According to the Laws of the Indies (1.VI, tit. III, law XVI), the *principales* were chiefs or nobles, but by this time, judging by the present, the *principales* must have been those who had fulfilled all the *cargos* in the *cofradía*, and had been *alcaldes* of the community. That nevertheless does not mean that they could not have also been descendants of the "nobles," since it was perhaps easier for the latter to serve on *cofradías*.

Along with these authorities, there would have been a number of *zahorines* (an *aj k'ij* is a specialist in time) called in to play their role in a charismatic way (through dreams, illness, or suggestion by another *zahorín*) and taught by the older *zahorines*. They would not have been recognized as authorities of the community but would have formed a consulting body of shamans with influence on several levels: those of the *principales*, *alcaldes*, *cofrades*, chiefs of lineages, and heads of households, for example.

My thesis here is that while the power of the formal community authorities was gradually waning, from 1871 onward, the *zahorines* were gradually acquiring ever more power, especially among those who attributed to them the power to transmit evil (even though they were not, properly speaking, witch doctors (*aj itz*: specialists in evil). During this period (1821–1871), however, the authorities had enough power over the inhabitants of the community (later municipality) that it is hard to imagine that the *zahorines* were frequently and powerfully at work.

Functions of Community Authorities

According to the Law of the Indies, *alcaldes* held "government of the peoples with regard to the universal," "could punish any Indian with one day in prison, six or eight lashes, for missing Mass on a Feast Day, or getting drunk, or committing any other similar fault," but in more serious cases, "the Indian *alcaldes* will have authority only to make inquiry, seize, and bring the wrongdoers to the jail in the Spanish town [Pueblo de Españoles] of that district" (1.IV, titl. III, Law XVI). They would presumably settle marriage conflicts that went beyond the capability of the witnesses from the corresponding lineages, and land conflicts between neighbors. With the help of the scribe, they probably also assigned the lands to be planted for the growing population. They also handled appointing the *cofrades* and undertaking customary and emergency collections, for example, in cases of conflict with the neighboring Chiquimulas.

With regard to the outside world, they represented the community, or *común*, to officials in the department of Sololá and the state in Guatemala City, especially in community land conflicts. It was probably the *principales*, as an ongoing body, aided by the scribe, who carried out the procedures in such conflicts, which went on for many years, and they informed the mayor about the sum of contributions that had to be collected for that purpose.

By means of the traditional 260-day calendar, the *zahorines* clarified signs in order to give advice. Their activities were probably limited to the community. It was also their function, as it is today, to divine the (nonempirical) causes of illnesses, for example, vis-à-vis the world of their ancestors.

The Priest

The priest, who in colonial times was the only Spaniard or native-born white man (*criollo*) allowed to live in an Indian town, did not live in San Antonio in the eighteenth or early nineteenth century, but operated out of San Pedro Jocopilas (until the mid-nineteenth century), from which he periodically came to celebrate mass. His disciplinary relationship toward the people in terms of dealing with drunkenness, unmarried couples living together, and nonpayment of taxes was handled through the *alcaldes*, who were charged with "oppressing them" (Indians) in jail for one or two days or with "whipping them" (Cortés y Larraz [1771] 1958: Point 8).

At the outset (1813–1820) of the period being described, it is clear that there is a relationship of mutual support between the *principales* and the priest, but it is from a distance. The priest is asked to provide information to the Audiencia on the need for money that people from San Antonio are struggling to collect in payment for rent of lands in Chuachituj, south of the current municipality. This money is for fixing the church, repairing the organ, recasting the broken bell, buying vestments, and also to set up a school. The priest writes favorable letters to the Audiencia, although he calls the people from San Antonio "careless" for having trusted the Chiquimulas without obtaining any collateral for the money loaned.

This same Dominican friar, Salvador Narváez, later (1830) presented a report in support of San Antonio against the actions of the Liberal surveyor Valerio Rivas, who sided with the Chiquimulas (Escribanía: Quiché 1.2).

There is documentation for 1849 indicating that the priest, Father Andrés Goicolea, comes to San Antonio from Santa Cruz del Quiché. He is well liked in Santa Cruz del Quiché, judging by the efforts made in 1849 to keep him from being transferred to Rabinal (Tzampop: 44–45), and well liked in San Antonio, judging by the stability and constancy of his visits—not a single one missed in twenty years, always with a charge of 12 reales for mass (Libro de Cofradías de Santa Ana).

A marked contrast can be seen after 1874: another priest appears, now charging 20 or 24 reales for mass. In another *cofradía* book, he leaves a record of his dissatisfaction when he says in 1876: "I celebrated the Resurrection Mass [Easter] and received 12 reales!!" (his exclamation points). Thereafter the continuity of visits is broken. The relationship is now apparently based on money, unlike that of Father Goicolea (Libro de Cofradía Santísimo Sacramento).

Hence, relations between the priest and community officials during the 1821–1871 period seem to have been friendly but with some distance. It is an indication that the resurgence of "pagan" traditions, which were reprehensible from the priest's standpoint, must not have been as strong as in other towns at that time. Nor did the priest apparently find any reason from within the community to stir up potential division.

Boundary Disputes

Next I will relate some of the boundary disputes for which I have found documentation. It is important to consider their extension over time and their magnitude so as to imagine the power that community authorities then had over their subjects, when jointly threatened by the outside enemy.

Land conflicts between communities in San Antonio and neighboring Santa María Chiquimula may possibly antedate the conquest (Popol Vuh 1968: 151), when the central triad of the emerging state of Quiché, comprising Quiché, Tamub, and Ilocab (now San Antonio Ilotenango), dominated the conquered Chiquimulas.

Elsewhere (Falla 1971a) I have presented Ilotenango's conflicts with the Chiquimulas, particularly after 1705, the date when lands in San Antonio were deeded. Although the boundaries did not satisfy both parties, judging from conflicts in 1708, they lasted until the following century. I have found a copy of the 1705 map (Escribanía: Quiché, 3.2., fol. 10 and 11), according to which the boundaries included all the areas in dispute except the one in the northeast, called Chuisicá, which was finally determined to belong to San Antonio in 1905.

The land scarcity of the Chiquimulas and Ilotenango's limited population on its own lands prompted continual invasion by Chiquimulas into Ilotenango lands. Starting in 1777, the Chiquimulas who had set themselves up on Ilotenango lands in Chuachituj, south of the current municipality, paid Ilotenango 125 pesos a year in rent, money that disappeared from the colonial coffers. The people of San Antonio repeatedly asked the Audiencia to give them that money, but as of 1820, the court record, which reflected a politically very weak structure, halted any direct action on behalf of the people of Ilotenango. Then came independence and, during the uprisings in Totonicapán, the complaint of the people of San Antonio was set aside and nothing was settled (Falla 1971a).

The enmities re-emerged after Guatemala City was taken by General Francisco Morazán (April 13, 1829) and a Liberal regime took power, which shortly thereafter passed a series of laws on labor and land tenure and rental (July 27). In the spirit of the time, it was declared: "let excess land from the fields of one town be granted to a neighboring one that needs it to be worked in common and also to extend its own" (Skinner-Klée 1954, Art. 21).

The Chiquimulas invaded land belonging to San Antonio with the support of the surveyor Valerio Rivas, who had presented a report to the government on the disparity of land in the communities. (The invasion must have taken place in early 1830.) According to the report by the surveyor appointed by San Antonio for its own defense, Manuel Vargas, on June 3, the Chiquimulas invaded the west side of the municipality from both north and south and came northward over the southern boundary from the land that the Chiquimulas were renting. The surveyor says that the law did not apply because seventy-two people from San Antonio, whom he lists, had been violently taken from their fields and could not plant now, and eight of them had houses on the lands invaded. The surveyor presents the map of another surveyor (Marure) who had made a survey of boundary markers in 1791. That map coincides with the 1705 boundaries as described.

The Chiquimulas also invaded San Pedro Jocopilas on July 16, 1830. A report by a friar who was passing through San Pedro states that the Chiquimulas had beaten five San Antonio people with sticks and that "all communication is cut off and it is clear that the intention is to cause a clash between the towns of Jocopilas, Ilotenango, and Quiché and that of Chiquimula" (Falla 1971a).

On October 9, 1831, the lawyer Francisco Antonio Madrid presented the conclusion of the commission set up to bring about peace between the two communities (Escribanía: Quiché 1, 12). He said that upon reaching the conflict site, he found the Chiquimulas and their supporters "wildly stirred up." He blamed the surveyor Valerio Rivas, who claimed to be the ultimate authority, based on rumor and according to the document of the pastor of Chiquimula, Salvador Narváez, who as a Dominican must have resented the Liberal government's recent decree expropriating property belonging to religious communities. The report went on to say that there were six victims in the town square of San Antonio, which the Chiquimulas entered when they invaded. He reversed the measurements of the surveyor Rivas and took the invaders to a hamlet in San Pedro Jocopilas, apparently the future municipality of Santa Lucía la Reforma. He needed twenty-five special "Dragon" troops from the squadron in Chinique (El Quiché) with a captain to take twenty-one Chiquimula Indians as hostages, and even so, he did not succeed in getting the *principales* to come forth until he got twenty-five more men as reinforcements from the political chief in Totonicapán. He thereby pacified the region and the Chiquimulas left the land they had invaded but not the land they rented in Chuachituj, which, according to the lawyer, Ilotenango had already lost to Chiquimula.

"To avoid disasters and claims that were constantly recurring," an effort was made in 1833 to survey the lands that the Chiquimulas were renting in San Antonio, San Pedro Jocopilas, and Santa Cruz del Quiché. The Chiquimulas were renting the land in Chuachituj from San Antonio. In 1841 the government sold this 41-*caballería* (approximately 4,550-acre) piece of land to the Chiquimulas, and the sum entered the treasury of San Antonio in 1845 (Escribanía: Quiché, 4, 14). Thus, San Antonio lost it for good and was probably very unhappy about that.

We do not know to what extent these events were influenced by the independence of the state of Los Altos—made up of Sololá (which included San

Antonio), Totonicapán (which included Chiquimula), and Quetzaltenango—which lasted only from February 2, 1838, to January 27, 1840, in an attempted uprising against General Rafael Carrera.

During all the years from the fall of President Gálvez (1838) to Carrera's victory at the Battle of La Arada (February 2, 1851), the government of the nation-state of Guatemala was weak vis-à-vis the native peoples because Carrera had to struggle continuously against Los Altos, after it declared itself independent of Guatemala, and against the Liberals inside and outside the state of Guatemala.

It is not clear what set off the next explosion. On December 6, 1850, around a hundred Chiquimulas invaded the hamlet of Sacxac in the west. The *justicias* and residents of San Antonio complained to the *corregidor* and regional judge in Sololá, asking them to put the invaders in jail because they paid no attention to them (Tzampop: 66–68).

On June 13, 1851 (Tzampop: 46–47), people from San Antonio again sent a note to the department chief in Sololá, this time blaming the Chiquimulas for the fire in their church, which may have happened the night before. The department chief answered them on June 25, asking them to come forth with information and evidence to be presented to the *corregidor* of Totonicapán.

A ruling issued October 14, 1862, at the request of people from San Antonio, stated that the Chiquimulas who were renting could not be expelled, that they must continue to pay their rent, and that if they did not pay, they would be expelled. The boundary markers were set up again with visible signs, but no boundary definition accepted by all parties was achieved.

In sum, the Chiquimula invaders, whose population had grown more rapidly after the conquest and had rebounded more quickly than that of San Antonio, did not remain within their own lands (see population figures below). The conflict involved the entire community, not only because the invasion came from three different directions (north, west, and south) and pushed many people off their lands, but because it had aggressively reached even the town square in San Antonio, where blood flowed, and according to the people of San Antonio, where the Chiquimulas burned their church. The conflict was bloody, with people killed, and as described by the traveling friar, it threatened to spread to the other communities that were also invaded.

In these conflicts, the external authority was shown to be weak and unable to deal with the heart of the problem. Central government power intervened only once, as far as I know, expelling the invaders, but it did not delineate the boundaries between the communities (except for the case of Chuachituj, which had been invaded over fifty years previously). Officials moved their forces only on extraordinary occasions, because their centers of action, Sololá and Totonicapán, were a day's journey away. Moreover, the weakness and instability of the governments of that period apparently gave a free hand to agents like the surveyor Rivas, who stirred up one community against another, and on the other side, to the commissioner and his battalion, which nullified the actions of the Liberal surveyor. The Conservative-Liberal rivalry can be seen pitting communities against one another. Finally, the very fact that both communities belonged to different *corregimientos*, or departments, often made it necessary to appeal to the central government, which was even farther away, in Guatemala City.

In such a situation, I argue, there could be no internal division in the community of San Antonio, which had to be united under a strong internal authority to battle these threats from outside the community. It is unlikely that there would have been an internal witchcraft battle in which *zahorines* were turned into witch doctors by the enmity of the contending parties. The friendly relations between the priest and the community reinforce this assumption. Moreover, according to informants, the rise of witchcraft is recent and dates from the years when land became scarce within the community, and the outside enemy had apparently been overcome.

From the Liberal Reform to the Revolution, 1871–1944

Population

At this point, the growth of the population of San Antonio (Chapter 2) as compared with that of Santa María Chiquimula should be recalled. To the Santa María figures for 1950 and 1964 in Table 4.5 I have added the populations of Patzité (1,289 and 1,777 respectively) and Santa Lucía la Reforma (2,912 and 4,651), which split off from Chiquimula.

The population increase of the Chiquimulas encountered a population vacuum in San Antonio during the nineteenth century, but when San Antonio's population began to recover in the late nineteenth century, the Chiquimulas had more and more people on lands near the municipal boundaries, and once these boundaries had been defined, it may be assumed that land scarcity led to increasing friction between neighbors in the municipality. My informants say, as already noted, that the rise in witchcraft in the years immediately preceding the explosion of Catholic Action was due to this scarcity.

Incursions of Liberal Capitalism

According to the policy of the Liberal government of the Reform period, large expanses of land had to be cultivated "using the many arms existing outside the general movement" of production, and "the free transfer of property" had to be encouraged, improving it for the sake of agriculture. The two measures that were part of this policy were the Regulations on Laborers and the Suppression of the Emphyteutic Annuity (Censo Enfitéutico) (1877). This policy meant extending the relationship of state control over the communities by reducing their isolation and the power of their officials, thus creating a setting propitious for witchcraft. I will now present my reconstruction of what happened.

On April 3, 1877, it was ordered that, upon request by a plantation owner or his agent, the political chief of a department would order that a crew of

TABLE 4.5. *Population of San Antonio Ilotenango and Santa María Chiquimula from 1524 to 1964*

Year	1524	1570	1675	1770	1893	1950	1964
San Antonio Ilotenango	3,700*	2,180	640	380	2,061	4,156	6,048
Santa María Chiquimula	1,920*	960	1,640	1,500	12,374	14,216	21,144

* Reconstructed figures.

workers be sent and would designate which town had to send it. Municipal mayors and their appointed aides were then obliged to provide the crew of no more than sixty laborers (Skinner-Klée 1954: 35–42).

I have not examined any documents on just how these requests were made nor on how the people of San Antonio reacted. I do know that those handling them were not ladinos, who were contractors and also mayors in other towns, probably installed through a fictitious election staged by the political chiefs, as happened in San Pedro Jocopilas (Ascoli 1973). It may be assumed that the process began through the indigenous mayors, who, under pressure, obliged their people to go work on coffee plantations in the foothills. I am assuming that the indigenous mayors and the authorities in general thereby lost power (although they could derive power to serve the purposes of the plantation owners), inasmuch as they were seen to be mere tools of the landowners and the political chief. Derivation of power was not used to resolve conflicts within the community. Rather, the hostility of the people of the towns toward ladino authorities and the society they served must have increased.

I have found no specific information on how the Emphyteutic Annuity was suppressed in San Antonio. Yet I should briefly reconstruct it, since this was the starting point for a new kind of land tenure, a shift from the previous communal form to an individual one, and therefore a new power base of individuals vis-à-vis community authorities.

The Emphyteutic Annuity (Censo Enfitéutico) was an institution whereby a land owned by the annuitant was handed over to an emphyteuta (the one planting on it) or lessee. The lessee was obliged to pay the lessor an annuity equal to 2 percent or 3 percent a year for the use of that property. Ownership of the land remained with the lessor, but according to the contract, which was for an indefinite time period, the lessor could not take the land from the lessee without his consent. Thus it was a perpetual rental arrangement. The community was the lessor owning the lands, and the lessee was the community member who had to make the annual payment.

The 1877 decree ordered that the lands were to be paid off by suppressing the annuity and communal ownership. To redeem them, the lessees had to pay the price for the lands to the community, but that money would be deposited in the Banco Nacional, where it would be paying 4% of the deposited amount for municipal expenses. If the lessee did not pay, he was thereby giving up the land he had, and it would be sold at a public auction. Likewise, if someone held lands that were communal property or town fields and no one was paying any annuity for them, that person was obliged to declare them. Two assessors would evaluate the lands, and whoever held them had to pay the assessed price to the municipality; if he did not pay them, he was understood to be waiving ownership of that land, and it would be auctioned off. Buyers of fields under this arrangement would then obtain a deed granted by the mayor or the *síndico* before a public notary or, in places where there was none, before the regional judge.

In San Antonio it may be assumed that before the 1877 decree, each household paid an annual fee for the land it worked. I do not know whether it was proportional to the amount of land worked. It must have been collected by the canton treasurers, vestiges of whom still remain. The land belonged to the community, which, through the mayor and probably in consultation with the canton *principales*, allotted it to whoever needed and asked for it. There must have been an awareness of what belonged to the lineages, or segments of them, on lands that they themselves had occupied for generations. The stability of surnames properly placed on the map, as still happens today, witnesses to that custom. The lineages or segments would have had their elders, who even today serve as witnesses in dividing up inheritance and in the traditional marriage, serve as judges in matters internal to the lineage or segment. There seems to have been no awareness that the cultivated land was rented by the community members from the community; rather, its ownership was perceived in concentric circles: first in the broadest circle, the community; next, the lineage and/or segment; and finally, the household group. If land was sold to a neighbor or someone from another canton, procedures would have to take place in as many places as the concentric circles that such an operation crossed, always within the community.

With regard to the decree, I do not know whether everyone possessing land paid, nor if they paid afterward for how many days or months, or how deeds were granted, and so forth. I was unable to study extensively deeds or entries in the registry in Quetzaltenango. In any case, the decree did away with the entire legal basis for communal ownership, and lands had to be registered with individual deeds before mayors, the municipal clerk, and the political chief in Santa Cruz del Quiché, who authenticated the signatures. Some lands must have then been entered in the registry office in Quetzaltenango.

Over time, disputes over land would have arisen between neighbors and relatives in San Antonio, and just as today, mayors would have been powerless to resolve them. The solution would ultimately have come from the regional judge. However, such disputes, involving both lawyers and money, seem to have begun to occur shortly before the revolution of 1944, according to available information. Between this period and 1877 there must have been no authority to resolve land disputes; neither the mayors in the community nor judges outside it would have resolved them. Into this vacuum and because of it, witchcraft must have flourished anew. Just as in the previous period the vacuum opened between community authorities and the central government, now there was one between community authorities and community inhabitants.

The beginning and end of this authority vacuum are not sharply defined. For a time it is likely that the mayors and *principales* (most of whom were simultaneously heads of their segments) continued to function as judges over communal lands or those of the lineage and segment. Likewise, for many people unable to pay lawyers, this vacuum had not ended. Nevertheless, this period marked the end of the community struggle against the Chiquimulas and against every other intruder who took advantage of the undefined municipal boundaries to claim empty land and seize it. Defining municipal boundaries could only be done by a strong government, such as the one begun during the Reform, which had penetrated far enough into the communities to impose forced labor and transform land tenure. Indeed, on July 5, 1877, against an appeal from San Antonio, which by way of exception was asking to be allowed east into Quiché lands, the central government ruled that the dividing line should be the canyon of the Jocol River.

On March 8, 1889, the western border of the municipality, from which the Chiquimulas had continually invaded, was settled. The Chiquimulas in 1887 had asked the president for some hamlets that, according to the 1791 map, belonged to San Antonio. They asked to go as far as the Tzununá River. In a compromise, the official decision traced a line down the middle between the borders that each contending side claimed as its own. At that point San Antonio definitively lost much of the land invaded by the Chiquimulas, though some remained on San Antonio's side because of where the line was drawn.

On April 1, 1889, President José María Reina Barrios approved the demarcation of the southern boundary with the Chuachituj lands. The 4,550-acre tract of Chuachituj had been sold in 1841, but the boundaries between this land and San Antonio were still not clear. Again, a partition was drawn halfway between the lines claimed by the two sides.

On January 24, 1905, President Manuel Estrada Cabrera finally granted the municipality title to lands in the northeast (Chuisicá) whereby the northern boundaries, which were still in contention, were set. In 1892, a group of five people from Quiché, apparently ladinos, had claimed some lands to the east of the straight line between Chucuchún and Xiguaná. The land was almost 225 hectares (561 acres), to be divided among the five. At the same time, a Chiquimula resident, probably from the hamlet that over time would become the municipality of Santa Lucía, together with several others, claimed all the land between a line somewhat farther east than that of the men from Quiché and all the area north of the Jocol River to where it ran into Camocutz Creek. The people from San Antonio then argued that they had bought this land (Chuisicá) from San Pedro Jocopilas, because it was then within the limits of the deed held by that municipality. They also showed that it was not unoccupied land, because eighty-five people from San Antonio had plots there, along with twenty-three houses. The engineer responsible for surveying suggested that this land not be taken from them for the "peace of the town of San Antonio, which is warlike when land is at stake," and from which a great deal had been taken since the eighteenth century.

Hence, after many court cases, in 1905 the president awarded the title to the whole municipality, in accordance with boundaries set in 1841, 1877, and 1889. According to this deed, which is still kept as a treasure in the city hall, the municipality's area covers 177 *caballerías*, 35 *manzanas*, and 4,373 v² (approximately 20,000 acres, calculated to the last square yard). Over time, San Antonio came to lose 139 *caballerías* (15,800 acres), almost its current area.

The disputes with the neighboring community of Santa María Chiquimula came to an end. The time when the community as such defended San Antonio's lands, because they were under its jurisdiction but not ownership, ended with the 1905 decision. From then on, everyone would defend his own land, and the community authority, having lost its role of representing the residents, lost the power granted by that role.[3]

Authorities

Authority continued to be vested in the two Indian mayors, appointed by the *principales* until 1935, when President Jorge Ubico began to have the political chiefs appoint an intendant. In San Antonio, the intendant was always a ladino. In 1945, the mayor was to be elected by popular vote, although in San Antonio the election was still done for some years through the *principales*.

In 1877 the community of San Antonio was raised to the rank of a municipality. In 1885 the president authorized the political chief in Santa Cruz del Quiché to appoint the municipal clerk instead of having the municipalities themselves do it. In San Antonio after the turn of the century, the municipal clerk was to be the first ladino to take up residence in San Antonio with his family, buy land, and open the way for other ladinos to settle there, even in the face of opposition from the Indians.

With the Reform of the 1870s, El Quiché became a department, with its own political chief and regional judge. Previously it only had a preventive judge, whose function was to advise the regional judge in Sololá of crimes committed, "sending the criminal along, if he has managed to imprison him" (1839 Constitution, Art. 77), but who had no power, for example, to move to seize goods without a prior order from the department judge (Art. 83).

As we have seen, the priest began to come from Santa Cruz del Quiché after 1850, but after the Reform period, monthly visits became more scarce and relations became more tense. The Reform government had decreed that the church could not hold goods and that religious orders were to be expelled. By 1893, for example, the priest came only once or twice a year, during Holy Week and for Corpus Christi (to offer a special prayer for rain). In 1907, the record of visits breaks off. According to informants, in the years before 1945 the priest came only three times a year, for the feast of San Antonio (St. Anthony; January 17), for Corpus Christi, and for All Saints (November 1–2). When the Missionaries of the Sacred Heart arrived from Spain in 1955 there were only three priests active in the whole department of El Quiché; the one in Santa Cruz served San Antonio. The Spanish group has as many as twenty-five priests or even more.

During this period (1871–1944), outside officials come even closer and in the person of the clerk, they reached the town itself, with the consequent effect of ending the municipality's autonomy. Since then, its officials have had less power, because they did not derive power from outside authorities. This is especially true of the *principales*, who have never made up a legally established body.

In terms of religion, however, the fact that the priest was not visiting regularly often left it up to the *principales*, *alcaldes*, and *cofradía* members to celebrate the feast days, and it allowed the *zahorines* to operate more freely and openly.

The Zahorines

I have already indicated that, according to the testimony of the parents and grandparents of my informants, "before"—without specifying when—there was practically no witchcraft. There was a great deal of land and some people even gave pieces of it away. On the basis of such testimony, it can be calculated that this "before" refers to two or three generations ago, in the early twentieth century, when, because it had extensive lands and little population, San Antonio was a wool-producing municipality with a large number of sheep. Since then, the number of acts regarded as witchcraft must have increased until the break in 1948. The number of *zahorines*—and their power—must have also increased.

It should be kept in mind that a *zahorín* (*aj k'ij*) is not the same as a witch doctor (*brujo*; *aj itz*). A witch doctor does evil; a *zahorín* does not. A witch doctor works for someone against that person's enemy: he "puts into him" an illness, a toad, even to the point of killing him. His mediators are the same as those of the *zahorín*: the deceased ancestors, the Sacred World, the wind. A *zahorín* operates in the open and is identifiable. A witch doctor does not, because he is censured by the community.

Yet a *zahorín* may be taken as a witch doctor. A person becomes ill and thinks someone is doing him harm. He goes to his *zahorín* to see why. The *zahorín* tells him that someone is sending evil his way and it has to be stopped with "traditions" (burning incense and candles, offering liquor in the hills, and so forth). Enemy and cause are identified. Perhaps the enemy has not gone to any *zahorín*, much less to a witch doctor, but when something happens to him, he also goes to his *zahorín* to defend himself against the other man. This mutual defense is not, properly speaking, witchcraft, although it is regarded as such by both enemies.

In other instances, when it is only a matter of making up for one's own sin in order to be cured, there is no witchcraft (according to the local belief). Ordinarily, this sin entails a social relationship that is injured or violated, often over a piece of land.

Hence, the ascendancy of the *zahorines*—whether these practitioners were regarded by others as involved in witchcraft or not—must have taken place as the authority of *principales* and mayors was waning, after the boundaries of the municipality were set and when, due to increasing population and the growing scarcity of land, one's enemy in San Antonio began to be within the community, replacing the outside enemy. It was also a time when land disputes could not be effectively resolved either by authorities within the community, who had no true jurisdiction over lands, or by those outside, to whom one could not go for lack of means, as well as other reasons. I reconstruct that into this authority vacuum, and under this growing population pressure on resources, going to nonempirical authorities, such as appealing to the dead and the saints through the *zahorines*, must have become more common. The *zahorines* grew in number because of the growing demand for their intercession and possibly because the priest was not there to put them down. Because the *zahorín* is ordinarily an elderly man who no longer works with his own hands in the fields, as their number multiplied, there were fewer *principales* who were not *zahorines* and thus some of the *principales* recovered their power, though now not for being *principales* but for being *zahorines*.

That is how I assume the process unfolded up to the 1930s, when, during the worldwide depression and the consequent widespread poverty, the power of the *zahorines* must have begun to wane because the demand for "traditions" must have fallen off, competition among the *zahorines* themselves must have been exacerbated, and thus their exploitation of their customers probably heightened. In 1934, President Ubico canceled the debts of the labor crew members, thereby opening the way to new alternatives and new power bases, as indicated in the chapter on merchants. At the same time, confidence in the outside world, which had dealt them so many blows since 1877 (such as the Regulations on Laborers), was gradually restored. This trust, which is the basis for the merchant's ideology, helped undermine trust in the *zahorín*, who was the bastion of tradition, of the memory of the ancestors, and of the power of the community as opposed to that of the outside world.

But in San Antonio it was not until after 1945, with the split in the national sources of derived power caused by the political parties, that those unhappy with the *zahorines* came forward and the first open rebellions took place. One of the first conversions in 1948 was a clear case of this type of rebellion (see next chapter). It was in this climate that Catholic Action arose.

Rebelling against the *zahorín* amounted to faith in a nonempirical healing power, and it entailed on the part of the dissident the need to gather together with other persons and to seek a source of nonempirical power to counteract that of the *zahorín*. This gave rise to the drive to proselytize and the insistence on praying together. This prayer in common was supported from outside by the church, whose priests were a source of nonempirical power. Once the priests began to openly support these rebellions or stir them up, even though they were not living in San Antonio, they became the *zahorines'* greatest rivals and adversaries. The Catholic Action group opened up to the priests with full confidence and faith, for from them came nonempirical power for struggling against the *zahorines*.

Opposition between the two groups, Catholic Action versus the Traditionalists, thus increased, with the priests communicating power from outside to the Catholic Action group, and the *zahorines* being the most hard-core group resisting conversions. The *zahorines* closed ranks, smoothing over their inner rivalries and divisions, and gradually stopped exploiting the group of Traditionalists for whom they were competing, thereby attempting to adapt to the outside world while trying not to become lax in their fundamental beliefs, such as the calendar. For their part, the priests preached conversion away from "witch doctors" and their diabolical customs, as we will see in the next chapter.

Conclusion

This chapter has delineated a series of factors involved in the increase of conversions through social reorganization at various levels. At this point I will recapitulate.

Resistance by sons to having their parents choose their wives, especially made manifest in the rise in the number of divorces, had an impact on the conversion movement, because, as my analysis shows, those who had rejected the wives chosen by their parents after having lived with them converted in proportionally greater numbers than those who had had a stable marriage. Nevertheless, by joining the new Catholic Action organization and through the power flowing from the Catholic Action board members and from civil and ecclesiastical law, converts whose parents had lost power, at least partly because of the land shortage and the gradual delay of the son's marriage until a more mature age, gradually recovered—now as parents themselves—the authority to keep the marriage of their children from dissolving and themselves from losing the gifts presented when requesting the hands of their daughters-in-law. The new organization, moreover, adapted to the rapid changes in marriage patterns required by the rising population by letting a son choose his wife.

The change in the one choosing the bride was presented as the symbol of a new organization, not only because in itself it was a useful adaptation, but because at the same time the overall superiority of the new organization was being extolled, in contrast to the threats and contempt out of which it arose, as was the inherent superiority of deriving power from outside. As a sign, this stance was indicating more deeply the need for the reorganization of a society whose population was growing faster than ever, spreading out geographically, becoming stratified, and struggling to break free from the constraints of the older generation.

Indeed, this demographic growth and the spread of the population in the municipality had the effect of increasing endogamy in a canton or within a group of two or three cantons. The *cofradía* system maintained by a substrate of marriage relationships between cantons was deprived of its support, and the converts, instead of serving in it, organized an alternative system of duties or *cargos* involving only those belonging to a canton or to a group of two or three neighboring cantons. The Catholic Action "center" was born, and as a canton organization, it withdrew from the requirements of serving in *cofradías* and extended its reach to the municipal authority, linking up with an organization on the municipal level that was standing in opposition to that of the *principales*, although its members were always under the mayor. It did not break away as a new municipality, replicating the old system of *cofradías* in the manner of some villages of other towns, which thereby became independent, but instead stayed within it. Thus there emerged a new level of articulation, halfway between the municipal and household levels, within the formal Catholic Action organization.

The emergence of the new formal organization was accompanied by confessional endogamy, which did not arise directly out of imposition by the church, but from some converts' experiences of death within their former organization (to be illustrated in the next chapter). Their connection to this organization had to be completely rejected. The church supported this tendency, which was akin to its own approach in this area. Proselytizing was encouraged (a trait that would distinguish Catholic Action from the Tradition and would distinguish the meetings taking place at centers from *cofradía* meetings) in order to obtain wives, either by converting them at the time of marriage or by increasing the number of entire households to join Catholic Action.

The formal organization was supported by a population of merchants who were building up capital, buying land, employing laborers, lending money, selling corn, and serving as baptism and marriage sponsors, thereby enhancing stable relationships, both inside the municipality and with people from the municipality working outside it. This resulted in a series of relationships that could have been independent of the formal organization, as happened with Traditionalist merchants who did not constitute a new intermediate authority over the Traditionalists of their canton under the authority of the mayor or the *principales*. In the new organization, however, it was the individuals whose power base was capital, transportation, and land, who likewise accepted the *cargos*, or supported those who did occupy them, thereby receiving authority over the converts and communicating their power so that the decisions of its board members would be carried out.

The division entailed in this stratification process was formalized with the open rejection by members of the new group of some of the principles or symbols of the traditional organization and those who defended it most tenaciously, the *zahorines*. The latter held a great deal of power in themselves, without being, as *zahorines*, a formally constituted authority, although many of them were also *principales*. I have already explained how, following the 1821–1871 period, there was an authority vacuum between national-level and community-level authorities, and that in the next period (1871–1944), it gradually shifted to the relationship between the community authority and the community inhabitants, primarily over lands. Then, among individuals, the demand for nonempirical resources rose during the world depression, and subsequently, with the changes brought about by the 1944 Revolution, those who felt exploited by the *zahorines* finally broke away from these practitioners and the entire system they represented.

Underlying this whole process in which such varied factors are at work is a common denominator, namely, the growing penetration of the outside world into a previously isolated community. This new influence is reflected in the rising living standard, which brings about a faster rate of population growth; the consequent effects of decreasing land per individual on the traditional basis of a father's power; the disruption of the community's exclusive organizations, which are difficult to adapt to a large population; the entry of capital through trade, with its consequent stratification and diffusion in the community; the penetration of the church and the extension of effective authority by the state—in short, a whole series of phenomena that cause the center of nonempirical power projected by its inhabitants to be shifted outside the community.

CHAPTER 5

Conversion

In this chapter we will study conversion itself using some examples of real people, which will be examined in terms of power. Then, drawing on these examples, we will test several hypotheses on the influence of some factors in order to explain the processes by which conversion occurs. We will then analyze the "rite" that consummates conversion, and conclude the chapter by summarizing the main aspects of the process.

I am here going to narrate and analyze the conversions of two individuals, one of whom converted the other, thereby passing onto him power derived from within the community. I have chosen these two conversions, first, for their dramatic effect, for they highlight the conflict within the power structure and the search for an adaptation to the environment in order to survive; and second, because in both instances these individuals are living with their parents, it will be possible to show how the opposition of these more powerful members has consequences for the rest of the household. I will narrate the conversions, analyze them in terms of power, and then try to compare them so as to draw out hypotheses to be tested.

Manuel's Conversion: No Power Derived from Within the Community

Manuel (fictitious name) broke with the Tradition in 1949, a year after two others from San Antonio had converted, one from the canton of Tzancawuib and the other from Canamixtoj. Although the other two converted before Manuel, they played no part in his own process.

Manuel was then 29. For ten years he had been living with a woman whom his father had chosen. He now had had four children by her, but only three of them were still living. Manuel, his wife, and his children lived in the same house with his father. His father was around 50 years old; his mother had died around twenty years before. His only brother had also died.

Manuel's father had not sought another wife, probably because he was a man with no land. The land on which the house they lived in was built did not belong to Manuel's father, but it had belonged to Manuel's mother's parents. Manuel's father had been born in a neighboring canton, and his life had been harsh and sad because he had borne the oppression of debts on the coast. His father had had to sell his land in order to pay off debt. That is why, upon marrying Manuel's mother, he went to live with her in her canton and with her father. Perhaps because they had had no male children, they left her an inheritance, an exception to the usual rules.

Hence, the owner of this land was not Manuel's father, but Manuel, who had inherited it from his mother. The land measured 80 *cuerdas*, counting the canyon. It was larger than what many had (15, 20, or sometimes only 10 *cuerdas*), even making allowance for the ravine, where nothing can be grown. Manuel grew wheat to sell and corn for their own consumption. He also rented land in La Estancia, a canton in the municipality of Santa Cruz del Quiché, in order to sell more grain. He often needed hired hands, recruited from among his neighbors. Many of his neighbors had worked for him at one time or another.

In addition, Manuel used to weave men's red sashes that he went to sell in the market in Chichicastenango; that was not the closest municipality, but it was closer to him than to the inhabitants in other cantons in San Antonio. He could get there in four hours. His wife fattened and raised pigs, just as other San Antonio women often do.

Manuel takes up the story in his own words:

> Then I got a fever in the middle of my body: one side of my body is hot and the other cold. And my body hurts. I went to a *zahorín*, my uncle Jerónimo, who is now dead. But before that I had been to see Antonio (another *zahorín*), also dead. I'm paying and paying money. Antonio said: "Your house is making you sick," and that I should go to Jerónimo's. Antonio says he knows how to ask for God's blessing, but does not know how to remove a spell that has already been cast. That same day I went to Jerónimo. He had his bundle of beans (*tz'ite'*). He told me, "You have an adversary." I told him that Antonio had sent me there. "Poor Antonio," he said, "yes it's true, he is unable to get rid of bad Tradition." He, by contrast, had been as far as Cunén, Uspantán, Chicamán . . . he goes there to cure all the sick.
>
> He began, and I worked a year with him. I spent Q 110 on him. And that was the end of my money. My wife sold her pig for Jerónimo's incense and liquor. I had planted 50 *cuerdas* of wheat. In June it was sold at a good price, but the money gave out. I was going to sell my land. The disease left my face and went down into my stomach like a ball. At night I'm about to die. I see what seem to be two men from Tzul come and take me by the neck and pull me back and forth. And I yelled. My wife got up, "What's

going on?" she asked me. And my father is still alive, and I'm coming to my senses saying that two men were killing me. "But there's no one here," they told me.

I went to Jerónimo, who begins other traditional practices. "Your adversary is putting in more resources, working harder against you . . . I'm going to strike some blows at him," he says. Jerónimo has candles. He has some black ones for evil that are dated, that came from Totonicapán. And we went up near his house to the aji'k (burning pit). I felt better for two or three days. But my stomach pain began again and I was on the brink of death. And my money ran out.

But I was a merchant in Chichicastenango. There was a man from Totonicapán there who sold clothes. I'm a weaver and I sell sashes. He was from Chimente, Juan. I told him I'm sick. He says he's going to tell me something in the afternoon, because "I'm busy now," he said. "I'm going to give some advice," he says.

I'm with my heart like this . . . At three in the afternoon I go over to be with him. And I spent it with him and told him all about my illness and what we spent. He says, "Look, how much money do those who believe in witchcraft make? Why are you believing the *zahorines*? That's fairy tales. This illness goes to shit if you believe in God. They're in business, they don't heal. You believe in God and you begin to believe right now." And he pulled a catechism out of the drawer, saying, "Recite prayers." But I don't know any prayers. "The Our Father," he told me. "How long I've known it!" I said to him. My grandfather had taught it to me in the Indian language. "Tomorrow you're not going to the witch doctor," Juan told me. "But [the treatment] still has some more to go," I said. "No, this is the work of the Devil," said Juan.

I never went back to Jerónimo. I'm now in pain with the pain in the stomach. "Begin to read today. You don't know how to read?" "No, just a little. I know the letters but I don't know how they're combined," I said. "Now begin to pray and you'll show people in your canton how not to believe in the witch doctor."

Two weeks later the illness went away. "And your illness?" my wife asked me. I hadn't felt which day it had left. I'm fine. "Let's try to pray more. Why believe in this witch doctor stuff?"

I said to my father, "Let's pray together." He knelt down with me, praying to God. My father had his divination beans (*tz'ite'*) and he also threw them in the canyon.

That was how Manuel was converted. Later he would go on to convert many others. He told all of them his story, as he told it to us. The first converts were four brothers who worked with him as laborers and whose father was dead. Later he won over one of Jacinto's brothers, whose story will be our second case. He had only done service twice in the *cofradías*, as the sixth *mayordomo* in 1944 and as the fourth in 1946, each time spending around Q 30.

Orders

We are now going to analyze this account, focusing on different aspects of the conversion process, which is a process of power. First, we will look at what I call orders of power: the *empirical order*, which can be verified by experience, and the *projected order*, which cannot be verified (see theoretical framework). In each order there are social units, power relationships, structures, and so forth, the existence of which can be verified in the empirical but not in the projected order.

In Figure 5.1, I have divided the two orders, the empirical and the projected. To the former belong those units whose existence and power may be verified by the senses, such as Manuel, his adversary, the *zahorines*, and their power in relation to others in the same order. To the latter belong those whose existence, power, and power relationship cannot be proven to the senses, such as deceased grandparents, the Sacred World, God, and the Devil. Both orders are intimately connected, according to Manuel's vision, because, for example, the *zahorín* himself has the power to cure him, thanks to his relationship to the deceased grandparents and to the Sacred World. However, I am assuming that just as Manuel's belief in *zahorines* may have an influence on his health and this influence can be verified, on the other hand, it cannot be verified that this influence comes from the deceased grandparents or from the Sacred World or from any other component of the projected order. I regard the projected order as nonempirical.

FIGURE 5.1. *Power structures before (I) and after (II) Manuel's conversion*

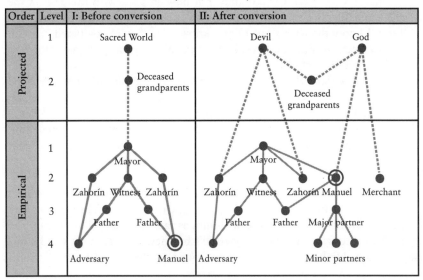

This distinction seems important, because we will be investigating the process by which complete adherence to belief is withdrawn from one element in the projected order and is attributed to another in the same order through conversion.

Units

The following units are involved in Manuel's conversion. We will go through Figure 5.1 from top to bottom, first in the power structure before Manuel's conversion (I) and then in the power structure after his conversion (II).

Structure Prior to Conversion (I)

Projected Order.   *Level 1*: The Sacred World, from which comes life through the deceased grandparents. The burning of incense and "traditions" of the *zahorines* are addressed to it.

Level 2: The deceased grandparents, who receive their power from the Sacred World and act as judges of their descendants who are in contention; the grandparents of Manuel's mother's segments and the mother of his adversary, who own the land that is apparently the basis of the conflict.

The ranking of the grandparents within the projected order is more complicated, but for the sake of simplicity I have eliminated it. If the conflict were between lineages, it would probably be the Sacred World, acting as a sort of mayor, that would have to resolve it.

Empirical Order.   *Level 1*: The town mayor. He does not appear in the story, but he is the highest authority in the municipality and oversees compliance with certain commonly accepted norms, some of which have to do with respect for the *zahorines*, their "traditions," and the beliefs underlying such "traditions" or rituals. Nevertheless, the mayor, as we saw in the last chapter, does not have the power to resolve conflicts over land. The mayor is the counterpart of the Sacred World in the empirical order.

Level 2: Manuel's *zahorines* and those of his adversary. They stand midway between the municipal level of the mayor and the level of the households. They have a more or less fixed number of clients from various cantons.

The witness for the dividing up of the inheritance is the oldest member of the segment or lineage of the parents of those in contention. This witness, who supports the parents' decisions with his authority and ought to settle land conflicts, has no power to act as a judge. Moreover, in this instance, this witness would not have authority over that conflict because the land in question is on the side of the mother's lineage.

The witness does not appear in the story, but in terms of the social organization of San Antonio, he should be mentioned. For the sake of simplicity I have not included the ranking of witnesses, which, like that of the deceased grandparents, is more complicated.

Level 3: The fathers of Manuel and his adversary. His adversary's father does not enter into the story; I reconstructed it. Fathers are the heads of the household.

Level 4: Manuel and his adversary. They are each under the authority of their father within the household.

Structure after Conversion (II)

Projected Order (as Manuel sees it).   *Level 1*: The Devil and God. With conversion, there has appeared a new factor, God, to whom Manuel attributes healing power with full assent, while he turns the Sacred World, which the *zahorines* entreat and expiate, into the Devil.

Level 2: The deceased grandparents. Conversion does not seem to have made the grandparents either favorable or unfavorable.

Empirical Order.   *Level 1*: The mayor.

Level 2: The *zahorines*, the witness, and now Manuel with the merchant. Through conversion, Manuel rises to confront the *zahorines* as the head of a group of associates that he himself converts. Over time this group will become linked to the regional Catholic Action organization, thereby benefiting from the power of that association. As can be seen from the story, it seems that the merchant was also a Catholic Action board member in his canton in Chimente, a village near Totonicapán.

Level 3: The fathers of the adversary and Manuel and the *major partner*, as I am calling the elder brother of the four converted brothers. Manuel's father, as a converted associate, stands on a level lower than that of Manuel.

Level 4: The adversary and the *lesser members*, as I have called the younger brothers of the four converts.

Manuel's Power Base

Manuel owns his own land, he is a weaver and a merchant, and he plants more than the average amount of wheat on rented lands. His various kinds of work enable him to have relationships in which he occupies a higher position. Any merchant who sells sashes is related to other weavers who work for him on the material that he provides them (even if they have their own loom); they are like his laborers. He also pays laborers to work and plant rented land. These relationships are temporary, but without them he probably could not have set up a lasting organization after converting. (Because these relationships are not involved in the conflict with his adversary, I left them out of structure I in the figure. I included them in II, now as lasting relationships on the way to being formalized.) As a merchant, he has horizontal relationships with merchants in other municipalities who provide him with information, which is a source of power. The merchant from Chimente tells him how he ought to become organized by "coming forward" and winning over followers, and offers him a vision of a movement that is emerging in nearby municipalities. By this time, Catholic Action has been set up in Patzité, Santa María Chiquimula, and Chimente. After his conversion, they invite him to those centers to take part in their meetings, where they each narrate their experiences and promise one another success. He is enabled to envision the possibility of having allies in the region sympathetic to his struggle, even though at that time they would not be able to defend him in conflicts within the community. Finally, the merchant offers him the remedy that can cure him, if he believes, and deliver him from the bankruptcy that is drawing near. His power base therefore lies in his holdings and revenues, his relationships with subordinates in the community, and his relationships outside the community, which open up new prospects for him.

Structures

Structure I: Before conversion

When Manuel seeks out the *zahorín* for healing, he is told of an adversary (whether real or fictitious) who is said to be using witchcraft against him, causing his illness and driving him bankrupt. In keeping with community principles, Manuel believes in the *zahorín*'s word. The *zahorín* holds the power derived from the units in the projected order, the deceased grandparents and the Sacred World. This power cannot be derived directly by people like Manuel, who have to make use of intermediaries, the *zahorines*. But the *zahorín* is competing with his opposite number to derive that power. This does not seem to go so far as to create enmity between the two *zahorines*, who are both under the mayor of the town. Although he is the guarantor of the community's principles, which are the basis for affirming belief in the *zahorines*, the mayor is unable to resolve land conflicts, and hence derivation of nonempirical power from the deceased grandparents becomes necessary, as we saw in the last chapter.

The fathers of Manuel and his adversary are not under the *zahorín* in the conflict, because the land belongs not to them but to their sons. Indirectly, in support of their sons, the fathers must have been on opposite sides, as becomes clear when Manuel's father is converted after he is.

Therefore, the entire conflict with the adversary, although it has some foundation in empirical reality (the piece of land), seems to be almost entirely of the projected order; hence Manuel's subordination to his *zahorín* remains tense until the break. It is what I could call a relationship of exploitation, borne by Manuel, who has no way of freeing himself from it.

Structure II: After conversion

Here the relationship of confrontation centers around Manuel and his former *zahorín*, plus the other *zahorines* and the mayor of the town who supports them. Just as in the previous structure, the confrontation relationship was almost completely projected, and because of illness an effort was made to seek out who the adversary was, here the confrontation means a struggle of visible, palpable agents, whose power can be tested as coming from them.

Even so, Manuel needs to derive power, so he thinks, from units of the projected order. This time he moves out of the *zahorín*'s domain and sees himself as the one deriving projected power directly. As noted, he then reverses the Sacred World's attributes of healing and turns them into attributes of causing sickness. Hence, he turns the Sacred World into the Devil and consequently leaves the Devil's domain and adheres to the unit that is the source of healing, according to the merchant, namely God. Manuel's opposition to the *zahorines* is projected onto the opposition between the Devil and God.

It seems that the deceased grandparents, who are persons of respect, have not lost their attributes of goodness, although for now healing is made to depend directly on God, nor does it seem that in Manuel's eyes the possibility of the *zahorines* deriving power from the grandparents is eliminated. The grandparents, who did believe in the *zahorines* and in the Sacred World, remain in an ambiguous dependence on the Devil (Sacred World), which at this moment of conversion is not given great attention because to do so would weaken the convert.

Manuel is now under the mayor, but opposed to him, even while not breaking this relationship of subordination. The formation of a group of associates, including his father, and the future merging of this group (center) with those of the entire municipality will force competition with the mayor and the *zahorines*, raising the conflict to the community's highest level of articulation. Then the power derived from department-level Catholic Action, the church, and the political parties will be utilized. This derivation here makes its way in through the window of the possible alliances that the merchant from Chimente opens up for him.

Regionalization of the alliances is replicated in the projected order, where the highest element is not a mayor of the community's deceased, as the Sacred World tends to be, but a God from whom incipient groups in different communities in the indigenous region and the ladino sector of the nation derive power, and to whom the newly converted merchants offer service.

Passage from One Structure to the Other

We now turn to the moment when Manuel's eyes are opened to the power with which he was previously unfamiliar. What aspects are at work in this change? How was it possible?

Manuel had previously been taken ill. The illness later changed and another type of illness with no physiological cause seems to have taken hold: consider the dreams that torment him and the speed with which he is healed. As he worsens, his anxiety rises, he makes repeated visits to the *zahorín*, spends more money, and comes close to bankruptcy—all of which augments his anguish. He feels he is in the throes of death. That is his condition when the merchant reproaches him for his behavior and assures him that the *zahorín* is nothing but a businessman who offers only what comes from the Devil, and that only God can cure him.

Thus far there has been an opposition between experience and belief. How is belief destroyed and its opposite set in its place? The destruction of belief (negative aspect) seems to be based on an intuition of a nucleus of truth (for him): the *zahorines* are businessmen. His subsequent reasoning can be explained from this starting point: it is in a *zahorín*'s interest that there be sick people; otherwise, he would be out of work. Hence, when someone gets sick, it is in his interest to keep him sick, and if someone is not sick, to make him sick. The rituals he performs, "the traditions" of burning incense, are to make people sick. Hence they are bad, all of them, and that there should be good and bad "traditions," as the *zahorines* say, is inconceivable. If they are always bad, the higher power source that gives them validity and healing ability, the Sacred World, must be evil. That is where the Devil comes from. Hence the *zahorines*, who are actually witch doctors, have to be confronted head-on and unflinchingly. Thus in Manuel's eyes they lose their healing capacity but can still induce sickness through the Devil. This assessment has changed their sign from plus to minus.

Very significant is the relationship between the loss of belief and exploitation, defined, as mentioned, by the almost complete absence of empirical content in the confrontational relationship or, more generally, by the almost complete absence of any empirical purpose for the units of the projected order. If relationships with the units of the projected order have no bearing on adaptation to the environment, they can be defined as exploitative relationships, and belief in them is likely to vanish.

The establishment of a new belief (positive aspect) takes place because it is shown to be an alternative endowed with power to cure him individually and enabling him to stand up to the *zahorines* socially—the individual and the social are mutually related. He anticipates that prayers and faith in God, which have healed other sick people, will again heal him (the individual), and many others will be able to be liberated from the *zahorines*' influence (the social), thanks to healing through faith in God. He anticipates that his own power, which is based on owning land, producing wheat on rented land, and relations with his laborers and with other merchants, will enable him to set up a combative organization (the social) against the *zahorines* in which a belief with healing capability is cultivated; by anticipating the existence of such an organization, he can, as of this moment, believe and be healed (the individual). It is for these reasons that he can accept this alternative.

Even so, this does not explain why he not only is able to see and accept this alternative, but actually does see it and accept it as such. Nor does it explain why adherence to belief, both the one abandoned and the one newly accepted, has to bear the characteristic of totality. I will try to elaborate on these points in the second case, on which there is more information.

Jacinto's Conversion: Power Derived from Within the Community

Manuel (from the previous case) began to win over Jacinto and his brother Francisco. There were five brothers: Francisco Number 1 (29), Lorenzo (25), Francisco Number 2 (20), Jacinto (13), and José (6). Only the first three were married. There were also three sisters, the oldest, between Lorenzo and Francisco 2, and the second and third, who were between Francisco 2 and Jacinto. Two of them had gone away to live with their husbands, so only the youngest was living with the five brothers and their parents.

Their father had 80 *cuerdas* of land. Before 1934 he had only worked on the coast, but after that he began renting a plot of land in La Estancia, Santa Cruz del Quiché, from the same ladino from whom Manuel had rented. But he never learned Spanish well.

In 1949, Jacinto, the primary narrator, who was then 12, began to go with his brothers to work on the coast. He first went to the Cerritos plantation in Escuintla with his older brother Francisco 1 to work planting tea and lemons. They were there for two months. Between the two of them they could do two days' work and earn Q 1.50, but Francisco only gave him Q 0.60. With that money they bought clothes and some extra things to eat that they did not get from their daily rations. They had to hand over the rest to their father when they returned.

The next year (1950) Manuel began to win Jacinto over. Jacinto visited Manuel's house to learn the catechism. Francisco 1 became angry. Jacinto warned Manuel, "Be careful with my big brother, he's going to stone you, believe me."

Manuel went to Francisco 1 and offered to give him work. Manuel says, "I asked Francisco to come work on 3 *cuerdas* with me. 'If you pay well . . . ,' he said. I'm going to pay you Q 1.50 (for the 3 *cuerdas*). 'Okay.' We went there and he began to talk. I showed him the little book with catechism drawings. The 3 *cuerdas* of work was measured out and he came to chat. I invited him to lunch and he started chatting again. We were talking for a whole day. It almost seemed to me he wasn't angry." This was how Manuel won people over: he told them about his own cure, and gave them explanations from the catechism, which he could then read.

A few days later, the elder Francisco and his father clashed because Francisco started refusing to hand over money so his father would not waste it on the *zahorín*. This was an open rebellion, because they were still living together in the same house, and the land had not been divided. Francisco would buy bread, fruit, chili, and other things for the kitchen, but he did not turn money earned over to his father.

At night Francisco would go to Manuel's house to listen to the explanation of doctrine, and he would come back at 11 P.M. or even later, at a time when everyone should be and was asleep. He also used to take his little two-year-old son with him to Manuel's house. Francisco's father would become angry and say that the child was going to become sick, and that because he was no longer providing money to perform "Tradition" for him, there would be no way to cure him and he would die. "But the kid is mine," Francisco would say. His father would answer him, "Go and ask for your land, your house, from Manuel!" Things went so far that one morning at breakfast time, when his father asked why he had gone to Manuel's the previous night, his father became angry and whipped Francisco with a leather strap. He also gave a slap in the face to the younger Francisco, who had begun to go along with his brother.

Jacinto, however, was withdrawing from Manuel because he saw that his father was so angry that it frightened him, and because he began to go to the coast with another brother, Lorenzo. In 1951 they went to the salt fields in the port, where Lorenzo earned Q 13 a week, but he drank it all away. Jacinto was very young and was not given work, so he spent his time with the San Antonio people, gathering firewood for them. Then a couple of years later he began to go out with Lorenzo to sell cheap jewelry from town to town and from one feast day to another. Throughout all this, the situation between Francisco and his father was so tense that Francisco asked to leave his house and asked that he please be given his plot of land to set up his house. He begged several times on his knees, to the point where the father decided to divide his inheritance among his five sons in the presence of the witnesses of his lineage. The elder Francisco would receive the old house, as demanded by Tradition, and the other children would have to put up their own houses on the land that was measured out to them. For now, since there was only one house, the elder Francisco was to occupy one room in the old house, while the father would occupy the other, with all the other sons.

Jacinto's father had sought a wife for him in 1953. Jacinto had a small market booth, but he sometimes left it to his brother Lorenzo to manage while he went to the coast with his wife. The elder Francisco worked with Manuel, weaving sashes. The younger Francisco is not mentioned, nor is José, who was still young.

At this point Jacinto, now 17, took sick. It began behind the heel of his foot, then went under the heel, and later onto his sole. Jacinto says that Francisco 1 would tell him:

> "You've gotten messed up for your disobedience. You have to observe Religion the right way. Otherwise, it's going to be worse for you." I thought, "That's foolishness." But Francisco said, "You're saying it's foolishness, and with your lips you're saying it is. This illness is like a tree that hasn't taken firm root in your body but that will do so." I came away thinking: My father didn't like Religion. My mother didn't either. My father slapped

my brother Francisco the younger in the face; he whipped my older brother with a leather strap. So I was in between.

At that time, my uncle José, the contractor, came by and took us to Guatalón, to weed cornfields, so I went with my wife. The work was over after two weeks. It was the time when a hundred-pound bag of corn was Q 15 (ordinarily it is between Q 3.50 and Q 5). I had a Q 5 advance, and my wife, Q 3. Between the two of us we put together around Q 12 for two weeks. "We're not going back home because there's no work," I told her in Guatalón. So we went to Progreso, below Escuintla, looking for work in cotton. We went even if only to clear fields, where you earn less than in the harvest. My foot became swollen. I suffered there. The work didn't give us enough for corn. I had left the business of selling small items with Lorenzo for him to handle for me. It was Q 28 in small merchandise. My brother began selling in Mazatenango and then he went to Escuintla, and he kept drinking the merchandise away. Through another person who was going to Escuintla, I asked him for Q 5. "I don't have money right now. So how am I going to get it together right away?" was his answer back to me, and he only sent two pounds of beans and two pounds of potatoes, one block of raw brown sugar, and fifty cents. It was only enough for bus fare from Progreso to Escuintla. We went to Escuintla and there I asked him for Q 10–15. He didn't give it to me. The next day he gave me Q 20 and said to me, "You handle the sales." And he didn't do any more selling. He no longer had any money. He just had Q 10. He went off no one knows where.

Jacinto kept getting worse. His brother Lorenzo did not help him in Escuintla. Here is Jacinto's story:

The time came when I had a fever, I couldn't walk, I couldn't eat. I was only drinking water. I didn't even go to the hotel, but just stayed in the sales booth. Someone from Momostenango threatened my brother with jail: "Dying at your sales booth is prohibited!" I was crying all the time out of my pain, and he didn't want to give me fare to San Antonio. Finally he gave me Q 4.00. I asked him for six. Four just covered bus fare. "I'm asking you for my money," I told him. But he just gave me four. And he went out to the streets. I was weeping in his sales booth. A man from Momostenango, who did business there, saw me and said, "Go home. If you go there to die, your parents will take care of you. Otherwise, who knows whether they'll bury you." My brother had bought a sheet from him that morning. "This illness is pitiful! You're going to give me back the sheet, and I'll give you back Q 1.50," he said to me. "If we fight with this jerk, fine." And the bus was waiting there. But my brother came and gave me Q 1.00, and as I was about to go, my brother said to me, "You're going away now, but you're a good believer in the Tradition. How are you going to get well, if at one time you're in Catholic Action and another time in the Tradition?"

His wife was along with him throughout this time. In his story, he does not mention her, although he always speaks in first-person plural. Later it will become clear that he had sought his wife during this stay in Escuintla.

Jacinto went back home and was bedridden for three years.

When the fever messed me up, I wasn't much of a believer in Religion, but I still feel it's the true Religion. My father would burn incense out in front of the house, and there I was praying the Creed, Our Father, and Holy Mary. I thought that what my father was doing was taking me to hell. My father went by himself to some men from Chiquimula, close to the boundary line. They told him that the time was near when "Your son is going to die." My father didn't want to tell me anything. My mother was going around sad. I was sleeping outside the house under the overhanging roof. My older brother's daughter told me, "Yesterday we heard some words." "What?" I asked. "That you're going to die," the kid said, "it's just that the time has not quite yet arrived, but you're going to die." They— the older folks—weren't telling me, just talking together inside, next to the fire. I was eating by myself. "You're going to die," said the girl. My older brother was studying doctrine. The kid, his child, also said, "You're going to die." So God is no longer forgiving me because I'm deceiving him.

I call my brother to ask Manuel whether I can come back to Religion. If I come back, it's to die in it. "I'm dying," I send word to him. "Let them bring me extreme unction." My father had said to me, "If you're going, go out to work and buy your corn," because I was eating some little tamales.

Manuel came when he had said he would. My father wasn't there because he was sleeping up on another property with his sheep. It was nighttime. When Manuel came, I was very ashamed. I seem not to be wearing any shirt, no undershirt, not even underpants. I was very ashamed. "What do I have for this Manuel to see?" I had entered Catholic Action about two or three months after him.

I asked him to see whether God would forgive me and whether I can return to Catholic Action. He says, "Probably, but you have to think just one way. Perhaps you're going to have the responsibility of being a board member or catechist. Perhaps you're going to go first to the church (to be married)." I told him I accept the doctrine, and I started to pray every day with my brother.

One day my father asked me, "Are you going to continue your Religion?" "Even if I die," I told him. "You want to die, as though you were more important than me. We've put aside money to bury you." I told him, "This land of mine that isn't willed to anyone, that I have not assigned because I didn't have a will, any brother who is willing to bury me, let it go to him." He said to me, "As if you have land that you've bought." "But you gave us that land without a will," I said. My father was angry. I told him, "Don't let those men come to burn incense. We're going to stone them, and I'm going to go to court to say that they were putting this disease into me, because these are things of the Devil." And he kept silent.

Then I began to study Religion. I had lost my wife in January. This happened in May; so a year later I was able to receive my First Communion. For two years I had no wife.

Jacinto improved, although not completely, and he went back to the coast with his older brother Francisco. He never went to a doctor. It did not even occur to him, he says now, because his father had no money.

Today (1970), only three of the five brothers are still alive. Lorenzo died without converting in 1960, and the younger Francisco died as a convert in 1966. Jacinto's parents are still alive, and they occupy a piece of land that belonged to Lorenzo and are raising one of his children. The youngest of the five brothers, José, became a merchant and married a young woman from Catholic Action, the daughter of one of the most well off merchants in the municipality. José grew up well disposed to Catholic Action and is still in it. The parents remain Traditionalists, and will probably die that way.

Power Structures of the Process

Seven power structures can be distinguished in Jacinto's conversion process (see Figure 5.2). In each, we will analyze the power bases and relations among the components. In a second section, we will analyze the movement from the sixth structure, just before Jacinto converts, to the seventh in which he does convert. This process lasted eight years, contrary to that of Manuel, which was over in a few days. Moreover, the delay before leaping to the last structure was very extended and offers a sharper view of the problem underlying conversion.

Structure 1: Before converting for the first time (1948)

The units in the projected order are, as they were with Manuel, the Sacred World and the deceased grandparents. In the empirical order, the mayor of the town is at the highest level of the structure; next the *zahorín* and the witness; then his father; and below Jacinto's father, his father's four sons, Francisco 1, Lorenzo, Francisco 2, and Jacinto. I am dropping the fifth son from the chart because he does not appear in the story.

The mayor is on level three. In Structures 6 and 7, where units outside the community are involved in the life of the San Antonio Catholic Action, I have added other levels. Thus in this structure, even if the mayor is on the highest level when compared with the others, he is only on the third level.

The power of sons vis-à-vis their father is weak, because the father has not divided his land among them. They are all subordinate to their father. They live with him, and if one gets sick, they all contribute toward paying the *zahorín* for his healing. Because there are several sons, however, some of them may have certain alliances among themselves against their father.

Figure 5.2. *Power structures in Jacinto's conversion*

Order	Level	1. Before conversion (1948)	2. Jacinto's first "conversion" (1949)	3. The two Franciscos converted (1950)

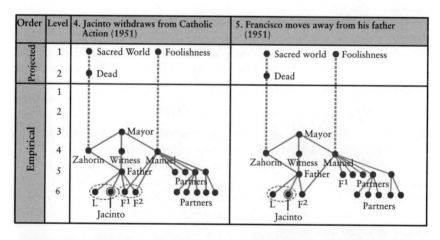

Order	Level	4. Jacinto withdraws from Catholic Action (1951)	5. Francisco moves away from his father (1951)

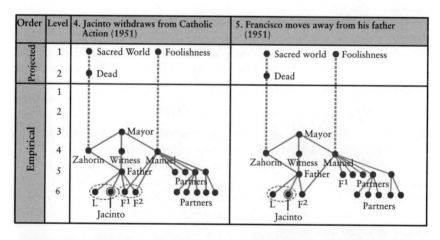

Order	Level	6. Jacinto separates from Lorenzo (1953)	7. Jacinto is converted (1956)

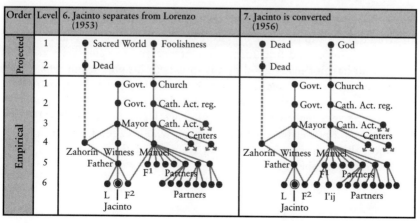

Structure 2: Jacinto "converts" for the first time (1949)

Manuel comes on the scene with his Catholic Action. With him, he brings the members who are converted: the four brothers. They are against the *zahorín*. They throw the powers in Jacinto's home off balance. Manuel draws Jacinto to class to give him catechism lessons.

His older brother Francisco, with whom he has worked on the coast, apparently not very pleased, reacts against Jacinto's conversion. From then on, Jacinto seems to be more in tune with his merchant brother Lorenzo, whose nature is more daring, than with the elder Francisco, who, for his part, seems to be allied with the younger Francisco. Jacinto's father does not seem to be worried about bringing Jacinto under control.

In the projected order, Jacinto now seems to see the opposition between God and the Devil (Sacred World) that Manuel preaches.

Structure 3: The two Franciscos convert (1950)

Through a work relationship and a long conversion (without illness), Manuel converts both Franciscos. These conversions are painful to the father, who threatens to disinherit his sons and goes so far as to strike them. At that point, the number of households converted rises to three and the members to ten, counting the three recently converted brothers. Manuel and his associates are collectively becoming stronger as Jacinto becomes weaker.

Structure 4: Jacinto leaves Catholic Action (1951)

Because he is working alongside his nonconverted brother, Lorenzo, Jacinto becomes disconnected from Catholic Action and from Manuel. Both are working as merchants far from San Antonio. Influenced by his brother, Jacinto regards the God of Catholic Action as "ridiculous" and, without giving it much thought, returns to being under the Sacred World. By this time, I know from other sources that the number of converts has grown to four houses and eleven men who are members.

Structure 5: The elder Francisco separates from his father (1951)

To avoid tension and to assure his future subsistence, the elder Francisco gets down on his knees and begs for his inheritance and to split away from his father, who has not made good on his threats to disinherit him. His father accedes, and the elder Francisco thereby rises to a higher level in which he no longer depends on his father either in terms of land or the household economy.

Francisco's independence will then influence Jacinto's conversion. He has also achieved a power base for his brothers, who also receive their land inheritance, although they do not separate from their father's household. There are now more members.

Structure 6: Jacinto breaks with his brother Lorenzo (1953)

In his illness, Jacinto gets no help from his Traditionalist brother, Lorenzo. He has a painful experience and almost dies. The only brother who represents the Tradition proves not to be a useful ally. He moves away from the Tradition and moves toward Catholic Action, the opposite pole.

Catholic Action becomes formalized in the municipality as the centers are linked to one another, and it becomes linked regionally with the one in Santa Cruz del Quiché, which is also above those in other municipalities. It is supported by the church. Although the point does not come up in the story, I know that during those years before the fall of President Jacobo Arbenz (in 1954), the church stood opposed to the government and communicated its support to regional and municipal Catholic Action groups against the authorities supported by the government.

Conclusion

In this transformation of structures, the *father* gradually loses power over Jacinto, loses two sons to Catholic Action, and divides the inheritance, while his oldest son becomes economically independent and lives in another house.

Catholic Action becomes stronger organizationally as more neighbors join and as it becomes formally organized municipally and regionally, although it does not draw power from the government.

Jacinto, who is going back and forth between his father (and the *zahorines*) and Manuel (and Catholic Action), loses more and more power from sickness, which keeps him from working, and from separation from his wife, which brings him to a situation where he is dependent on his parents for food and clothing. On the other hand, he loses his ties to the Tradition when he breaks with his brother and his Traditionalist wife and owns some land.

The balance of power between the father—whose power base is weakening but still powerful in relation to Jacinto, given his increasing destitution—and Catholic Action, which is growing ever stronger, is upset by other changes in the structure and in the decision-making process that Jacinto undergoes.

The Move: Final Structure and the Decision-making Process
Structure 7: Jacinto definitively converts (1956)

When Jacinto finally converts, his power base is minimal. He has lost his wife, he is prostrate in bed, he cannot work, and he is dependent on his father. The now grown-up sons of the elder Francisco play a part in persuading him.

Regionally, Catholic Action is being supported by the central government, and the municipal centers derive this power to struggle against Traditionalist mayors, as the one in San Antonio still is at that moment.

Back home and alone with his illness, Jacinto slowly enters into the great crisis of indecision and doubt, which increases his fever. That fever may in turn sharpen the opposition of the two poles between which he is torn. He says, "I went away from Religion, and I came back." He finds himself pulled between his father and Manuel; between the *zahorín* and Manuel; between the Sacred World and God.

He looks clearly at the two alternatives but does not opt for either. The first means staying with his father, whom he fears as the one who has reprimanded and beaten his brothers, and on whom he is dependent because he is unable to work and has lost his wife. His father gives him shelter and food. His mother, who has always supported her husband, washes his clothes. Even so, he "feels" that the *zahorines*, at the behest of his father, are sending him off to hell.

The second alternative is to go over to Manuel. The idea is attractive because he "feels that it is the true Religion" and that prayers can save him from his illness, so much so that he secretly prays the Our Father, Hail Mary, and Creed. Nevertheless, this alternative is not clear, because he is held back by a great shame toward Manuel, and does not know whether God will forgive him. If Manuel forgives him, God forgives him. But he has often laughed at Manuel and has called his advice "foolishness," inventions not to be taken seriously. He has deceived God and Manuel, because when he first joined Catholic Action, he told Manuel that he would follow him, but then he moved away. Both alternatives are ambiguous to him because both have positive and negative sides.

On the one hand, if Jacinto remains with his father in the Tradition, Manuel's God is "foolishness" and the Sacred World will save him through Traditionalist incense. If Jacinto goes over to the Catholic Action group, Manuel's God cures him and the Sacred World is the Devil. Staying or going over means thinking that you are staying or going over; it is something in the mind. The projected order is defined with one value or another depending on whether he remains in the Tradition or goes over to Catholic Action (empirical order). But the reverse is also true: Jacinto will go over to Catholic Action or not, depending on whether the units of the projected order are defined positively or negatively. At the basis of his indecision lies this "vicious circle" between the vision of the projected order and the vision of the empirical world. This is the problem of conversion.

At the time of indecision, both orders and both alternatives seem to be lacking in fixed value: "I would go over to Religion and then come back." At one moment he places a positive value on God and Manuel, at another, on the Sacred World and the *zahorín*.

His indecision, which apparently could continue indefinitely, is suddenly set off balance by an external factor. The *zahorines* give up on him: "They tell my father that the time is approaching when 'your son is going to die.'" A relationship is suspended because Jacinto's father is not going to go back to the *zahorines* to have them burn incense for Jacinto, and one power unit declares itself impotent to cure Jacinto. This statement does not mean that Catholic

Action can save him, because the other relationship, that Manuel be willing to forgive him, still has to be established. Hence he does not yet lose faith in the *zahorín*'s judgment that he must die.

The *zahorines* give up on him probably because they think nothing can be done with him, and in order to avoid being blamed for his death, they would attribute it to the grandparents or to the Sacred World, speaking through the *tz'ite'* (the red beans). Ultimately, everyone has to die, as the Traditionalists repeat with some insistence when they bury their dead in front of Catholic Action members, who make fun of the ineffectiveness of the *zahorines*. Their verdict would not have to be to their discredit because even if Jacinto should convert to Catholic Action, which according to them has no nonempirical healing power, he would die in the hands of Catholic Action in any case.

Jacinto's father, nevertheless, does not tell him of the *zahorines*' prophecy, perhaps because he thinks it would draw him away from the Tradition or would speed him toward death. The news reaches Jacinto through the children of the elder Francisco, and in a tone of reproach for his failure to be converted.

Jacinto tells them, "I would be better off dead." He views death as an escape from the tension that he is suffering between the two sets of units. Death looks appealing to him, he is willing to accept it, because this tension is killing him. Paradoxically, through death he wishes to escape from this tension that is killing him and that, for him, means death.

The restructuring that he yearns for but has not been able to find now approaches him with the presence of death. This restructuring means a total loyalty such that Jacinto will declare to his father, "I will keep following my Religion even though I die." This total loyalty includes in its horizon the acceptance of death. Unless death is accepted there is no total loyalty, and without total loyalty, there is no restructuring for Jacinto. However, if death is approaching him in any case and becoming inevitable, the risk of accepting it is becoming almost unavoidable. In seeing himself pressed to accept it, any possibility of doubting is being closed off, and he moves to suspend reason as though he really were dying.

Survival is thus forcing him to leave doubt behind. Indeed, his own lack of a stance (his doubt and indecision) amounts to his inability to attribute to the Sacred World or to God a quality of power great enough to demand total loyalty from him. However, when Jacinto surrenders to one of the two with complete loyalty, he will then be granting it power. But he can find no other reason for conferring this power or surrendering with total loyalty than that of survival. Hence, survival is forcing him out of his doubt. If he does not surrender or does not grant this potential, thereby accepting death, he sees that he will remain in the state of tension that is killing him and that he will die. But the compelling reason of survival overcomes the opposition of doubt: that is, he gives his total assent not because he sees that the Sacred World or God (and the *zahorín* or Manuel) has a potential that can demand such assent, but because he needs to give his assent to survive. Hearing through the children that death is near closes off for him not one alternative or the other (Sacred World or God) but actually removes a deeper alternative, namely, that of being able to doubt and to remain undecided, as opposed to not doubting and opting for something. In other words, it is as though the news were telling him that if he wants to live, he has to decide for something with full assent and loyalty. So as not to die, he then begins taking the steps toward giving up the reason that has kept him stuck between the poles of doubt, in order to give his assent and loyalty with totality to that which has in fact been appearing more viable to him, namely God and Catholic Action. (He has said that he "feels[!] that it is the true Religion.") What remains to be seen is whether Manuel and God will accept him.

The restructuring is complete when it is accepted by Manuel, the representative and president of Catholic Action. It is a true "rite of passage," as Jacinto tells it: "When Manuel came, I felt very ashamed. I seem not to be wearing any shirt, no undershirt, no underwear. I felt very ashamed. 'What do I have for this Manuel to see?' I had entered Catholic Action about two or three months after him."

Manuel's acceptance, indicated by his visit and presence, influences Jacinto's restructuring; it is not simply a seal on a restructuring that has taken place beforehand. Manuel's acceptance radicalizes (totalizes) Jacinto's loyalty and assent, which has already been shown in Jacinto's initiative in calling Manuel. As in rites of passage, this radicalization occurs enveloped in a feeling, which, to use a metaphor, melts in an instant and makes a person's insides malleable. This malleability, this kind of intoxication and loss of meaning, is needed so that the logical impasse, which has remained so sharp and hard, may dissolve, not because it objectively ceases to exist, but because the mind perceiving it becomes clouded and confused to the point where it does not focus on the limitations of that logical fork in the road that was holding it immobilized, but instead lets itself be moved, not by the reason of one of the two contrary poles (because neither has sufficient reason to elicit a total assent as such) but for the sake of sheer survival. Hence, once one has been moved, one seizes the (empirical and projected) pole that one has most been approaching for reasons not entailing this totality (assent, loyalty), and one holds on with all one's might.

In this instance, the powerful feeling that comes pouring into Jacinto's mind is shame, whose deep meaning for someone from San Antonio, and its relationship with *aguardiente* (grain liquor), a ritual drink that removes shame and makes alliances possible, would require an extensive analysis that cannot be performed here (see also Chapter 4). Briefly, shame and its substitute, liquor, occupy the place of mediators between opposite poles, because they change the mind (liquor "changes the blood"). Shame, a feeling that painfully makes its way in like a thorn (*qu'ix*, which means both "shame" and "thorn"), means death of reason for Jacinto, a death Jacinto has been avoiding vis-à-vis Manuel.

The last bastion resisting change is Jacinto's relationship with Manuel. This relationship has become one of shame, because the basis on which the feeling of shame rests consists in seeing as true what used to be seen as a deception (i.e., that one changes in relation to another). If these two points occur, Jacinto will be changing vis-à-vis Manuel, and his change will be shame toward Manuel, who sees it as deception.

Indeed, when Manuel enters, Jacinto feels that Manuel's gaze is denuding him of the "structure" (clothing) that constituted the deception toward Manuel and toward himself and that was preventing the relationship of domination-submission between them. Hence the powerful feeling of shame pours forth.

But to be precise, it is not the feeling itself that confuses logical reason, but rather the vision—prior to the feeling from which it springs (and perhaps might not spring)—of his very person being threatened in its need to subsist vis-à-vis another who is pressing him for the relationship between them to be reformulated if he wishes to continue in existence. Thus concludes the very moment of Jacinto's conversion, and his assent and loyalty toward Manuel and his organization become total.

The upshot of the conversion is that Jacinto begins to get together with his elder brother Francisco and pray with him, and he takes a stand toward his father. This association is the result of the change in the structuring that has taken place. He always remains under his father's power because he is his son, but now he is under Manuel, not the *zahorín*.

Jacinto tells his father that he will follow his Religion "even if I die." This does not mean that the total loyalty is never going to crack again, and that since he has already left Catholic Action once, it could never happen again. Yet that seems unlikely, given the deep and painful character of this most recent conversion to Catholic Action.

He threatens the *zahorines* that he will stone them and bring charges against them in court, because the "Traditions" are making him sick, as if they were witchcraft, and the mayor can imprison witch doctors.

Jacinto recovers, although not completely. The differences between the sickness in his foot and that of his doubt become clear. The one in his foot is not fatal, but that of his doubt truly was, he thinks. He recovers and seeks work outside the municipality, this time with his brother Francisco 1, far from his father's influence. Over time, he makes his First Communion, the significance of which is similar to fulfilling a *cargo* in a *cofradía*. He has to study the catechism, learn to read on his own, and later to write. He gets married and then performs several duties (*cargos*) as part of the elected leadership in the Catholic Action center in the municipality. He has never been wealthy, but his voice now has weight even in meetings of centers from other cantons.

Regarding Jacinto's father, it would be illuminating to analyze his resistance, which has continued to the present, indicating that he gives complete assent to the Tradition, but I have no information on this. Later, however, I will offer a vision, albeit from afar, of the resistance of fathers and *zahorines*.

In conclusion, in view of the rigidity of the logical structure and the impossibility of finding reasons to surrender with complete loyalty to either of the opposite poles, the Sacred World or God, the news of the *zahorín*'s decision that they are giving up on him frees Jacinto from some of the power being exercised over him and sends him toward death. The immediacy of death illuminates his reason, impelling him to emerge from doubt, and that means survival. In order to survive, he accepts the risk of death entailed in a total assent and its corresponding surrender, and embraces the death of logical reason, which was holding him paralyzed before his option. He sends for Manuel. But the restructuring is completed only when Manuel accepts the establishment of the new power relationship. Manuel's symbolic entry into Jacinto's house culminates in this vision of his own deception and nakedness that was blocking such a relationship, which provides the basis for the powerful and pervasive feeling of shame. Loyalty to Manuel and Catholic Action becomes total; conversion is complete. Frequent association with his converted brother, the attack by the *zahorines*, his recovery, his departure to look for work, and his advancement in Catholic Action positions all follow from his conversion.

Hence, the crucial ingredients in the conversion itself were the *zahorines*' decision to end the relationship, the immediacy of death, and Manuel's kindness when he arrives, as a sign of the new relationship: two relationships with death between them.

Comparison of the Two Conversions

An examination of the two cases has enabled us to come to a deeper understanding of the conversion process and the problems entailed in it. By comparison and contrast, I will now seek to summarize some of the factors examined so as to test them further on.

At the Household Level

One difference between the two conversions lies in the fact that Manuel is, and always has been, the owner of his land and house; he is not economically dependent on his father; he earns more than his father; his father is widowed, whereas he has a wife and is almost 30 years old. Although Jacinto owns his land, he received it as an inheritance from his father; he has no house of his own; he is dependent on his father; he is earning nothing (after he becomes sick); his father has a wife, whereas he is alone; and he has barely turned 20. Thus, Manuel has a great deal more power for making the break entailed in conversion, while Jacinto has to derive that power from another source.

I hypothesize that, as a rule, few instances of conversion will occur while one's father is alive, and fewer still if the father owns the land and lives with the dissenting son.

Kinship

Manuel and Jacinto also stand in contrast with regard to the power inherent in kinship. Jacinto derives power from his two brothers who are already converted, one of whom lives in his own house. Manuel, on the other hand, has no brothers.

The work relationship strengthens the kinship relationship between brothers, whether it be to resist or to hasten conversion. In Jacinto's case, when he breaks off the work relationship with his merchant brother who remains with the Tradition, the conversion process is set in motion.

I therefore hypothesize that the extension of the conversion process beyond the household takes place through kinship between siblings, particularly male siblings, or through patrilinear relatives (cousins). Additionally, it appears that this process is strengthened or weakened by work relationships.

Rising to a Higher Level

Manuel can move up one level of articulation, from confronting his adversary to confronting the *zahorines*, because of his relationships of superiority over his hired workers. Jacinto, however, does not have such relationships and cannot do this. He merely supports Manuel's confrontation with the *zahorines*.

I presume that in the conversion process, those who have relationships of superiority over other individuals will make more converts than those who do not, and will occupy leadership in the formal organization. (This hypothesis reiterates the stratification process described in the last chapter.)

Derivation of Power from Within the Community

As a pioneer, Manuel has no power coming from within the community, and he makes up for it with his own power. Jacinto is almost completely lacking in his own power, and he makes up for it with power derived from the formal organization of Manuel and his associates in the vicinity.

I hypothesize that the derivation of such power is necessary for the movement to grow, and that the influence of such derivation will be illustrated in the geographical spread of the converts concentrated in certain cantons and settlements.

Derivation of Power from Outside the Community

Manuel derives power directly from outside the municipality through his trade relationships. He receives information on the success of the movement elsewhere. When he himself is cured, the movement can begin in his own community. Jacinto draws power indirectly through ties that are already formally organized at a stage when the organizations are receiving political support from the church on a national level.

I hypothesize that derivation of power from outside the community must have been a requirement of the movement and that the growth of the movement will have been marked by the stages in which it increased, as will be shown when the story of Catholic Action is told in Chapter 6.

Initiation

Both conversions (but especially Jacinto's, with its long indecision) include the three moments of the *rite of passage*: separation; liminal state in which one belongs neither to the social group from which one is separating, nor to the one that one is joining; and adhesion. The second moment, the liminal stage, entails a vision (and perhaps a feeling as well) that one is nobody, because one is not in any social group, neither one nor the other. It is a social death that brings the one in crisis close to physical death.

I presume that a proportionally high number of conversions will be occasioned by critical situations in which death draws near, such as illness, economic failure, accidents, and the like.

Testing the Hypotheses

It would be logical to follow the order of the previous section considering the hypotheses presented, but in order to situate the process in a geographical framework, we will first study the hypotheses about the derivation of power within the community and then take up the one having to do with the household and the relationship between fathers and sons. Finally, we will study resistance to conversion and the initiation that takes place in conversion, which in the next section of this chapter is examined as a ritual.

We are leaving aside the hypothesis on the ascent in level because it is implicit in the previous chapter, and that on the derivation of power outside the community, which is considered in Chapter 6.

Geographical Extension as an Expression of Derivation of Power from Within the Community

I stated that derivation of power from within the community was necessary for the Catholic Action movement to grow, and that the influence of such derivation would be shown in the geographical advance of converts, scattered or concentrated in certain cantons and hamlets. I will now illustrate how that process of geographical extension took place.

I will utilize Map 5.1, on which I have shown the original locations of the centers, each bearing a number indicating the chronological order in which the center was built, and the zones where Catholic Action converts are the majority, the minority, or are completely absent.

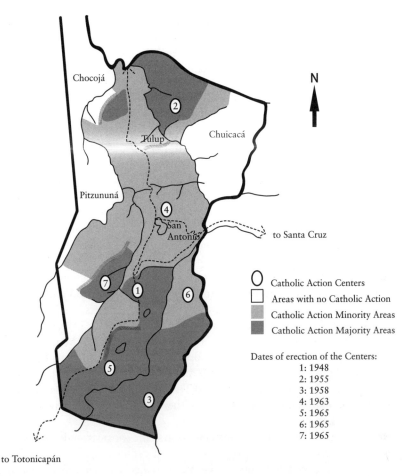

MAP 5.1. *Areas of Catholic Action concentration and location of Catholic Action centers in San Antonio Ilotenango*

Intracommunity derivation is expressed in the continuity of the zones where Catholic Action has a majority, located in the southern part of the municipality, and in the absence of Catholic Action in areas to the north and in the western strip of the municipality. It can be seen that the influence of conversion, which began most strongly in the centers in the south, had not succeeded in penetrating these more distant areas, into which, I assume, conversion would have spread had they bordered on the original focal point.

The *chronological order in which the centers were built* also indicates the geographical pattern of the derivation of power. Centers 1, 2, and 3 are the original focal points where the first convert derived power from outside the municipality. But No. 1, located alongside the road from Totonicapán and Santa Cruz, also served as the coordination point of the other two centers. Then, No. 2 broke off to the north and has not succeeded in extending its power, probably because of its isolation from the rest. Number 3 also broke off from No. 1 to the north, leading to a loss of some of the drive in the south. Number 5 also split away from No. 1, toward the south, and later No. 7 split away from No. 1 toward the north, while No. 3 gave birth to No. 6 off to the north. The order in which the centers broke off shows the influence of proximity to Center No. 1, located in the southern half of the municipality, from which all except for No. 2 have split away.

Derivation of power is hindered by *geographical features*, especially rivers and mountain ridges. The western strip and the northern area (Pitzununá and Chocojá) are cut off by the Tzununá River; and the Chusicá triangle in the northeast is isolated by the Jocol River and other creeks. Ridges and rivers surround and protect people in Tulup from the influence of Centers 2 and 4. A ridge prevents Centers 5 and 7 from occupying areas to the east where Catholic Action is in a minority.

Derivation of power from within the community is greater when an organization has been formalized (center). Thus the areas where Catholic Action is a majority extend out from five centers, for example, Tzancawuib for No. 1, Chuijoj, which is now almost a canton, for No. 3, and Chichó and Xebaquit for No. 5, or where it only reaches a few nearby hamlets, such as around Centers 2 and 7 (Centers 4 and 6 are exceptions).

Around Center No. 4, which does not govern a majority, there are typical *influences of resistance*. Center No. 4 operates in the central town of the municipality, where its power is probably diluted by the presence of ladinos and that of merchants who have established Traditionalist ties, as explained in the previous chapter. (Center No. 6 has neither a majority nor a minority: 50 percent are Catholic Action members.)

Why conversion became most influential first and most strongly in the south and not in the northwest or in the municipal center must be explained by derivation of power from outside the municipality. At that time, most merchants were located in the south, probably because the road between the department capitals of Santa Cruz del Quiché and Totonicapán goes through the southern cantons. By contrast, the road that goes through San Antonio itself is an offshoot from that highway, and the one to the north is not open all the way to Santa Lucía la Reforma (which in any case is not a department capital) because a bridge is missing. Hence, it may be assumed that when conversion has jumped to areas that are not contiguous, in many instances it must have been due to merchants who were influenced by conversion outside the municipality, and who, even though they happened not to live in the areas where merchants were concentrated, introduced the new belief in remote areas, where they remain a minority to this day.

To observe the process in greater detail, I have prepared Map 5.2, showing the gradual growth of conversions in two hamlets in Sacxac from 1960 to 1970. It is an expansion of a portion of the majority zone surrounding Center No. 7 in Map 5.1.

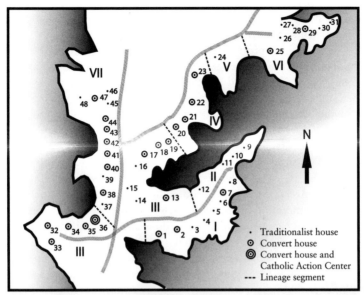

Source: Enlargement of aerial photograph by the National Geographic Institute (1954)

MAP 5.2. *Growth in the number of households converted from 1960 to 1970 in the hamlets of Chicalté and Chuichop of the Sacxac canton*

Again, derivation of power entailing conversion takes place because of *contiguity*. Catholic Action existed in the municipality in 1948, but it was not until 1961, with the conversion of the first household in the hamlet, that the process was set in motion. Once that happened, the result over ten years' time was that twenty-five of the forty-six households in both hamlets converted.

Yet the mechanisms of contiguity must be distinguished from those of kinship. They reinforce one another, but, as will be explained in the next section, they are distinct. To test the former as distinguished from the latter, attention must be paid to the influence from segment to segment (not related by blood but nearby) of the lineage rather than to the influence from neighbor-relative to neighbor-relative of the same segment. In this sense, my point is illustrated by the conversions in the 1962–1964 period, when influence extends from one segment to another (from III to VII), and especially in 1965–1966, when it extends to three more (I, IV, and VI) because conversion moves to nearby nonrelated neighbors.

Even in this microcosm, geographical features exert their influence. It is significant to note how four years go by and conversion still does not jump over the small crest of the hill and spread through the segments that face a different canyon, even though there are houses from the same segment on the other side of the hill (III), and it reaches a different segment on the same side of the hill before reaching the same segment on the other side. Thus, the geographical feature constrains the influence of conversion, not only between different segments, but even within the same segment.

In this instance, it is probably more a matter of the outward effect of conversion, determined by the geographical feature, than physical distance. The hill in question can be crossed in fifteen or twenty minutes, and some houses on either side are as close as or closer than some from segments on the same side of the hill. But the loudspeakers from one side of the hill are aimed west, whereas those on the other point eastward, or toward the other segments from the other side of the canyon. To be converted means allowing Catholic Action members to pray in your house and letting the neighborhood, and if possible, the whole canton, know through the loudspeakers. Who becomes aware of the conversion varies, depending on whether one lives on one side or the other of the mountain. Revealing oneself means overcoming resistance to doing so, and that is easier if others have done so than if one is alone. Hence I said that this geographical feature that rises up in the way determines the effect of conversion toward the outside. The center had to be set up (1965) for conversion to leap over the geographical feature and extend its power to the other segments. Since then, conversion is not reaching into different segments, but is extending through houses of segments already reached.

Contiguity is only one necessary (but not sufficient) condition for power to be derived and for conversion to extend and multiply in different hamlets and cantons. Some segments are surrounded from the standpoint of contiguity (see V) and yet resist conversion, because there is not enough power to convert them, while on the other hand, there are converted houses in the more isolated hamlets where Catholic Action is in a minority that do not spread Catholic Action because they do not have enough power to do so. Territorial proximity is hence a necessary condition, but unless power that can be transmitted is on hand, it is not enough to extend conversion. Derivation outside the hamlets and the canton takes place through a merchant (House 36), whose house later becomes the site for the center.

In conclusion, there is a geographical pattern of growth in the number of converts. They spread by maintaining some proximity, which in many cases is true contiguity, of areas where a majority of people are in Catholic Action. There are areas isolated from the focal points for the spread of Catholic Action where no other explanation need be sought for the absence of Catholic Action than distance. These areas are set apart by geographical features like rivers, which not only separate physically but also confer on their inhabitants a certain common identification with regard to the rest of the municipality.

The geographical pattern expresses the derivation of power from neighbor to neighbor of different segments, and derivation between relatives in the same segment should not be confused with derivation from nonrelated neighbors. (How it operates between neighbors and relatives will be seen later.) The establishment of a center (formal organization) leads to greater power, the derivation of which in nearby areas can be seen in the majority presence of

Catholic Action in cantons or in adjoining hamlets. Proximity or contiguity is a necessary condition for power to be derived and the number of houses to be multiplied, but power drives conversion. Hence, the case of houses not converted when surrounded by converted neighbors has to be explained.

Kinship

I said that the conversion process was extended beyond the home through kinship between siblings, especially male, or between patrilinear relatives, such as children of one's father's brother. My second hypothesis was that the process is bolstered if there are shared work relationships. Let's test these hypotheses below.

We will study the conversion process in one of the patrilinear lineage segments (VII) of the hamlets of Sacxac (Chicalté and Chuichop) from the previous section (cf. Map 5.2) and then confirm our findings with data from other segments.

Lineage Segment

The patrilinear segment is composed of four subsegments (A, B, C, and D), which contain three, three, two, and four houses, respectively. All together the segment is made up of twelve houses extended in a row, one next to the other, along the level area between the top of the mountain ridge and the sharp drop of the river canyon. It will be noted that such a distribution makes the closest relatives, such as brothers, immediate neighbors, while more distant relatives, like cousins or uncles, are somewhat more distant neighbors.

Diagram 5.1 represents the genealogical representation of the segment. The houses have been numbered just as they are on Map 5.2. It is clear that geographical distance corresponds to distance of kinship. (Lineage, segment, and subsegment are explained in Chapter 2.)

Placement in the Process in the Hamlets

Let us situate the conversion process of the segment within the conversion process of the two hamlets Chicalté and Chuichop. (For a more detailed explanation, see Falla 1970.) In 1970 there were 46 houses in the two hamlets, 25 of them already converted and 21 unconverted (see Map 5.2). The conversion process began, as noted, in 1961, and, properly speaking, it has included only 20 of the 25 converted houses. The other five houses were put up between 1961 and 1970. The individuals forming the household in each of these five new houses were already converted when they separated from their fathers or brothers, because they had converted where they were raised. Hence, I say that the conversion process did not involve them as individual units and only involved 20.

The timeline of conversion and building houses can be summarized in Table 5.1. The houses of the particular segment being studied are underlined.

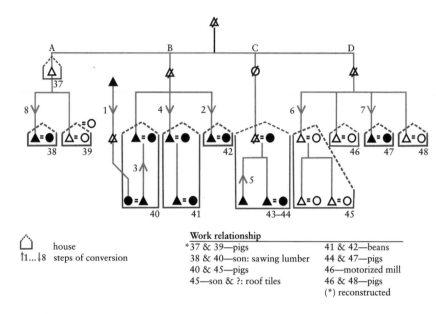

⌂ house

↑1…↓8 steps of conversion

Work relationship

*37 & 39—pigs	41 & 42—beans
38 & 40—son: sawing lumber	44 & 47—pigs
40 & 45—pigs	46—motorized mill
45—son & ?: roof tiles	46 & 48—pigs
	(*) reconstructed

DIAGRAM 5.1. *Lineage segment corresponding to VII in Map 5.2, with converted houses (in black) and nonconverted houses (in white)*

Conversion of the Lineage Segment

We will divide the process of segment conversion into eight steps (see Diagram 5.1). However, only six houses will be converted through these eight steps, because the conversion of one house is frustrated after a few weeks, and converting the next house requires two steps, first that of two members, and then that of the other members of the household in different years. The first four steps convert the houses in subsegment B; the fifth step, that of subsegment C; the sixth and seventh, the two of subsegment D; and the eighth step, one in segment A. The informants providing the account are two center presidents who witnessed and promoted the conversions of all these center members.

Subsegment B.   *Step one*: House 40 (1961). A father and his only son, both married, lived in this house. The father was 59, and the son 24. The son had been living with his wife for seven years and they had a six-year-old girl. Both father and son worked dealing in pigs, which they bought in San Pedro and San Antonio and sold in Totonicapán. They traveled with the father in House 45. The son also worked sawing lumber with a relative who lived nearby in House 38.

The son fought with his wife, and she went off to her grandparents' house in a distant canton. The son became remorseful and went to ask her to come back. The girl's grandfather made it a condition that he accept Doctrine and be converted, otherwise he would not return the girl. The son accepted and was converted. His father, however, did not want to convert. When the Catholic Action members came by at night in response to the son's invitation to pray in his house, the father left the house.

Step two: House 42 (1962). In this house lived a man, 37, and his wife and children. None of the sons was married yet. He worked alone dealing in beans, which he bought in San Antonio, San Pedro, or Santa Lucía and sold in Totonicapán. Sometimes he traveled as a merchant with his nephew (House 40). He was the younger brother of the father in House 40, who refused to convert. His nephew was already converted, as we saw. Upon coming back from the town square on Tuesday he was talking along the way with his nephew and another man, who would later become the center president, a neighbor slightly farther away. The two were urging him to become converted and stop drinking. One of his sons took sick. Instead of going to the *zahorín*, he went to his nephew and to the one who would become the center president, who went with other members to pray in his house.

Steps three and four: Houses 40 and 41 (1964). This is the same House 40 as in step one, and the house of his other brother. They were converted together.

The composition of the home in house 40 has already been described. In House 41 lived a man, 41, with his wife and a son, 21, with his wife. They worked as dealers in beans, which they bought in San Antonio, San Pedro, and Santa Lucía and sold in Totonicapán, traveling with his brother from House 42.

Thus in these three houses (40, 41, 42) lived three brothers, the oldest in 40, the one in the middle in 41, and the youngest in 42. The oldest one refused to be converted, even though his son had already been converted. The one in the middle was not converted, while the youngest one was.

The two unconverted brothers were converted as follows: a child of the youngest one had died. The other two brothers were with their younger brother

TABLE 5.1. *Chronology of converted houses and houses built in the hamlets of Chicalté and Chuichop in Sacxac (1961–1970)*

Year	Number of house converted	Number of house built
1961	36, 34, 35	
1962	42	
1963	32	
1964	40, 41	
1965	22	
1966	29, 1, 2	23
1967	43	17
1968	47, 13, 18	19
1969	21, 20	33 and 44
1970	7, 38, 25	

Notes: a. Numbering corresponds to Map 5.2 and Diagram 5.1. b. Numbers of segment in the study (VII) are underlined.

at the wake. The relationships between the three brothers were tense at that moment. To pay for his child's funeral the youngest brother had sold a piece of land to the middle brother. This plot bordered on the oldest brother's land, and so the oldest brother was angry at his other two brothers, and while they were having breakfast at the wake he uttered a harsh word against them. The middle brother lost his temper and threw a bowl at the oldest one's face, taking off a piece of skin. The fight was serious and the oldest one ended up in the hospital in Santa Cruz del Quiché, and the middle one was jailed there.

The middle brother encountered Christian Doctrine in jail and was converted; the older one pondered things in the hospital and, upon leaving, he joined Catholic Action (three years after his son).

Subsegment C.   *Step 5*: House 43–44 (1967). This is a single house, which two years after being built was split into two. In one house lived a widow with her two sons, the older one, 32, with his wife, and the younger one, 17 and unmarried. The older one was the head of the household, not the widow. He dealt in pigs between San Antonio and Totonicapán together with his uncle from House 47. The deceased grandmother of these two brothers and the deceased father of the three brothers who were now converted were brother and sister.

The older unmarried brother brought conversion into the house. When the Catholic Action members sang at night in the homes of his nearby relatives, he says that "it was painful to him." He heard the loudspeaker as he was already in bed. "I'm crying," he used to say.

The older one used to drink, and he once had Q 54 stolen from him when he was passed out drunk. He had also had another unpleasant experience because the *zahorín* who did divining for his widowed mother had taken advantage of her and left her a son. For these reasons he sent his younger brother to a rosary that was being sung for nine nights at the home of another neighbor, not a relative, in preparation for a mass that was going to be celebrated at that house. On the third day, the older brother happened to pass by as they were putting up the loudspeaker. He was on his way to get some liquor. The center president asked him when he was going to be converted and he stayed for the rosary. They then agreed upon the date for his conversion.

His widowed mother was against it, as was his wife, but he said that if his wife was unwilling to accept Religion, she should leave. The night of his conversion, when the "brethren" came to pray, his wife hid in the ravine, and the next day she went off to her mother's house, taking their little child with her, but she returned the following day.

Subsegment D.   *Step six*: House 45 (1968). Three married couples were living in this house, the father, 53, and his two sons, ages 25 and 23, with their wives. They worked as pig merchants between San Antonio and Totonicapán, traveling together with their cousin from House 40. The youngest son made clay tiles (I do not know with whom). The now deceased father of the head of the household was a brother of the deceased grandmother of the brothers in House 43–44 and brother of the father of the first three brothers converted, in Houses 40, 41, and 42.

The head of the house had joined Catholic Action because he had heard the loudspeaker at his relatives' house at night, and when his children took sick, one with fever and paroxysms and the other with pain around the waist, he called on the Catholic Action members and they prayed and gave them medicines, urging them to go to the doctor in Totonicapán, until the children were better. The head of the household was converted. His wife, however, who was the daughter of a *zahorín* in another canton, refused to be converted, and when two Catholic Action members came to pray in their house, she just sat down and watched. She threatened to go back to her parents' home. Her *zahorín* father was performing "Traditions" from afar, as his daughter had asked him.

Because of his wife, they left Catholic Action after a month. At a rosary the head of the household told the members that they should not come back. "Maybe when my father-in-law dies," he told them. The 23-year-old son likes Catholic Action, but his father does not allow him to go.

Step seven: House 47 (1968). A man, 41, lived in this house with his wife. He was the third brother of the head of the household who went back to the Tradition. He worked as a pig merchant between San Antonio and Totonicapán with a nephew from House 43–44. He drank a lot and spoke against Catholic Action, for example, saying that its members gave their wives to the priest.

He was converted at the same time as his brother. He explained that there would be no one to perform "Tradition" for him because he did not know how. But when his brother went back to the Tradition, he did not. His wife had a sister in Catholic Action.

Subsegment A. *Step eight*: House 38 (1970). In this house lived a man, 25, and his wife. His father, who was still alive, was a brother of the now dead parents in the subsegments already mentioned. His work was sawing lumber with the first convert in the segment, the one who had lost his wife in a fight and had gotten her back under the condition that he be converted. Both were approximately the same age, although the first convert was his nephew to the second degree.

The first convert advised him to be converted. His father, who was a pig merchant and lived in his own separate house, did not want his son to convert. He answered him, "If you don't give me permission, what if I get involved with another woman?" His brother had two women. His father replied, "That's up to you."

This takes the conversion process of the lineage segment up to 1970. All of *segment B* (three houses) and all of *segment C* (two houses, one built after conversion) are converted. In *segment D* (four houses), only one is converted, and in segment A (three houses) likewise only one is converted.

Informants offer the following reasons for the lack of conversion in these houses. The three in *segment* D: one returned to the Tradition because of the strength of the *zahorín* father-in-law; another (48), a pig merchant, seems not to have been the object of enough pressure from a converted brother; while the third (46) is unlikely to be converted, according to the center president, because his wife is the sister of a rich Traditionalist merchant and he owns the only motor-driven corn mill in the two hamlets, probably purchased with money loaned by his brother-in-law. It also seems that 46 and 48 work together in their pig business. The two in *segment* A: according to the center president, the household of the father (37), as an old man who does not speak Spanish, naturally resists, and the brother who deals in pigs like his father (39) is unlikely to be converted because he has two wives.

Processes Recurring in the Segment

In the account of these conversions, we find some processes recurring. First, conversion takes place in concentric circles, the inner circle being that of several brothers (for example, subsegment B), then that of relatives living in the vicinity of these brothers (subsegment C), and finally that of relatives from the same segment living somewhat farther away from the original focal point of conversion (subsegment D). In all instances they are male relatives connected along patrilinear lines.

Confirmation of These Processes

Table 5.2 supports my contention that the trend of conversion from brother to brother is common to the two hamlets. Of the sixteen converts who have brothers in another house in these hamlets, fourteen have the support of a brother in Catholic Action. The same trend can be noted in nonconverts: of thirteen who have a separate house, twelve are supported by Traditionalist brothers. Hence, I deduce that there is a tendency to derive power from a brother, either to be converted or to resist conversion.

Likewise, the table confirms the tendency to derive power from patrilinear relatives in the same segment when there are no brothers. As in the case of the segment studied, these are usually patrilinear first or second cousins. Of the nine converts who do not have a brother in a separate house, seven have a male relative from the same segment in a separate house who is converted. Of the nine nonconverts who have no brother in a separate house, all nine have a male relative from the same segment in a separate Traditionalist household.

This concentric-circle pattern, with brothers in the center and then relatives who are not brothers but living nearby in an outer circle, can be verified on Map 5.2, which shows how converted households first appear in the immediate vicinity of the lineages and then conversion spreads to more houses in the vicinity, but not those of brothers of the initial core.

TABLE 5.2. *Brother-to-brother and member-to-member (nonbrother) relationships in the same segment in Traditionalist and Catholic Action houses in two hamlets of Sacxac*

Houses	Traditionalist	Converted	Total
One of whose members has <u>brothers</u> in another house . . .	. . . and these brothers are Traditionalists = 12	. . . and these brothers are Catholic Action = 14	26
	. . . and these brothers are not Traditionalists = 1	.... and these brothers are not Catholic Action = 2	3
	Subtotal = 13	Subtotal = 16	29
Some of whose members only have <u>members from the same segment</u> in another house . . .	. . . and these members are Traditionalists = 7	. . . and these members are Catholic Action = 9	16
	. . . and these members are not Traditionalists = 0	· . . . and these are not Catholic Action =0	0
	Subtotal = 7	Subtotal = 9	16
that have no <u>brothers</u> or members of the <u>same segment</u> in another house	1	0	1
Total	21	25	46

Shared Work Relationships

We have now established the first part of the hypothesis stated above. The second has to do with the influence of work relationships on conversion, either for resisting it or for driving it forward. The segment studied has a monopoly on trade in piglets raised in San Antonio, San Pedro Jocopilas, and Santa Lucía la Reforma and sold in Santa María Chiquimula, San Francisco el Alto, and Totonicapán. It seems to be a specialization—inherited from one's father throughout this segment—that came from Momostenango almost a century ago and took root in this locale, which is located between the sites for purchasing and reselling. The pattern within this specialization is that if one member of a segment has changed religious affiliation, he tends to bring into that affiliation the segment member with whom he works and travels; however, the specialization does not require that all segment members work together, and some can be converted while others are not.

In this sense it stands in contrast to segment II, in which none of the houses has converted, because all the adult (married) men in the segment belong to a sarabande musical group: marimba and saxophone players, drummer, and so forth. Here, either all are converted or none are. But they cannot all be converted, because Catholic Action has prohibited marimba groups because they promote drinking, and because the head of the group is a *zahorín* from another canton and the father of some of the marimba players.

TABLE 5.3. *Number of individuals in two hamlets of Sacxac who work with a brother or relative from another house, or not, by worker's religious affiliation*

	Work with brother or relative of another house			Do not work with brother or relative of another house	
	Trad. w/Trad.	Conv. w/Conv.	Trad. w/Conv.	Trad.	Conv.
	12	8	2	23	20
Subtotal		22		43	
Total			65		

Coming back to the segment studied, further precisions could be made about the *degree* of the need for collaboration in the various kinds of work done by members of this segment (and by others). For example, sawing lumber necessarily demands that there be at least two men, one on either end of the saw. Making roof tiles also means working necessarily in a team of four or five, one bringing water, one molding, another handling the oven, and so forth. A pig merchant could travel alone if he were only taking a few animals, but when there are twenty little pigs, it is hard to handle them by oneself. A bean merchant can travel alone, although it is a good idea to travel with people one knows, especially if one travels some portions on foot and spends the night outside market towns. Finally, the one with the motorized mill does not need help from anyone outside his house, because his wife can run it and she can deal with customers.

I assume that the gradation in the need for working together, depending on the type of occupation, has a differentiated influence on conversion, although in the scant figures from six hamlets of workers (see Diagram 5.1), it cannot be determined. The only thing shown is that the religious affiliation is the same for both members of a pair of workers, except in one case in which there was agreement, but it was then undone (case of frustrated conversion: House 45).

In the two hamlets under study, there are 65 working men: 22 of them work with a brother or a relative of another house, and 43 do not work with a brother or relative of another house. Of the 22, there are 12 Traditionalists in work partnership with Traditionalists, 8 converts with converts, and only 2 of a work pair in which one is a Traditionalist and the other a convert. The remaining 43 men in the two hamlets do not work with other men or relatives from another house in shared work. Only in some instances do they work together with brothers or sons *within* the same household.

From these numbers it can be seen that there is a very high correspondence between the collaboration of brothers or relatives and religious affiliation, even if they live in different houses. This is what I sought to prove in the second part of the hypothesis above.

To conclude, it may be noted that in the forty-six houses in these hamlets, there are six converted outside merchants and two Traditionalist outside merchants, thereby confirming the connection between outside merchants and conversion established in Chapter 3 (the pig and bean merchants mentioned above are not outside merchants because they operate within the region).

Conclusion

The two hypotheses stated at the beginning of the section are now confirmed: first, the conversion process takes place through kinship between male siblings and then between patrilinear relatives; and second, that process is strengthened by work relationships between brothers or relatives.

Son's Power vis-à-vis His Father

I have hypothesized above that there will be few conversions while one's father is alive, and fewer still if the father lives with the dissident son and therefore still owns the land. This hypothesis is illustrated in the segment under study, because in only two of the six converted houses does the son convert while the father is alive. In one of these cases, the son does not live with his father (House 38), and in the other, he does (House 40). In this latter case, even though the converted son lives with his father, he is the only son and the father will not be able to disinherit him because he has no other sons to whom he can leave an inheritance. There is also the case of one of the sons in House 45, where conversion was reversed. He says that his father does not allow him to be converted.

Let us again look at the forty-six houses of the two hamlets together to see whether this hypothesis is confirmed (see Table 5.4). I must first explain how I define "son" and "father" here. "Son" will be a male who already has a wife, and if he also has male children, they do not have a wife. This means a married man who is still not a father-in-law of his son's wife, or one who is not *chuchkajaw* (through his son). "Father" will be a male who has one or more married male children. That means a man who is now a father-in-law of his son's wife—he is now *chuchkajaw*. Keep in mind that the term *chuchkajaw* means the father or mother of the spouse of one's child. It is something like "co-in-law" (*consuegro*; see Chap. 2). "Sons" may or may not have a living father; they may or may not live with him; they may be only sons; or they may decide against their father or not.

Turning again to look at the forty-six houses in the two hamlets (Table 5.4), we find twenty-five converted households. Of these twenty-five households, only twenty existed at the time of conversion. The other five broke off from the twenty after the latter converted. These twenty were already constituted as social units when they made their decision to accept conversion.

In eight of these twenty, a son had a living father, whether he was living in that same house or in a house other than that of his son. In the other twelve houses, the sons did not have a living father.

TABLE 5.4. *Houses of hamlets in canton of Sacxac by categories shown (1970)*

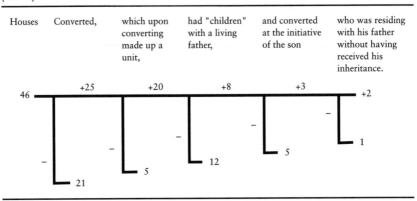

Houses	Converted,	which upon converting made up a unit,	had "children" with a living father,	and converted at the initiative of the son	who was residing with his father without having received his inheritance.
46	+25	+20	+8	+3	+2
					1
	–	–	–	5	
–		5	12		
21					

Only three sons from the eight houses took initiative against the resistance or inertia of their fathers to convert the house in which they were living, constituting 15 percent (3 of 20) of the conversions. In the other five houses (of the eight), the fathers took the initiative, or 25 percent of a total of twenty conversions. Finally, in the remaining twelve conversions within these twenty converted households, the ones taking the initiative were sons without living fathers (see Table 5.5).

This seems to bear out the hypothesis that there are few cases of such conversions in which the sons go against the father's wishes. What is lacking, however, is a precise comparison with the Traditionalists, which I cannot make because I do not have information on the sons who met with resistance from their fathers, who did not allow them to be converted.

The approximate comparison that *can* be made is based on the number of sons with and without living fathers among converts from the twenty houses and Traditionalists from the twenty-one houses. The reasoning is that if there are proportionally more sons with living fathers among the nonconverts than among the converts, it is because living fathers keep them from converting. Table 5.6 below offers the evidence and confirms the assumption.

The difference between converting or not arises from the number of cases of sons with a living father who live in each house: the eight converted sons with a living father live in eight houses (one per house), while the fifteen nonconverts with a living father live in fifteen houses (1.5 per house).

This is all the evidence I can present to corroborate the part of the hypothesis having to do with the difficulty in converting faced by sons while their parents are still alive. With regard to the second part of the hypothesis, having to do with the influence of *residing* with one's father, which means that the inheritance has not been imparted to the son, we can compare the number of sons (converted or not) who live with their father, with those (converted or not) who do not live with their father (Table 5.7). The reasoning is that if living with one's father has a negative influence on conversion, among converts there ought to be proportionally fewer sons living with their fathers than among nonconverts. That is not borne out by the evidence presented, however. Hence the second part of the hypothesis is not verified.

Resistance

I have hypothesized that the cores of resistance to conversion will be found among those individuals who are most initiated into the Tradition. I said that the degree of initiation of such individuals would be measured by the number of step-by-step rites of passage covered within the Tradition. By way of examples, I mentioned marriage, *cargos* of *cofradías* in hierarchical order, becoming a father-in-law (*chuchkajaw*) through the marriage of one's son, and the rise to *principal*, especially inclusion in the group of *zahorines*. Correspondingly, I said that nonconverts would be older than converts.

TABLE 5.5. *Person taking conversion initiative in houses in two hamlets of Sacxac*

Person initiating conversion		Houses converted
Fathers		5
Sons	with fathers alive	3
	with fathers not alive	12
Total		20

TABLE 5.6. *Sons converted and not, in two hamlets of Sacxac, by whether father is alive*

Sons		Converted		Total
		Yes	No	
Father alive	Yes	8	15	23
	No	12	11	23
Total		20	26	46

Note: Totals of converts and noncoverts do not add up to total of houses converted or not, as children are counted here and several may live in one house.

TABLE 5.7. *Sons with father alive in two hamlets of Sacxac, converts or not, depending on whether they live with their father or not*

Sons with father alive		Converted		Total
		Yes	No	
Live with father	Yes	7	11	18
	No	1	4	5
Total		8	15	23

First, with regard to (traditional) *marriage*, or *c'ulnem*, described in Chapter 2, it is difficult to find any way to prove this hypothesis because, before they reach the age at which one passes through that ritual, men and women in this society are under the guardianship of their parents or anyone replacing them, and hence few are converted before taking a wife or husband. Before marriage, individuals have practically no power, and so although they are not initiated into marriage—an initiation that would act on them as resistance to being converted—they do not have the power to convert even if there is no resistance.

The only evidence I can offer to show the effect of resistance as a result of initiation in marriage I obtain from data on divorce. The argument is that through divorce (leaving the woman chosen by one's parents) one rejects the initiation signified by the traditional marriage, and hence individuals who by their own choice have negated the meaning of traditional marriage at some time would be more willing to convert than those who have not negated it. The data should indicate that among those joined in marriage who have not yet been initiated into other rituals (*cofradía*, for example), those who have left the women chosen by their parents have converted in greater numbers than those who have not left them.

I do not have precise data because I do not know which *cargos* in a *cofradía* each individual has served. I therefore cannot isolate the initiating factor of such *cargos*. Nevertheless, I can eliminate the factor of becoming fathers-in-law. If we take those who have gone through the marriage rite but are not yet fathers-in-law and compare the divorced to the nondivorced, we obtain the following results that tend to bear out the hypothesis: half of the twelve converts have left their wife, while of the eleven nonconverted only around a quarter (3) have done so (see Table 5.8). (I have not included in this total the sons whose fathers are alive, so as to have better control over those whose decision is freer because they are not dependent on their fathers.)

A second initiation rite that could be a factor in resistance to conversion is service in the hierarchically ordered *cofradías*. In the previous chapter, we found that 22 percent of the converts had done service in the *cofradías*, as

TABLE 5.8. *Men who have been married, are not fathers-in-law, and whose fathers have died by now: converts or not, whether divorced or not (in two hamlets of Sacxac)*

Sons		Converted		Total
		Yes	No	
Divorced	Yes	6	3	9
	No	6	8	14
Total		12	11	23

Note: Divorce = abandonment of at least one woman to whom one was joined by the traditional marriage ritual, *c'ulnem*.

TABLE 5.9. *Houses, converted and not, whether they are of fathers-in-law or not*

Houses		Converted		Total
		Yes	No	
Of fathers-in-law	Yes	7[a]	10	17
	No	13[a]	11	24
Total		20	21	41

Note: [a]This figure does not correspond with the figures of 8 and 12 of Table 5.4 because there the issue was children (8) with living parents, even if not converted, and here the issue is only converted parents (7). Of these seven, only four took the initiative of converting.

opposed to the general population (including converts), for which the figure was 44 percent. I should also state that in those percentages I did not isolate the initiating factor of other rites, such as becoming a father-in-law or a *principal*.

A third rite is that of becoming a father-in-law, or *chuchkajaw*. Here I am referring to the traditional marriage ritual itself, but in terms of what is done by the parents, rather than the son. When the son rises to a higher level, they also rise. Moreover, the main actors in the traditional wedding are the parents of the young people getting married. They pay the expenses (see Chap. 2).

Those who are fathers-in-law, I assume, are less likely to convert than those who are not but are married. The data from the two hamlets of Sacxac seem to confirm this assumption, inasmuch as of the twenty houses converted, seven are of fathers-in-law and thirteen are not. Of the twenty-one nonconverted houses, ten are of fathers-in-law and eleven are not (see Table 5.9).

Comparing the average age both of the four fathers-in-law who take the initiative to convert (42.4 years) and of the other three who do not take the initiative to convert (50.2) with the average age of the fathers-in-law who presumably have the initiative to resist (60.7) sheds light on the likely existence of other initiation factors that are stronger when one is older, such as inclusion among the *zahorines*. Thus it is verified that those who are fathers-in-law tend to be harder to convert than those who are not, although I have not excluded other higher-level initiations.

Fourth is the initiation of becoming a *principal*. Here I define the *principales* as those who have fulfilled the *cargos* of town mayor and *alcalde* of the *cofradía* of San Antonio, which is the most important *cofradía*. They are now taking it easy and in principle become part of the council of elderly men who will designate the candidate for mayor, the *mayores*, *auxiliares*, and *alguaciles*. To this day, there has been only one case of a *principal* (who was not a *zahorín*) who has converted, out of the twenty-two men who have served in the *alcaldía* of the *cofradía* of San Antonio. Ordinarily they are older people, who are now fathers-in-law. Thus, here it can be seen how being a *principal* (in the Tradition) embodies an initiation *within* the Tradition that is even more resistant to the pressure for conversion than being a father-in-law.

The fifth initiation step that lends resistance to conversion is that of being a *zahorín*. In the whole municipality there are fifty-eight *zahorines*, only some of whom are *principales*. Because of their advanced age, almost all are fathers-in-law, or *chuchkajaw*, hence another word for *zahorín* in Quiché, besides *aj k'ij*, is *chuchkajaw*. None of these fifty-eight *zahorines* has converted during the twenty-two years in which Catholic Action has been in existence. Their resistance can be regarded as rock-hard. (Today, in 1970 there are fifty-eight of them; twenty-two years ago there must have been more, hence the number of *zahorines* who could have converted is greater than fifty-eight.)

These *zahorines* extend their power over other houses of relatives, primarily sons and daughters. They have an influence on them, even though they live in separate houses. This influence is noted especially in the cantons like Chichó and in hamlets like those studied, where conversion has been pushed almost to its maximum limit, and according to the center leaders, "those who remain aren't going to be converted, because the only ones left are the *zahorines*."

In the twenty-one houses in the hamlets of Sacxac, three are those of *zahorines* and eight more are of the sons (four) and daughters (three) or grandchildren (one) of *zahorines*. They add up to eleven, that is, over half of those who have not been converted (see Table 5.10). Indeed, there is no former *zahorín* among the converted, nor any house of a son, daughter, or grandchild of a *zahorín*.

In the canton of Chichó, where pressure for conversion has been even stronger, twenty-seven of the forty-six houses are in Catholic Action, eighteen are Traditionalist, and one is Protestant. Among the eighteen Traditionalist houses

TABLE 5.10. *Reasons for resistance to being converted of the twenty-one unconverted houses in the two hamlets of Sacxac*

Reason for resistance	Explanation of reason	Houses	Fathers-in-law
Zahorín	Is a *zahorín*	3	3
	Has relationship to a *zahorín*:		
	—sons	4	2
	—daughters	3	2
	—grandchildren	1	0
Traditionalist	—Now old	1	1
	—Brother is Traditionalist	1	1
	—Rich wife is Traditionalist	1	0
"Tradition"	—Two wives	1	0
	—Liquor makers	1	0
Conflict	Overland with Catholic Action relatives	2	1
Inertia	Lack of strength	3	0
Totals		21	10

DIAGRAM 5.2. *Kinship relationship of nonconverted House 8 of the two hamlets of Sacxac with* zahorines

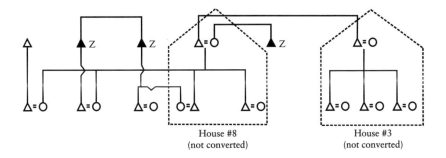

House #8
(not converted)

House #3
(not converted)

there are six unconverted houses of *zahorines* (with seven *zahorines*) and two unconverted houses with a brother and grandson of *zahorines*. Taken together, these eight houses are almost half of the houses not converted. None of the twenty-seven Catholic Action houses is that of a *zahorín*, and only one is home to a grandson of a *zahorín*.

A *zahorín* wields influence through his kinship relations, which are mutually self-reinforcing. One example can be found in the interconnecting relationships of the members of House 8, whose head is married to the sister of a *zahorín* from another canton, one of whose sons is married to the daughter of another *zahorín* from another canton, and in turn (something that escaped me in classifying my data) two of his daughters are married to sons of two *zahorines,* who are brothers in another hamlet. At the same time, according to my informants, the head of House 8 influences his brother (House 3) to keep him from converting, even though this brother has no closer relationship to *zahorines* (see Diagram 5.2).

The average age of these ten *zahorines* (three from the two hamlets of Sacxac and seven from Chichó) plus another eight from Xebaquit is approximately 67. Although the information on ages comes from Catholic Action informants, who are younger than the *zahorines*, and tends to be exaggerated, in any case the high average age of *zahorines* is in keeping with their role of praying for others and answering requests for consultations when they can no longer do farm work. Of these eighteen *zahorines*, three are under 50, the youngest being 43, who has a large clientele. This information indicates that although the number of *zahorines* is going to decline, the *zahorines* are not going to disappear at least in the next twenty or twenty-five years.

In Chapter 3 (note 2) I explained the depth and intricacy of the belief practiced by *zahorines* in using the traditional calendar.

With regard to the hypothesis that converts will be younger than Traditionalists, it is confirmed according to the data from the two hamlets of Sacxac, inasmuch as the average age of heads of household of the twenty converted houses at the time of conversion is 38.5 years, and the average age of heads of household of nonconverted houses is 48 years. Although men as young as 20 or 25 or even younger have begun the conversion of a house, nevertheless the average age of the rebellious individuals is higher (38.5).

Finally, I want to say something about other factors of resistance that have been mentioned in passing in the section on kinship when dealing with a single segment. Of the twenty-one houses in the two hamlets of Sacxac, eleven have not converted (see Table 5.10) for the already presented reason having to do with *zahorines*; another three because of Traditionalist relationships with people related to *zahorines*; another two because their behavior (making clandestine liquor or having two wives) is incompatible with what is preached by Catholic Action but not with the Tradition; two more because of a land dispute with Catholic Action relatives; and finally three out of inertia, for lack of pressure to convert. Pressure is connected to geographical extension and to the increase of the number of converts in other hamlets and cantons.

What is allowable in the Tradition as opposed to Catholic Action doctrine includes other kinds of conduct, the most characteristic and well known of which is getting drunk (*chupar*). Drunkenness, however, seems to be a more ambiguous behavior than the clandestine manufacture of liquor, for example, because of its harmful effects such as wasting money, getting into fights, and so forth, which are experienced more close at hand. When someone drinks in excess, "there's a place to get a hold on him," as one Catholic Action leader observed. It is not the same as when he does not drink and is not hostile to Catholic Action.

To summarize what has been presented in this section, the numbers of those who have not yet become fathers-in-law but have rejected the traditional marriage ritual by getting divorced; those who have served in *cofradías*; those who are fathers-in-law and enjoy the respectful relationship of *chuchkajaw*; the only *principal* in the municipality who has been converted; and the complete absence of converted *zahorines* in the entire municipality—all point to a graduated series of initiations that increasingly solidify resistance to anti-*cofradía* beliefs. The fact that unconverted heads of households are older than those who are converted reflects the chronological sequence of such initiations: those who are older will usually have gone through more steps of initiation. Finally, the search for other categories of resistance among those who are unrelated to *zahorines* gives us a range of reasons, some of which have to do more directly with what is empirical and less with initiation, such as not losing one's role as liquor manufacturer, land conflicts, having two wives, and so forth.

The levels into which each of the steps considered give initiation are at the same time levels of articulation of power. I have therefore not sought to present initiations in isolation from the power structure. I have only sought to show the source from which I am assuming that absolute adherence to a belief comes, which is initiation (the rite of passage to reach these levels of power). Simply being at a higher level of power is not the source of an absolute adherence, although being at a higher level of power usually implies having passed through steps of initiation.

Initiation

I have assumed that, given the structure of the act of conversion, which includes the three elements of the rite of passage (separation, liminal state, and adherence), and given the liminal state as a social "death" (not belonging to any unit), situations of being close to physical death would make it possible to express this social death and would facilitate conversion, and that a high number of conversions would be caused by *critical situations* in which death is near.

When converts are asked why they converted they tend to answer in one of the three following ways: (1) that it was because of "temptation," and they tell the story; (2) by a decision (*por voluntad*, "will"), and they tell the story; or (3) they simply tell the story. Here I will relate critical situations to conversions because of "temptation."

"Temptation" means some great suffering, such as one's own sickness or that of one's children or one's wife, which entails expenditures of money for the person in question. It can mean the death of one's child or wife, or some other misfortune, such as falling into a ravine, losing one's sales operation, and so forth. *Temptation* is something opposed to *salvation*, and it has a nonempirical connotation because it is believed that some nonempirical element such as witchcraft, one's deceased grandparents, fate (*la suerte*) managed by inconceivable forces, or God is involved.

Conversions by *decision* imply that there was no temptation nor was the person forced one way or another, but that Catholic Action was attractive because of the singing, friendships, lessons in how to read, and so forth. Nevertheless, some say it was "by a decision" in order to avoid telling the story of a fight with a brother or some other humiliation. In these cases, the story told by other people then reveals more.

Conversions of the latter type include those implying a degree of pressure through human beings, which is regarded as independent of nonempirical forces. Such is the case, for example, of someone who converts because he does not find a bride among Traditionalists or because he needs money or because he wants to avoid division in the home.

The situation that immediately brings about conversion and that makes up the heart of the story told by the convert or by a third person familiar with it I will here call the *occasion* of the conversion. My reports on the occasions for conversions for the two hamlets of Sacxac and for converts in the fifth center (cantons of Chichó and Xebaquit) come mainly from other people who were actively involved in winning over the person in question.

In the two hamlets of Sacxac, of the twenty houses converted, twelve were conversions *by temptation* and the rest were *by decision* or by pressure. Of the conversions *by temptation*, five were because of a sick child (three) or wife (two); five because of the death of a relative: children (two), grandchildren under their care (two), and a sister (one); one because of witchcraft over his land; and one because while drunk he lost his selling booth (see Table 5.11). Of the remaining eight, which are not well classified as "by decision" or by pressure, three were through the influence of the converted brother or wife's brother; three because of the influence of the children or of the convert's wife, who were attracted to Catholic Action; and two because of a fight that took one to the hospital and the other to jail.

In the seven instances of a "father" who converted in the two hamlets of Sacxac, two have been conversions at the initiative of the son, and the other five were at the father's initiative. The first two have been by temptation; four of the remaining five have been by temptation. These data point to a trend in which a greater crisis is needed for one who is more deeply initiated (the father) to be de-initiated from the previous religious affiliation; those who are barely or less initiated (the sons) in the older form of religion can be de-initiated without a crisis.

Regarding the twenty-one nonconverted houses, I have also investigated whether there might have been "temptations" such as those that served as the occasion for Catholic Action members to be converted and to what extent they might have had an influence. Although the information gathered does not present so many temptations of suffering among the unconverted as in those who converted, I have become aware of "temptations" in eight houses: deaths of sons, death of a daughter, illness of children or of the head of the house himself, falling from a tree, and a house catching fire. However, the persons who suffered such temptations remained rooted in their belief and continued going to the *zahorines* despite the Catholic Action members who were trying to take advantage of such situations to win them over.

The information on the fifty-one persons who converted by their own decision in Chichó-Xebaquit confirms the hypothesis on the large number of conversions through temptation. In these two cantons, twenty-six of the total conversions were by temptation. Again we find illness, whether of oneself

Table 5.11. *Occasions of conversion "by temptation" in two Sacxac hamlets*

Temptation	Houses
Illness	
—of children	3
—of wife	2
Death	
—of children	2
—of grandchildren	2
—of sister	1
Witchcraft on land	1
Loss of selling booth	1
Total Conversions	12

(eight), of children (ten), or of one's wife (two); the death of a child (three) or of a wife (one); and dreams of bad omens (two).

The economic aspect enters into all instances of temptation: illness drives people deeper into debt to the point where they cannot endure what they later regard as the exploitation ("they only do it to get money") of the *zahorines*, so they then go to the Catholic Action leaders. If there are *zahorines* in the house or very close relatives who are *zahorines*, this aspect of economic exploitation does not exist because no payment is required of them. This aspect brings the individual to the brink of destitution, and death places his very survival in jeopardy.

In all instances, Tradition is referred to as a system of beliefs and practices whose most genuine representative is the *zahorín*. When what is later regarded as a failure of the Tradition is experienced, the way is opened to the loss of faith. Those who are not converted are very reassured in their beliefs, especially through the influence of the *zahorines* operating through their relatives, and they reinterpret the failures of the healing rituals.

Most of the "temptations" have to do with illness or death from illness. It seems that at the beginning of the conversion movement, Catholic Action was evidently more successful in restoring health than later, perhaps because at that time the Traditionalists were more reluctant to use medicines, whereas in the past few years some pills are now accepted, although there is still a resistance to injections. Nevertheless, it cannot be attributed to the movement of modern medicine, because some converted despite the death of their children, and others who used medicines were converted through faith in prayer as a nonempirical instrument of healing.

According to one Catholic Action leader—and this is what he preaches—illness comes from two causes: from God or from neglect. If it is through neglect, medicine is available; if it is from God, prayer is available. One cannot always tell the difference. Both means have to be used. But if it is a matter for prayer, one has to let God take the sick person if He wishes. Hence, he is very insistent on this point to the one who is going to convert, apparently more now than before, and emphasizes that he must be ready to accept death as a consequence of the illness for which he has sought the help of prayer in Catholic Action, and that he must not return to the Tradition if his child dies. If the prospective convert is not wholeheartedly resigned to the death of the child, this leader does not regard him as well converted.

Thus I have shown how, in a high percentage of cases, the liminal state of conversion has been brought about by critical situations that are regarded as "temptations."

Conversion "Ritual"

Here I want to show how the last step in conversion takes place in a kind of initiation, and how this ritual signifies and achieves the completion of the conversion with its characteristic of total adherence.

When an individual finally decides to convert, he notifies a Catholic Action member, who in turn goes to a catechist or, if this member is a catechist, to the center president. The president notifies the Catholic Action members in the class or, if no class day is coming soon, notifies all the members through their catechists to come together on a particular night to the house of the one who is to be converted.

When the time comes, the one to be converted and his family are waiting. They have swept the house and sometimes have spread pine branches on the floor, as they might for a feast day. At the appointed time, the Catholic Action members arrive with battery-operated lanterns or *ocote* wood torches. The one who seeks to be converted goes out to the entryway and invites them into the house. In one corner lies the sick person, perhaps close to death. Near the wall is a small table with some saints' pictures and a couple of candles.

The members come in, but do not sit down. They all stand facing the head of the household. The president begins to speak: "We knew you wanted [true] Religion." "Yes," the new convert says, "I am putting this Tradition aside, because I'm just wasting money for nothing. Perhaps my son will recover with Religion."

The president begins an exhortation, speaking softly but firmly. The man listens to him with his head bowed and his arms crossed, occasionally answering "yes, yes." The president tells him:

> Maybe your son will not get better . . . we can't say whether he will get better because only God knows. Does your wife intend to be converted? Because if she's burning *pom* [resin] off somewhere else with a *zahorín* while you are converted, it may happen that between the two of you, you will kill your child because you're engaged in deception. Whether he is going to get better . . . only God knows. God isn't a child. God isn't a toy. You can't tell him yes today, tomorrow no. If your son dies, he dies.
>
> And suppose today you see a sign in the night: some owls gather together, or some cats or coyotes come in . . . what are you going to say? What if you find some big snakes on the path tomorrow? What if an uncle of yours or a brother comes over to reprimand you? It's the Devil who has brought them. . . . And he's going to say that your son is going to die tomorrow. Are you going to get frightened? If you are converting just to see whether your kid gets better . . . let him die! And what if you have a dream at night: a bunch of coyotes, or being bit by snakes, or you're riding a white animal—that's the casket—or a small airplane comes to the house bearing the casket, or you're riding in a truck, or your house is on fire, or the house has no door, or the community house where the body is held for burial is opened up. Are you going to think that you're being told that Religion is of no use? When you throw out this bundle [i.e., Traditions performed, evil actions that fall upon a person to kill him or her], you don't look back.
>
> Religion demands work: class, going to mass, studying doctrine. Mass takes away a day of work. Since you're used to working seven days a week

. . . now, after we are converted, we no longer work on Saturday. Sometimes we don't work on Wednesday as well because of class; not Saturday
or Tuesday [market day]. So do we die? It's rest for our bodies. When we're
not in Religion, our bodies work all year long, and they seem to wear out.
Sometimes we plant and nothing grows. And we plant piglets [we raise
pigs] and they die. Now in Religion we allow our body to rest.

And our family: we used to go to a feast, but all we did was drink liquor.
We've got ten or fifteen quetzals, so where do we go to spend them? To the
cantina. And we've got children and family. The kids are crying and there's
nothing to give them. And there's nothing to give our wives.

Since the same has happened to some of the other members, they add,

Yes, that's what I went through. I spent the thirty quetzals on liquor. And
my wife is there waiting for the money. Yet other women have a nice loaf of
sweet bread, and they're eating, and they're eating. But my family is weeping. That's a bad example. It's true what they're telling us.

The president continues:

Now, after being converted, the feast day comes, and you go happily
down the street. You go to mass and come out and eat well. Your children
are happy and are eating oranges and candy. The children are happy and
we are also happy with God. You come home, and your coffee is prepared
and the meat is cooked. . . . And how happy you are with God . . . and the
kids are happy . . . good food, meat, coffee, or perhaps something else.

That's what Religion gives us. And when illness comes along: we pray to
God and confess our sins on our knees before God.

The man says, "Yes of course. That idea seems good to us."

When the talk is over, they begin the rosary. They light some candles. Everyone kneels down before the saints' images, the women on one side, the men on
the other.

After the rosary, the one being converted and his wife take out their *tz'ite'*
bundles and hand them to the president. And when the leaders have the bundles
in their hands, they pray all seven creeds and a prayer to Saint Michael the
Archangel. The conversion is completed. The president and his catechists then
throw the bundles into the ravine.

Then the convert offers a cup of coffee to the Catholic Action members, but
the president and his catechists refuse it: "We didn't come for love of a cup of
coffee, but for love of God." Thus they finish. They come back to pray at
night two or three more times.

The structure of the conversion "ritual" is made up of the threefold elements of the *rite of passage*: separation, liminality, and adherence. Separation
is signified by the removal of the *tz'ite'* bundle from the house; liminality by

the preaching of the leader, who reprimands the neophyte and conjures up for him fearful situations; and adherence by the entry of Catholic Action members into the house. The chronological order is reversed: the members come in first, and the *tz'ite'* is handed over last, but this reversal seems accidental.

The handing over and removal of the *tz'ite'* (separation) involves rejecting the *zahorín* and making a break with Tradition as a source of life; rejecting the belief of the Traditionalists as harmful and rejecting the Devil, who brings death to someone lacking the *tz'ite'*; and risking death, which is entailed in getting rid of this symbol that is so prized by the *zahorines*. The *tz'ite'* bundle is handed over to the president along with sculpted stones, stone axes, glass crystals, and mementos from one's ancestors, all of which are to be thrown into the ravine, a site that symbolizes the presence of the Devil. The *tz'ite'* departs from the house and the evil (illness, etc.) with it.

The leader's sermon (liminality) places the neophyte, who has never previously submitted to his authority, in a situation of inferiority and humiliation, which is enhanced by the presence of the members, before whom he has declared his impotence. They look through him with their gaze, and he hunches over. The spatial arrangement and the leader's words tend to make the neophyte see himself as of little worth, as no one socially, as one who has just broken away from the social group of his faith and does not yet belong to the other one, which for him is still new and unknown.

In this situation of inferiority, as in initiation into the Mysteries, all sorts of fearful situations pile up, such as, for example, dreams of a bad omen, songs of animals, disputes among relatives, all of which can later make the convert waver in his faith. As frightful as they might seem, they are all deceitful signals that lead to death. The aim of piling them all up together is to ground the neophyte, whom liminality makes pliable, in the truth of his new faith.

Liminality is most radicalized in the acceptance of death (of his son, in the case described) for incomprehensible reasons. Now it is not only situations of fear and apparent signs of death that are faced, but death itself through faith in a life that overcomes daily death. One who accepts death in this fashion, in some way truly dies and rejects the opportunism of conversion, which would make it a false conversion.

The result of liminality is the total adherence of faith indicated by the entry of Catholic Action members into the house. Expressions like "you throw out this bundle, you don't look back," "God isn't a toy," "Let him [his son] die!" or other often-used expressions like "it has to be well planted," "with a single heart," and so forth assume this total adherence, which accepts death rather than abandoning faith.

The entry of the Catholic Action members, the third element of the rite, means total adherence to belief in the power of Catholic Action prayer. Along with the Catholic Action group, the house is permeated with a concentrated power that has its effect even on the sick bodies of those dwelling there who accept it. It also means joining Catholic Action: as it enters the house, the house joins it.

The results achieved and signified by the ritual are courage against the threats of the *zahorín* and at the same time marvelous enjoyment—"you go joyfully down the street"—partly the result of a reorganized attitude and partly of a rejection of ways of life like drunkenness and dependence on the *zahorín*, which they regard as destructive and exploitative.

The actual embodiment of the structure of the "ritual" is flexible (hence the quotation marks). The accent is on what is fundamental, namely the entry of Catholic Action into the house, the removal of the *tz'ite'*, and the liminal preaching. Whether the Catholic Action members are received sitting or standing, the neophyte is by the altar or by the sick person, the members accept coffee or not, are all accidental. The rite has been created only recently, the details are not set, and compared to the rites traditionally practiced with the *c'ulnem*, or traditional wedding, it seems utterly disorganized.

Because of its very flexibility and novelty, the rite includes greater scope for the improvised word, although there is always insistence on certain ideas for the repetitive message (the words are always the same) or actions (gestures, movements, and so forth). Hence, the rite is not, so to speak, very "ritualized." It seems that this is the way all rites that entail rebellion against one social group and entry into another recently established one ought to be.

The conversion rite thus serves to signify, complete, and totalize the individual's conversion vis-à-vis the group. It serves to express the state of liminality that the neophyte has suffered (such as illness, death of a child), relinquishment of the previous group, and adaptation to the new one. The rite de-initiates the neophyte from the principles in which he had previously been initiated through rites of passage within the previous social group and initiates him, because of his state of pliability, into the sharply etched principles of the new group. Thus the neophyte's faith is radicalized (total adherence).

Conclusions

From the foregoing, I conclude that there are certain constants in the various processes that bring about conversion. First, in the *household*, I found a certain tendency for conversion to be easier for sons when their father was already dead, but I was unable to prove that conversion is inhibited when the son lives with the father, a sign that the inheritance is not yet distributed. I was unable to corroborate other possible hypotheses, for example, that it would be easier for an only son to convert, because data were insufficient. Nor was I able to measure in economic terms (amount of land; income from other sources) a father's power over his son.

Nevertheless, the father clearly has more power than the son, and in all instances when he is a *zahorín*, he has prevented his son from converting. It seems that there is an analogous influence over their sons by *principales* and fathers (fathers-in-law) who are further along in age. In such cases, the degree of the father's initiation, which is ordinarily an indicator of his power in the community, gives the father power to resist.

In most cases of conversions of households containing fathers and married sons, it is the father rather than the son who has taken the initiative in conversion. In such cases, he tends to be younger, on average, than fathers of married sons in nonconverted homes. The age may indicate the unequal degree of initiation into the principles of Tradition.

Second, at the *Catholic Action center* or before the center is set up, at the level of the *lineage segment* or *canton*, I found the derivation of power operating through neighbors: first through brothers, then cousins or uncles on the father's side, and then nonrelated neighbors. The bond of kinship between brothers and patrilinear relatives is strengthened by shared work relationships, which in theory are closer the greater the need is to work together due to the type of work. This work relationship is found at the root of many pairs of relatives, who almost always coincide in their religious affiliation.

The influence of kinship becomes all that much stronger for putting up resistance to conversion when the focal point of resistance is a person who is more deeply initiated. Thus a *zahorín* is able to control more distant relatives, such as his grandchildren, and relatives who are not neighbors, such as his granddaughters. Likewise, it must be kept in mind, as stated in the last chapter, that through their daughters some Catholic Action members have been able to convert her husband and sometimes even his father.

I have not researched relationship by marriage, but the information from the last chapter and the contraction of the area where brides are sought leads one to think that some influences between nonrelated neighbors are probably reinforced through marriage alliances.

In all these processes through the demographic changes presented in the last chapter, it is clear that this society has been adapting without breaking an area of interaction that is more or less equal in size, where kinship relationships are the foundation for social organization.

Beyond kinship, there is simple contiguity. I have found geographical proximity to be a necessary condition for derivation of power. The areas more densely populated by converts are next to one another. The areas devoid of them are connected on the outskirts of the municipality, farthest away from communication with the department capital. Rivers, and sometimes hills, have an isolating effect and determine the identification of small hamlets or groups of segments walled up behind them.

The establishment of a formalized center in a settlement or a canton grants it more derived power. Some centers have been quite prolific, giving rise to several others, even at the expense of being left with fewer members. That is how the movement has been able to make its way into a great portion of the southern part of the municipality.

Some centers have pressed proselytizing to the point of reaching a limit of possible conversions. The only ones left in their hamlets are *zahorines* and those closely connected to them, or a few others who because of some special circumstance are out of the firing line of conversion (for example, they spend much time on the coast or in Guatemala City). The group of hamlets in Sacxac has almost reached its limits of potential conversions. The cantons of Chichó and Xebaquit of Center No. 5 are even more saturated. The total adherence of the few *zahorines*—some of whom are destitute—to their traditional beliefs is all the more dramatically demonstrated.

Third, *in the community* the seed of conversion has entered areas isolated by geographical features through merchants who picked up the seed from others in the municipality or outside the municipality, or sometimes through marriage relations.

Fourth, the *initiation factor* comes into play both for putting up resistance and favoring conversion. In the first instance, it is an initiation carried out through rites of passage within the Tradition. The effect of such initiation, judging by the signs of behavior, is total adherence and loyalty. Many of them, one thinks, would rather be killed than waver. For them, the apparent failures of the Tradition, when their children or grandchildren die on them, are not failures. They are reinterpreted as the implacability of destiny.

In the second sense, initiation is regarded as a new belief, opposed to the traditional one on points regarded as fundamental, such as the calendar and the *tz'ite'*, and it takes place through a crisis (in most cases) and is completed ritually through the stage of liminality. In many cases, a crisis is needed to separate (de-initiate) the neophyte; but just as some (the *zahorines*) can no longer be de-initiated, so there are others who do not need such a crisis just to be initiated and are converted by their own choice. Such tends to be the case in the conversion of the younger men.

By overcoming the crisis through conversion, the individual attains a new adaptation to the environment. This adaptation has consisted, according to the converts, primarily in being liberated from *zahorines* who were deceiving them and also in other effects such as overcoming drunkenness, being healed, opening up to the influence of the modern world, and so forth. It is likely that some feel such exploitation more than others because a *zahorín*'s sons, daughters, grandchildren, and brothers do not pay him for his "traditions," while those who are not his close relatives do pay. Thus, just as I have not been able to isolate from initiation the effect of this exploitation, I have not been able to isolate it from the level of power to which it gives access.

CHAPTER 6

Power Derived from
Outside the Community

In this chapter I attempt to show the effects within the community of power derived from outside of it. I will not be able to study the structure of this power at the department or national level in any detail because to do so would become very extensive. I will simply take my place within the community to observe the lines of the derivation of power, as if I were looking out a window at the national and regional structure. Hence, these observations on regional or national processes will remain hints and paths for further research.

Political History of San Antonio: 1945–1970

In pursuing the effects of power based on sources outside the community, I provide an account of the municipality's political history, noting how changes of government and constitutions, the operation of political parties, and the activity of the church and other institutions nationally and even internationally have an impact on events in the municipality. The development of Catholic Action is central to the political history of the municipality, as we will see.

My sources are oral and written. For oral sources, I am relying on information from Catholic Action people, thereby placing limits on my knowledge of those opposed to Catholic Action and also about the 1945–1954 revolutionary period, because my informants did not experience the internal politics of the municipality during that time, either because they were children or because they were away from the municipality trying to earn a living. The written sources are the municipal records to which I had access—thanks to the mayor in the 1968–1970 period, who belonged to Catholic Action—the records of some canton centers, and the records of the municipal headquarters of Catholic Action in Santa Cruz del Quiché. I was unable to get access to the official records of the government office in the department capital, which would have been very rich in precise details.

I will divide the account into four periods: (1) immediately before 1945; (2) 1945–1954; (3) 1954–1963; and (4) 1963 to the present (1970). The year

1945 marks the beginning of the revolutionary governments (following October 20, 1944); and 1954 marks the fall of the revolutionary governments and the establishment of right-wing regimes, starting with the invasion of Colonel Carlos Castillo Armas from Honduras in June 1954. In 1963, Colonel Enrique Peralta Azurdia seized the government.

I will weave the story of the events at the municipal, department, and national levels, showing how they relate to Catholic Action, and then I will set forth a comparative analysis of the various periods.

Before 1945

The period before 1945 is of interest here because it is when the Catholic Action movement arose in the Indian highlands of the country. In 1934 the first two local founders of Catholic Action were converted independently of one another. They belonged to different municipalities of Totonicapán: Santa María Chiquimula and Totonicapán itself. Both sought support and guidance from the Franciscan pastor in Momostenango, a municipality in Totonicapán, who told them that they should each win over five men, and that each of these five should likewise win over five more, and so forth. This first group was called the Society for the Propagation of the Faith by the priest, and it was centered in Momostenango.

The "seed" soon spread. A center was set up in 1937, with a board of directors made up of a president, vice-president, secretary, and treasurer, in Santa María Chiquimula. The president was one of the first two converts. In 1944 the seed spread from Chiquimula to Patzité, the first municipality to receive it in the department of El Quiché. The bearer of the seed was a merchant. Around 1945 it spread to Santa Lucía la Reforma, also from Chiquimula. Both Patzité and Santa Lucía, we should recall (Chap. 4), are municipalities whose people are entirely from Chiquimula. It is therefore likely that the shared origin and proximity helped extend the movement to these municipalities before going elsewhere, such as to San Antonio.

At this time there were only three priests in the entire department of El Quiché: in Santa Cruz del Quiché, Joyabaj, and Nebaj. The priests worked with the *cofradías* and had apparently learned to live with their "excesses." They also tolerated the activities of *zahorines* and their rituals, which the church was later to regard as heterodox. By contrast, the Catholic Action movement was dividing hamlets and municipalities, even though they had no resident priest, because the movement demanded that the *zahorín* and certain central symbols like liquor be given up.

We should bear in mind that political parties were not operating then. The municipal mayors, then called "intendants," were appointed by the department political chief. In San Antonio, the intendants were always ladinos, while the rest of the town council (a *síndico* and six *regidores*) was appointed each year by the *principales*. In addition to the mayor, there was a ladino clerk, appointed by the office of the department political chief.

1945–1954

Church and Government

October 20, 1944, marked the fall of the Liberal junta that had replaced General Jorge Ubico for three months after the downfall of his fourteen-year government. Presidential elections were soon organized, and political activity began to flourish and gradually made its way into municipal populations far from Guatemala City.

After winning a popular election, Juan José Arévalo took office as president in early 1945. A new era of democracy was beginning for the country. The constitution was radically revised. According to the new constitution, which was passed in 1945, mayors were to be elected by popular vote within the municipalities.

In San Antonio, there was no election for mayor in 1945. Instead, the San Antonio Indian who had been appointed by the department chief two years after the revolution, to replace the ladino intendant from Santa Cruz del Quiché, acted as mayor.

The church also made its way into the municipalities early in this period. In 1945, Rafael González was made auxiliary bishop of Los Altos, with the see in Quetzaltenango. He organized Catholic Action on the diocesan level, utilizing the existing Society for the Propagation of the Faith, changing its name and making it a part of national Catholic Action and further energizing it by visiting even faraway towns and cantons on muleback. The bishop covered several departments, because the diocese of Quetzaltenango, then one of the country's three dioceses, was made up of eight departments, including El Quiché.

Municipal Politics

A year went by and in late 1945 the mayor was elected by "popular vote." As was the case until 1964, popular election amounted to being designated by the *principales*. In 1945 they picked for mayor a prestigious man who knew how the mayor's office worked because once before (1939) he had served as alternate to the ladino intendant at the behest of the indigenous town council. He took office, but, curiously, shortly before his period was to conclude (October 1946) he resigned, as noted in the records, "out of poverty." It seems obvious that something was afoot beyond the scope of his authority and the decision by the *principales*.

For the next period, which began in February 1947, an indigenous man who had many contacts with ladinos was chosen to be mayor. He was a merchant who bought goods in Mexico and engaged in contraband. By contrast with the mayor from the previous period, he had never served in the municipality as *síndico* or *regidor*. Hence we can see that even though the *principales* appointed him, the hierarchical tradition of fulfilling *cargos* was being violated and that, accordingly, some strong pressure was being imposed on the *principales* to appoint him. I assume that the pressure came from the ladinos.

It must have been the ladinos who injected the spirit of the 1944 Revolution into the municipality. Yet they never appear on the municipal payrolls, whether as mayors, *regidores*, or *síndicos*. For the 1947 period there seems to have been an agreement between ladinos and *principales* whereby the *principales* would designate a candidate to the liking of the ladinos, even if he was an Indian.

The two ladino officials in the municipality, both of them from outside the area, knew how to profit from the revolution. First, all wage debts that had then been pending for around seven years were canceled. Besides that, a position was created for a clerk at Q 15 a month. Likewise, before Christmas in 1947, the town council decided, presumably by pressure from its officers, to grant those officers a yearly bonus of a month's pay because they were worse off than the teachers in town, who were also ladinos, inasmuch as they had no vacations. Yet the mayor, who was Indian, would continue to serve for free until 1956.

The economy of the municipality was able to sustain such spending because of the municipal autonomy acknowledged by the 1945 constitution, by which the municipality could charge fees (Art. 202). The 1947 mayor had been able to start a market day in the town, and it was possible to charge a fee for the use of the square. Moreover, through the governments during the revolution, municipalities received certain funds from the recently created Department of Municipal Credit. However, there is no reason to think that the municipality of San Antonio became a desirable location for unemployed ladinos, as was the case in other towns.

In terms of the formation of political parties, it was around the 1947 mayor and his son, who was married to a ladino woman, and other ladinos in the town with indigenous ancestry that the group formed that later was to be called "communist" and "pro-Arbenz." Not forming part of this group with a ladino image, however, was another family of ladinos that had no indigenous ancestry in the municipality and had a larger amount of land than the average outside the municipality. Presumably this family of ladinos without marriage ties within the municipality was opposed to the "communists."

Nevertheless, politics seem to have been excluded from the choice of mayors by the *principales*, because the next seven (1948–1954) were not only continually designated by the *principales* but—contrary to the case of the 1947 mayor—all had first been either *síndicos* or *regidores* some years before being designated. It therefore seems that the *principales* allowed themselves to be politically pressured by the "communists" in the 1947 mayoral election, a pressure that led to the resignation of the highly esteemed mayor in 1946. In subsequent periods, the *principales*, who governed the not-yet-clearly-divided indigenous majority in San Antonio, upheld the tradition, above and beyond the political power that was held by the ladinos and a very small group of ladino-tending Indians.

Observing the seven mayors designated up to 1954 by the *principales*, it should be noted in advance that the stability based on election by *principales* lasted until 1964, and that this stability was quite solid in comparison with the changes in the municipal government after the 1964 mayor. Indeed, of the sixteen mayors in the 1945–1962 period, only one resigned (the one in 1946) and another was deposed in 1951 for "abuses against persons" (I do not know whether that term was used to cover up political enmities), in noteworthy contrast to the three or four resignations in the municipal period since 1964 (as we shall examine below).

Catholic Action and Anticommunism (1948 Onward)

I have said that the division within the indigenous population had not yet given rise to two rival bands with approximately equal power. Catholic Action came into the municipality in 1948 through three different cantons along separate paths. None of the first three converts was aware of the other two at the time of their respective conversions. The first was a 38-year-old merchant in the canton of Chiaj, located in the middle of the southern part of the municipality. He says he used to drink a great deal out of sorrow over the loss of his wife, but then a merchant from Chiquimula that he met in Escuintla began to convince him "to put his vice aside and believe." For three months he hesitated, but he finally made his decision and began to go to the class every Thursday in Santa María Chiquimula, four hours away on foot. At the time of his conversion, he married another woman, whom he brought from a distant municipality. His new wife did not want to be converted and resisted what her husband was saying during the first three months of their marriage. She finally gave in and together they both learned to pray and sing. They used to sing and pray by themselves in the church in town; people thought they were crazy and came up to them to ask what they were doing. Little by little, others joined in and he gave each of them a catechism. They managed to set up a small group of ten or twelve, most of them merchants. In 1947 they all celebrated Holy Week with the members of the *cofradía*. The *cofradía* members did not like praying in Spanish, but they put up with it. Catholic Action had not yet become a focal point of division.

Likewise, in 1949, another merchant, this one from the canton of Canamixtoj in the north, received the message from Santa Lucía la Reforma and converted. His decision was made out of antipathy to the *zahorines*, because his first wife had died on him despite the traditional rituals he had performed and paid for. The third merchant was from Patzalá, and as we learned in the previous chapter, he received the seed from a merchant from Totonicapán in the market in Chichicastenango.

Catholic Action found itself enlisted in the church's national movement against "communism." The rise of "anticommunism" started in 1948, when leftists murdered Colonel Francisco Javier Arana, who was seen as the future candidate of the right and was then chief of staff of the army. Agitation in the country prompted the organization of the Anticommunist Party and growing antigovernment opposition.

In 1950, the First Eucharistic Congress was held in Guatemala City. To it came rural representatives from around the country, many of them Catholic Action members. The impressive large gathering had political implications, because it showed the strength of the church and of "anticommunism." The first convert from San Antonio, who still had no fellow members, attended the congress. He was representing around fifteen members who lived near his house in the canton of Chiaj. He had no banner to carry because the center had not yet been formally organized. He recalls that in 1951 he attended another large gathering in Guatemala City, this time with a banner, but still no one was with him.

During this period the archbishop traveled around the country, accompanied by the image of the black Christ from Esquipulas, as a standard-bearer of "anticommunism" and head of the Guatemalan church. For his part, the auxiliary bishop of Quetzaltenango continued his rounds spreading Catholic Action, starting it in some municipalities and officially confirming it in others, such as in San Antonio, which he visited in 1952 after passing through Santa Cruz del Quiché.

As the word went around that the bishop was coming, the first convert, who now served as president of Catholic Action in San Antonio with approval from Quetzaltenango, sought help from fellow Catholic Action members in Santa Lucía la Reforma so that they could welcome the bishop together. On this occasion, they joined the two Catholic Action groups operating in San Antonio, the one in Chiaj and Patzalá in the south, and the one in Canamixtoj, which attended classes and meetings in Santa Lucía, to the north.

Arriving with the bishop was a catechist who preached movingly in the Quiché language. Listening to him were not only the Catholic Action members but also other people from the municipality, including the *cofradía* members and some *principales*, who had gathered to welcome the bishop. The catechist unleashed an attack against the *zahorines*, candles, and "drinking." That point marked the beginning of the division: on one side stood Catholic Action, now grouped on a municipal level and visibly supported and confirmed by the bishop, with a total of around thirty members who had been won over; and on the other side, the Traditionalists, who rose up against Catholic Action "because they wanted to take away the Tradition." Several days later they threw stones at the president of Catholic Action in a canyon and beat him with sticks.

Agrarian Reform and Political Consciousness (1952–1954)

A year earlier, in 1951, the Anticommunist Party had been established in Santa Cruz del Quiché, and it subsequently established a branch in San Antonio,

where one of the first three converts became its president. He brought together other Catholic Action members in his canton. They formed the core of
the "anticommunists" and presented an electoral slate (1952) in opposition to
the *principales*, who probably supported the "communists" because they were
in the government. The *principales* won the election once more.

Nationally, in 1951, Colonel Jacobo Arbenz had become president. During
his uncompleted term, leftist tendencies came to the fore even more. Thus,
June 1952 saw the enactment of the Agrarian Reform Decree, which was to
have an impact on a good portion of the country. In Santa Cruz del Quiché,
the rural surveyors measured the land of a Spanish contractor and money
lender, who also had a clientele in San Antonio. There does not seem to have
been any measuring of land in San Antonio, because it was a municipality of
smallholdings, where land was not sharply concentrated under one owner.
Only a few were likely to be afraid of the decree, one being the president of the
"anticommunists," who had over a *caballería* (111 acres) of land, although
the soil was quite sandy.

Many people from San Antonio who worked on the coast or in the coastal
foothills on coffee farms, or on leased lands, or in the salt flats near the port,
experienced the political agitation of that period, although as a rule they were
not actively involved in pressing demands for land or in making labor demands. For example, in the salt flats, the labor union ordered the indigenous
laborers, many of them from San Antonio, not to go out to the yards until the
owner agreed to a wage increase. "If you don't go along with it," the labor
union ladinos from eastern Guatemala told them, "we're going to hack you
off the job with machetes." Thus by supporting the strike by ladino workers
they were able to have their pay rise gradually from Q 0.75 to Q 1.50 per day,
even though Q 0.75 was attractive pay for people from San Antonio. "That's
already pay for someone well-educated," they said. Others went to the labor
courts, with the encouragement of the union, or took over farms following
Communist Party leaders, or volunteered to help defend against the airplanes
of Castillo Armas, it was reported.

What these workers experienced at that time, without a framework for understanding what politics was about ("we had no idea then what politics
meant"), was reinterpreted in the light of the organization of parties within
the activities of Catholic Action in the municipality when they came back to
San Antonio after being driven away from the coast as cotton growing expanded in the 1960s. In San Antonio they did not adopt the positions of their
fellow workers from the Arbenz period, because the national situation and the
local context made that impossible. However, they retained a clear picture of
what they had seen, even though they did not share the experience of the
leaders who were jailed and tortured and some of whose comrades, say the
people from San Antonio, disappeared into the sea.

Summary

Concluding this period, we may reconstruct what alliances existed in the municipality in 1953 and 1954, noting that the ladinos with kinship ties in the area, as well as a few ladino-tending Indians (with ladino children or grandchildren) in the town were active in the "communist" group. Opposed to them was the "anticommunist" group in the canton with the largest amount of uncultivated land, all of them Indians with ties to Catholic Action, and ladinos with no indigenous ancestry and with land outside the municipality, who would support the "anticommunists" at election time but did not belong to their local affiliate.

In this opposition there does not seem to have been any special effort to win the mayor's post. The concern of the "anticommunists" was to defend themselves against any possible invasion of their lands, and that of the "communists" was to benefit from the national government and to combat the money lender in Santa Cruz del Quiché who had a number of debtors in San Antonio. Both concerns were beyond the reach of the local town government.

The *principales* would stand by the government, albeit with some ambiguity, because even though they probably were not directly attacked by the "communists," who let them choose the mayor every year, they nevertheless must have felt threatened by the revolutionary ideology that their adversaries presented as opposed to worship of the saints, private ownership of the land, and individual marriage (the rumor against "communists" was that marriage should be collective).

In addition, they were afraid that "communists" were concealed within Catholic Action, because its members preached against the Traditions of the saints; they were allied with the money lender, who would indeed come to seize many lands in San Antonio; and they went to confession to the priest, who, according to some Traditionalists, took advantage of women under cover of the sacrament.

For its part, Catholic Action did not have a great deal of power because only forty-six households were converted in 1954, and the power derived from a departmental church with only three priests and a circuit-riding bishop for a huge diocese came down to echoing the national "anticommunist" stance. Finally, the party supporting it was in opposition to the government and did not grant its power directly to the Catholic Action board but to a canton group.

Judging from events some years later, what concerned Catholic Action was gaining control over the church building in the town and the mayor's position, which was tied to the legal right to the church building. In this local concern, Catholic Action ran up against opposition from the *principales*, who were little concerned with national developments and what happened there.

TABLE 6.1. *Approximate growth of Catholic Action by year and by center, 1954–1969*

Center	Year center formalized	Houses converted per year			
		1954	1959	1964	1969
Number 1	1951	4	17	37	55
Number 2	1955	11	17	24	30
Number 3	1958	11	22	39	53
Number 4	1963	12	21	33	52
Number 5	1965	4	11	29	74
Number 6	1965	4	7	15	26
Number 7	1965	0	0	14	36
Total		46	95	191	326

Source: Lists from informants and Catholic Action records and attendance books.

Because of the diversity of levels at which the interests of "communists" and "anticommunists" and between the *principales* and Catholic Action were at odds, groups as unlike as the *principales* and the "communists" could support one another, as could the "anticommunists" and Catholic Action to some degree, as we shall see from subsequent developments.

1954–1963

Castillo Armas overthrew the Arbenz government in July 1954, utilizing the religious symbol of the Christ of Esquipulas, which the archbishop had previously taken on pilgrimage throughout the country, and harnessing anticommunist support from the church. Consequently, the country was then opened to foreign clergy, and churches were given legal status in the Constitution (Art. 50). On the other hand, the organizations of the lower classes, such as labor unions, peasant leagues, and agrarian committees, which had been active in the previous period, suffered repression.

Religious Conflicts

In 1954, shortly before the fall of Arbenz, a conflict broke out in Santa Cruz del Quiché between *cofradía* members and *principales* on one side, and members of Catholic Action on the other, who then numbered around three hundred. This conflict was to have a counterpart later in San Antonio, whose few members of Catholic Action were still traveling to Santa Cruz del Quiché. The conflict was over the procession of the Buried Lord during Holy Week. *Cofradía* members had not wanted Catholic Action members to take part in the same procession with them, even though the *cofrades*, who were few in number and old, had barely been able to carry the image by themselves. Regarding themselves as the majority, the Catholic Action members proposed that they carry the image the next year, this time leaving out the *cofrades*. They went directly to Castillo Armas, who was now head of state. He listened to them personally and decided in their favor, ordering that the department governor's office step in to take away the keys for the procession platform from a *cofrade*. To defend themselves, the *cofrades* were reduced to burning a great deal of *pom* (resin from a tree) so as to invoke the power of traditional practices to try to cause the church choir loft in which Catholic Action members used to sing to come crashing down in punishment. The conflict occurred in late February or early March 1955.

Shortly afterward, in that same year, Spanish Sacred Heart Missionary priests arrived to take charge of pastoral work for the entire department of El Quiché. Their presence was soon to be the object of one of the first Catholic Action conflicts in San Antonio.

The first serious conflict between Catholic Action members and the *principales* in San Antonio occurred on June 28, 1955, and centered around symbols (as had happened in Santa Cruz del Quiché). Catholic Action members had ordered six pews to be made for the church. But the addition of these pews meant taking over the church, because the pews would impede the Tra-

TABLE 6.2. *Number of houses in the whole municipality of San Antonio in 1970, by religious confession: Catholic Action, Protestant, Traditionalist, and 1/2 (houses with members belonging to different groups)*

Canton	Catholic Action Center	Catholic Action	Protestants	Tradi- tionalists	1/2	Total
Chiaj						
Tzancawib	No. 1	16	13	61	2	92
		39	2	37	3	81
Canamixtoj	No. 2	30	4	106	1	141
Chuijoj[a]	No. 3	53	6	35	2	96
Chuijip	No. 4	18	17	52	1	88
Chotacaj		11	8	69	1	89
Xejip		23	2	92	4	121
Chichó	No. 5	29	1	14	1	45
Xebaquit		45	1	32	3	81
Patzalá	No. 6	26	0	30	1	57
Sacxac	No. 7	36	10	145	3	194
Total		326	64	673[b]	22	1,085[b]

Source: Informants' lists.

Notes: [a]Chuijoj is half of the canton of Patzalá.

[b]The total number (1,085) and the number of Traditionalists are probably greater.

ditionalists from burning candles on the floor. The Traditionalists removed the pews, kicking them and breaking one of them. The governor stepped in and came personally to San Antonio on July 7 because the members of Catholic Action presented a complaint against the mayor, the *síndico*, and other "Catholics," as they called the Traditionalists.

It was July and it had hardly rained. Corn had gotten expensive throughout the country, possibly due to the change in the government, repression, and the return to the status quo before the land reform. A hundred-pound bag of corn was costing Q 15.00 (vs. Q 3.50 in 1970). The Traditionalists complained to the governor that Catholic Action was responsible for the lack of rain because of the hindrances they were creating to their rituals. They also complained that they were being called "witch doctors," that processions were being prevented, and in general that the Tradition was being changed. That was why it was not raining. Catholic Action members, however, blamed the Traditionalists for having taken the pews out, for keeping them from saying prayers in the church, for calling them Protestants and communists, for falsely accusing them of having books from Russia, and for insulting the priest, calling him a communist and saying that he took advantage of women under cover of confession. They also accused the Traditionalists of playing the marimba in church and drinking and dancing there.

The governor ruled in favor of Catholic Action, indicating that the Catholic religion was free and could not be imposed on anyone. Marimba-playing was forbidden in church, and the benches were put back, once the broken one had been fixed.

The next conflict took place one year later on September 18, 1956. It was Tuesday, a market day, when the priests from Santa Cruz del Quiché showed up in San Antonio with a Canadian priest, who had recently left China, to place him in charge as pastor. They had previously advised the Catholic Action leadership and the mayor's office of this appointment. They got out of their car and went walking through the beautiful two-story convent, tranquilly talking about what would need to be repaired. The building dated back to colonial times, but no priest had lived there permanently for centuries. As they departed, the priests promised to return a week later.

The following Tuesday around five of them arrived at 2 P.M. People were occupying the town square. The municipal *síndico*, who had belonged to the "communist" group during the Arbenz period, stirred up the people to charge at the priests and yelled at them, "We don't want priests here. All they are is clever exploiters. They just come to make money. Foreigners, communists. Three masses a year is enough. Let's mess them up now, and if they come back, let's kill them." The Catholic Action members—who are called "catechists" in the complaint before the regional judge—were in the church. The *síndico* (not the mayor, who was a weak man) went into the church and brought out the catechists, kicking and shoving them. That night one of them was taken to the hospital in Santa Cruz del Quiché to treat his head wounds. The priests fled in their car and, in view of this reaction, did not install the pastor in San Antonio but instead placed him in Patzité, where Catholic Action had more members.

The *síndico* did not go unpunished. He had another enemy, the Spanish labor contractor in Santa Cruz del Quiché, mentioned in the discussion of the previous period. This labor contractor and money lender had a number of debtors in San Antonio, especially among people who lived near the town. One of the ladinos, who had been in the "communist" group, had his eye on the house of one of the debtors and advised them not to pay. In order to demand payment, the money lender came personally to the court in San Antonio in 1956. The *síndico* then had him jailed and it took a truckload of soldiers brought in from the military base in Santa Cruz del Quiché to get him released. The Catholic Action leaders, with the influence of the money lender and a top leader in Castillo Armas's Liberation Movement and possibly the governor, who was a friend of the money lender, had an arrest order put out for the *síndico*. He fled to the coast near the Mexican border, but he was eventually caught in 1957 and imprisoned for nine months. "The enemy of Catholic Action, enemy of the priests, enemy of the MLN [Liberation Movement]," as a document in the Catholic Action files puts it, thus fell in defeat. The money lender was able to claim the lands of those in debt, including their houses in some instances. He then sold them to other people in the town.

Victory in this conflict spurred conversions, and the second Catholic Action center was set up in San Antonio, apparently at the suggestion of the priests.

Another conflict between Traditionalists and Catholic Action broke out in 1962, this time in a canton, over the building of a school in Chiaj, where Catholic Action had more households. The Traditionalists in the canton were against building the school, even though a committee including both Traditionalists and Catholic Action members had been set up at the suggestion of the school district supervisor in Santa Cruz del Quiché. Catholic Action members, who were enthusiastically behind the idea, began to lay adobe bricks for the school. A group of Traditionalists, numbering between 100 and 120, came to the construction site, some with machetes, others with sticks, yelling, "We don't need the school. Our fathers didn't have one. Later our children don't want to work. They learn to steal there, to be lazy, they learn evil prayers and bad words. They don't respect their fathers and mothers. Our fathers didn't have a school. They set up *cofradías* and followed Traditions, and we have cash. What good will a school do us?" Catholic Action members were not intimidated, and they continued building. The military base in Santa Cruz del Quiché gave them twenty truckloads of stone. The National Committee for Building Schools gave them other materials such as cement, roofing sheets, and paint and paid for the construction chief. The local men provided their labor, and they completed it in 1967. They built a school that went on to have more students than the one in the town.

This school had begun in 1962 with the first grade in a private home; in 1963 it had a second grade, and the next year the first three grades. People from the southern cantons of Xebaquit, Chichó, Patzalá, Chiaj, and Tzancawuib sent their children there, at first only those in Catholic Action, but later Traditionalists as well. The school was the first Catholic Action project that was not purely symbolic.

The number of converts continued to grow. By 1964, four centers had been organized, with a total of around 191 converts (see Table 6.1). Despite all the conflicts in which Catholic Action was involved as it grew in membership and strength, the 1954–1963 period was one of stability for the municipal government. Each of the six mayors who served, all of them appointed by the *principales*, finished his term.

Political Conflicts

National events caused a great deal of political instability. In July 1957, President Castillo Armas was assassinated and three parties took part in elections to replace him: the MDN (Nationalist Democratic Movement);[1] the PR (Revolutionary Party), which claimed to be the heir to the ideals of the 1944 Revolution; and the RN (National Renewal), which under another name had supported General Miguel Ydígoras Fuentes in 1950 against Arbenz. The winner of the 1958 election (after the 1957 elections were declared fraudulent and a government junta was created) was Ydígoras Fuentes, who took office in March 1958.

This was the period when the Christian Democrat Party was born, although it was officially suspended from 1961 to 1966. In Santa Cruz del Quiché it would establish ties with Catholic Action, partly because one of its top leaders, René de León Schlotter, had good contacts and could present proposals to the German bishops' Misereor Foundation, which provided ample funding to the Social House of the priests in Santa Cruz del Quiché, to Radio Quiché, and to a model farm in Chitatul near Santa Cruz. At first, René de León and the Christian Democrats used to stay at the religious house. They thereby established the necessary contacts with Catholic Action leaders in El Quiché, and at the initial organizing meetings, those leaders were invited to form part of the party leadership in Santa Cruz.

That was how the Catholic Action group in San Antonio became affiliated with the Christian Democrats. The Catholic Action leaders used to travel to Santa Cruz for a weekly class. During the class, a leader would tell them in the Quiché language for whom they should vote. That was also how a branch was set up in San Antonio, which in the 1960 election presented a slate in San Antonio. Some claim that it won by two votes, although when the votes were reexamined, it lost to the candidate of the *principales*. Throughout this period the *principales* always presented a candidate for mayor.

Although the Christian Democrat Party was forced to suspend activity in 1961, in the record book of the affiliate in San Antonio I found an entry for November 7, 1961, with the names of the same slate that was installed in the municipality on January 1, 1962. I interpret this as a ploy by Catholic Action and the Christian Democrat Party in San Antonio, in the sense that when they could not register their candidate, they would include the opposition candidates in their record books so as to leave a record that they had had a candidate that year and that they had won.

Summary

This period could be summed up as follows: Catholic Action gained strength in the department and the country as a whole, initially with the support of the government's anticommunist movement. It was aided by the priests, whose ranks grew to twenty-five throughout the department, and indirectly by long-standing anticommunists in Santa Cruz del Quiché, like the money lender. Although the Traditionalists continued to designate mayors, they did not achieve any prominence while Castillo Armas was alive. Afterward, with the emergence of competitive elections, they sought power through a political party.

With the death of Castillo Armas and the birth of the Christian Democrat Party, Catholic Action entered a new phase, now linked to that party. This union would lead it to a position of organized opposition to governments further to the right than the Christian Democrats.

Conflicts between Catholic Action members and Traditionalists occurred in the town in regard to the occupation of the church and around accepting a priest, and at the canton level around the school in Chiaj. Although one conflict was religious and the other was not, both involved resistance to the acceptance of power from outside the community that was making its way into the life of the people of San Antonio, and Catholic Action was more adept at this than were the Traditionalists.

The struggle over the church, which was to return, would become the battleground for the mayor's office. The *cofradías* of the *principales* and Catholic Action, both organizations devoted to ritual celebrations, became rivals for control over the site of their celebrations. This competition both reflected and concealed the struggle for the mayor's office, which, as both contending parties saw it, was a decision-making center that exercised its control over ritual organizations, which were themselves a path to that control. It was especially important to occupy this decision-making center, because it was the locus that would receive derived power from the state.

For this very reason the ladinos, who were more active in the earlier period when national interests were at stake, now took on an appearance of passivity. They were not interested in taking over the church building, and hence they were also uninterested in winning the mayor's position. No source of revenues related to the municipality that might be the basis for potential jobs emerged during this period, because although people were slightly better off, the municipality continued to be poor.

1963–1970

In March 1963, Colonel Peralta Azurdia carried out a coup in response to a threat of the left returning to power. A constituent assembly was then formed, and the legislation it passed included a requirement that political parties would need a minimum of 50,000 signatures to be registered. Three parties were registered: the MLN (National Liberation Movement), a wing of the previous MDN; the PID (Institutional Democratic Party), sponsored by the head of state; and the PR (Revolutionary Party). The first two were right-wing, and the third moderately left.

The Christian Democrat Party (DC) was not given approval, because the student sector of the party refused to accept the conditions imposed by the head of state and rejected his call for them to collaborate. This was also the beginning of a new stage for the DC, because many party leaders who were willing to collaborate left the party, and the student group, which had been more energetic in visiting local party organizations, won the support of the General Assembly. With the departure of right-wing leaders, the party tilted further leftward. The students, who were in contact with Marxists in the university and were receiving guidelines from Pax Romana, the international Catholic student movement, to "Christianize the university," were active in politics, and they moved the party in a new direction, under pressure from their more leftist opponents in the university.

Municipal Period 1964–1966: Innovations

The government appointed people to occupy positions on the town council for 1964. A Catholic Action member recounts that he himself suggested the names of the members of this town council through a high official at the supreme court, who in turn passed them on to the governor of El Quiché. The man appointed mayor was a merchant and labor contractor who did not openly side with either the Traditionalists or Catholic Action. He seems to have been on the fringes of the "communists" during the Arbenz period. He was married to a ladina and his sons were ladinos. Thus, it seems that because of his open record of relations outside the municipality, he had enough departmental connections to have influence in the governor's office and be established as mayor, independent of Catholic Action influence. On April 3, 1964, he was sworn in by the regional judge and the Secretary of Justice, with the governor in attendance.

In that same month of April 1964, Credit Union Circles, which were under the cooperative that had been set up by one of the priests in Santa Cruz del Quiché, were started in San Antonio. That same priest had also given 500 quintals of fertilizer to the first Catholic Action center in San Antonio, then the most active center, to be resold at Q 4.80 a bag, rather than the going price of Q 6.80 at stores in Santa Cruz del Quiché. We will later see how this price difference put the store owners on their guard and set Catholic Action in opposition to them and to the regime.

The credit union was linked to fertilizer. The president of this center was a promoter of both the Cooperative Circles and the sale of fertilizer. Catholic Action members who accepted the fertilizer also enthusiastically began to save little by little in order to receive a loan, should they need one, up to double the amount they had saved. Thus, over time, six circles were established, two in

Chiaj, one in Chichó, one in Patzalá, and two in San Antonio itself, with a total of eighty members. For the most part, Traditionalists did not take part in these circles, and they remained cautious and reluctant to accept fertilizer, the acceptance of which became a symbol of success for Catholic Action members.

Shortly afterward, in Santa Cruz del Quiché, problems arose between the governor during the Peralta period and the Santa Cruz cooperative because fertilizer was being sold at a lower price. The powerful ladino merchants in Santa Cruz felt threatened by the cooperative, which had brought fertilizer prices down and could likewise compete with them in other products. They went to the governor, and after a threat from the government, passed on by the nuncio, that either the priest who had organized the cooperative had to leave or they would expel from the country all the Missionaries of the Sacred Heart of Jesus who were working in the department, his superior exiled him to Guatemala City. Instead of declining, the cooperative doubled in size within two years, and reprisals were unleashed against Catholic Action in Santa Cruz and in the nearby municipalities that became aware of these events.[2]

On November 12, 1964, the same governor, who had little use for Catholic Action, visited San Antonio in connection with road repair in the town, and he offered to help the municipality by getting it a tractor. He encouraged the town to set up a "Friends of the Town Committee" to take charge of repairing the old school building in the town and bring in safe drinking water. It is said that, in view of what Catholic Action was accomplishing, he wanted to prod the Traditionalist group to respond to the people's material needs. The committee was set up on December 29, 1964. Its president was a rich merchant who was one of Catholic Action's main foes. All the indigenous members on the board were Traditionalists. A ladina also held a position on the board, and a teacher in the town served as both treasurer and secretary. This committee was the first formal organization that the Traditionalists set up to resist or eliminate Catholic Action, which by this time was well organized in the municipality.

That was where things stood when conflict once more broke out between Catholic Action adherents and Traditionalists in San Antonio. It was a Tuesday in April, a week or two before Holy Week. As in 1955, the dispute was over rights to control the use of the church. There were six side altars where candles were burned. Under the guise of repairing and cleaning the church, Catholic Action members went at them with pickaxes and began to remove bricks from the church. People on the Friends of the Town Committee, commonly called the "townspeople," rose up and went to the mayor's office to present a complaint and ask that the wreckers be jailed. The mayor called in the Catholic Action leaders, who yelled at him while the other side was also yelling, and he ended up making no decision, agreeing with one side and then with the other. The "townspeople" therefore went to the governor, who was friendly to them, and accused the mayor of not serving his town. Summons were sent to the disputants, the governor came to the town, and on Monday of Holy Week both sides leveled accusations at the other. Finally, two board members of the first Catholic Action center, the president and vice-president, leading Catholic Action for the entire municipality (although strictly speaking they were only board members of their own center), were jailed. The reason given for jailing them was that they had collected money without authorization. This was the money that they had collected for repairs. The "townspeople" returned from Santa Cruz to San Antonio that day in an express vehicle, quite satisfied to have left their adversaries in jail. It was a victory that was supposed to last for many years, they said, because the governor had explained to them that the punishment would be from "eighteen to thirty years in jail."

The Catholic Action members went to work to get the prisoners released. They went to the governor and offered him money to get them out quickly, because if they waited for the court process it would take several months. They wanted to show their enemies that Catholic Action members "moved quickly and were sharp." The governor flatly refused, even if they gave him Q 1,000.

Money flowed in all these developments. The owner of the bus lines in San Antonio had loaned the Traditionalists Q 1,000 for legal documents and bribes. I do not know in whose hands it ended up. For their part, the Catholic Action members collected around Q 300 from some of the better-off merchants. They were disturbed because they thought the conflict could last for several years.

The Catholic Action members then went to the regional judge, and one of the merchants gave him a Q 50 "gratuity." The judge issued a ruling in which he declared the prisoners free of any crime and ordered that they be released immediately. The governor wanted to stop the judge from freeing them, but the latter angrily answered him, "You do your job, and I'll do mine." Five days later, they were free, and left Santa Cruz by night in an express car.

Then, in order to defend his flock, the superior of the priests in El Quiché, on the basis of the church's legal identity, set up a "Projects Sub-Committee of the Parish of San Antonio Ilotenango." The charter was finished on January 12, 1965, several months after the conflict, and the registry book was authorized as of October 20, 1962, several years before. It is known that these dates prior to the events were written in to legitimize the acts of which the Catholic Action members were being accused. In that record, it is established that the tally-sheet records for voluntary contributions would be printed. Then in another record, dated April 14, 1964 (*sic*), it is recorded that a decision had been made to repair the church, and again the tally sheets are mentioned. Apparently, in haste, the date was mistakenly recorded as 1964 instead of 1965. This served to provide legal legitimacy for collecting money, repairing the church, destroying the side altars, replacing the floor, and so forth. Legally, the church building was directly under the church.

It was at this time that a Central Board was organized for Catholic Action in San Antonio, because previously the existing centers did not have a municipal-level board above those at each particular center. Catholic Action in San

Antonio thereby acquired a greater degree of independence from Santa Cruz del Quiché, because the Central Board would be responsible for dealing with certain matters previously reserved for the board in Santa Cruz, such as permission for couples to marry.

Taking advantage of the fact that Radio Quiché had been set up by the priests and inaugurated in September 1965 and was now operating, and that radios could be bought on time through the Philips outlet that had recently opened in Santa Cruz, the leaders in San Antonio, who had been going to Santa Cruz on Tuesdays to listen to the class in order to then repeat it in San Antonio the next day, stopped making this weekly trip. The radio station broadcast the class directly on Wednesday, and the members in the various municipalities like San Antonio gathered to listen to it directly. Catholic Action in San Antonio thus became more independent, even though the leaders no longer had the opportunity to strengthen certain contacts with leaders in Santa Cruz.

When they learned that the two men jailed were free, the "townspeople" went to work again. They sent briefs to the court, but these were simply filed away. I do not know whether any further "gratuity" was given to the judge or the secretary, but a merchant who is a friend of the secretary commented to other friends: "I'm going to give this roll of material to the lawyer or the judge, so Catholic Action will take firm hold." He wanted Catholic Action to be firmly rooted in San Antonio. The judge's secretary passed on the word, "No problem, they've already brought another brief. Let them fire off lots of them. There's money here for lawyers."

In 1965, the use of chemical fertilizer became more widespread. This was the year when Center No. 5 (Chichó-Xebaquit) was in full bloom, after it broke away from Center No. 1 with only fourteen households, probably because of competition between two fertilizer merchants, one in Center No. 1 and the other in Center No. 5. By the end of the year, Center No. 5 had doubled its number of households. This rapid growth would continue more or less at the same pace in the following years, because in late 1966 there were thirty-six households and in late 1967 there were sixty-four. Growing use of fertilizer went hand in hand with the growth of Catholic Action in these cantons.

It was around this time that the peasant league also arose in San Antonio, as I will be noting in the next section. Centers 6 and 7 were also set up in 1965, perhaps reflecting the impact of the church's victory and of chemical fertilizer (see Table 6.1).

Meanwhile, the Traditionalists kept sending legal briefs against the mayor to the Ministry of Government in Guatemala City and Santa Cruz del Quiché. The mayor is said to have grown weary, and he eventually resigned. His alternate, who was on the side of the "townspeople," took office on August 10, 1965, but only a few months had passed when the former mayor presented a document against his alternate, accusing him of siding with the "townspeople" and not being a true justice of the peace. The former mayor claimed that when a politician from Santa Cruz del Quiché came to San Antonio one day, the mayor had left his office with him and had gone with the "townspeople" to examine the second floor of the convent.

On February 14, 1966, the governor—a different one from the previous one—showed up and dismissed the mayor and, as an interim appointment, installed Regidor No. 4, who was illiterate. The first former mayor and another Catholic Action merchant got together and personally presented the governor with a candidate to replace the interim one, who, being unable to read, was unable to do the work. The governor examined this candidate to see whether he could read and write, and on May 9, 1966, he was appointed mayor by a gubernatorial decree to replace the illiterate interim figure. That mayor completed the two-year municipal period during which four mayors had gone through that position.

In national elections held on March 6, 1966, the PR unexpectedly defeated the governing PID and the MLN. The Christian Democrat Party was not allowed to be registered prior to the election, but a few months later it was officially recognized before the PR began to guide the nation.

Elections were also held in San Antonio for the 1966–1968 period. For the first time the results went against the choice by the *principales*, who, along with the "townspeople," went with the MLN Party. Catholic Action members, on the other hand, tried to be officially registered under the Christian Democrat Party, but since that was impossible, they gave their support to the PID, whose local group was led by the former mayor from the previous period who, on his own, sought a Catholic Action partner, one who was intelligent but a "drinker." The Catholic Action leaders did not agree with the choice of candidate and presented their own slate, but they delayed and meanwhile the candidate presented by the former mayor from the previous period had already been registered. In the municipal elections, the PID triumphed over the MLN, while the PR, which won the presidential election nationally, had no representation.

Municipal Period 1966–1968: Five Mayors

The new mayor took office on June 15, 1966, and the maneuvering soon began. It was set off when the first *regidor* got drunk and insulted the mayor. In response, the mayor had him jailed, but when he came out, perhaps out of spite, the first *regidor* went to the governor's office to present his resignation. It was his first step in attacking the mayor, who belonged to Catholic Action even though he used to drink too. The first *regidor* was an MLN Traditionalist, who for the sake of minority representation[3] was on the town council, most of whose members were Catholic Action adherents and belonged to the PID.

The next step was probably begun through the influence of the "townspeople" in the regional court or at the governor's office. The PR was in office in the national government, but as we have seen, it had not supported any of the parties in San Antonio for the municipal election. However, for the "townspeople," who had no departmental connections through the *cofradías*, it would be easier to change parties than for Catholic Action members, whose diocesan board members had commitments to the Christian Democrats. It seems that at this point the "townspeople" began to tilt toward the PR and to win over some of the officials in its administration.

The fact is that the regional court fined the mayor in early August, because he had not come to the governor's office after taking office. That prompted the mayor to get drunk. That night, while the mayor was drinking, the *alguaciles* had three men jailed for being out in the street in violation of the curfew imposed by the suppression of guarantees then in effect in the country. The next morning, in the absence of the mayor, who was out drinking, the *síndico* and the first alternate *regidor*, both members of Catholic Action, released the men who were in jail. When he came back to his office, the mayor became angry, insulted the *síndico* and the *regidor*, and accused them of having taken a bribe for the prisoners. Perhaps still drunk, the mayor wanted to jail his two fellow council members. Seeing this, the other *regidores* made a common front against the mayor and threatened to resign. The two leaders from the first Catholic Action center tried to mediate in the dispute, but the mayor went to the governor's office, where he presented his irrevocable resignation. The governor accepted it but was not pleased. The procedure went to the Electoral Tribunal and the first alternate *regidor* took office as the mayor's replacement on August 9, 1966.

This mayor, the second in the line of mayors of this period, did not last even three months. The "townspeople" accused him of being unable to write. He had learned to read on his own, and he could sign his name, but no more. The "townspeople" wanted the first *regidor* who had resigned right after taking office to be made mayor.

Aware of his very weak position, the new mayor went to the governor's office with the clerk one day before his adversaries did, and there the fourth *regidor*, a Catholic Action member who was a contractor and could read and write, was appointed mayor, even though he wasn't present. They informed him after his appointment, but he was unwilling to accept until finally he received a telegram from the Electoral Tribunal, ordering him to take the position or go to jail. This happened in late August or early September 1966. He was the third mayor during this period.

The "townspeople," who had been humiliated because they had shown up at the governor's office one day late, did not give up. One of them, a merchant, went to the labor inspector in Escuintla to get documentary proof that this person (the mayor) was a labor contractor and hence could not be mayor. He distributed four copies of the documentation, one probably to the Ministry of Governance, another to the governor's office in Santa Cruz del Quiché, another to the regional judge, and finally one to the Electoral Tribunal (each costing Q 25).

In order to come out on top, this merchant, who was eyeing the mayor's position himself, was having conversations with an opportunistic departmental politician who had been in the PID, but who had switched to the PR because it was then the party in power. Through this man's influence, his own insistence paid off in the Electoral Tribunal, which sent a note indicating that even though the mayor could not be forced to resign because he was a labor contractor, if he wished, his resignation would be accepted, and in such a case, the fifth *regidor*, who was able to read and write, would replace him. This *regidor* was a Traditionalist.

When he received the note, the mayor lost heart and resigned. He seemed happy, because "the Q 15 I earned as mayor was nothing compared to the Q 400 that I could earn with a truckload (of people)." This happened at the end of March (Holy Week) 1967. Succeeding a drunk and an illiterate, he was the third mayor dismissed in less than a year.

The new mayor, like the two preceding him, had interim status. The country was under a state of siege, and thus elections to replace the mayor could not be held in the municipality. In December 1967 the elections could finally be held, and so the mayor changed for the fourth time. In this election, the Catholic Action group for the first time presented a candidate under the Christian Democrat Party, which was now registered as a party. The "townspeople" presented the merchant who served as an intermediary under the PR banner.

The results, according to someone who was then a *regidor* and a member of Catholic Action, gave the Christian Democrats a 70-to-65 victory over the PR, but the departmental Electoral Registry stepped in to arrange votes in favor of the PR. Neither side had many votes because many people were on the coast harvesting cotton. Taking office as the fifth mayor was the PR merchant who was aligned with the "townspeople." He was an opportunist who has subsequently sought to be on good terms with Catholic Action as well.

During his six months as mayor, construction began on the new school in the town, which had been suggested three years previously by the governor, who was opposed to Catholic Action. He also replaced the municipal clerk with one from the PR. At the beginning of his term there was Q 700 in the treasury, but six months later there was simply a Q 254 debt. It was rumored among both Catholic Action members and Traditionalists that embezzlement had occurred around construction of the school, that this money had been used to pay for roofing on the school or wire fencing at a price over the actual one, and that the mayor and the clerk had pocketed the difference. However, with the support of the party in power, the mayor concluded his term.

Next came the 1968 election for mayor. With the aid of a Christian Democrat leader in Santa Cruz, the Catholic Action group registered their slate under this party. This was one of the few municipalities in the department of El Quiché that was able to do so. The "townspeople" supported the PR, the party in power.

This time the Catholic Action candidates were well chosen. The mayor had been president of Center No. 1; the *síndico*, president of Center No. 5; the first *regidor*, one of the main promoters of the school in Chiaj; the second *regidor*, a recently converted well-off merchant; and the other candidates for the council had likewise served as center leaders. They represented almost all the centers and cantons, most of them were merchants, and almost all had been or were board members of their centers. The candidate for mayor, moreover, had more godchildren than almost anyone in the municipality. With these people, the slate could bring in voters who did not usually vote, and once elected, it promised stability such as the other municipal councils whose selection had involved bypassing the *principales* had not had. It should also be noted that this slate upheld a principle that the *principales* used to apply in choosing their candidates, namely, the hierarchical order by which one does not serve in a municipal position without having first done so in the *cofradía* or vice versa. For Catholic Action, their *cargos* on the board were tantamount to those of a *cofradía*.

Indeed, the Catholic Action candidates won 101 to 75. On the afternoon of the election, a formal agreement was drafted in San Antonio in the presence of party representatives to prevent a subsequent fraud, but once more the ballots were taken to Santa Cruz del Quiché, where 20 Christian Democrat votes were annulled and 6 PR ballots were added, leaving a tie. It was then said that the Christian Democrat candidate had been jailed in 1965 in the conflict over the altars, and that the victory would therefore go to his opponent.

In Guatemala City, however, the record from the electoral tables in San Antonio was respected (what influence was brought to bear I do not know). Moreover, with regard to the accusation against the candidate for mayor, a lawyer advised a board member to prepare a certification to the effect that although the candidate had been arrested, he had not been sentenced, and that he take this to the Electoral Registry, which he did. He himself identified the ballots that had subsequently been stained after voting in San Antonio and so had to be declared invalid in Santa Cruz del Quiché, and the mayor's position was awarded to him. Catholic Action thus won in San Antonio for the first time.

On September 11, 1968, two days before the council took office, the Town Improvement Committee was set up with two *principales* from each canton on it. The municipality gave them a meeting site in the old school and a room on the second floor of the religious house for *cofradía* matters. The members were not the same as those on the Friends of the Town Committee, which had been set up in December 1964, but Catholic Action members saw both committees as more or less the same; the people on both were allies. The Traditionalists became established with a formal organization in order to assure that they would have a couple of meeting places before the opposition mayor took office.

Municipal Period 1968–1970: Stability

By way of exception, this mayor's term was peaceful and stable. On the day that his two-year term ended and he turned over the position in 1970, he furnished the *principales* with an account of the projects he had carried out: he had paid off the debt and left Q 100 in the treasury; built municipal toilets for Q 360; bought a plot of land to extend the cemetery; provided economic help for building the school in Patzalá Canton (see the next section for a detailed narrative); inaugurated telephone service; established fees for the purchase of pigs; made efforts to get electric power in the town; and in fact INDE (National Electrification Institute) began to install connections a few months after his term ended.

1970 Elections

The time arrived for elections for the next period, which was to begin in 1970; these were also presidential elections. Catholic Action members chose their candidate for mayor in a meeting held in their chapel. They held a voice vote, choosing their candidates from possible names written on a blackboard. The one chosen to be the candidate for mayor had been president of Center No. 2 and had learned to read on his own, but he was barely able to write. He was intelligent, had been a merchant, and owned cornfields on lands that he leased on the coast. After leaving the coast, he had lost some of his money, and that was probably why he did not have many baptism ties. The others on the slate (for *síndico* and *regidores*) were chosen by the Christian Democrat representative in San Antonio, a former Catholic Action board member and also a merchant.

The Traditionalists presented two different slates, one under the PR and the other under the MLN-PID coalition. The first slate's candidate for mayor was the former deal-making opportunistic mayor from 1966, who had served for six months, the last in the series of five mayors. The candidate for the second slate was the *fiscal* of the Traditionalists, who is like a lifelong master of ceremonies, chosen by the *cofradías*.

Why did the Traditionalists split into two slates and run the risk of dividing their votes and losing? One explanation is that because these were also presidential elections, they would have a greater chance of winning with the party in power. Another explanation is that the first slate with the PR had been presented by the candidate for mayor himself, with his own characteristic personal flair. Probably both motivations were at work, and the Traditionalists had a few votes for the PR to keep him happy, while the majority went with the coalition.

The Traditionalists' second slate included two Protestants for the first time. It is curious that these people, who call politics dirty and reject the saints, should have allied with the Traditionalists. The pastor was related to the political intermediary of the "townspeople," who is not a fervent Traditionalist.

The Christian Democrat political representative in San Antonio engaged in systematic propaganda by visiting each of the centers on Wednesdays, when the members were gathered for the class being broadcast by radio. Some center leaders welcomed him, but others were cooler, and one even courteously refused to allow him to speak, because according to guidelines from the bishop of El Quiché, propaganda was prohibited in the chapels. However, in this case, the members asked the leader to allow it, first announcing after the class that people were free to remain or to leave as they saw fit.

The recently set up Radio Utatlán station played a role in this 1970 election, but I have not been able to establish just what it was. It must have competed with Radio Quiché, which was run by the priests. The new station aired some complaints against the priests for "meddling in politics" even though they were foreigners, sometimes mentioning their full names; the traditions and *cofradías* were supported in their celebrations; and, in general, a different channel was opened up, not only for presenting paid ads by political parties but also for giving voice to personal resentments or to contesting groups that had no opportunity to express themselves over Radio Quiché. Radio Quiché broadcast paid ads by all parties, thereby conferring on those who were against Catholic Action a certain seal of approval, but it would not have been a means for sharp attacks, much less if they were against the church.[4]

On the eve of the deadline for registering slates, the Electoral Registry returned the Christian Democrat slate to Catholic Action members because there was a discrepancy between the name of a *regidor* on the slate and on his personal identification card. It was a ploy by the party in power to block the Christian Democrat slate at the last minute. The Christian Democrat representative in San Antonio, together with the one in Quiché, handled all the required procedures very quickly and managed to have the slate registered correctly before the registry was closed.

The result of the vote on March 1, 1970, was 130 votes for the CD, 115 for the MLN-PID coalition, and 15 for the PR. Although Catholic Action and the Christian Democrats won, and there was more participation than two years previously, thanks to the presence of twenty women at the polls,[5] a certain lack of discipline could be seen, because one whole center did not show up to vote and at another there was known to have been resistance to voting on the part of influential leaders. Catholic Action members seemed to be growing weary of the message of the political representative, who always spoke to them of major victories and immediate changes, such as raising wages on the coast, through the Christian Democrats ("this time yes"), but the Christian Democrat victory never came about.

On election day, the votes were counted at the election tables in the presence of the party representatives; the ballot boxes were then sealed and sent directly to Guatemala City. The unofficial results were broadcast immediately over Radio Quiché to prevent them from being changed as they had been three and two years previously. The Christian Democrat mayor took office a few months after the election.

Nationally, the coalition won. Although they had lost in the municipality, the Traditionalists would enjoy government support, and soon they would pull political strings to place their own man as mayor, after having the Christian Democrat and Catholic Action mayor overthrown.

Before the mayor was overthrown, there was yet another struggle between Catholic Action and the "townspeople," which occurred in August 1970. The "townspeople," led by the political go-between who was also a merchant, and with the help of lawyers, sent a document to the Ministry of Governance presenting complaints about the Spanish priest, the clerk, the mayor, and Catholic Action, because they were not allowing them to continue with their traditions. Specifically, they said that the mayor had not yet appointed the traditional *chajales* (caretakers of the church) and that the earlier decision about the one holding the key to the church was not being observed.

The document was not signed by the political go-between who was fanning the dispute, but by the *alcalde* of the *cofradía* of San Antonio, the most important *cofradía* in San Antonio, who, when argument broke out between the two sides, got cold feet and kept silent. The document was repetitious and unclear and was drawn up by a ladino in Santa Cruz, probably a *güisache* (someone who acts like a lawyer without being one), who was the source of some expressions and arguments that the local Indians do not normally use but that were designed to appeal to higher authorities, such as indicating that the Traditionalists were being insulted with the expression "profane Catholics" (it should be "pagan") or "wild Indians." He mentioned the Spanish priests using public opinion against Cardinal Casariego, who was born in Spain and who at that time was being bitterly harassed by the group of Guatemalan priests called COSDEGUA (National Council of Priests of Guatemala) in Guatemala City. Finally, the document accused the municipal clerk of election fraud in the recent election.

The interim governor summoned the two parties and brought them face to face. For one side there appeared the political intermediary, the *alcalde* of the *cofradía* of San Antonio, plus other Traditionalists; on the other side, the mayor, the clerk, the visiting priest (not I), and some Catholic Action leaders. After a discussion, they agreed that the main key to the church would remain in the hands of the sacristan of the Traditionalists, who begrudgingly was forced to accept it in order to open and close the church daily or pay someone to do it, because he lived in a canton far from the town. The Catholic Action sacristan still had the key to the side door of the church and a copy of the key to the upstairs of the convent, which had previously been solely in the hands of the Traditionalists. The validity of the previous election was not questioned, nor was the clerk challenged.

The battles continued and, as mentioned, there came a point when the mayor was deposed, and an arrest warrant went out for him. He ran off to the coast. With 326 households in 1970 (see Table 6.2), Catholic Action seems to have reached a plateau, probably due in part to the impossibility of governing cleanly and peacefully while in opposition to the governments in power at the national level.

In a four-year period (1966–1970), four chapels were finished: in Center No. 6 (1966), in Center No. 2 (1967), in Center No. 1 (1969), and in Center No. 5 (1970). The first three, which are smaller, entailed spending of around Q 700, plus the contribution of adobe bricks made by the members, their voluntary labor helping the builder from Santa Cruz del Quiché, and the lumber and land donated by some of the members—altogether totaling some Q 5,000. The chapel at the center is the most visible symbol of the organization's existence, and it represents the irreversibility of the conversion process.

Summary

In the country as a whole during this period, Christian Democracy moved further toward the left and into opposition to the two administrations in power, that of the head of state Colonel Peralta and that of the elected president Julio C. Méndez Montenegro. The party supporting Catholic Action thereby led it into opposition and into the risks that entailed, while the Traditionalists usually sought support from the party in power in the national government.

The stability of the alliance between the Christian Democrats and Catholic Action, not only in San Antonio but in the entire department, was due to the connections between Catholic Action in municipalities and in the department capital. As long as the alliance was maintained in the capital, it would hold up in the municipalities. This way of working contrasts with that of the Traditionalists, who switch parties, always pursuing the one in power. They have no departmental organization (e.g., departmental *principales*), and their alliances are made for specific elections. That does not mean, however, that Catholic Action is monolithic; some centers or groups have other ideas. Divisions within Catholic Action appear to be more noticeable the larger it becomes.

During this period, when factional splits opened up within the Catholic Church worldwide, in Guatemala some priests gradually broke away from the positions of the hierarchy. Catholic Action, which constituted almost the entire flock served by the priests from Quiché, with encouragement from some of them, assumed the consequences of opposition to the interests of more powerful people in the department and to the regime from which those people sought help and which supported them.

Nevertheless, the Catholic Church, whose legal standing improved after 1956, used its influence to protect municipal Catholic Action centers and their leaders. Likewise, the Christian Democrat Party, which has followers in the department capital, protected its grassroots supporters who give it power. Sometimes the existence of two authorities (department governor vs. regional judge) and the opposition between them, which was helpful to the Catholic Action leaders, was a reflection of clashes between parties that both the department leaders and the priests could utilize in the defense of municipal-level Catholic Action.

These eight years (1963–1970) covered three municipal periods. There were four mayors in the first period and five in the second. This instability reflected that of the country itself, which was under a de facto government and a state of siege. Although paradoxically, while it might seem that centralized decisions would provide greater stability, that was not actually the case, because bringing influence to bear on the appointment of mayors required a great deal of intrigue, the mayor appointed did not have popular support, and, in some instances, he had not even been consulted before being designated.

That instability was also the result of a lack of experience of popular elections in the context of party struggles. Until that time, mayors had been appointed by the *principales*, and the election was practically a fiction. More recently, by contrast, mayors did not have the support of the *principales* and those chosen had previous responsibilities in the *cofradía* or in Catholic Action before becoming mayor.

That instability also derived from the fact that neither of the groups, Catholic Action or Traditionalist, had a clear preponderance over the other. Both had departmental and national support. Contributing to this balance is minority representation, by which the losers have some people in the mayor's office, and the possibility of mayors being replaced.

The stability of the most recent period was due to the power and agreement of those on the town council, which practically canceled out the Traditionalist *regidores*. It was also due to the mayor's popularity in terms of baptismal sponsor ties. The harmony of the Catholic Action local administration was respectful of the Traditionalists.

Derivation of power tends to legitimize the mayor by means of the state apparatus. Access to agents of this machinery then becomes crucial. Ordinarily, for each of the contending groups, we find a community middleman who has no funds and is probably financed by the party during election time; a group of merchants in the community from each contending group, which finances the requests of the intermediary; some advisor in the department capital for each group; a lawyer or "self-taught lawyer" eager to earn a few quetzales; and influential persons who tilt the decision of the governor or regional judge. In theory, the groups contending at the municipal level, particularly the *principales* and *cofrades*, stand apart from all this intrigue that feeds off these conflicts and therefore has an interest in them.

Derived power has yielded material projects such as the school and access to chemical fertilizer. While these innovations have been utilized by members of Catholic Action, they have also increased their numbers. In the next section, we will analyze in greater detail derivation of this type of power in the case of Patzalá Canton.

Other Sources of Derived Power

Here I want to describe some other sources of power that have not been explained in the account of the municipality's political history, but that in one way or another have been involved either in the growth of Catholic Action or in determining which side holds the mayor's office. I did not include them in the account of political history because they were somewhat on the margins of the conflict between contending religious groups and doing so would have been a digression.

Third Order Franciscans (± 1965 to 1970)

The group of the devotees of Saint Francis (*sanfranciscanos*), or the Venerable Third Order of Saint Francis, is made up of a small group of eleven men and their wives, nine of them professed and two novices, which operates within Catholic Action but is independent of its leadership structure. All belong to Catholic Action, several of them hold or have held leadership positions in Catholic Action, and it has the appearance of an elite cell that is inside it but that is not quite of it. They are said to perform more prayer and penance than others. They do not drink at all, and they reproach those who get drunk. One of them wanted to physically beat up the president of the Catholic Action central office because he had gotten drunk and was setting a bad example. They claim to have a greater hold on salvation. They sit in the front of the church wearing a scapular that covers their chest and shoulders and a rope belt. On third Sundays they meet to pray all fifteen mysteries of the rosary, and a few years ago, when a Franciscan priest was pastor in Patzité, they used to go periodically to that municipality to meet with their fellow Third Order members there.

The "seed" of the Third Order was brought to Patzité around 1965 by a merchant who then visited the Franciscan priests in Guatemala City to enhance his organization and message. However, shortly after the Franciscan left his parish, the other priests, Missionaries of the Sacred Heart who cover the whole department without the help of any other congregation or religious order of priests, decided to disband the Third Order in Patzité because they saw it as divisive.

The Third Order Franciscans who were left in San Antonio complained that the priests ridiculed them for their rope belts and scapulars, and have criticized them in public "because all they do is pray and pray and aren't concerned about planting." The devotees of Saint Francis have tried to confer some kind of legitimacy on their order by going directly to the bishop and asking him to grant approval to the group's charter. The bishop, who is not a member of the congregation of the priests and is not a Spaniard like them and so is lacking in power, has kept them at arm's distance.

Although no split has taken place because the bishop did not support them and because the Franciscans in Guatemala City are very far away and would not have any interest in supporting them, the lines where a division could take place are nonetheless plain to see. The fissuring force driving them is a tendency to set themselves apart from Catholic Action, although without rejecting it completely since they themselves have served as its leaders and were among its promoters. The tendency to set themselves apart accentuates religious practices and zeal for the original morality of Catholic Action. Curiously, some of their members have been noteworthy in local politics, inasmuch as both Catholic Action mayors (1968 and 1970) have been Third Order Franciscans.

Evangelical Protestants (± 1958 to 1970)

Drawing comparisons between Catholic Action or the Third Order and evangelical Protestants would not make either side happy, but in terms of power structures, their similarities are quite revealing. The evangelicals (pentecostals) have derived their power from the Church of God (Iglesia de Dios). According to some of its pastors, the Church of God has about 15,000 members in Guatemala. It expanded throughout the country rather than in a localized area because it did not attend the synod in which Protestant churches divided up the country's territory among themselves. It is headquartered in the United States and is organized under a general supervisor and a twelve-member Consulting Council. Regional supervisors are under the general supervisor. Central America is a region, and under its supervisor is the Western Territory of Guatemala, under which in turn is the pastor responsible for the district that is headquartered in Santa Cruz. Finally, that pastor is over the pastor of Chuicacá in Santa María Chiquimula.

The pastors of San Antonio originally belonged to the same district, and even though they split off and came under the Independent New Jerusalem Church of God—whose main pastor is headquartered in Santa María Chiquimula—some of their members still attend the annual conventions of the Western Territory, where five thousand pentecostal participants gather in the village of Chiquimula in Chuicacá. Attending these week-long conferences are indigenous people, ladinos, and American ministers, who stir up one another's enthusiasm to maintain themselves in the faith for a whole year.

San Antonio has two small churches of the Independent Church of God, with a total of sixty-four households in the entire municipality, although they are concentrated in the central cantons, especially Chuijip and one hamlet or another in Chiaj. Conventions are held each year in both chapels, with visitors coming from nearby municipalities. At first the only chapel was in Chuijip, very close to the town, but recently an internal conflict has led to the splitting off of another, which began to operate in the private home of one of the "brethren." Both acknowledged, however, that they are under the Independent Church of God in Chiquimula, which also supervises six other chapels in other municipalities.

The first Protestant convert, who is now pastor of the first small church, was a Catholic Action member who around 1958 went over to the Protestants. He had been a stratum B merchant in Izabal. Later he converted a group of relatives and traders who did business near him in Izabal, and he put up the church alongside his house in San Antonio. Another merchant from Izabal is the second pastor in this same chapel; he converted his children and siblings in Chiaj, where he lives.

It is rumored that in 1969 an internal conflict broke out, the upshot of which was that the group centered around the second small church in the town split away. The pastor in Chiquimula then conferred the rank of pastor on one of the merchants in the new church, a truck owner whom the congregation chose by vote.

Comparing the growth of Catholic Action and Protestantism, we may ask why one movement developed more vigorously than the other. The reason does not lie in the kind of beliefs or worship, such as that the evangelicals have rejected the saints and speak in tongues (glossolalia) with everyone trembling. One-third of the households in Chuicacá are pentecostal and are thus on a par with Catholic Action and the Traditionalists, each of which also has approximately one-third. I believe the reason lies in the difference in the power available to Catholic Action and evangelical Protestantism in San Antonio. The Catholic Church in Quiché has more power than the Church of God in Quiché or the Independent Church of God in Chiquimula. It has a group of priests devoted full-time to their parishes who are organized as a strong community throughout the department, with resources overseas and a connection to the national church, which has majority status. By contrast, in the Church of God in Santa Cruz (not the Independent church in Chiquimula), the ladino who is the immediate supervisor has to watch over his store in Santa Cruz, which is his livelihood; he seldom goes in his own car to the chapels in other municipalities (not every week, for example, like the priest does); no other pastor helps him; he has no ties to a majority church, whose higher authorities can wield pressure on behalf of grassroots groups. The Church of God's greater weakness in terms of number of pastors, time devoted, sources of income, means of transportation, and national connections explains the higher probability of small churches breaking away, as compared to Catholic Action. Divisive tendencies also exist in Catholic Action, with competing boards and groups of cantons that react against the central leadership, but these are countered not so much by the leadership in Santa Cruz del Quiché as by the priests. Chuicacá, by contrast, because it is a village in Chiquimula, has served as the site for periodic massive conventions, and judging by the size of its chapels and other installations, it has received more economic help, as well as personal visits from supervisors and missionaries from the United States.

The Peasant League (1965–1970)

Around 1965, under the government of Colonel Enrique Peralta Azurdia (1963–1966), efforts got under way to organize a peasant league in San Antonio, the aim of which would be to defend the rights of indigenous people vis-à-vis ladinos and the authorities. A man from San Antonio, along with others from Santa Cruz del Quiché, attended a short course in Guatemala City organized by people who would then go on to set up the Guatemalan Federation of Peasants, a Christian Democrat Party spin-off, with the same leadership as the party. It was legally recognized in January 1967.

Shortly afterward, apparently that same year, a man from Santa Cruz del Quiché was appointed as the regional salaried extensionist to promote the growth of peasant leagues in the municipalities. He came to a canton in San Antonio and organized a board there by holding an election from candidates' names written on a blackboard. The local people were not familiar with this voting method, so the board members thus elected were all merchants, some of whom employed day laborers in the municipality.

While approval of the by-laws was being pursued through the Ministry of Labor, the league members—who numbered thirty persons, all of them in Catholic Action—held meetings every two weeks under the direction of the president, who was both president of the Catholic Action center in Chiaj and the promoter of the Cooperative Circle in Chiaj. As these meetings took place, specific objectives were proposed, some of them suggested by the regional delegate. For example, the league could help do away with (unpaid) voluntary labor imposed collectively by the municipality for road repair; it would struggle to get pay for the *alguaciles*, who in other municipalities had to serve the whims of the ladinos; it would press those who hired workers to give a day's wage for Sunday, which they had off; it could bypass the contractor who arranged for labor crews to go to the coast by having its own leadership operate as a contractor; it could also rent a piece of land for a crop school and a meeting place, purchase a medicine kit for curing sick members and build up a fund to help those who might fail for other reasons, and finance the construction of a larger classroom in the Chiaj school. Later we will see how this wide range of goals, some of which overlapped with those of the Cooperative Circle, was an indication that organizing the league had not responded effectively to people's needs.

The by-laws of the Peasant League of San Antonio, which had not been approved during the Peralta administration, when the governor had also been opposed to the cooperative in Santa Cruz, were approved by the new PR government with a ruling on November 22, 1966, a few months before the Peasant Federation itself was established. According to the by-laws, the board formed a five-member executive council and a three-member consulting council. The league could have affiliate sections in the cantons, with at least twenty members under three leaders. The monthly dues would be Q 0.10.

With the approval of the by-laws, facilitated by the inauguration of the new administration, which promised to do more to encourage grassroots organizations, and with the parallel growth of Cooperative Circles nourished by loans for chemical fertilizer, many members of the circles signed up for the league, which soon had fifty members, all of them in Catholic Action. Nevertheless, two years after being officially authorized, the league began to languish. Some of the aims it was pursuing had been attained, but others had not. Work on municipal roads was reduced from three days to one day per person every six months, and a little money had been gathered for the school classroom. Nothing else had been accomplished, and these two points were not achieved through a new and different kind of combativeness, because reducing road work was part of the anti-Traditionalist thrust (inasmuch as communal work was a long-standing tradition) and the classroom was a mutual-aid type of project.

Some of the other unmet goals ran against the grain of the league leaders, who themselves hired day laborers; therefore, getting paid for the seventh day of work did not seem to be a matter to be struggled for, nor did raising the rate for a day's pay from Q 0.60 to Q 0.80, as some of the more goodwilled among them might have been willing to do if pressed. Their comment was, "Are we somehow large plantation owners?" and so they evaded any commitment. Moreover, being merchants, they did not have the experience of being contractors, nor did they need to go down to the coast, and so they did not even try to do away with that kind of go-between.

Finally, other goals such as getting pay for the *alguaciles* and renting the site and field for agricultural experimentation were not met, because those served by the *alguaciles* are not only the ladinos, who are very few in number, and because they did not have money to lease land and there was no incentive to grow crops together.

There were other reasons for the decline of the league. The president resigned when he was made town mayor in 1968, and as mayor he recognized the need to require "voluntary" work because the municipality had no money and he was under pressure from the Highway Department, which had a tractor but needed help to fix the road leading into the town. Members of the league began to be called "communists," a term even more off-putting for other merchants who also belonged to Catholic Action but not to the league. One criticism was that it did not accomplish anything practical ("Does it give us anything to eat?"). Finally, the political climate in the country became increasingly repressive, and some of the department priests who did not want "to become involved in politics" were hindering the Quiché extensionist by not letting him use a room for courses in other municipalities.[6] The only power that the federation could provide the league in the municipality was simply the organization at the department and national level. For example, to raise pay for workers on the coast, the majority of people in the highlands would have to be brought together. Such linkages were far from being achieved.

Decline of Cooperative Circles (1968–1970)

As the league's activity languished, so did the Cooperative Circles, which were attached to Catholic Action centers. The promoter of the circles became mayor in 1968, and because of his new obligations, he no longer collected what the members had saved each week. Collection stopped completely in January 1969 (as can be seen in the records of the Chiaj circle).

A similar decline could be seen in other circles, even though the person in charge did not change, thereby suggesting other reasons, for example, that after 1967, the Santa Cruz del Quiché Cooperative became more cautious about lending, in view of bad experiences with delinquent debtors, and it granted loans only to those who had more in savings and who had a record of paying on time. It took more time to grant a loan, up to a month and a half, and the cooperative began to demand the deed to one's land as collateral. The upshot was that those who had more money saved up—amounts such as Q 180, 150, or 125—dealt directly with the cooperative in Santa Cruz without going through the man in charge of the circle, who used to gather the money each week and take it to Santa Cruz. Thus, as practically all the circles attached to Catholic Action centers became defunct, the board members in charge of the circles lost the support of people who had come together drawn by a 1 percent monthly loan as compared to the 5 percent or even 10 percent ones offered by ordinary money lenders. Catholic Action thereby lost the impetus from their attached credit union circles.

Independent Projects from Catholic Action and the Municipality (1967–1970)

The derivation of power from outside the community, independent of the mayor's office and of Catholic Action (and therefore threatening to the centralizing authority of the mayor's office and Catholic Action leaders), is even more apparent in the building of the school and the road in the canton of Patzalá. Analysis of this process will make clearer the division evidenced in the building of the school in Chiaj, which was promoted by Catholic Action leaders in competition with the municipality, then held by the Traditionalists, as recounted in the previous section. The process that spurred the growth of Catholic Action in Chiaj was, by contrast, a hindrance in Patzalá, which was not fully incorporated into Catholic Action's decision making.

In September 1967, Joint Action (the national community development program under the presidency) authorized the formal document constituting an Improvement Committee in the canton of Patzalá, along with its president and other officers. Three of the four board members belonged to Catholic Action, but the treasurer was a Traditionalist because it so happened that the man chosen was the canton treasurer, who from time immemorial had collected contributions for celebrations. The document was passed to the department governor's office, and everything was in order.

Joint Action has a local office (No. 7) in Santa Cruz del Quiché. The center's coordinator and staff are made up of an agronomist, a social worker, a teacher, a home educator, a nurse, and several social promoters—all under the regional director in Chimaltenango, who was then an agricultural engineer.

The Improvement Committee was formed to widen a road so that vehicles could reach the canton directly from Santa Cruz del Quiché in order to build the canton school, which was needed because the children, more and more of whom were attending the school in Chiaj, had to cross a canyon every day to get there. The committee's purpose thus entailed breaking away from Chiaj, the initial Catholic Action center, and becoming more independent of the town in terms of roads.

Bridge and Road in Patzalá Canton

Before the committee was created, the people of the canton experienced a conflict with Chiaj, and that gave the people in Patzalá a sense of identity that enabled them to undertake the job by working together as a whole canton. As some put it, "We saw that we could." The conflict arose around the construction of the four footbridges that cross the Jocol and Joj Rivers at several places in the municipality and connect Patzalá with the four southern cantons (Chichó, Xebaquit, Chiaj, and Tzancawuib) on the one side and with the municipalities of Patzité and Quiché. These bridges consisted of two or three large pine trunks, which were cut down in the mountains and had to be brought in by a group of men working together.

The inhabitants of the four cantons refused to show up when summoned to work. They had no interest in the other side of the river, except for those who took a few corn husks, squash, and ears of corn to sell in the little market in Chuicacá by crossing through Patzalá, or the few merchants who did business in the Patzité market. However, the people in Patzalá had to cross the Jocol River to go to Santa Cruz del Quiché and Patzité, whose market they went to more often because it was close. So the people of Patzalá, upset because they had contributed to the school in Chiaj that benefited these four cantons and now were not receiving any return, decided to put up one of these bridges by themselves. They erected it in two days (they saw that they could).

In previous years, the greater connection through marriage between these five southern cantons was probably at the root of the solidarity and cooperation that kept communication open. Being related by marriage entails frequent visits back and forth. By now, however, such ties were diminishing, as we saw in Chapter 4.

Both Catholic Action members and Traditionalists gathered on a hill where formerly they used to come together with drum and flute to undertake communal work on trails and bridges. There they chose their board and decided, as mentioned above, to go to Joint Action, with which they already had ties through the building of the school in Chiaj. A large number supported the board chosen there, as over eighty men, most of them in Catholic Action, signed the formal record establishing the committee.

After the leaders went to Joint Action and the governor's office, the widening of the road began. Joint Action provided the materials, which were brought in from Chimaltenango and Guatemala City: 70–80 quintals of reinforcement rods, 50 bags of lime, and 50 bags of cement to build the conduits that would protect the road from being washed away by the rain. Forty conduits were made in twenty days along the Joj River, each man doing three days' volunteer work under the direction of a master builder from Santa Cruz.

Money had to be collected to pay for the master builder, continual trips by the leaders, and other expenses. This led to some friction, first with the treasurer, who was also treasurer for the canton and had Q 108 in cash left over from contributions from years past, which had been contributed for masses and feast days. A small group of Traditionalists opposed letting this money be used for construction projects by the new committee, and they presented a complaint, drawn up by a self-taught lawyer, to the governor. With the help of Joint Action, the committee presented another document drawn up by the judge's own lawyer. The governor summoned both parties and ordered the treasurer to hand over the money or face jail. The argument was that the treasurer was not authorized to collect money in his canton. It did not matter that this had been a custom for centuries—he was not legally authorized and "therefore" had to hand it over to the treasury of the new committee. The poor treasurer, trembling, counted the money in the governor's presence and handed it over to the board of the committee, which then replaced the treasurer with a new one from Catholic Action.

School and Politics

After finishing the conduits, the Improvement Committee started work on the school, and Joint Action hinted that the municipality ought to help. The committee leadership went to the mayor, who had been a Catholic Action board member in Chiaj, but he refused to make any contribution: "When did you come to tell me you were meeting? I don't have any money."

The people of Patzalá, who had helped with the school in Chiaj, were now upset that the former board member in Chiaj was unwilling to help with their school, even though the municipality had contributed to the school in Chiaj. The cantons were in competition, and a canton was in competition with the municipality.

The people of Patzalá, however, with the support of Joint Action, an agency of the Revolutionary Party administration, were intent on getting the best of the Christian Democrat mayor. The governor summoned him, along with the mayors of Patzité and San Pedro Jocopilas, where canton schools were also being built. These mayors were apparently willing to make the contribution, but the mayor of San Antonio blithely said, "No, colonel, I'm not willing, because they haven't told me when they meet." The governor threatened to have him taken to the regional judge, but at this point the ladino municipal clerk of San Antonio, who had come along with his mayor, stepped in and advised him to contribute by paying for the master builder.

The master builder was hired by the municipal clerk, who was a man from Santa Cruz del Quiché. According to the account of the man from Patzalá, who is the source of this entire sharply etched story, the clerk took advantage of the occasion to make a deal with the Santa Cruz builder for Q 225, provided the builder would make a deal with the mayor for Q 300. The clerk, who gave the builder a Q 200 advance, did not want to give him the remaining Q 25, and so the builder himself revealed the scheme to the people of Patzalá. The ladino clerk thus pocketed the Q 75 difference.

To have an idea of the material benefits of power made available from the outside, I here present a detailed list of the contributions received from Joint Action, the Rural Social and Educational Fund of the Ministry of Education (requested through the teacher), and CARE (the two institutions used by Joint Action for handling the funds).

Joint Action:	**CARE:**
65 100-lb. bags of lime	pipes
90 m2 of bricks	
95 metal roofing sheets	**Municipality:**
2 doors	Q 225 to pay builder and assistants
8 gallons of paint	
2 rolls of barbed-wire fencing	**Canton:**
	Q 200 (Q 2 each) lumber for beams
Rural Social and Educational Fund:	430 days of labor on adobes
12 desks for five students each	Q 50 for inauguration
1 blackboard	

Joint Action not only provided material benefits, but through the support of the government, it backed up the committee in its decisions: "Oh, the committee is strong" (for forcing people), said one man, "otherwise we go to the governor's office."

The school was dedicated in February 1970 after three months of work and just a month before national elections. The invitation to the inauguration was issued by the committee, the municipality, and Joint Action. Several vehicles went to the hilltop where the school was built, as the road could now be used. According to the inauguration program, outsiders attending included the regional Community Development director, staff from the local Joint Action center, the school district supervisor, and the priest, who said a mass. Some of those who came took advantage of the occasion to pass out propaganda for the PR, which was then in office. The building of the school simultaneously with those of the other nearby municipalities, San Pedro and Patzité, had clearly been timed to coincide with vote-getting.

According to the informant from Patzalá, "People accepted the PR papers. Some acted stupid. They said, 'How can they do this for election day?' As we had explained, 'Act like you don't know anything, ask for things. Deep down you know what you're going to do, when the actual day comes . . .'" On the other hand, the person who acted as a middleman with the Christian Democrat Party reproached them, saying, "The PR, which is yelling about the school, has to be confronted. They have no right. It's just a dedication." But someone else replied, "Let them talk there. Let them give us things. I can ask them how I should vote, to keep them happy." But the party representative answered, "It looks like you're afraid to raise a challenge. You shouldn't accept these papers . . . ," to which the other man said, "You can have a wad of papers in your pocket, but it doesn't mean you believe . . ."

In fact, on election day in March the Catholic Action members from one of the centers in Patzalá did not show up to vote in San Antonio, as indicated in the previous section. Others, however, did accept the government's help but still voted for the opposition party.

As far as the school itself, the dedication served to validate the committee's activities that some people from Patzalá had resisted. Some of the parents who had been uncooperative now sent their children, and of the 130 children in the canton aged 7 to 12, according to the 1967 census, 40 regularly attend the school. Sixty children fit in the classroom.

Summary

Thus far we have seen how a good number of the canton's inhabitants came together outside of the control of the mayor and of Catholic Action to derive power directly from a government development agency that was theoretically apolitical but that had support from the governor in its actions, especially around presidential election time. We have also seen how a group of Traditionalists was opposed to this initiative, but made the mistake of trying to use power not from the development agency but instead from the governor, as was done during the conflicts over the municipality. Likewise, some Traditionalists did participate in the effort of the committee leaders, all of whom were Catholic Action, because the rivalry from which the committee arose was not between Catholic Action and Traditionalists but between canton and municipality.

Catholic Action probably gained prestige in the canton and around the center, because the board members were Christian Democrats, but the tensions with the mayor, a former leader in Chiaj (Center No. 1), and with the Christian Democrat go-between, also a former leader there, would inevitably diminish the movement's strength at the municipal level. This tension in Catholic Action did not occur in building the school in Chiaj, because the mayor was not in Catholic Action and outside power had served to build up the five cantons in the south, where Catholic Action had a majority, against the center of municipal power. Likewise, when the school was built in Chiaj, the Christian Democrat Party was not operating legally, and in 1966 Catholic Action had been told to vote for the PID, the party in power, and hence deriving help from the development agency did not entail any betrayal of Catholic Action's party, as it did now on the eve of elections.

The derivation of power from a development agency without the departmental church or Catholic Action serving as intermediary signified a possible weakening of Catholic Action in the municipality. By comparison with derivation of power from the cooperative or the peasant league, it is clear that the latter are not formally in Catholic Action, but nevertheless they have Catholic Action leaders who are advised by priests. If Catholic Action members in the municipality go to these department leaders, as long as the latter are not separated from Catholic Action leaders in Santa Cruz del Quiché, they are strengthening municipal Catholic Action and are strengthening themselves as Catholic

Action leaders when they grant power. By contrast, the canton committee was deriving power from an agency whose members were not in Catholic Action, were mostly nonindigenous, and had no links to the priests. If this agency granted power, the tie between municipal and department Catholic Action was not thereby strengthened. We will now see how Catholic Action is weakened in a canton when power is derived from sources other than the church. This time it is a private foundation that is granting power.

Agricultural Projects with Different Relationship to the Church

A few days after the March 1970 election, Joint Action organized a course on agriculture at the Social Work House in Santa Cruz del Quiché and invited two young men from Patzalá to attend. (I do not know whether this was a way for Joint Action employees to protect themselves vis-à-vis the impending change of government and of the political party in power.) The two men returned from the course and formed a group of thirty-five men, which first took the name Agriculture Association and then changed it to Farmers Association to have more leeway in their goals. The board was composed of major Catholic Action figures. They then sought to have the association approved by the governor so they could get a loan from the bank to buy chemical fertilizer. When the governor told them that having approval from his office did not suffice for obtaining loans but that their by-laws had to be legally recognized, and they did not have enough time or money for that, people at Joint Action put them in contact with leaders of the Penny Foundation, a private institution for providing credit to rural communities that demands only a list of the applicants, a diagram of the location, and a document from the municipality indicating residence and the good behavior of the applicants.

At around this time CENDAP (National Center for Development, Training, and Productivity), another private organization, organized a radio-broadcast course on agriculture in several municipalities of Quiché through Radio Quiché. Priests were brought in to help get the canton groups going. In San Antonio, five groups were organized with fifteen men each, gathered around their radio, papers in hand, and a group leader. Insistent visiting by the priest overcame some reluctance by the Catholic Action members who met for the classes. The course lasted about three months. Participants met in the afternoon to listen to the radio and hear the explanations, which the group leader then repeated in the indigenous language, with a tone of religious exhortation, while his disciples dozed off. They did some practice planting, which did not yield much. But the participants stayed together for three months in the hope of getting chemical fertilizer at low interest rates.

In Patzalá, the CENDAP Circle competed with the Farmers Association. Some in the circle criticized the association for having Traditionalists and for being a "witch doctor group" that was selling the canton out to the PR. They said that the activity of the circle was better because it was done in the United States, whereas that of the association was done only in Guatemala.

However, the CENDAP Circle in Patzalá did not get fertilizer loans for its members, whereas the association did. Since no one in the circle had his land properly registered in his own name, members could not get loans even in someone else's name. So "they didn't get anything" after having spent "the whole day wandering around."

From the Penny Foundation, the association was able to get 191 (100-lb.) sacks of fertilizer and 57 (110-lb.) sacks of urea, worth Q 1,487.00 at 10 percent a year, payable in one year. Each sack thus cost them approximately Q 5.20, as the merchants sell it. Hence the twenty-five members of the association who in the end signed the last request saved almost Q 700.

The organization of these two groups displays two types of derivation of power: from a private foundation that is independent of both the church and government; and from another organization that is also private but in which the departmental church is involved in the derivation. Some participants in the first group might not acknowledge the church as an authority, but not so in the second. These differences caused bad feeling between both groups, suggesting that one way by which the conflict between Catholic Action and Traditionalists might be reduced would be the growing involvement of private or state organizations linked directly to associations in the cantons, thereby undermining the unity of Catholic Action.

Treasury Guards (Guardia de Hacienda)

Around twenty-one Treasury Guards work in the department of El Quiché, most or all of them from other departments. Their work is divided into five zones, one of which includes the municipalities of Sacapulas, San Bartolo, San Pedro Jocopilas, and San Antonio Ilotenango. The guards are under a chief, whose headquarters is in Santa Cruz del Quiché; he in turn is under the Director of the Guards in Guatemala City, who in turn has been under the Ministry of Governance since the Revolutionary Party took office in 1966, rather than that of the Treasury, as was the case previously. The guards move from one area to another to confiscate clandestine liquor. They earn Q 65 a month, minus the contribution to social security, the party, and other benefits, leaving them around Q 61. The chief earns Q 125. In addition, Ron Botrán (a rum manufacturer) pays them Q 5 for every clandestine still seized, most of which goes to the chief, with a small proportion for the guards. Finally, both the chief and the guards supplement their pay with numerous bribes.

Falling prices for clandestine liquor is one indicator that the number of clandestine liquor manufacturers is growing around the country. The producer (*cuxero*) is now selling a jug (roughly four gallons) to the bar owner or reseller at Q 2.25. Fifteen years ago it sold for Q 3.00. During the Ubico period it was not sold (at least not in San Antonio) because whereas a producer today risks only a few months in jail, then the common practice was to invoke the justification "shot while escaping."

A squad of four guards comes to the municipality approximately every other month. They usually come with a list of names of people fingered by complaining neighbors (catechists are accused of presenting complaints). From Santa Cruz the chief gives the mayor prior notice that the squad is coming. The guards also receive in code a telegram with the names of bars that pass the chief a monthly Q 20 contribution so that they will not be searched with no advance notice. Some bar owners in turn pass the word to the producers in the cantons so that they can hide their barrels. Even so, the guards go into some houses by night without presenting any court order (which is against the law), even when constitutional guarantees in the country are not suspended.[7] They seize manufacturing operations and often accept Q 50 bribes from the producer. Sometimes, however, even after the bribe is taken they still imprison the producer, and that angers the victims. However, to protect themselves from a possible riot, the guards make it a rule never to be by themselves.

Treasury Guards thus find themselves in a situation in which they must demonstrate their effectiveness by seizing an average of three factories per visit, and yet they must do so despite the network of bribes directly connected to their chief, and they must supplement their own income with bribes, as their superiors do, of whom one guard says, "all they do is get fat on other people's work." Liquor producers are under the fierce outside pressure of these agents whom they pay bribes, and yet they keep the price of clandestine liquor from dropping to the very bottom. Consumers are passing their surplus on to the manufacturer and the guards, both of whom are concerned not to let such a rich source of income be blocked up.

We may assume that this network has been becoming more firmly established over time, and that the individuals who have gained most power are those who through their regional connections have been able to make deals with the head of the guards and manage to protect the producers in the ravines and their customers, while those who do not so avail themselves are at the mercy of those very guards. These bar owners tend to be in the town (not in the cantons) because the center of communications (telegraph, a leak from a *regidor*, or even the mayor) is in the town. Through their regional connections, such individuals tend to be middlemen for political parties, and given the political nature of the positions of department chiefs, intermediaries tend to belong to the party in power, thereby reinforcing the anti-alcohol ideology of Catholic Action, which is linked to the opposition party.

Military Commissioners

Across the municipality are about twenty military commissioners, two in each canton, who are under a chief commissioner from one of the central cantons. They are chosen by each mayor for his term of office and are answerable to the commander of the military zone in Quiché. By contrast with other areas in Guatemala (Adams 1970: 199), where the institution of the commissioners has served as a direct instrument for repression since 1954, in San Antonio the military commissioners act as more powerful *alguaciles* who jail drunks on feast days, help maintain order, and provide assistance during recruitment of soldiers for military service. I have no indications that they have been involved in the conflicts between Catholic Action and the Traditionalists.

Conclusions

Next I will carry out a cross analysis of various aspects of the power structure during the periods outlined and examine how they fit in with the birth, growth, and stagnation of Catholic Action.

Increasing Available Power Sources

The domain under which the population has been living is becoming more pluralistic. In Ubico's time, there were no power sources outside the community from which its population could oppose the government. It is unlikely that there could have been a divisive movement spreading through the area at that time.

In the next period, when political parties came on the scene, the independent centers of power multiplied, and Catholic Action emerged by deriving power from the church and the anticommunist movement. It did not gain momentum, however, until the interests granting it power seized the government (1954), gained strength from state power, and for one or two years again centralized power by suppressing political parties and supporting the church as a bulwark of anticommunism.

With the 1957 election following the assassination of Castillo Armas, and with the growing influence of the church, which receives money from outside the country, power at the national level fragmented, and Catholic Action allied itself with the Christian Democrat Party, which would go on to oppose the government. The church granted it power by defending it with its own legal standing, with its influence, and with its link to innovations such as fertilizer. For a time the church almost completely mediated the derivation that granted control over the environment (e.g., credit), and it was not until the last two years that other sources granted their power to Catholic Action members or to both Catholic Action members and Traditionalists, independently of the church. This new multiplication of power sources has lessened the effect of the church's power, which, since the entry of chemical fertilizer, has not been able to introduce any other technological or organizational innovation with a similar impact. The result has been that Catholic Action has been brought to a standstill in the number of its conversions and in the radical nature of its stance.

It is likely that with increasing road communications and people's greater participation in politics, the power sources interested in manipulating votes will keep growing and hence the mystique of Catholic Action will diminish. The political inclination of such groups for or against the government, and for or against the interests of the dominant groups in the country, will keep the division between Catholic Action and the Tradition from being healed, possibly until a new division emerges, this time horizontal, between units that belong permanently to different power levels within the community.

Fighting Only over Symbols?

During the periods described, conflicts have been sharpening over the derivation of legitimacy from the state (for mayors), and disputes have developed over the society of the past (Tradition) or over the institution outside the community, the church (Catholic Action). Although these conflicts have had an indirect impact on the adaptation of individuals to the environment (rebellion against exploitation by *zahorines*) and they reflect increasing friction and envy between residents over land, they have not really been over resources, but over symbols.

Prior to the Ubico administration, however, the conflicts were not over symbols but over the coercion by ladino units outside the community in terms of debts and forced labor on roads and on coastal plantations and the advent of ladino outsiders into the community. During the Arbenz period, as well, even though this exploitation did not disappear, conflicts were centered around specific resources such as the land of the money lender and of those who owed him, the land of the slightly better-off residents, and certain interests valued by ladinos that are difficult to specify for lack of information but that entailed the subversion of power structures on the national level, based on ownership of large agroexport plantations. Because people in the community were rather equal and their interests remained primarily local, the land conflict did not stir them up nor did they split over it.

The conflict over internal symbolic legitimization began to arise as a response of individuals to what they regarded as exploitation by those who were manipulating those symbols, the *zahorines*. The national opposition, then, even though it had different interests, granted power to the struggle against the validity of those symbols, and the church, as an outside body, served to legitimize new symbols.

When the fall of Arbenz caused land conflicts to be suppressed in the municipality and everywhere else in the country, the struggle over symbols within the municipality was intensified. As the legitimizer of the new symbols, the church represented nationally the triumph of that suppression.

It is plausible that if the struggle over resources had been allowed to be pursued nationally, and if it had entered the community more forcefully, the battle over the validity of symbols—which in the minds of the people in the community had nothing to do with the issue of land struggles—would have ceased to be important.

The battle over nonagrarian symbols, when seen in parallel to the repression on a national scale, moved to a different arena, especially when the group rebelling against the traditions (Catholic Action) obtained a local power base equivalent to that of the traditional group. This new arena was legitimization by the state. The validity of the state as a legitimizer was not called into question, as happened with the internal symbols, but rather the competition began to be over deriving that legitimization. It was a battle over political symbols, not a battle for direct control over the physical environment (means of production, land, and the like) or a battle over simply religious symbols.

Here again the power structure was reflected on the national level, where several parties would succeed one another in power (from the PID to the PR and then to the MLN-PID; from the right to the moderate left and back to the right), thereby demonstrating a balance of forces in which no authority is backed by a power clearly greater than that of its opponents. In this oscillating back and forth, derivation of legitimization becomes more important in terms of retaining the image of legality with the population and of manipulating government power. In this state of fluctuation, the derivation of external power from a particular bloc does not reach the point at which it can impose a new order and support the interpretation of its legitimization with force.

With the appearance of new sources of power outside the community (the Penny Foundation, for example), which claim not to be tied to any symbol such as a religious or political creed, "race," or such, the struggle seems to center around the derivation of that power. Although these sources of power offer technology or financing (fertilizer, money), nevertheless, because of the need to repeat the derivation every so often, the power granted places the units deriving it at the mercy of those above them. Fertilizer credit, for example, is renewed each year and one has to be in good standing with the foundation to receive it; however, land, for which the national ideology was struggling in the Arbenz period, would have become a power base whose ownership did not have to be legitimized every year. Thus, the recent derivation of power from technology places the community in a state of ongoing dependency on these sources.

Competition over the latter sources of power displaces the conflict over the valuation of the community's internal symbols, insofar as those sources are independent of the institutions that validate them, such as the church; but it ties the groups that depend on them even more strongly to the national interests of those sources, whether they are private sources of credit or, even worse, wholesale dealerships. In the case of wholesale dealerships (recall Chap. 4) that operate through intermediaries in the community (merchants), stratification within the community is reinforced and tensions rise further between the intermediary (who is also a money lender) and the population he supplies.

Hence an area of conflict emerges that is possibly going to divide the community horizontally. With this new division, the conflict over internal legitimization of symbols will gradually be replaced by conflict over the resources themselves, because the debts entail repossessing land, and the ground will thereby be prepared for violence encouraged by outside forces.

Regionalization, Nationalization, and "Village-ization"

The development of Catholic Action brought with it a process of regionalization, the steps of which should be examined by comparing the forms of derivation of power of the movement. In its origins, it was based on the informal relationships between merchants from nearby municipalities. The convert comes to depend as an individual on the organized center of a neighboring municipality, such as Chiquimula and Santa Lucía. His conversion is radical, but his confrontation with his adversary, the *zahorín*, takes place initially between individual and individual. Only when the convert wins over more individuals who recognize him as a leader does the confrontation move up a level: the first convert and his followers versus the *zahorín* and his. The need to get out from under the power of the *zahorín* to achieve this confrontation is what makes the first convert enlist other converts.

At this stage (1948–1951), the new converts' relationship to Catholic Action in the nearby municipality was similar to that of the evangelical Protestants in 1970, who derived power from the Independent Church of God in Chiquimula, but it differed insofar as the Catholic Action organization in Chiquimula did not grant legitimization to the leadership of the neighboring municipality because it was at that time under the bishop of Quetzaltenango and it did not have the authority to grant such legitimation, whereas the Independent Church of God does grant it. Likewise, Catholic Action in the neighboring municipality operated at the same level as that of the incipient organization in the Chiaj canton, for example, in San Antonio.

Given the incipient nature of San Antonio's Catholic Action organization, and the model in Chiquimula, its first leader was impelled to go to Quetzaltenango in 1951 seeking legitimation from the bishop. His center, as symbolized by its authorization to have a banner, then began to depend on a regional network of power that was quite extensive (the whole diocese of Quetzaltenango) but that had little power to offer from a distance. The confrontation continued within the canton.

The next year (1952) the confrontation expanded to include the bishop himself and his aggressive catechists. Until then, even though conversions might be as radical as described, opposition had not emerged within the municipality, and a degree of collaboration between Catholic Action and the Traditionalists had been maintained, albeit with some reluctance, in joint processions. Opposition emerged when the legitimization granted by the bishop was made manifest to the municipality, and when the two Catholic Action groups, one with a board and the other that still did not have one (Chiaj and Canamixtoj), united to form one group.

Catholic Action converts in San Antonio and in the other municipalities served by the pastor in Santa Cruz showed that they were under the bishop of Quetzaltenango by going weekly to the bishop's representative in Santa Cruz. The center of the region to which Catholic Action in San Antonio was attached gradually became Santa Cruz, thereby reducing the limits of the regional network from the entire diocese down to the parish of Santa Cruz and its nearby municipalities. The first converts from these municipalities and their leaders met in Santa Cruz each week and were given guidance.

With the change of government (1954) and the larger number of priests in Santa Cruz, Catholic Action grew and the center in San Antonio split in two. The conflict had now made its mark on the municipal level, and the leaders of the first center plus those of the second were acting together to deal with the conflicts, even without a common organization. Properly speaking, they were both under the priests in Santa Cruz and later they were under the diocesan board, which was made up of Catholic Action members in Santa Cruz. Their orientation to Santa Cruz as a center of derivation of power and legitimation increased as more Catholic Action centers emerged in San Antonio.

With the creation of the diocese of Sololá and the appointment of its first bishop (1955), the already weak ties to Quetzaltenango were cut. No significant communication was established with Sololá as the headquarters of the diocese in terms of visits by Catholic Action members, and the region was increasingly defined as the department of El Quiché, inasmuch as the congregation of priests covered the entire department and only that. Ties to Sololá were definitively cut in the late 1960s when Quiché became a diocese.

As a result of the conflicts in 1965 the central board was formalized in San Antonio, with the other canton centers under it. The derivation of legal status for this formalization once more came from outside, from the church. When this more encompassing organization emerged, the intensity of regionalization subsided. Ties with the diocesan board in Quiché were not cut, but communication between the boards in the canton centers and with the diocese now passed through the central board in San Antonio. Municipal Catholic Action grew stronger with this greater degree of autonomy, but its regional ties were weakened. These ties have been sustained by the radio station, but they are now more institutionalized and depersonalized. Canton leaders no longer go to Santa Cruz del Quiché to attend class and they no longer have the chance to establish personal ties with diocesan leaders or with the leaders from cantons or centers from other municipalities. The growth of Catholic Action in the region has made it impossible to maintain such ties. Even though there has been no return to the situation of the *principales*, who had no committee of *principales* to turn to in Santa Cruz del Quiché, the trend is toward less regionalization, which had been necessary in view of their initial weakness.

Although Catholic Action is in theory organized nationally, with a president headquartered in Guatemala City, and it is conceivable that power could be derived from the national level, the scope has actually not gone that far. Indirectly, however, insofar as the internal division in the community has made it necessary for each of the parties in conflict to go not only to municipal but to national units, such as the Ministry of Governance, and to become familiar with how decisions are made and engage in deriving power from the state, some steps have been taken toward national connections, albeit among a small number of people comprising those who operate as intermediaries. The derivation of national power from other sources, such as the peasant federation, parties, and private foundations is increasing people's awareness of belonging to the domain of the nation, however slowly.

At the opposite pole, however, with the formation of new canton centers caused by population increase and stratification, a stronger linkage has emerged between the municipality and the households and lineages. This process, which could be called "village-ization" (*aldeización*; *aldea* = village), is being bolstered by state development agencies or by credit foundations, which, unable to manipulate the entire municipality, grant power directly to canton committees composed not only of people from Catholic Action centers but also including some nonmembers. The building of schools at the centers, alongside the chapels, also extends the relationship to Traditionalist children who would not enter Catholic Action chapels. This process, which is rooted in the gradual reduction of kinship ties, goes hand in hand with keeping a certain limit on the number of persons one deals with face to face, which is necessary for keeping ties personal and preventing them from becoming anonymous.

In short, the limits placed on Catholic Action in the municipality were slowly reduced as its growing grassroots strength led to the formalization of new levels of power in the municipality. The creation of the center gave rise to the "village-ization" process, while the ties to national centers of power has gradually strengthened relations at the national level. In their opposition, the Traditionalists have also followed the same process, although they have no equivalent to the church to link them regionally or nationally and thereby to legitimize their internal symbols.

Liberation

To what extent has the Catholic Action movement been a social process of liberation from oppression? I will try to make my answer nuanced by presenting various stages of the process and utilizing information from earlier chapters to achieve a synthesis.

Accounts by converts generally point to the dramatic overcoming of an oppressive situation of indecision that was tormenting them and that often threatened their very existence (health). According to the narrative testimonies, in overcoming this indecision—which also reflected a lack of definition toward the power domain the converts existed under—an oppressive relationship (to the *zahorín*) was broken and an almost unlimited horizon of hopes was opened up. The latter was expressed in terms of "salvation," unexpected "miracle," joy, singing, and unusual courage, to the point where the converts' enemies began to make fun of them because "they thought they were gods," because with their behavior they were proclaiming "that they were no longer going to die." The unexpected irruption of something from outside went hand in hand with the vision of the opening of the limits on the situation of poor farmers. They experienced the previously closed possibility of accumulating wealth, the sources of which were outside the community and which they had not known how to handle before.

Oppression by *zahorines* was the culmination of a process that began with rising population, land scarcity, the disappearance of the enemy nearby in the Chiquimula community, and the consequent weakening of authority within the municipality. In this process, the authority of the *zahorín*, as a person whose power lay in the nonempirical belief in his ties to one's deceased grand-parents, to the Sacred World, and to the transcendent realm in general, was strengthened to the point where, probably as a result of the crisis of 1930, his decisions, solutions, and orders became economically intolerable for a sector of the population that no longer trusted in his nonempirical healing powers. It is therefore important to show that the *zahorín* was not always an oppressor or felt as such by his clients, and that he could most certainly recover his status as a respectable person worthy of trust for advice and even for healing. It is also important to mention that the intolerable domain of the *zahorines* was the counterpart of the loss of control they had as *principales* and as part of the municipal authority. Most of them were also *principales*. In other words, since these elders gradually lost their strong authority over the people as *principales*, they exerted their authority as *zahorines* in an intolerable way.

Oppression by the *zahorines* was differentiated, and so was the reaction to them. Their sons and daughters, their brothers and sisters, the sons and daughters of their brothers and sisters, and their sons-in-law and daughters-in-law all remained faithful to them. Because the *zahorines* were generally older men devoted to praying and "performing traditional rites" due to their inability to wield a hoe any more, the number of people under their domain through kin-ship has been large. Their personal relationship would keep them from squeez-ing these family members economically.

Liberation from the *zahorín*, which meant that the dissidents had to form their own groups, was extended along geographical and patrilinear kinship lines. Another influence prompting a differentiated reaction by people was the requirements of their work, which either demanded working together or made it desirable.

As division gradually spread throughout the municipality, the *zahorines* must have loosened their oppression over those who were not their relatives in those parts of the municipality where Catholic Action had not become a majority. Merchants with business interests in the town and political intermediaries began to derive power from outside the community for themselves and for the *cofradías* so they could become formally organized and counteract the power that the dissidents were deriving from outside. Thus, opposition within the municipalities in a country with a power structure with multiple domains returned power to the authorities of the opposing units to the extent that they were acting as true authorities. Within Catholic Action, which was very well organized, individual sorcery was eliminated; presumably it must have declined within the Traditionalist community as well (although it has not disappeared) insofar as individuals had to be connected to the committee, which was in fact set up as a defense against Catholic Action. Oppression by *zahorines* accordingly dropped off, and the dissident liberation process likewise slackened.

In the eyes of converts, this liberation also broke down the former limits on accumulating wealth. Curiously, the movement was the analogue to the way capitalism came back into the community. In 1876, when the Decree on Laborers was issued making labor on coffee plantations obligatory, there was enough land in the community for people to be self-sufficient with their crops and sheep and to trade for what they did not produce. Local resources were sufficient within a particular standard of living, which, however, was an expression of the limits imposed by the colonial period. As population rose, local resources became insufficient. The growing extortion of forced labor during the crisis of the 1930s and the decline of local resources per individual led the Ubico administration to cancel debts in 1934 and replace them with the Vagrancy Law, which indirectly expressed the reasons for that measure: forced labor was unnecessary (and harmful) because the resources of the communities were insufficient and would force the community's inhabitants to leave it to seek a livelihood elsewhere. Hence it was said that those who were not working on their own lands had to prove that they were working on the plantations, that is, that they were not vagrants.

By de-linking debtors from the plantations, this decree enabled them to pursue trade outside the municipality. The number of merchants grew, the scope of their operations expanded, and some experienced earnings beyond their dreams. Earlier I referred to this experience as paralleling liberation, but in this regard it was not liberation from the *zahorín* but from the limits imposed on the people of the community by their resources. These limits were reinforced by the *cofradía* system, which leveled out those who might advance dangerously at the expense of their neighbors. Now, however, money was causing disruption in a way that far surpassed anything they had experienced or imagined before.

Assuming that the nineteenth-century forced-labor law was an oppressive intrusion by capitalism, this was another wave of capitalism, but unlike the previous pattern of extracting surplus labor from the community by keeping its inhabitants in an egalitarian poverty, this one was going to enrich the community in a differentiated manner and stratify it through the emergence of previously nonexistent levels of power that would become formalized in organizations, such as the centers in the cantons. In tandem with this stratification process there emerged a rebellion against the *principales-zahorines* and the *cofradías*, which in turn increased the need to derive power from outside. This derivation was made possible by the existence of sources of power outside the community and by the means that the intracommunity higher-level units had available to them to bring about that derivation. The root experience of power outside the community would be at the basis of belief in "salvation," likewise coming from outside the community.

However, with the economic boom of a few merchants who began to amass lands in the municipality, thereby leaving failed debtors landless, the stratification process that had raised them up simultaneously closed off the rise of those who were left under their domain. Tensions began to form, and although they were mitigated by relationships of kinship and baptism sponsorship, the distance between some residents and others in terms of unequal power has continued to grow. The liberation of the merchant who tells how he was converted and became rich has become, as the opposite side of the same process, the beginning of the oppression of his debtors and hired laborers.

The process of stratification and oppression is being reinforced as the wealth concentrated in the center of the country utilizes the roads recently paved to Santa Cruz del Quiché to sell vehicles to the merchants, establishing an ongoing relationship with them and introducing technology, such as chemical fertilizer, electric devices (radios, mills, loudspeakers, and so forth), and farming technology (for the moment, only hoes). The merchant who has ongoing ties to dealerships that provide him with merchandise on consignment (with no interest!) draws earnings that are proportionally quite high by selling it in the community on time and with interest.

Catholic Action, which was a liberating movement and which gave the Traditionalist population an opening to what was new from outside, is weakening, becoming stagnant, and turning into an institution that is tending to become overorganized, to specify its rituals in detail, and to pursue its own self-maintenance.

The future will probably see the population, now split vertically, divided horizontally. It must be stressed, however that any prediction will inevitably be influenced by events outside the community, such as the invention of some applicable new technology (seed), an increase or decrease of energy (electricity, price of oil), commercial agriculture, an increase of tourism, political support for the cooperative movement, support for grassroots small farmer organizations, and especially the tendency to centralize power in the state.

Just as stratification might not have been transformed into a movement organized in rebellion against traditional beliefs had there not been (as there in fact was) a structure of many domains outside the community, so the future will be shaped by the combination of these and other factors outside the community.

CHAPTER 7

Conclusions

Theoretical Summation

I will now attempt to pull together the factors that, in my analysis, were involved in the conversion movement studied.

Power Base

As San Antonio became increasingly connected with the rest of the country, and particularly with Guatemala City through trade, some individuals found themselves increasingly capable of confronting traditional community authorities and rejecting long-established practices, such as that of redistribution, that were defended and enforced by local authorities. An important component in this newly felt power was found in conversion to Catholic Action, a process that not only involved a new basis of belief but also provided access to power sources at higher levels, both departmental and national. The conversion effectively established new sources and bases of power within the community and linked the actors with sources of power beyond the municipality's borders.

Weakening of Authority

Contributing to the weakening of the traditional local authority and helping to unleash the conversion movement was the fact that population was increasing at an accelerating pace. This had an influence on the change of geographical marriage patterns and required the emergence of an intermediate organization (the Catholic Action centers) with power extending over a smaller geographical area. Although the formation of these centers did not imply different beliefs, it nevertheless initiated a divisive dynamic that would facilitate the rejection of such beliefs prompted by other factors.

In addition to population increase, the growing power of the state to deal with border conflicts between communities helped weaken community authorities. When the defining of municipal limits led to the disappearance of the common enemy outside the community, and resources (land) grew scarce as a result of population increase, the municipal authority lost the sense of being the coordinator of the community's struggle, and so tensions between individuals grew. Those occupying existing positions of authority enhanced their power through the recourse of exercising traditional belief systems to legitimize their control over people. Witchcraft spread to such an extent that those suffering from the excesses of the now-weakened authority rebelled against the authorities who relied on their belief that they could defend people against witchcraft, and they rejected their legitimacy by withdrawing their faith. The dissidents included both individuals whose power base had grown and those whose power base was very limited and who depended upon existing relations within the community.

Liminal Step

Conversion (which was implicit in this rebellion) from one belief, accepted with characteristics of totality, to another belief often arose out of a crisis (such as illness, death of a loved one, or failure) that was ritually reinterpreted as a step across the threshold to membership in a new or different social group. The crisis, which, because of the nature of faith as totality, could have been resisted (as indeed it often was) by always reinterpreting the failure of the former belief, was not overcome by those who had been ritually less initiated in the basic principles of the traditional society in terms of the numbers of rites of passage covered on the hierarchical ladder. Hence differentiated initiation tends to explain differentiated de-initiation (conversion).

Derivation of Power from Within the Community

Other factors can explain differentiated conversion, that is, why some individuals have joined the ranks of the movement while others have either been indifferent or have gone into open resistance: proximity and neighborhood, kinship, work relationships, and shared residence. We have studied these factors within the framework of the derivation of power, so that it can be generalized that they are more influential to the extent that they entail a greater loss or gain of power for the convert, as the case may be.

Derivation of Power from Outside the Community

The existence of opposing national-level units capable of granting power and legitimizing the dissident units on lower levels within the community seems to have been a factor that was absolutely necessary for the conversion movement. Thus, acts of rebellion were not more or less sporadic, but gave rise to an organized movement that in rejecting the legitimacy of the traditional units was affirming the legitimacy of the new ones. In the next section, we will see that the intolerability of the authority that led to the crises described above, in a situation of a unitary domain on the national level, caused acts of rebellion even to the point of physical aggression against the units holding that authority (for example, by killing the *zahorín*) but not a movement that rejected legitimacy. It is hard to conceive that in a situation where domains were unified, a movement would have arisen and would have taken on the characteristics of totality proper to conversion. Tensions and adjustments would have taken place, but a situation would not have arisen in which one could speak of conversion as a complete change of adherence.

Power and Initiation

Finally, we may indicate that all the factors considered above may be subsumed into two irreducible concepts, namely, *power* and *initiation*: power, whether one's own or dependent on others, at different levels of society as the driving principle for bringing about conversion; and initiation, as the totalizing principle that communicates to resistance or conversion the character of adherence above and beyond the influence of any power. Within the concept of power are subsumed the growth of the power base of individuals through trade; the formation of a new social level within the community; the prompting of the rejection of fundamental beliefs; the weakening of authority on various levels; derivation of power within the community conditioned by proximity and neighborhood and made possible by relationships of work, kinship, and residence; and, finally, the derivation of power from outside the community. The concept of initiation encompasses the generation of full assent to certain beliefs through hierarchically ordered rituals such as marriage, the duties within the *cofradías*, and so forth, and the overcoming of the crisis of conversion ritually reinterpreted as crossing a threshold.

In this study I have focused primarily on the analysis of power. This does not mean downplaying the importance of the factor of initiation and its effect on the totality of assent because, as I state in Chapter 1 and demonstrate in Chapter 5, this aspect of conversion cannot be interpreted solely as adaptation to the environment.

Just as both elements, power and initiation, are irreducible, they are also inextricably connected. When the change of the physical and social environment places in crisis the adaptation of the person who is reluctant to give up his beliefs, he can be impelled to the edge of his own destruction (de-adaptation). As we studied in Chapter 5, at the moment when the individual accepts his own destruction (death) he fashions his own affirmation. The dialectic of this change, which takes place through leaps, contrasts with the ongoing adaptation conceptualized in power.

I have no intention of claiming that this totality is not a source of power and that it may not be conceptualized as cultural power, but only that this totality draws its power from the rejection of the power represented ritually in initiation. The leap of conversion is therefore a dialectical process of adaptation for which one has run the risk of utter de-adaptation.

Exploitation and Faith

Exploitation is the de-adaptation of a subordinate by the power of another who constrains the control over the environment that he should have. When the relationship of subordination is grounded in belief in the legitimacy of that relation, liberation from exploitation is conditioned on losing faith in that legitimacy and in the emergence of faith in its opposite. This process of liberation, which implies having the power necessary for bringing about that readaptation, is a conversion process. Acceptance of death and discovery of new meaning offers light and courage with effects that can be verified, even in health, and that can energize major social changes.

Faith, or total assent, may be utilized by an exploiter; but when it seeks a basis for legitimacy in a liberating alternative, it is not only the instrument of a liberation from exploitation, but it also bears within itself "a new life" as expressed by the ritual symbols that seal liberation. Hence faith should be distinguished from its utilization, and it should be said that when it opposes exploitation, faith takes on characteristics of human fulfillment such as joy, hope, and courage, which are not expressed in exploitation.

Faith can be utilized by an exploiter, either because the conditions for power, whether one's own or not, are not sufficient for beginning to rebel, or because the exploited have been initiated into the fundamental beliefs that grant legitimacy to the exploiter, or both factors are combined to different degrees. Then the utilization of faith is necessary for the exploited. Indeed, because this is the case for most Third World peoples, the proper vision of the dimension of faith ought not to begin with its utilization for exploitation but with the process of liberation, because that is where its best expression is to be found. In that case, the full assent of faith in a situation of exploitation is conceived as a core of resistance to exploitation and as a liberating seed that should not be ruled out when the moment for political praxis arrives.

Violence and Conversion

Assuming that between these two aspects, initiation and power, it is power that provides the forward drive, we now ask which of all the factors subsumed under "power" has been decisive for producing the conversion movement: the new power base? the formation of a new level of articulation? the weakening of internal authority? the derivation of power from outside the community?

In answering this question we are aided by comparing San Antonio with the Tzeltal community of Amatenango in Chiapas (Nash 1967, 1970) where, prior to the accelerated changes in recent years, there has been a culture and social structure similar to that of San Antonio, particularly with regard to the practice of witchcraft. Although changes similar to those in San Antonio have taken place in this community, in Amatenango they have not produced a conversion movement. The comparison thus becomes very suggestive for intuiting the decisive factor in that movement.

Comparison between the two communities also sheds light on the reason for the very high murder rate (forty-eight homicides in fifteen years: 1950–1965)[1] in the tiny town of Amatenango, with its 1,900 inhabitants, all the more so because one might assume that in Guatemala, where turbulent political violence has been commonplace since 1960, the bloodbath would be greater in San Antonio than in an isolated community in a stable country like Mexico. Why, in communities resembling one another in terms of belief in witchcraft and in their assumption that it has influence on people's lives because of their ancestors, has the result of the reaction to witchcraft in one case been the conversion movement and in the other a rash of murders?[2]

In going through the various factors noted above, we find, first, that in both communities a new power base has appeared: in Amatenango through the concentration of cattle (up to 200 head in one case) in the hands of individuals and the manufacture of clandestine liquor, and in San Antonio through trade. Second, in both communities a new level of articulation has emerged, that of cattle raisers and of the two opposed cooperatives with members mixed from the traditional two rival sectors in Amatenango, and in San Antonio that of merchants and the two contending organizations they maintain, the *cofradía* and Catholic Action.

Third, internal authority has been weakened in both. In Amatenango, stratification and the ladinization of some individuals have withdrawn power from the *principales* and the healers (*curadores*, equivalent to the *zahorines*), placing individuals who had not passed through the traditional hierarchy of *cargos* in positions of authority such as that of municipal president. The authority of the two supreme healers has weakened even more through the envy awakened by the aggressivity of the powerful. The number of acts of witchcraft has multiplied as have the number of healers operating outside their systematic hierarchy. The result of the rise in witchcraft and healers has been more murders, to such an extent that the crimes in which there has not clearly been a suspicion of witchcraft, such as those caused by cattle rustling or competition over women, would apparently not occur without the climate of violence fueled by envy and suspicion of the influence of sorcerers.[3]

In San Antonio, authority within the community has been weakened by causes such as population increase, gradual decline of resources, and so forth, which I assume must also have occurred in Amatenango, but stratification and ladinization gave rise to a new organization for growing in power. Then the individuals who created and utilized it entered into competition not only with the *principales* and *zahorines* who had risen to authority through the former organization (the *cofradías*), but with all those who were identified with it. The opposition of the two organizations over power won for the *principales* a support such as they had not had before the division. Then, whereas in Amatenango the new power base of some individuals did not serve to support the two opposing organizations (the cooperatives) and between the latter there arose no problem of beliefs, in San Antonio the recent superordinate units split and supported the two rival organizations, and between them there subsequently emerged a problem of belief to justify the legitimacy of their already existing organizations.

The weakening of the *principales* and *zahorines* in San Antonio shortly before that organized division took place did not lead to the murder of the assumed sorcerers or their clients, but to the rejection of the *zahorines*, whose clients the converts used to be. Whereas in Amatenango the climax of oppression expressed in an extreme fear of witchcraft broke out in a series of murders of either the sorcerer or his client, in San Antonio witchcraft experienced in illness was overcome by conversion. In Amatenango the vitality of faith in the healing power of a healer was depleted in confrontation with his opponent, and probably more trust was put in a weapon than in the healer to stand up to one's enemy, but in San Antonio there was a positive rejection of faith in one's own *zahorín*, and aggressivity was not turned against the possible witch or his client, but rather against the exploiting *zahorín* himself, who made one believe that he would bring healing but (according to the convert) he was actually making one ill so as to collect more money.

Within this difference between killing the enemy sorcerer or refusing to believe in one's own *zahorín* there has been a deep constancy shared by both communities, and this is what makes the comparison so rich. What is constant is that although in principle people in San Antonio deny faith in the healing power of their *zahorín* and therefore of any *zahorín*, they have nevertheless retained an unquestioning belief in their destructive power and in their connection to nonempirical units (ancestors, for example). People in San Antonio continue to acknowledge such power, but they do not fear it, because conversion has raised up a healing power (of "salvation") vis-à-vis any *zahorín* firmly set in the overwhelmingly superior multitude of Catholic Action members. Thus while overcoming fear of witchcraft, they have retained belief in witchcraft, as is likewise true of people in Amatenango.

Why within this common background has the difference indicated above arisen, one that is theoretically so subtle but whose results are so different? It is my impression[4] that the answer to that question revolves around the kind of derivation of power from outside the community. Amatenango is under a basically unitary domain, while San Antonio is under a multiple domain. Even though Amatenango is connected to San Cristóbal de las Casas by the Pan-American Highway (40 kms.) and has ladinos present and operating at the higher levels of articulation, such as teachers, the doctor, the priest, and two nuns (the latter supported with outside money)—all of whom enable people in Amatenango to derive power—and even though through its officials it may possibly bring the murderer to the justice system or call federal troops, for example, to install the proper mayor, nevertheless, the power granted by the state in such matters cannot be derived in any other way than through the official party, the PRI (Institutionalized Revolutionary Party). When the people of Amatenango sought refuge under the opposition party (PAN) for the first time in history, they learned that "nothing can be achieved with a municipal president backed by the PAN because the PRI is the party that really has control over regional and national offices" (Nash 1970: 251). Without an opposition party that is strong when compared to state power, it is difficult to imagine how there could have arisen an organized movement bearing "salvation" to counteract witchcraft. In San Antonio, by contrast, we have seen how the movement emerged due to a weak state and opposition parties comparatively stronger than those in Mexico.

Among the powers outside the community, the power of the church as a decisive factor for initiating and developing the conversion movement is ruled out because in Amatenango a priest and two sisters live there, whereas in San Antonio there is no more than a visiting priest serving the Catholic Action community. Hence, the Catholic Church, which served as a channel for the conversion movement, as did the Protestant churches, could not have aroused that movement within a structure of practically sole political control.

We are nevertheless left with two objections related to factors whose influence is not cleared up. The first has to do with the power, albeit within a unitary domain, of the state over the community. According to Nash, as the power of the government strengthens the officials in the community, the number of murders will drop. She states that the recent opening of the Pan-American Highway has coincided with the rise in the number of murders, possibly because increased communication has weakened the independence that the municipal government needs to rule on the permissibility of some deaths as resulting from legitimate self-defense. According to this explanation, one would have to reach one of two conclusions with regard to Guatemala in the time of Ubico, when there was a single political domain: either that the municipal authority in San Antonio[5] was even more consolidated than that of Amatenango over its members, or that in the person of the intendant, the outside authority was articulated with greater power than was the case in Amatenango, which is itself part of a far larger country. The power vacuum caused by the weakening of municipal authority in San Antonio and postulated for the rise of witchcraft would not be large enough to provoke the climate of murder in Amatenango. The magnitude of the political power vacuum outside the community would then explain whether there would or would not be murders in a unitary domain. The phenomenon of attacks on sorcerers would then disappear in the transition toward a better articulation of the community with the state. But the existence of the conversion movement within an internal structure of powers that are being loosened continues to postulate the existence of a multiple domain.

A second objection has to do with the difference in the source of the recent power base of one community and the other. In both, the experience of capital buildup has made it necessary to question the ideal of egalitarian redistribution in the system of *cargos* and *cofradías*, but it can be objected that the cattle raiser (in Amatenango) has not had to travel outside his community nor to become familiar with the values of the ladino world like an outside merchant (in San Antonio). In both cases, the experience of capital buildup has received a distinct coloring to which the conversion impulse could be attributed.

I respond to this doubt by accepting the particular impulse of the merchant's experience as set forth in Chapter 3, but I deny that it is the decisive factor. This is because of the multiplicity of the domain, and not because of trade. Even outside the area of greater trade centered in San Francisco el Alto in the western part of the country,[6] there are communities where the conversion movement has taken hold, such as in Santa Eulalia, department of Huehuetenango (Davis 1970),[7] and in the Ixil area in the northern part of El Quiché (Colby and Van den Berghe 1969).[8] If that is the case, even though the movement has grown stronger in concentric circles from San Francisco el Alto and its environs, with the differentiated stratification of each circle caused by trade, trade has nevertheless not been the decisive factor because the conversion movement has also occurred in these communities that do not have outside merchants.

To conclude this section on the relationship between violence and conversion, I would like to speculate briefly on the reason for the absence of political violence (now not under situations of witchcraft) in San Antonio. Whereas elsewhere in the country the multiplicity of the political domain has created a climate fostering political assassination, in San Antonio it has led to a clash of legitimizing symbols. I ask what factors would make San Antonio a setting for political violence?

My answer is rash, because no detailed studies have been published on violence in ladino, let alone indigenous, communities. The reasons would have to be sought in the proximity of national conflict in terms of guerrillas and government counterinsurgency in such a way that religious division would fit, in general terms, with the armed confrontation. Witchcraft becomes irrelevant when faced with brute force.

The Indigenous Future

Conversion and Identity

Finally, I ask, how has the conversion described in this study contributed to the future of indigenous people in Guatemala? Has it meant a step toward their disappearance or has it been rather a process of adaptation for survival?

On the one hand, the conversion movement entailed a greater degree of cultural ladinization: learning Spanish, demanding schools and literacy, extending the trading area, close connection with ladino power units outside the community, gradual loss of municipal independence, acceptance of beliefs backed by a ladino authority, and so forth. Although I have not heard converts explicitly accused of ladinization in San Antonio, in other towns with a higher proportion of ladinos, such as Tecpán (Cabarrús 1973), resistance by Traditionalists to the incursion of the ladino world, its domain, and its beliefs include such an accusation. Thus, the loss of cultural signs proper to the indigenous community could have weakened the identity of many people in San Antonio and could have helped dissolve a large number of indigenous people into the ladino population.

Yet, as we have seen, conversion did not entail loss of identity by indigenous people nor could it have involved such a dramatic struggle with the Traditionalists, had that opposition not had to remain within the terrain of the same identity, not only as Indians, but indeed as San Antonio Indians. Hence, the battle ultimately was about the possibility of translating that very identity into a different organizational shape. The loss of proper cultural signs was accompanied by other replacement signs, which even though they were ladino in origin, were assumed as their own, and once they were assumed as their own, were no longer ladino signs.

One group saw Catholic Action as a betrayal of the beliefs of their ancestors and a refusal to acknowledge oneself as their descendant, whereas for the other it was the way to adapt in order to continue to be socially recognized as children of those ancestors, albeit with a belief that was fundamentally different in some respects. While conversion represented for some a rejection of identity, for others it was the only way to affirm it, given the circumstances.

Moreover, these were not visions of two different groups; rather, both were struggling within the same individual when he entered into the liminal situation. The risk of losing one's own existence, amply spelled out in Chapter 5, may thus be understood as the risk of losing one's social identity.

Inasmuch as this new way of being indigenous was not limited to San Antonio, but extended throughout the western highlands, judging from the ethnography reviewed in Chapter 1, a previously closed option was opened to the indigenous people, one different from social ladinization. The 1950 and 1964 censuses reviewed (Early 1974) indicate that for the eight highland departments (Chimaltenango, Sololá, Totonicapán, Quetzaltenango, San Marcos, Huehuetenango, El Quiché, and Baja Verapaz) where religious division has been observed among the Indians, there is only a slight decline in indigenous identity from 81.85 percent (1950) to 81.6 percent (1964), which is less than the decline in national percentages (55.8% to 50.4%). The persistence of an equal proportion of Indians in the communities confirms that religious division in them means that ethic identity is being retrieved there, even under oppressive circumstances, such as having to pay for them with pieces of one's own culture.[9]

Ladinization and Researchers

Integrationism

A view in which conversion is seen as retrieval of identity questions the assumptions of the integrationist understanding of ladinization that characterized the anthropological literature of the latter half of the 1950s (Adams 1956). Adams (1956: 213–244) defined ladinization as the result of a twofold process, that of social mobility, by which an individual abandons the customs of his group in order to join another, and that of transculturation, whereby an entire community becomes culturally more like another. To understand the transculturation process he classified communities in a continuum ranging from traditional indigenous to those that are ladinoized to the new ladino communities. The assumption in such a typology that I am questioning is that a more ladino-tending community is closer to abandoning its ethnic identity than one that is less ladinoized, because I have observed the process of strengthening indigenous identity through cultural ladinization.[10]

Furthermore, although the conversion process may have meant a degree of cultural ladinization and initially might entail friendly relationships with ladinos, the growth of such religious organizations among the indigenous peasantry has reaffirmed the interethnic tension within communities where ladinos occupy a higher level of power within the indigenous majority that they exploit. This reaffirmation, sustained with power derived from non-Indian sources outside the community, has been recently displayed during the 1974 national elections. While the traditional Indians in the *cofradías* have tended to make deals with the interests of the right-wing administration that supports the local powerful ladino, the Indians about whose identity outside observers have raised doubts have gone over to opposition to the government by affirming their ethnic character vis-à-vis the local ladino. The well-known victory of the opposition in Chimaltenango illustrates the massive support of the ("ladinoized") indigenous vote.[11]

Colonial Situation

Another vision of the loss of ethnic identity, which is questionable from my material, particularly given the division of labor and stratification (trade and capital buildup) that accompanied the phenomenon of conversions, conceives of the Indian as a product of the colonial period: "Oppression made the Indians . . . ," and hence "the disappearance of the slave and of oppression has to cause the transformation of the Indian into something different" (Martínez Peláez 1971: 594–618). However, the existence of merchants who devote themselves to trade through most or all of the year, who have become wealthy through the surplus value of goods, and who have become exploiters without ceasing to be Indians indicates that ethnic identity can rise to different levels of power or cross social-class boundaries. Hence, although before the conquest there was no relationship of contrast vis-à-vis the Spaniard, the native-born white, or the ladino for identifying oneself as an Indian, it is not the oppressive aspect of that contrast relationship that made the Indian.

This is why I do not regard it as correct to conceptualize the indigenous population in Guatemala as the oppressed class, as presented by one current of Guatemalan sociology (see Guzmán Böckler and Herbert: 1970). In contrast to Martínez Peláez, these researchers include the indigenous bourgeoisie as a stratum within the indigenous class. The resulting confusion has provoked considerable comment,[12] although it has not been emphasized that these writers are on the mark in pursuing the national-level discrimination of Indians in the class structure, that is, in the fact that, for the most part, indigenous people belong to the oppressed class, and the oppressor class is predominantly ladino.

The Community

Following Cabarrús (1973), and on the basis of my material, questions may be raised about the notion of Stavenhagen (1972), who, using Wolf (1960), tends to situate the indigenous identity in "the quality of social relations found in communities of a certain type and in the self-image of the individuals who identify with such communities." These communities are said to be of a closed corporate type "whose members are bound by certain rights and obligations, which have their own forms of social control, particular political and religious hierarchies, etc." (Stavenhagen 1972: 199). According to this definition, San Antonio is a closed corporate community. Hence my material does not directly refute this view.

Nevertheless, if it is admitted that ethnic identity encompasses various levels of power, there is no reason why, as long as some type of organization exists, it may not also encompass levels of power higher than those of the community, whether corporate or not. In his study of Tecpán, Cabarrús mentions "indigenous professionals" and their associations made up of a single community or more than one, who live in the capital city, with broader domains than that of the community, and who work in a bureaucracy or the university.[13] The recent emergence of this new way of being Indian, which, like conversion, prompts an accusation of ladinization both from Indians linked to the community and from urban ladinos threatened by their presence, demonstrates the enormous flexibility of a people who struggle to remain in history, even though they have surrendered their culture in order to survive.[14]

A New Stage

The recent emergence of this new way of being an Indian marks the opening of a new period in the adaptation of Guatemala's indigenous people. La Farge ([1940] 1959) divided the sequence of indigenous cultures into five periods, the last of which opened with the Liberal Reform in the last century. Goubaud Carrera (1959) added a sixth beginning with the year of the October Revolution and its social transformations in 1945. Here we have the impression that a new period is opening up as individuals occupy levels of articulation above that of the community and yet do not relinquish their identity even while occupying them.

The reasons given by Palerm (1972) for the crisis and critique of integration in Latin America also apply to this phenomenon. According to him, "the possible reasons for the sudden crisis of the centuries-long process of ethnic, social, and cultural integration in Spanish America," are to be found in the hemisphere-wide influence of the Indian, Chicano, and Black movements in the United States; unemployment caused by the mechanization of the countryside; and population growth in indigenous areas. These apply to the phenomenon described because the revalorization of ethnic minorities and their despised cultures is channeled by way of the literature of anthropology and other social sciences issuing from universities. Individuals who used to conceal their identity, now finding themselves in a setting more favorable to their culture, are encouraged to maintain it. The first ones to see this change in the atmosphere are those who move about at higher levels of articulation rather than peasants or those who live in the community.

Unemployment caused by the mechanization of export agriculture encourages greater schooling in the communities that used to provide labor (Hodara 1972). Moreover, in indigenous communities like San Antonio, schooling is one of many facets of closer articulation of the community with the surrounding ladino world. Hence, the pioneers in the struggle for new schools in the cantons have been those who have been involved in the conversion movement. Recall the case in San Antonio of the schools in Chiaj and Patzalá and the tensions with the Traditionalists. Schooling has been the main route for rising to levels of power outside the community. Concern for education is new in San Antonio, hence there are still no indigenous students who go on to high school in the department capital, let alone enroll in the university. In other communities, however, that process has taken its course in a number of individuals who are not merging into a ladino sea, but are instead organized into associations. These include extensionists, university students, agriculture specialists, nurses, radio announcers, teachers, and the occasional lawyer.

Demography affects employment and is also a reflection of hidden trends that come to light only through analysis. The centuries-long trend for the percentage of Indians in the country to decline recently seems to have halted. The figures for the years 1788, 1893, 1950, and 1964 have declined as follows: 78 percent, 65 percent, 53.5 percent, and 42.2 percent. By contrast, according to the 5 percent sample for 1973 (Dirección General de Estadística 1974), the percentage has risen slightly, to 48.7 percent. If there is a classification error, as has been shown to be the case for the 1950 and 1964 censuses (Early 1974), it may be assumed that in this most recent census the error was greater, given the decline in signs of differentiation, such as distinctive dress. This phenomenon, which places in crisis the traditional ideals of *mestizaje* and social and cultural integration, goes along with the emergence of higher levels of power in a society resisting ladinization.

Access to this new stage with major consequences for Guatemalan national identity has meant that indigenous people have had to overcome a crisis similar to that of conversion when they leave their community (Cabarrús 1973). Breaking with peasant society likewise calls into question the ethnic identity that seemed inseparable from the situation of the peasant community. Overcoming the crisis has meant a beginning of a twist in their own indigenous identity, without going back to being peasants. Identity is then vigorously retrieved, the previously despised symbols are given new dignity, and the sense of belonging to the indigenous sector takes on new life with a system of signals intended for communication with urban ladinos. That revitalization then comes back to peasants and non-peasant residents of peasant communities through the connections that groups of professionals living in the main cities maintain with educated Indians living in the communities.

The university and the church have helped strengthen that revitalization. The first anti-integrationist book (Flores Alvarado 1968) was the work of a university anthropologist and lecturer. The "Declaration of Barbados" (1971), which attacked missionary ethnocentrism and its discriminatory character and endorsed a liberating anthropology, has stimulated priests to renew their thinking and to change their stance in their pastoral work. Some groups of them have discovered the message of the incarnation of Christianity in indigenous cultures proposed by Vatican II and officially assumed for Latin America by the CELAM Department of Missions in the Melgar document (1968). The church has organized gatherings in various dioceses in Guatemala to listen to the Indians themselves and that has given rise to a reconciliatory tendency, which returns to the community to heal the division between Traditionalists and members of Catholic Action, even to the distaste of leaders of the latter.

Predictions regarding the potential for change among the indigenous population on the national level offered by this new stage would have to start by considering that "Indians and ladinos who wield any power at any level of articulation within the power structure of the nation *fully aim to keep and increase it*" (Noval 1972: 18; emphasis added). Hence, what may be anticipated is neither the disintegration of the Guatemalan nation nor the formation of an Indian or Quiché nation. A play of interests in the power structure enhances the unity of the nation, therefore, nativist expressions of disintegration must be interpreted as manipulation needed by ladinos or Indians who are expressing themselves in this manner to retain and increase their power.

A more careful study of the phenomenon would have to analyze the different positions in the national power structure of individuals who have left the countryside. Such an analysis would be subsumed within the "middle classes" who are divided politically into "a small group, generally intellectuals, which joins the revolution: [and a] vast majority that adheres to the parties or political behavior of the bourgeoisie," their conduct thus being a "reflection of the contradictions between the classes that are structurally basic to society (bourgeoisie and proletariat)" (Torres Rivas 1973).

In this view, the ideology of ethnic revitalization will be used for opposing interests: either, for example, to rationalize support for the government as advantageous for indigenous people, or to proclaim the need for radical changes, supposedly to destroy discrimination felt, studied, or pondered. The power structure divides the Indians from the middle class, just as it generally splits the middle class, which has never formed a party. Hence, the formation of an indigenous party led by the middle classes seems impossible. Indigenous people realize this when they express yearnings for broad national and even international unity: "It's not we who divide ourselves, it's they who divide us."

All of this means that ethnic revitalization among middle classes or urban sectors outside the indigenous communities has something ambiguous about it. When it contributes to the valuing of indigenous culture and enables indigenous men and women to have a free choice of options really open for them to change, then it carries a banner of justice. But when social identity is placed above human equality and hinders the critique of exploitation in the name of a racially privileged people or pulls people away from the struggle for the oppressed under banners of ethnic organization, then that identity is only a mask that thwarts the liberation of men and women, indigenous and ladino.

Epilogue

This book was first a doctoral thesis that was completed in 1974 and was published in its original form by the press of the University of San Carlos in Guatemala in 1978. I think it had a substantial impact in Guatemala for several reasons, starting with the fact that it was the National University of San Carlos that took it on, made it its own, and publicized it. Another reason was the title, *Quiché Rebelde*, which was not the title of the thesis itself. It captured the public imagination, because at that time the lid was being lifted on the power of the indigenous insurgency in the northern part of Quiché. The rebellion alluded to, however, was not a guerrilla but a religious rebellion, a modern rebellion against traditional beliefs; that rebellion had a liberating, but primarily symbolic, power. Yet, I have the impression that this rebellion was seen to be very closely connected to the indigenous rebellion, and, as became apparent, this perception was not off the mark.

Another reason for the book's impact was that it contained a great deal of information and was the outgrowth of fieldwork that perhaps in other countries is taken for granted, and there is nothing special about it. But in Guatemala, especially in times when increasing repression makes writers say nothing or write about earlier centuries rather than write about contemporary topics, the book was seen as a contribution to knowledge of the country and to the developments then taking place. Readers who delved into it found themselves defending the book, even though its very title would have discredited it with conservative sectors. These latter sectors came to appreciate it later.

A final reason for its impact was that, taking these previous reasons into account, in mid-1979 the Association of Guatemalan Journalists awarded it the Golden Quetzal, the highest prize given to any book published in Guatemala. That award gave the book the final boost it needed to be disseminated throughout the university, where it was adopted for classroom use for several years and reprinted several times; it was also studied by church people (Bishop Juan Gerardi, the martyred bishop of Quiché, was one of them), and in the tumultuous 1980s it was read in guerrilla camps. I suppose the army also studied it. Later on, it was helpful to development organizations, and it spread through the municipality of San Antonio, where its few readers kept it buried underground during the dark years, and then later took it out proudly, because, they said—so I was told—"This town has a book written about it!"

I have stayed far away from San Antonio. The last time I visited it before leaving Guatemala for a number of years was in 1979, when I passed by at night to leave the Golden Quetzal award with the former sacristan so that it could be kept in the municipality. I did not go back there except very briefly in 1994 with a priest who had been there for some years and wanted to show me the changes that had taken place. To this day I have not been able to return, and I am venturing to write this epilogue on the basis of reports from other people and superficial knowledge of a neighboring municipality, Santa María Chiquimula, where we Jesuits have been doing pastoral work since 1987.

When I was doing fieldwork in San Antonio Ilotenango (1969 and 1970) it was inconceivable that many of the kinds of things that have happened could occur in such a tranquil place. I am going to focus on four points that have a certain chronological sequence: the army repression starting openly in 1979; the influx of development organizations starting in 1988; the impact of infrastructure investment; and the religious situation among groups that have been traditionally divided but are now closer. Then I would like to offer some reflections on the book after thirty years, and to note some lines of study that I think are important for the present.

Army Repression

I had not yet finished writing this book when, in late 1972, I connected a group of university students and young Jesuits with San Antonio. I recall the outpouring of enthusiasm of the young students, men and women, from the city, who had dreamed of doing something in the indigenous areas of the country and were now getting such an opportunity. They committed themselves to making a suspension bridge over the Jocol River in the canton of Canamixtoj for schoolchildren. Some were architecture students. They wanted to build something in order to become rooted in the midst of the people. They did not stay long because, shortly afterward, the group shifted the center of its activities to Santa Cruz del Quiché, the department capital, a larger and more important place with greater organizational influence. There they made contact with Catholic Action leaders. Their organizing work, which was based on doing literacy work using the Paulo Freire method, took root, and on May 1, 1978, it emerged publicly as a formally established group under the name Committee for Peasant Unity (CUC). The word "Kuuk" also means "squirrel" in Quiché—a symbol of agility, a kind of "nahual" of this peasant organization.

After the Spanish embassy massacre on January 31, 1980, the nature of CUC changed, and it turned to armed struggle. The occupation of the embassy had been organized by the popular movement, especially the CUC. The massacre showed that open and peaceful movements would not bring about any change. This act of repression was blatant proof, and its effect in Quiché was electrifying. From that point, CUC gradually began to change into a guerrilla-linked organization, then a seedbed for guerrilla members, and later a guerrilla force, so that only its name was left. Things moved very quickly. Although the effect was felt primarily in Santa Cruz and its nearby cantons, which was the political center of Quiché, San Antonio was also included.

This was the atmosphere in which 39 people were massacred in the canton of Sacxac in San Antonio on Tuesday, December 23, 1980. It was a market day, just before Christmas, and things were bustling. On the road from Santa Cruz to San Antonio, guerrillas stopped a pickup truck of men who said they were pig merchants—actually they were army spies. The guerrillas took the truck, and the spies made a report to the army. Around 11:30 A.M. the helicopters began to bomb the canyons. Everyone gathered in the town square was trembling with fear—but no one was killed by the bombing itself. The army sent its infantry to the canton of Chiaj and set up a roadblock there on the road to Totonicapán, but with no results. Then the column of soldiers left from there and went through the canyons to the canton of Sacxac, the hamlet of Chuichop, crossing the fields of corn that were being harvested, and going into houses and killing people indiscriminately. Most of the victims were Traditionalists because, trusting in the army, they had not fled from their homes. This was one of many massacres of civilians who had absolutely nothing to do with the insurgency, and were even opposed to it. One of those killed was a powerful merchant who had a store and trucks; the soldiers accused him of helping the guerrillas with food. The soldiers were following the strategy of fish and water: "if you can't catch the fish, drain the water." The guerrillas were the fish, and the civilian population the water. But the water was really blood.

Before and after this horrifying event there were twenty-nine cases that I have been able to document, almost all caused by the army or army-connected forces, especially a small massacre of people from another municipality who must have been encamped in a remote corner of San Antonio, in the hamlet of Chocajá. Some of these people were involved in the preparation of this book as informants, for example, Don José Guch, the merchant who had the dream about the green parakeets and offered us his testimony and his human warmth (chapter 3). Below I copy the names that appear on the REHMI Report (Interdiocesan Project for the Recovery of Historical Memory) (ODHAG 1998) and the Historical Clarification Commission (CEH), along with some that I was able to check directly on my very quick visit in 1994.

Late 1979: criminals from San Antonio pretending to be guerrillas attacked a pickup and some trucks on the road from San Antonio to Totonicapán, killing a merchant named Antonio Gómez Ajpop. As a result, merchants in San Antonio made an alliance with the army G-2, and soon the bodies of the seven criminals turned up in the park in Santa Cruz with cardboard signs tied onto them and signed by the ESA (Secret Anticommunist Army) (unpublished document in the REHMI Report).

August 1981: in the canton of Chichó, army troops captured Petronila González (75 years old) and another person. They were taken to Chiché, El Quiché, and were executed there (CEH 1999: 850).

May 2, 1982: Matías Osorio Cor (54 years old) was abducted in the department of El Quiché (ODHAG 1998: 380). He was a Christian Democrat mayor of San Antonio Ilotenango in 1970.

May 21, 1982: Antonio Tiu Gómez, a member of Catholic Action in San Antonio, was shot dead in Salcajá, Quetzaltenango. He was on the army's list and had moved away (CEH 1999: 793).

July 12, 1982: José Guch Tiu (50 years old), his brother Martín Guch Tiu, nephew Pedro Guch Yat (22 years old), and Antonio Guch Ajanel from the canton of Chichó were abducted on the road from Lemoa to Chichicastenango. The bodies were found along with the burned truck in the canyon. José Guch was one of the most powerful merchants in San Antonio and one of the main Catholic Action members. Alongside the bodies was found the documentation of an army confidant (ODHAG 1998: 359 and personal report).

February 26, 1983: massacre of displaced people. In the hamlet of Chocajá, army troops killed Vicente Pérez Lainez, Lorenzo Zapeta, and Encarnación, Lucía, and Estela, whose surnames are unknown. They captured Isabel Lainez López, who was president of Catholic Action, his daughter Rita Guadalupe Pérez Lainez, and two other people. They were never heard from again. Diego Pérez Lainez (nine years old) was wounded, captured by the soldiers, and released nine months later. In March of that same year, a newborn girl died as a result of the move that the population felt forced to make (CEH 1999: 1099). The people massacred in this instance were not from San Antonio; their surnames are typical of the municipality of Santa Cruz. They probably moved to this remote hamlet of San Antonio to escape from repression. They were scattered groups of what would later be called Communities of People in Resistance, but they were soon dismantled in southern Quiché.

June 24, 1983: Lorenzo Xanté Xic killed in the canton of Sacxac (ODHAG 1998: 318). He was a Catholic Action board member.

1983: in the canton of Sacxac, army troops wounded and captured Carlos Pérez Lainez of the CUC. He has been missing since then (CEH 1999: 1200).

January 24, 1985: Antonio Lobos Córtez (27 years old), killed in the canton of Patzalá (ODHAG 1998: 226).

April 19, 1985: in the canton of Chiaj, members of the Civil Self-Defense Patrols with their faces covered captured María Sampor Cor at her home.

For fifteen days she was raped and then killed. Her body was found in a nearby canyon (CEH 1999: 1380). The surname is probably not Sampor, but Tzampop.

The total number of persons is 29.

From this list it is evident that Catholic Action was constantly under repression from the army, which regarded the Catholic Church and all of its organizational expressions as a focal point of the insurgency. It is also clear that the merchants, as the most dynamic portion of the population, were hit by both sides: by the army, which regarded some of them as a base of support for the guerrillas, and by the guerrillas, which took their vehicles. It is not surprising that this sector was to emerge later as a force for unifying the people and holding them to neutrality, as was necessary for survival.

This list does not compare in the number of victims with those from other towns in Quiché. San Antonio was not one of the towns suffering the most repression because it was in a corner of the department of Quiché backing up to the department of Totonicapán. According to the REHMI Report (ODHAG 1998: 530), 263 of the 422 massacres recorded for the entire country took place in Quiché, but not a single one took place in Totonicapán. Nor were the insurgent forces very organized in San Antonio, because San Antonio was on the boundary between the two guerrilla organizations, the EGP (Guerrilla Army of the Poor) in Quiché and ORPA (Organization of the People in Arms) in Totonicapán, and the western area where the people speak Mam.

The fact that the repression was of lesser intensity made it easier for the people in San Antonio to enter more rapidly than others into the push for development. It can be contrasted, by way of example, with another municipality in Quiché, San Bartolomé Jocotenango, which was under heavy military occupation until 1996 (González 2001).

Influx of Development Organizations

Entry into San Antonio

According to a short monograph by a university student who visited the municipality in the early 1990s (García Vettorazzi 1996: 101), in order to escape this unbearable war-generated violence, the people of San Antonio became internally reunified and asked both the army and the guerrillas to withdraw their forces. The student does not say just when this happened. The process must have been very complicated, and it is not clear just who in San Antonio was involved (they seem to have been mid-level merchants) nor who spoke with the army (which was growing ever stronger) and with the guerrillas (growing ever weaker), nor what the conditions of the agreement were. It is hard to imagine that the army would have acceded to a neutral position. The fact is that the local population came together in 1986, when the national government passed into the hands of the Christian Democrats after years of de facto military regimes. San Antonio achieved a level of trust from the military that made it possible for contacts to be made with development organizations.

In 1988, Alvaro Colóm, a textile engineer and private consultant (and presidential candidate for the left in 1999) came to San Antonio with a World Bank project designed as a pilot plan for setting up compensation funds within the neoliberal framework. Through the offices of the local Catholic priest, he established contact with a leader of the Charismatic Renewal, a group that had split off from Catholic Action in the 1970s. People were suspicious and reserved, but they were now free of the obligation to participate in civil patrols organized by the army. The military loosened its control over this community long before it did elsewhere, allowing other civilian forces to come in.

The project consisted of a loan to pay seventeen seamstresses. The engineer had helped set up a textile factory (*maquila*) in the indigenous town of San Pedro Sacatepequez, known as the "Taiwan of Guatemala," near Guatemala City. San Antonio was not a good site for an assembly plant given the distance and the lack of infrastructure. But it could take advantage of its tailors, who came on the scene in 1970 to fill the vacuum left in the domestic market by San Pedro when it turned to export. According to Colóm, the aid project was a success, and the people repaid the loan. Other reports indicate that years later this cottage clothing industry found itself competing with other nearby towns, particularly Chichicastenango.

A further step in development and connecting with civilian forces took place in 1991, when the charismatic leader who had contacted Colóm was a member of the municipal corporation. The mayor of San Antonio, with the help of CDRO (Cooperation for the Rural Development of the Western Highlands), an NGO (nongovernmental organization) supported by the party in power, had brought the population together, organizing the main population centers, cantons, and hamlets to form an association that would be called ADISA (Association for Integral Development of San Antonio Ilotenango). The Improvement Committees of the eight population centers were represented in it, and the leader of the charismatics had been made director of the association. There was a great deal of connection and overlap between the municipal corporation and the association, because the founding members were members of the corporation, the mayor supported the organizing process, and the director of the association had the support of mid-level merchants. The latter had insisted on becoming unified in order to save themselves from repression and had held discussions with the army, and probably with the guerrillas as well (unbeknownst to the army) to keep from being caught in the crossfire.

Let us note in passing that it was a Catholic charismatic who made contact with outside development groups and who seems to have served as the go-between in the difficult process of achieving unity. Catholic Action was still too suspect to show its face.

At around this time, Colóm happened to be flying over in his helicopter, because he was president of FONAPAZ (National Fund for Peace). This government agency had been created that year, 1991, to deal with the population affected by the armed struggle. Colóm was on his way to Ixcán, but he could not get in because of poor weather and decided to land in the wonderful little town of San Antonio, whose colonial church and religious house made it recognizable from the air. To his surprise, he found the leader of the World Bank project assigned to the municipality in a meeting with the ADISA leadership. This man assailed him for not helping San Antonio, and pointed out that ADISA was in existence and that the people were well organized. Even though San Antonio was by now outside the war area, Colóm decided to make this municipality a model of production projects and of the institutional enhancement of local power.

FONAPAZ and then FIS (Social Investment Fund) were the means by which an array of projects for potable water, health care, schools, and electric power were launched. During the war, the Reconstruction Committee, which was the army's development tool, had also introduced potable water into the town of San Antonio and had opened up roads.

In 1994, the community told FONAPAZ that they needed to go beyond social investment to production projects. FONAPAZ sought the best advisers for agricultural diversification and dairy farming and initiated a project worth millions coordinated and set up by Israeli technicians. The dairy project began with 42 Jersey cows and was intended to expand to 600 cows in barns so as to sell milk even in Guatemala City. But when Colóm left his position, FONAPAZ cut off technical and financial assistance. The upshot is that according to some reports from the area, now there are only 15 cows left and "far from providing milk they are a wretched sight." The immediate problem was procuring feed for the animals and the structural problem of the instability of government plans, because each administration leaves unfinished what the previous one has started. But some agricultural projects have been successful, such as production of tomatoes and snow peas, which are sold outside San Antonio and even exported.

Development Trends

I have neither data nor space to provide a year-by-year account of development in San Antonio and its connection to politics and forces within the municipality. Instead, I will indicate only four of the more noteworthy features.

Development Organizations

In 1999, a wide range of organizations were working in San Antonio. These included SODIFAG (family), PAIN (boys and girls), SERJUS (legal services), CDRO (development), CADISOGUA (development), ASODESPT (development), PADEL (development), FUNCEDE (development), PROYECTO KICHÉ (development), and INTECAP (nutrition). The presence of so many organizations in a small municipality does not seem conducive to either development or institution building. Because they typically have political sympathies, they are often at odds with one another. There also may be contradiction between sources with stronger financing such as USAID (U.S. Agency for International Development), which through an American company called Nexus has made a subcontract with FUNCEDE (Central American Development Foundation) and the European Union, which operates through PROYECTO KICHÉ. Even so, it seems that both financing sources support ADISA and the municipal corporation, which have kept most of the NGOs linked with their counterparts.

Political Developments

Four national and seven municipal elections have been held from 1985 to 1999. In national elections (for president) a different party has won every time (DC, Christian Democrats, in 1985; MAS, Solidarity Action Movement, in 1990; PAN, National Action Party, in 1995; and FRG, Guatemalan Republican Front, in 1999), but the Christian Democrats have won six of the seven municipal elections (for mayor of San Antonio). This indicates a certain stability of the internal forces, despite national instability. This is probably due to the predominance of a group with driving force within the municipality, and its longstanding relationship of trust with some NGOs, a relationship firmly grounded in personal ties between outside staff members and some leaders in San Antonio.

The energizing and unifying group does not bring everyone into a single political party. Its unifying strength has been waning; for example, in 1985 when direct military rule over the country ended, the Christian Democrat candidate for mayor got 72 percent of valid votes, whereas in 1993 the figure was down to 56 percent. (I do not have the figure for 1999.) In other words, there was little political division immediately after the repression, but it has gathered strength even though one group holds onto majority status, and they are the ones driving development forward.

Position on Indigenous Rights

In May 1999, a national referendum was held on four proposed changes in the Constitution. After the peace had been signed in 1996, the agreements had to be implemented, including the agreement on the Identity and Rights of Indigenous Peoples, signed in March 1995. The first question on the referendum was about the agreement: "Do you ratify the constitutional changes approved by the Congress of the Republic in the area of 'Nation and social rights': YES or NO?" It amounted to defining Guatemala as a multiethnic, multicultural, and multilinguistic nation, a hotly debated issue that pitted the most powerful organizations in the country, such as CACIF (Coordinating Committee of Agricultural, Commercial, Industrial, and Financial Associations), against indigenous organizations represented in COPMAGUA (Coordinating Body of Organizations of the Maya People of Guatemala). San Antonio voted overwhelmingly YES: 396 out of 444 valid votes that Guatemala ought to be a multiethnic nation. This lopsided vote was 89 percent as compared with 43 percent of the votes for YES on a national level. Even so, this victory of the Yes vote in San Antonio was quite relative because the participation of voters was quite low (only 11 percent of all voters), and the true winner was the absentee vote, even more than on the national level, where participation was 19 percent. Plainly, it cannot be concluded that the ethnic identity of the people of San Antonio is in crisis: quite the contrary, it is clear that there is no consciousness or information in most people in this municipality on the need to give political expression to the right to identity. It makes no difference to the people whether Guatemala is declared to be a multiethnic nation or not. Even so, the defeat of the NO is likely to have opened the eyes of the party that won the national elections, the FRG, so that it will try to have a more decisive influence in San Antonio, by manipulating religious groups, as we will note below.

Leadership Group in the Municipality

We have seen that there continues to be one group remaining on top in San Antonio, whose political expression is the Christian Democrat Party. In religious terms, it comes from the union of two organizations, Catholic Action and the Charismatic Renewal. Although historically there have been tensions between them, as we will see further on, when politics enters the picture, they seek shelter within the same party. Both belong to the Catholic Church. They are not closed but try to make alliances with some Protestant churches. The current mayor of San Antonio, for example, is a Protestant. I assume that they also seek support from the traditionalists. Apparently what makes it possible for such alliances to be forged is the fact that most of them are merchants who do business outside San Antonio; the real driving force is not so much religious ideology as the open and enterprising ideology typical of such merchants.

It also seems that this merchant sector is the one that has been most open to the great new feature of migration to the United States. We do not have figures, but the reports point toward a growing wave of migrants to the north, albeit with ups and downs. By the same token, seasonal migration to the coasts has dropped, and the traditional institution of the labor contractor who used to take crews of workers to the plantations after advancing them money has disappeared. On the other hand, today in San Antonio there are "coyotes" who take young people to the United States for a hefty sum of money. Only merchants can pay such a sum, not the poor in the municipality. Remittances are presumably coming from the United States and they strengthen this dynamic group, comprising merchants doing business outside the municipality, which is now under one party and whose religious expression is Catholic Action and the Charismatic Renewal.

Impact of Infrastructure Investment

Although investment in infrastructure and production has not lifted people out of poverty, it has been producing many changes. These changes have been reinforced by the other phenomena noted, such as migration to the United States, the increase in the number of merchants and their wealth, the initial inroads of television, and factors whose origins we do not know, such as planting of marijuana on municipal lands and the existence of bands of criminals that carry out robberies on the roads.

The gravel roads that wind through the canyons connecting almost twenty population centers in the municipality, as well as the municipality itself with neighboring municipalities, have reactivated a regional market that extends into remote corners of the countryside. Means of transportation have increased to move people and goods. There are now one hundred pickups, whereas in 1970 there was only one. Dollars from the United States, transformed into cement, lumber, and steel reinforcement rods, can be taken to the cantons to make houses with material from the outside. There are now stores and small markets in the cantons. The paved road connecting San Antonio to Santa Cruz in twenty-five minutes opens up the services of the department capital to the people. Sick people can be taken quickly to the hospital at night. Students can live in the town of San Antonio and attend school in the department capital.

Health has improved. In 1998 there were 126 deaths in the current population of around 15,000 inhabitants, whereas in the 1965–69 period deaths averaged 170 a year in a population of 7,000 inhabitants. Measles, which in the past could kill 300 children in a year, is now under control. There is a health center with a doctor, a nurse with a degree, and five nursing aides. Moreover, 84 percent of the houses are connected to water. People no longer have to go to dirty ponds to get water to cook or bathe in summer.

Thirty years ago there was no electric power in the municipality; now 30 percent of the houses have electricity. Electrification allows for stores (refrigerators), faster sewing machines, musical instruments, and TV sets in homes, which enables people to make a business out of showing films on video. Tailors can extend their work hours. The whole pace of life is imperceptibly changing, and people in the countryside are becoming more sharply stratified.

Many schools have been built with the social investment funds (FIS). There are now fourteen schools, whereas thirty years ago there were only three. These schools serve a school population of 2,118 children with 51 teachers who teach in Spanish, although a number of these teachers may be Quiché-speaking. Only six cantons have a bilingual preschool. The impact of the erosion of indigenous culture is growing, although illiteracy is still about 74 percent. However, many of these young students, both male and female, will gradually join the ranks of so-called indigenous professionals who leave agriculture, craftwork, or trade behind and move about within a regional society, without losing their own identity. Even so, it seems that the number of indigenous professional people in the municipality is still very low. The ideal for someone in San Antonio is still to be a merchant, not a student. The success of some merchants who have even reached the top levels of CACIF is a great stimulus to young people. (Statistical data from FUNCEDE: 1996 and Grupo Mega: 1999.)

Religious Division

I earlier mentioned the religious groups that are behind politics. Thirty years ago the population of San Antonio was sharply divided into three groups: Traditionalists, Catholic Action, and Protestants. The process of division had been brought about by a conversion movement that was deep in two ways: it caused profound change within people, and it overturned the foundations of the community.

The arrival of the Catholic Charismatic Renewal movement in the mid-1970s split Catholic Action. Its external manifestations were applause, speaking in tongues, healing, prophecy—in short, a series of "charisms" that result from a joyful exaltation where there is not much room for reason. Like Catholic Action, it had come from outside. It responded to emotional needs, like the pentecostal movements, but it was a Catholic alternative. In the years when the insurgency arose and the social commitment of the Catholic Church was more explicit, the charismatic movement was another spiritual and millenarian expression, disconnected from the seemingly imminent change toward which the revolutionary groups were pressing. The charismatic movement was very much out of tune with a church that was socially committed, as was the hierarchy in El Quiché. The diocese was headed by Bishop Gerardi, who was assassinated many years later. He was responsible for San Antonio from Santa Cruz. He was very concerned about the charismatics, because they had built a separate shrine on their own and were threatening a schism.

When the army began to kill priests and the bishop himself barely avoided being ambushed on the road heading up to San Antonio, all the outside pastoral agents, from the bishop to the last nun, withdrew from El Quiché. This happened in mid-1980. The charismatic movement must have found itself with more room to operate because the army regarded Catholic Action as the religious incubator for the guerrillas.

The internal division in the Catholic church in San Antonio does not seem to have led to a new conversion movement. Both movements, Catholic Action and the Charismatic Renewal, remained under the same religious domain (the church) and, as already noted, under the same political domain (the Christian Democrat Party). After 1988 neither of them was really a conduit for development, and both were somewhat weakened. Development, as we have said, was being pursued directly by the government and by other nongovernmental organizations, not by the church. The situation was very different from that of the late 1960s, when, for example, priests from Santa Cruz and Catholic Action were instrumental in introducing chemical fertilizer, and the adoption of this technology was initially seen almost as a symbol of rejection of the Tradition.

The internal division was skillfully halted in the mid-1980s by a priest living in San Antonio, who, even though he was not indigenous, learned Quiché, and gained people's trust. The reconciliation was not easy because it went against the mindset of a good portion of the clergy and of the groups that were at odds. Neither Catholic Action nor the Renewal was suppressed, and the charismatic movement was given the same status as Catholic Action, by offering it a representation on the highest body in the parish and recognizing its right to be represented in parish councils and to meet for prayer in separate places and at different times.

It should also be noted that a movement based in Totonicapán and encouraged by the development organization CDRO sought to remake the social fabric of communities and sectors in an organization called POP (which means "woven mat" in Quiché). At meetings of these organizations there was no talk of religious divisions, or the army, or the guerrillas.

Protestants, according to all indications, have grown enormously in membership and in numbers of churches. Their growth would have been even greater had there been no Charismatic Renewal, which enabled Catholics to remain in their church and shelter themselves somewhat from repression. In 1970, some Protestants worshiped in their houses in the cantons, but there were only two chapels, both of the New Jerusalem Church of God and both near the town of San Antonio. Currently there are 26 small churches throughout the municipality. Growth has been considerable. Openness to dialogue varies a great deal among Protestants. Some participate with Catholics in the same political party, the Christian Democrats. Other groups are more closed and are said to be forbidden to listen to the radio or read a newspaper.

With regard to the Traditionalists, a distinction must be made. On the one side is the structure of the *cofradías*. When I visited the municipality in 1994, I was told that only two of what used to be eight *cofradías* were still remaining. As the backbone of the traditional organization, they have been dwindling and will probably disappear or their function will change. In January 2001, the feast of San Antonio was sponsored jointly by Catholic Action, the Charismatic Renewal, and the *cofradías*—something that would have been inconceivable thirty years ago. The *cofradías* are apparently seeking the help of the church simply to continue to exist.

Then there are the "Mayan priests" who used to be called *zahorines*, or in Quiché *aj q'ij* (specialist in the day) in the singular or *aj q'ijab'* in the plural form. They are experts in the Mayan calendar, which is still used and whose value is being retrieved nationally by the movement of Mayan priests. Unlike the situation thirty years ago, these priests are now organized nationally in a number of associations supported by non-Mayan cultural or ecumenical religious organizations. For example, there is an ecumenical association called Guatemalan Christian Action, which has helped the Mayan "Chilam Balam" Council of the Quichés obtain its legal papers and allows them to use its meeting place in Santa Cruz. Many Mayan priests from San Antonio are members. This council in turn is part of a broader organization, Oxlajuj Ajpop.

The more advanced members in this movement see the very organization of the *cofradías* as a product of Spanish colonization, and the ritual of the *cofradías* is being displaced by celebrations in the hills by Mayan priests. There is an effort to go back to the deeper roots of the culture of one's forebears, without outside interference. Yet in San Antonio these celebrations are not separated from the Catholic Church, because after the rite of the Maya priests a hilltop mass is celebrated at their request in a close relationship with the Catholic priest, who is himself Quiché.

A very important role in this close relationship has been played by the movement toward enculturation in the Catholic Church that emerged from Vatican II but reached Guatemala only slowly. The conclusions of this book, which were written in final form in 1974, pointed toward the birth of this trend toward valuing Maya symbols, language, beliefs, and the ancient ceremonies. Enculturation means presenting the Christian message from within the culture. The aim is not to break the culture unless it is oppressing the human person, and to value and promote whatever is positive, holding to religious freedom as a fundamental premise. The Catholic Action movement of thirty years had no hint of enculturation.

Likewise important for this development has been the formation of indigenous Catholic priests (Mayas), young men who after many years of seminary training return to their people and are challenged by the beliefs of their ancestors. Today a Quiché priest serves San Antonio and has a very close relationship with the *aj q'jab'*.

According to some of the more organized Maya priests from outside San Antonio who are in contact with the Maya priests within, the most important thing is not religion but Maya spirituality. We do not know to what extent the Maya priests in San Antonio would insist on this distinction. According to this way of thinking, Maya spirituality is an essence. It not only is shaped in rituals and prayers but permeates everything: it harmonizes nature and the humanity of living beings; it promotes consensus in decisions. That is why when consensus is betrayed or manipulation takes place, conflicts are heightened. Conflicts—and indigenous communities are full of them—are not only the absence of that spirituality, but are also the expression of a sensitivity that has been defrauded. Maya spirituality makes everyone equal, but at the same time it stresses the need for hierarchy by which one rises in service to the community, as it were, in steps. In this spirituality, older men and women are the source of spirituality and deserve the respect of all. Even though women have not inherited land, Maya spirituality does not discriminate against them, because men consult them about everything. This essence gives life to all things. The earth is alive, time is alive and is possessed by vast energy flows. The earth may not be abused; it is our mother. Time cannot be desecrated; it is set within people's blood. One can feel it vibrate when the flows are set in motion. It announces dangers as well as opportunities. Equality is not monotony. Maya spirituality is in the marimba that cries out; it is in the multicolored clothes of the women. The four-sided view of the world, apparently very rational, is given colors: red where the sun is born, black where it dies. Birth and death are mediated by the green in the center of the world. When a wedding is celebrated, the "holy drink" (alcoholic) is placed at the center of the house so it can mediate the contradictions. It is where the center of the world is located. In the south is the tender yellow of children, and in the north the white of old people, and the line uniting them again passes through the green in the center of the sky and the sea. Maya spirituality may be described by many traits, but it cannot be defined in rigid concepts, like religion, which divide human beings.

The poetry and utopia, however, cannot keep us from seeing how hard it is to reach this spirituality as a common substrate under different religions. There may be an environment of coexistence between the different religious groups, but this does not mean that the problem of division does not remain latent, today more as a purely religious difference without the other social implications embodied thirty years ago in the difference between Catholic Action and the Tradition.

Finally, we want to say something about religious indifference and cultural erosion. I think it is important to stress that there is more to the religious phenomenon than listing the religious groups described. If that were the case, we would not understand the more overwhelming changes wrought by globalization, and we would be left with some mechanically applied labels. In each religious group there are varying degrees of participation and a growing number of people who are indifferent to religious expressions and to this underlying Maya spirituality. Sometimes deepening poverty does not allow for participation—religion flourishes where there are surpluses, as it used to flourish among the native-born upper class, the oligarchies. Sometimes the influence of development organizations disconnected from the churches makes religious practice superfluous, and money, alcohol, and sex corrupt leaders in the municipal capital, where the bars are near the NGO offices. Sometimes globalization through migration to the United States and the mass media have a strong eroding effect on the cultural foundations of the people. Criminal activity (robbery along the roads) and marijuana cultivation cause some people to keep their distance from the open religious organizations that condemn such activities. All these processes of modernization and globalization have to do with indigenous urbanization, something that has not been much studied, but which is increasingly important. "In a number of Latin American countries around half—or even more—of the indigenous are now living in urban areas and they work in productive activities other than agriculture" (Bascuñán and Durston 1999: 190).

Reflections Thirty Years Later

Such is the picture of the municipality that I have been able to put together from afar, with the help of some people knowledgeable about San Antonio. At this point, looking at what has changed, I can deal with answering the question that several people have asked me: how do I feel as I look back? Where was this book on the mark, as I look at it from a distance, and what flaws did it have or what was missing? My assessment will be very succinct.

Perhaps the first point on which it was on the mark was the decision to study a community not in isolation from outside influences, but as part of the nation of Guatemala. Research into the community led me to become very deeply involved in indigenous culture and life and made me see Guatemala from below, through a lens tinted very differently from the glasses I was wearing. I think that the wealth I found there is in this book. Not just that, however: what was happening in the community was very connected to what was happening in the nation. Power is the glue, across cultures, that connects the different levels, from the individual who changes religion to the nation that splits in half, passing by way of households and the community. At that time, anthropological studies were connecting community and outside influences. But I think in this study this relationship is advanced systematically, using the concept of power, as I have already said.

Second, the focus of the study was on the mark inasmuch as it did not originate in a laboratory but from the concern of the population, which at that moment was plunged in religious division. That gave the study vitality. We were—the people and I—involved in the same crisis. This focus had the effect of making the study intellectually stimulating by placing the horse ahead of the cart, rather than the other way around. That is, there was a question to be answered, put simply: "Why do people change their belief?"—an easy and clear question that would gradually center both the fieldwork and the writing of the dissertation. The question was the horse and the answer (this book) the cart. At the same time, this question was consonant with a personal and professional question that aroused me passionately, as a priest and student of theology, a point that at the time it did not seem relevant to bring out specifically in the book: how does all of this stuff about faith operate in social reality, and how does it combine with what goes on in people's minds and hearts? When I began to study anthropology, I had just completed four years of theology study in Innsbruck, where the topic of faith was central to modern reflection on Christianity. That led me to locate one area for a response in power, but it was incomplete—a further explanation had to be sought, because power by itself did not explain the break and the totalizing aspect of belief and hence the radical nature of conversion. That was how I took up the aspect of initiation, which, even though it does not completely explain the mysterious leap of faith, at least shows the liminal context in which it takes place. For all these reasons, it seems to me that the focus of the study was on the mark.

Third, I think that the choice of the community was also on the mark. I sought a small community for the ease it would offer for the research. I looked for a Quiché-speaking community, because that was the majority language in Guatemala. I looked for a traditional rural community because indigenous culture would be denser there, so much so that you could almost cut it with a knife. But all these things were not the center and essence of what was on the mark. What was on the mark—half luck, half intuition—was the choice of a community in the department of El Quiché. For me at that time Quiché was like a faraway mysterious place filled with experiences, perhaps somewhat mythical. This was not so much because of the studies that had been done, such as that of Colby among the Ixils or Bunzel in Chichicastenango, but for the sheer resonance of the word in my imagination. I don't know whether it was by coincidence or, as I say, by intuition, but the study of this community turned out to be for many people a gateway into the heart of contemporary events in Guatemala. Although this book perhaps deals with something rather specific, the conversion movement, and even though it is focused on one community lost among the canyons and mountains, it gets to the root of many things that happened later and are still very much with us today.

Looking at where it was off the mark, its flaws, and what is missing, I find many things, but I will focus on three main ones. The first is the source of information. Although the research was on a totality, the municipality and its conversion process, my informants were limited to one-third of the population, those who had been converted. I do not mean that I did not speak with Quiché Maya Traditionalists, but the perspective did not come from that sector of the population, nor did it come from the Protestant population. In addition to this limitation imposed by the situation (my status, religious affiliation, and the limited research time), there was another limitation particular to that time. We were still not aware of gender, and so the perspective of the study was from a male viewpoint. I decided not to learn Quiché for use in interviews, for lack of time and because some linguists told me that fieldwork could be done in Guatemala without knowing the indigenous language well. Since I was not fluent in the language, I was unable to approach women to listen to their voice. This is another flaw of the many that can be found in this work.

A second defect, related to the previous one, is that there was no analysis of the content of the religious beliefs to see, within the break entailed in conversion, what was retained as a common substrate and what changed. I was aware of that while writing the dissertation, but I was under time constraints, I did not have enough information on the topic (although loose data could always be soaked up like a sponge), and what I had already analyzed and written was coherent and appeared to be complete. In this I was not consistent with my desire to write something complete, rather than just to fulfill the dissertation requirement. I failed to enter into what is now being called Maya spirituality in San Antonio.

Finally, a third deficiency is that it is to some extent a cool study. I put a lot of thought into connecting all the parts into a logical whole—I have no problem with that now. The theoretical framework was useful to me, and perhaps I was too attached to it. Nor do I have a problem with that. I was very analytical, sometimes subtle, which on first reading may look repetitive, even though it is not. Nor am I speaking of this as a deficiency because it is cool. What I mean is that when I did this study I had still not experienced the inner death that I speak about in the book, even though I was already forty years old. I spoke of something that I understood and for which I felt compassion, but I had not experienced it personally. The study is not a cry of the heart—that was something missing from it. It is a work of adult youth, funny as that may seem. It is good, I think, but still lacking in the integration of head and heart.

Further Lines of Research

In closing, I am going to mention a couple of lines of study, each with many ramifications, that I think are important for the present.

First, I think that the tradition in anthropology of studying indigenous communities has to be continued, especially by simultaneously studying several communities spread across the map so as to be able to find contrasts around the focus of the research. I think that there ought to be an emphasis on the immediate historic background of violence, but without thereby letting the research get caught in sterile ideological arguments. The focus of study ought to be on the impact of globalization on the culture of these communities. I have in mind the impact of migration to the United States; the effect of market ups and downs and free-trade treaties on agriculture, artisan work, and other types of products; the impact of investment in textile industry (*maquila* plants) near indigenous towns; the impact of structural adjustments and social compensation funds; growing drug crops (marijuana) and involvement in crime; the new appreciation of what is ethnic; media penetration; and so forth. For all of that, anthropology has a very valuable experience that other disciplines do not, although it ought to learn from them as well. What must be studied is not simply the impact of globalization on the economy and the society of these communities, but also its impact on culture, understood as values, symbols, beliefs, rituals, and the meaning of life. I think that the sector that ought to be singled out in such studies is that of young people, with a gender angle, because young people offer a clearer X-ray photo of cultural breaking points—how young people, for example, see the impact of migration to the United States, how they go about getting there, how they stay in touch with their family, how marriage ties are broken, how their identity suffers, and so forth. Likewise, how young women see the impact of working in factories (*maquila* plants), how having a salary affects their relationship with their parents, how they again fall under the male control of their bosses, how they relate to nonindigenous fellow workers in the plant, and so forth. We have the impression that in-depth case studies can be complemented by studying the community qualitatively and quantitatively. Such a study has to be open not only to the nation, as this one was, but today even more to the globalized world.

A second line of pursuit is studies of the indigenous urban population, an area that is problematic and almost ignored by researchers. In Guatemala and elsewhere in Central America this phenomenon is becoming increasingly important. Here I only want to offer some suggestions in the form of some rather disorganized questions. What happens with indigenous municipalities that are being absorbed by large cities like Guatemala City and Quetzaltenango, and what is happening with indigenous towns that are municipal seats growing in population and becoming small cities, standing in contrast to their peasant hinterland? Is migration to the cities crystallizing in more or less homogeneous urban indigenous barrios that are related to their community of origin? What is the future of the indigenous population living in the poorest places, such as the canyons on the rim of Guatemala City, full of indigenous people who because of poverty are prevented from maintaining the connection with their community of origin and are captives of drugs and youthful violence? On the other hand, how are the indigenous social classes of merchants, landowners, and professional people in cities like Quetzaltenango related to the ladino sector, and what role will they play in forming a multiethnic nationality? Likewise, the indigenous associations with their myriad acronyms, each claiming to represent the indigenous world, supported by NGOs: what kind of grassroots support are they gaining and how are they coordinating so as to one day really represent the indigenous sector on a national level? What purpose is served by areas for coming together, like the park in the center of downtown Guatemala City on Sundays, to form a network of young people who get to know each other and get married? Will the political groups with different strategies flow together into a united force or will they be fractured by external or internal forces? Finally, what are the trends in Guatemalan indigenous communities in the United States, such as that of the Kanjobals in Los Angeles, who maintain their identity, keep sending remittances, and talk directly by cell phone to their relatives in the village?

A third line of inquiry, related to these two, is research into the process of making Guatemala a multiethnic, multilinguistic, and multicultural nation, as it has been formulated in one of the peace agreements. Even though that definition has been formulated, reality is not created by decree. The thrust of that social process has to be researched so as to find its strengths and opportunities, its weaknesses and dangers, and to help at least diminish the massive discrimination that still exists in Guatemala—as was made evident in the extreme polarization before the May 16, 1999, referendum, when that definition of the Guatemalan nation was rejected. On the one hand, the process of empowerment of the groups representing the indigenous sector on the national level, such as the Coordinating Body of Organizations of the Maya People of Guatemala, must become known, as well as how rooted they really are in the vast rural and urban masses (or are they just isolated leadership structures?) and their relationship to the education system as a channel of access to various levels of power (Maya University and the like). On the other hand, we need to know to what extent ladino society is softening or becoming more rigid in all its points of contact with the indigenous population, and to what extent the perception of the ladinos that they are the only sector representing the Guatemalan nation is being changed. We must delve deeper into their weak and threatened identity, but also discover the riches of the ladino subethnicities in the various regions of Guatemala, and the connection between ladino rural communities and urban society. Study of this issue ought to bear in mind the relationship between the two sectors, not only at the level of rural communities as traditional anthropological practice has done, but also nationally. It is difficult to incorporate this issue into a research project because of its breadth, because of those aspects of it that do not lend themselves to analysis (like everything having to do with content of identity and elements of consciousness), and because of the difficulty of generating in-depth analyses. Nevertheless, I believe that this issue is very important for the future of Guatemala—because, in it, justice and the harmony and social respect of the citizenry are at stake. It seems that the rejection in the referendum of the idea of Guatemala as a multiethnic, multicultural, and multilingual nation should be regarded not only as a "lost opportunity," but rather as a stimulus to "reinvention," as Susanne Jonas so aptly suggests in a recent book on the peace process in Guatemala (2000: 217).

—Ricardo Falla
March 2001

Bibliography

Bascuñán, Eduardo, and John W. Durston. 1999. Globalización, tratados comerciales y autodesarrollo indígena en América Latina. In Rolando Franco and Armando Di Filippo, (eds.), *Las dimensiones sociales de la integración regional en América Latina*, 181–209. Santiago: Comisión Económica para América Latina y el Caribe (CEPAL).

Comisión para el Esclarecimiento Histórico (CEH). 1999. *Guatemala: Memoria del silencio. Tomo VIII: Casos presentados. Guatemala.*

Fundación Centroamericana de Desarrollo (FUNCEDE). 1994. Diagnóstico del Municipio de San Antonio Ilotenango, Departamento de Quiché. Internal report. Guatemala.

García Vettorazzi, María Victoria. 1996. Poder local y desarrollo en los municipios de San Antonio Ilotenango, Quiché y Sololá, Sololá. Ph.D. diss., Facultad de Ciencias Políticas y Sociales, Universidad Rafael Landívar. Guatemala.

González, Matilde. 2001. *Continuidad e imagen de un poder ejercido "durante años."* AVANCSO (forthcoming). Guatemala.

Grupo Mega. 1999. Análisis del Municipio de San Antonio Ilotenango, Departamento de Quiché. Internal report. Guatemala.

Jonas, Susanne. 2000. *Of Centaurs and Doves: Guatemala's Peace Process.* Westview, Colo.: Westview Press.

Oficina de Derechos Humanos del Arzobispado de Guatemala (ODHAG). 1998. *Guatemala nunca más: Informe del Proyecto Interdiocesano de Recuperación de la Memoria Histórica. Tomo IV: Víctimas del conflicto.* Guatemala.

Theoretical Framework

In order to comprehend the religious conversion movement, I make use of two main theories, that of power and that of liminality.

Theory of Power

Conversion is a moment in a process of adaptation by an individual or a group to the environment, whether it be the world of nature, such as land, water, and all resources, the world of the surrounding society, or both. Because conversion entails the abandonment of a broader social unit encompassing the individual, from which one breaks away to join another or to fashion one, the result is a confrontation of individuals or groups of individuals in their struggle for adaptation, as is abundantly illustrated in the body of this study. Hence there is a political side to conversion, that is, it involves a power relationship, which is understood as suitable control over the environment. To control the inherently limited environment vis-à-vis other individuals who are trying to control it means adapting to it and having power.[1]

Power is an aspect of every social relationship because life in society is a way of adapting to the (physical) environment, and because in society, just as other individuals can be a help, so also by their very existence they are at least a potential threat. It therefore follows that power is always reciprocal, that is, neither of the parties in competition for control over the environment ever has total or zero control. The existence of one of them, as tenuous as its control over the environment may be, limits the other's power.

Power may be *independent* (one's own), by which control over the environment is based on the potentiality (intelligence, technology, weapons) of the unit, or *derived*, when it is based on the potentiality of another unit from which it receives it. In this case, the deriving unit is said to be under the domain of the unit from which it receives or derives power, because the domain of one unit over another takes place when one unit has greater control over another's environment than the latter does itself.

Both units are then said to operate at different *levels of articulation*. But if both confront one another, each having a control over the environment that is independent of the other, they operate on the same level. These concepts of independent and derived power, domain, and diversity of levels I have found useful, inasmuch as the confrontation of individuals, one converted and the other not, sometimes even within the context of the household, requires a framework that shows how this confrontation is related to behavior at the municipal and national levels. Unless I articulate the power relationships between levels, I cannot draw out the vision of the structure, and the phenomenon will only be partially explained.

Another distinction that I have found useful is that of the *reality potential* and *cultural potential*. "Potential" is a primitive concept that cannot be properly defined: it is the capacity that consists of the qualities of persons, social groups, technological resources, and so forth, by which one unit can control the physicosocial milieu vis-à-vis another. Because the units (individuals or a set of them) are sociocultural subjects, two aspects of their potential can be distinguished, one of them having to do with the "actual potential of the unit to act in some specific way in a real environment" and the other pertaining to "what the people believe is the potential of the unit, the rules, the proscriptions, and the special values they attribute to it" (Adams 1970: 48). The first is called reality potential and the second, cultural potential. Just as a unit's real potential changes when its internal organization changes or when the conditions of the environment change, so also the cultural potential changes when the definition of the unit by its members or the definition of the unit by other members of the environment changes.[2]

Those beliefs that are ordinarily called "supernatural" can be regarded as a kind of cultural potential, continually put to the test, reinterpreted, confirmed, or rejected in view of the experienced result of what their potential is. A god, a deceased grandfather, a *zahorín*, a priest, a fortune-telling rite, or a piece of incense may be regarded as charged with both types (inseparable aspects) of potential: one that they have by the influence that the belief, as an instrument of the unit for controlling the environment, exercises over its bearer, inasmuch as this belief is an item of knowledge and all knowledge can transmit power. I am assuming that this aspect of the cultural potential *is verifiable*. The other aspect is what the person or persons in the unit believe that they have, but actually *it is not verifiable* that they have it. Let us suppose, for example, as observers and interpreters of social life, that it is not the god, not the dead person, and so on, but the image—insofar as it is known—that communicates the potential because we assume that the influence of these units cannot be experienced as coming from them. Thus it is possible to put forward a difference that Adams (1970: 50) only hints at when he speaks of the "nontestable, non-verifiable content" of many beliefs. This difference is that there is one cultural potential that can be experienced, that is, whose fit to reality can be established, and another that cannot be experienced; for example, the cultural potential of the deceased person in the eyes of the living relative cannot be experienced, *insofar* as the person is dead (not insofar as it is from the image of the dead person while alive). If it cannot be experienced, then it is attributed by the sociocultural power unit. The process by which this potential is withdrawn from a unit is made manifest precisely in conversion.[3]

Some beliefs are more resistant to change than others. Although the facts seem to contradict them, they are maintained because the facts are reinterpreted, as when a diviner fails to diagnose an illness and then attributes his ineffectiveness to mistakes in the rite or in the attitude of those present. One particularly resistant type of belief is that which is based on what I could call the *total loyalty* of an individual to a social unit. Total loyalty can be defined as the willingness of the individual to put the social unit and belonging to it ahead of anything else, even to the point of destruction and death. Because I do not know the (internal) attitude of individuals, I base my interpretations on their words, deeds, facts of their life, and so forth, when I assume that particular individuals maintain such total loyalty to a particular unit at a particular moment.[4]

The totality of this loyalty is a quality that the individual *attributes* to the social unit to which he or she belongs, because this totality, as is made clear in this study, is disproportionately greater than the power base that the social unit controls and can control, and the reasons that demand absolute loyalty cannot be proven to be enough to demand it to that degree. That is why the aspect of totality of such loyalty has to be regarded as a notable type of nonverifiable cultural potential.

> If the concepts have reasonable (and crucial) congruence with experience, they are rewarded. If their beliefs do not work, then, over a period of time, variations are conceived of and tried. It is well documented that all belief systems carry a great amount of nontestable, non-verifiable content, and so most meanings do not change drastically merely due to failure in the external world. There are points, however, where some individuals lose their faith and try new meanings. (Adams 1970: 50)

The aim of this study is to make clear where this point is at which individuals lose their faith, that is, which individuals they are, their social characteristics, and the circumstances in which they must find themselves in order to lose their faith. As stated, it will be those who are maladapted, who upon losing control over their milieu need a new set of beliefs. Yet this generalization, although it leaves open the possibility of some other kind of explanation, cannot explain why under equal circumstances of being maladapted and in crisis in relation to their milieu, some individuals only reinterpret their faith, while others lose it.

Finally, I use the concept of *operating* (or operative) *unit* (Adams 1973: 119–133), which in this study I call a "social unit." An operative unit is a set of actors who share a common pattern of adaptation to an aspect of the environment. The actor may be the individual or an operating unit. In terms of six traits, Adams divides the units into three types and seven subtypes (see Table A.1). The six traits are:

1. The members have independent powers;
2. They are identified by their common membership;
3. They grant powers reciprocally;
4. They assign powers in a centralized manner;
5. The center (leader) wields independent power; and
6. The center delegates power.

The three types of units are: *fragmented, informal,* and *formal.* In the first type (fragmented), the members have at least a common adaptation pattern, for example, parallel or complementary behaviors toward aspects of the milieu, but their activity is not coordinated. The fragmented unit can be the subtype of *aggregated and individual* units and that of *identity.* The first subtype contains only the first trait, and the second, the first two traits. Examples of the first subtype are buyers in a market, and students in a class. Examples of the second are ethnic groups such as native people in Guatemala.

What distinguishes the second type (informal) is that the activity of its members is *coordinated,* but they do not receive power delegated from the center (leader, authority). This type contains the following subtypes: the *coordinated* unit, properly speaking, that of *consensus,* and the *majority.* They are distinguished by having traits three, four, and five. An example of the coordinated subtype is a set of leaderless hunter-gatherer families who act in a way that is based on the reciprocity that unites them; another is members of American political parties. Examples of the consensus subtype are buffalo hunters who for a portion of the year needed the coordination of a leader. The majority subtype is exemplified by Plains Indians in the United States with police societies capable of wielding coercion.

What characterizes the third type (formal) is that the center already has so much power that it can delegate it. This can be the *corporate* unit if it has all six features; and an *administrative* unit if it has the last two (center with independent power and delegation of power) but the other features may or may not be present. This last unit is a residual category. The state is an example of the corporate unit, and the bureaucratic units of complex societies exemplify the administrative unit.

While fragmented and informal units lack *authority,* the others have it. In the remaining informal units (consensus and majority), authority is based on the leader's *ability,* and for formal units, on the possible use of *force.*

Theory of Liminality

Because total loyalty cannot even in theory be explained by the concept of a controlled environment, given that the environment, as I have already hinted, is always less than a reason that can demand total loyalty, in order to explain

TABLE A.1. *Opposition of units encompassed in a larger unit of another nature*

Types of Operating Units / Independent variable traits	Fragmented		Coordinated	Informal		Corporate	Formal
	Individual & aggregated	Of identity		Of consensus	Majority		Administrative
Members have independent powers	+	+	+	+	–	+	var.
Members identify their common membership	–	+	+	+	+	+	var.
Members grant reciprocal powers	–	–	+	+	+	+	var.
Members allocate powers (centrally)	–	–	–	+	+	+	var.
Center (leader) exercises power independently	–	–	–	–	+	+	+
Center delegates power	–	–	–	–	–	+	+
Type of authority	None			Ability	Centralized		Power

this loyalty I invoke another concept: initiation rites (Van Gennep 1908; Turner 1967, 1969). Through the liminality phase of such rites people are initiated into the fundamental principles (suggesting a total loyalty) of a society. Conversion, by which an individual is initiated into a new social unit with total loyalty, resembles an initiation rite.

Three phases have been distinguished in initiation rites: (1) separation from a state or social unit (in the broad sense), (2) liminality (*limen* = threshold), and (3) joining another state. The rite transforms the neophyte because it changes him or her from one state to another. The passage from one state to another is commonly symbolized by death (separation), burial (liminality), and rebirth (adhesion). The moment of liminality, which is situated between the two moments of separation and adhesion, is the one in which the person, by virtue of the ritual, belongs neither to the previous state or unit nor to the one following. The liminal person, who is in a situation of liminality, cannot be included in either social category; he or she therefore does not make sense. Such a person combines the coincidence of opposites and personifies the absence of logic and rationality. Having been excluded from all social categories and dispossessed of the kinds of status that go along with them, all that is left to the liminal person is the bare fact of being a person. Hence, when several individuals go through such a period together, the relationship of "communitas" (being siblings without categories) and equality between them stands out in relief. The only thing they have left in common is the uniqueness of the person. Thus, a powerful outpouring of feeling is commonly unleashed by the impulse of the ritual.

The cycle of socialization is made up of a series of initiation rites, which in some societies stand out in sharper relief. In becoming socialized, the individual goes through those rites and gradually achieves an ever higher status ascribed to the new state. With its mysterious and sometimes grotesque symbolism, the initiation rite represents the basic principles of society and communicates them to the individual who participates in the rite. It is assumed that passing through the liminality period—precisely because it entails stripping one's belonging to one state or another—better disposes the individual to "internalize" the teachings symbolically expressed in the ritual. I understand "internalization" to mean the quality by which such an individual will be found to be more resistant to abandoning the principles and basic beliefs thereby transmitted. It can be assumed, for example, that a person will be less likely to give up such principles and beliefs (i.e., to which he or she has been converted)—which he or she perhaps does not go out to defend in periods of tranquillity—the greater the number of initiation rites through which he or she has passed step by step.

Here I assume that such initiation rites take place in every society and that initiation is defined by the three periods described above, namely separation, liminality, and adhesion. Moreover, I understand basic principles or beliefs to be those that at least sometimes demand total loyalty.

The conversion process has certain characteristics that set it apart from that of socialization. In conversion, the individual rebels against (separates from) certain basic principles and beliefs of society, and either forms the core of a new social unit adapted to him or her or joins an existing one that he or she finds more suited. In socialization, on the other hand, the individual adheres more and more firmly to those basic principles and beliefs and adapts to the already existing social unit. Even so, both processes resemble one another in the three phases described, because conversion, as the initiation rite, includes the moment of separation from the unit against which the individual is rebelling; that of liminality, for the person converting does not belong to either unit; and that of joining an already existing unit or starting one.

Given this resemblance, it may be assumed that when two units clash over some basic belief (which requires total loyalty), the crises of adaptation to the milieu will be described by members of these units as liminal periods, and they will take advantage of them to proselytize. For example, illnesses of individuals will be interpreted by members of opposed units as an argument for one unit or another's inability to cure the ailment, and undecided individuals will waver back and forth between the opposing arguments (because they will not be able to decide to belong to either one—they will be in liminality). They would not be wavering back and forth if they were not in a crisis of adaptation and had not in some fashion lost control over their environment.[5]

Although in the conversion process the liminal person is not, properly speaking, going through an initiation rite during the crisis of adaptation, since he or she is not subjected to either social unit and therefore is not subjected to their rituals, nevertheless, when he or she finally decides in favor of one and submits to the initiation rite to enter the new unit, at that point, by virtue of that rite he or she symbolically goes through the three phases of separation, liminality, and adhesion previously experienced in a nonritual manner. Thus the crisis of adaptation is reinterpreted as ritual liminality and further light is shed on the explanation of the loss of total loyalty, with which I was not satisfied if it had to do only with control over the environment. To what extent both standpoints are truly in dialectical opposition is a matter that goes beyond the limits of this study.

Notes

Foreword

1. Many of his works that remain in manuscript are available at the library of the Centro de Investigaciones Mesoamericanos (CIRMA) in Antigua, Guatemala.

1. The Study

1. [To designate the accepted form of religious belief and practice in San Antonio, Falla uses the term used by the people themselves, *costumbre*. The literal meaning of the word is "custom," which suggests that its center of gravity is a series of ritual practices more than a set of firmly defined doctrines or ethical practices. To some extent, *costumbre* represents a survival and adaptation of pre-Columbian religion (such as the use of the 260-day Maya calendar), but in other respects it derives from popular Catholicism in Spain, as practiced by the religious brotherhoods known as *cofradías*. Practitioners of *la costumbre* by no means deny the authority of the Catholic Church, but their religious practice depends relatively little on priests, whom they might see only on special occasions, such as annual celebrations for patron saints. In this translation, *Costumbre* (which Falla puts in upper case), is rendered as "Tradition," and its practitioners are called "Traditionalists." Trans.]

2. "Convert" in this study refers to those who have embraced the particular form of Catholicism known as "Catholic Action," thereby breaking with the religious and cultural forms known as "Tradition" (*Costumbre*).

3. The word *zahorín* has a pejorative sound today, but that was not the case thirty years ago. A new term, "Maya priest" (*sacerdote maya*), is now used in Spanish.

3. Trade as a New Source of Social Power

1. In 1876, the political chiefs were ordered to send plantation owners the number of laborers they needed, up to 110, from Indian towns. The next year regulations were established for the monetary advance that was to be given to crew members, and borders of departments were opened so that laborers could cross them going from the towns in one department to plantations in another. Obligatory work on plantations

was suspended in 1894, but it was replaced by that of road building. Only those who owed more than 30 pesos still had to work on the plantations. The world financial crisis of 1929 caused debts to rise to an intolerable level, and in 1934, two years after the uprising and slaughter in El Salvador (La Matanza), all debts in Guatemala were pardoned, but the vagrancy law was imposed.

2. Below I explain what I understand by the term "spiral" and discuss in greater detail how the 260-day calendar works (as it is understood in San Antonio).

In San Antonio, the *zahorines* use the 260-day calendar, made up of twenty days and thirteen numbers. The twenty days are: *[noj], tijax, kuwuk, ajpu, imox, [ik'], akabal, c'at, queme; queme; [quiej], k'anil, toj, tz'i, batz; [e], aj, ix, tziquin, ajmak*. The ones in brackets are also Lords of the Years, as I will explain. The days are combined with thirteen numbers, for example, March 9, 1971, was 3 *noj*; March 10 was 4 *tijax*; March 11, 5 *kuwuk*, etc. The cycle repeats after 260 days (20 days x 13).

There is also a 365-day solar year. It is known to exist because some say that the year begins on a date that falls between March 9 and 13. It has a moveable beginning. Since this year has 105 days plus the 260-day year, if, for instance, in 1971 the solar year begins on 3 *noj* (March 9), the next year (1972) it ought to begin 5 days (100 + 5 = 105) after 3 *noj*, that is, on 8 *ik*, and so forth. (Further on we will see that because 1972 is the beginning of a twenty-year unit, it does not begin on 8 *ik*). Each year begins on one of the four days bracketed above: *noj, ik, quiej*, and *e*, which are the Lords of the Years. Each day is not only under the influence of the Lord of the Day but also that of the Lord of the Year. The heart of the day is thus within the heart of the year.

A further complication comes from leap years, which make the beginning of the year moveable. For example, 1964 was a leap year and the year began on March 10. However, 1965, 1966, and 1967 were not, and they also began on March 10. But 1968 was a leap year. Then our (Gregorian) calendar adds one more day to them, so the day when their solar year begins is set back in accordance with our first day. Without such a correction, the beginning of the year would move forward indefinitely not only vis-à-vis our year, but vis-à-vis the sun, and thus it would no longer indicate the time for planting, as it used to do. So a correction has to be made every twenty years by having the year begin five days later, or on March 13. Thus the five days that the beginning of the year had been moving back during those twenty years are gained back. This correction, for example, took place in 1972. Then the year does not begin on the Lord of the following year but it is leaped over. For example, if in 1971 the year began on 3 *noj*, in 1972 it did not begin on 8 *ik* but on 13 *quiej*. This is not explained by the *zahorines*, as far as I know, but it follows logically. Moreover, I have verified it by checking dates with *zahorines* separated by over twenty years.

It also follows that because every 100 years, except for those divisible by 400, are not leap years, there is another correction every 400 years, that is, every 20 by 20 years, and this period ought to have its Lord and successively each multiple of the number of years of the previous unit by 20 (e.g., 400 x 20; 8,000 x 20; 160,000 x 20).

Every Lord of a unit of time is within another larger unit, as if it were in concentric circles. As they are related and time begins to grow by the smallest one, when the circle is completed, another broader one begins and so forth. This is what I call *spiral* time. As time goes on, the circles get bigger but each circle is drawn on the pattern of the previous one.

Although I am not aware of anyone who explains this whole idea, the *zahorines* handle it in their divining with beans (*tz'ite'*), and they must intuit that they are handling something very intricate, something that provides an explanation for all events in the world submerged in time. This vision of time incarnate in the life of human beings and society, which corresponds to the units with their Lords, is the conceptual and unitary elaboration of the faith of the *zahorines*. Here is found the reason for their wonderful resistance to the invasion of new beliefs. It is a kind of reason that has taken on life through ritual: that of the initiation through which they have become *zahorines* and the rituals of their divining practices. It is no wonder that among younger generations the disorderly growth of society and its stratification has the effect of disturbing the compact order of this worldview and understanding of society. (This note includes some very valuable information provided by Domingo Ramírez, who was born in San Antonio, and who, although he is not Indian, has a mastery of Quiché and has put into writing many traditions of the town, including that of the calendar.)

3. In San Antonio, the acceptance of chemical fertilizer provided an opening of the traditional barrier holding peasants back; nevertheless, they subsequently realized that they were now dependent on technology.

4. Social Reorganization

1. Only through the average amount of land owned by level A, B, and C merchants, which is around 64 *cuerdas*, did I deduce that at least the thirty-eight merchants in these levels used laborers, because the approximate amount of land that a man without sons can cultivate by himself ranges between 14 and 20 *cuerdas*, which at a rate of five days' work per *cuerda*, would occupy him 75–100 days a year. But there are other merchants, those who have sales of Q 150 or more, who also employ laborers, because they earn more in business than from working in the field, regardless of the size of their land. However, they give work to one or, at most, two laborers.

The one who has the most land, who cultivates 300 *cuerdas*, sometimes employs twenty men and around ten women. He also has two long-time trusted laborers, who handle weighing what workers have picked.

2. I here follow Wolf's (1966: 3–7) conception, according to which the peasant is forced to hand over his surpluses to the dominant group. In this conception, the peasant can do no more than survive and is incapable of investing such surpluses.

3. Davis (1970: 56–65) states that, starting in 1888, the lands of the future ladino municipality of Barillas were taken away from Santa Eulalia; that the Indians struggled at that time to register the community land plus extra lands in order to defend themselves from ladino invasion; that in 1902 those deeds were given to them, and that as the result of a law in 1905, individual titling of lands whose titles had been received in 1902 began. Davis shows that this is where we find the historic root of today's factionalism.

6. Power Derived from Outside the Community

1. MDN (Nationalist Democratic Movement) was a party organized in 1957 to continue the Liberation Movement of Castillo Armas.

2. This same priest would later be involved in the efforts of the Melville brothers, then Maryknoll missionaries, to organize labor crew members in leagues, against the will of their bishops. The Melvilles later had ties with the guerrillas. The priest who

organized the cooperatives then distanced himself from the Melvilles, who later left the country.

3. Article 101 of the Law on Elections and Political Parties provides rules for granting positions on corporate bodies, including municipal councils, to minority parties.

4. In early 1970 the price of radios had dropped dramatically from five years previously, and one could be obtained for Q 22 with a Q 5 down payment and Q 3 a month for six months. According to figures gathered in 1970 from several cantons (305 Catholic Action households from four different cantons), 36 percent of the houses in the municipality in 1970 had at least one radio, a figure that indicates the rapidly increasing power of radio.

5. Illiterate women were granted the right to vote for the first time in the 1965 Constitution.

6. The extensionist's wife was mysteriously murdered in 1971.

7. Article 57 of the 1965 Constitution: "One's home is inviolable. No one may enter another's dwelling without the permission of the person living there, except with a written warrant by a competent judge and never before 6:00 A.M. or after 6:00 P.M."

7. Conclusions

1. The murder rate is 251.2 per 100,000 for Amatenango, as opposed to 31.9 for all of Mexico.

2. Amatenango is a municipality that is practically entirely indigenous, with a core of 1,900 inhabitants and four nearby neighborhoods. The center is divided into two endogamous sections that have traditionally been opposed to each other and were governed by two *principales*, two supreme healers, the president, and the *síndico*, plus their staffs. The president and *síndico* alternated between the two sections every three years.

3. Of the thirty-six murders examined by June Nash, in eight cases the victim was a healer (there are only twelve in the core of the town), in nineteen the motive for the crime was suspicion of witchcraft, and in all cases, after the murder took place, the local inhabitants discussed whether it was because of witchcraft or for some other reason.

4. Here I speak with the caution of one whose knowledge of Chiapas comes only from books. There would also have to be a comparison of communities in Chiapas with different murder rates. The independent variable would be the magnitude of the power vacuum mentioned earlier.

5. I have not heard from informants in other communities in Guatemala, nor have I read in the ethnographic literature that murder as a result of witchcraft was widespread in the time of Ubico.

6. The area of greatest trade with the center in San Francisco el Alto is limited by a circle formed by Santa Cruz del Quiché, the city of Huehuetenango, the city of San Marcos, Coatepeque, Mazatenango, Sololá, and back to Santa Cruz. San Antonio is inside this area, which is economically privileged in comparison to the other two larger circles. The second circle is bounded by Jacaltenango, Soloma, Nebaj, Uspantán, Joyabaj, Chimaltenango, Cotzumalguapa, Tiquisate, Retalhuleu, Pajapita, Malacatán, Tacaná, and back to Jacaltenango. The third is located beyond these boundaries (Smith 1972).

7. Santa Eulalia is located at the far limits of the second circle of stratification.

8. Nebaj is located in the Ixil region, which marks the northern limit of the second circle of stratification. Cotzal and Chajul, farther to the north, also belong to the Ixil area. Division has recently been reaching the area of Alta Verapaz; however, there the double domain does not seem to take effect due to the isolation that hinders the derivation of power.

9. The anthropologists who participated in the symposium on interethnic friction in South America that took place in Barbados in January 1971 said of this oppression: "The indigenous policies of Latin American governments themselves are aimed at the destruction of the native cultures. . . . In view of this situation, states, religious missions, and social scientists must assume inescapable responsibilities for immediate action to end this assault, thereby helping to serve indigenous liberation" ("Declaración de Barbados" 1971).

10. The "integrationists" of the 1950s were witnesses to the process of ladinization that could be seen in the period between the censuses. Social processes shape their interpretation. When they change, the interpretations, as reflections of society, also change. I am not thereby denying influence in the opposite direction, of the researcher and analyst on society. Today it would be well to restudy the identity of some communities in the eastern part of the country that could be adduced as examples of the abandonment of identity through transculturation. Such is the case of the community of La Montaña in Jalapa (Adams 1970: 202), which, even though it has lost the indigenous language, retains its awareness that its identity is different from that of the ladinos in El Progreso, but whose inhabitants do not like to be identified as the "little Indians" of the East. In April 1973 they spilled their own blood over recently planted land in a boundary dispute with troops brought in by ladinos from El Progreso.

11. According to a reporter for *El Imparcial* (March 5, 1974), the opposition got almost twice as many votes as the government-sponsored coalition. Traveling through the municipalities of the department, I was able to confirm that those results are basically accurate. I spoke to people who were familiar with the results from the voting tables. The official results were changed to benefit the right-wing coalition of parties as part of a general fraud.

12. See Aguirre Beltrán 1971, Torres Rivas 1971, Carmack 1972, and Noval 1972.

13. Guzmán Böckler, Quan, and Herbert (1971) also refer to one hundred families of the indigenous bourgeoisie taking shape, made up of owners of commercial and shop-based businesses and owners of lands in Quetzaltenango. Their children have continued the activities of their fathers or have devoted themselves to intellectual pursuits (p. 6). Their capital buildup comes from the period after the world economic crisis of the 1930s. Here I especially have in mind those who leave their community to go away to school.

14. Cabarrús (1973) shows the flexibility of identity that is shaped by different cultures and structures. What needs to be studied now is not only that identity can be shaped in theory, but that in particular settings it is likely to be so formed.

Appendix: Theoretical Framework

1. The use of the concept of power to explain national phenomena has been outlined and systematized by R. N. Adams (1970: 31–123). The exposition that follows is based on some points that are fundamental to understanding his theory or that, even if

not elaborated by him, will serve as a starting point for formulating my hypotheses and for examining my material (also see Adams 1973).

2. This difference between reality potential, a potential that the unit is actually proven to have, and cultural potential, a potential that the unit (or its members) thinks it or another unit has or a potential that another unit (or its members) believes that it has, is a replica of the distinction drawn by Linton (1936: 361) between cultural patterns and actual behavior, based on a "happy quality that all men have of thinking and believing one way and acting another."

3. Adams (1973: 109) deals with this issue when he speaks about the "domain of God" or the "domain of the Devil." He says, if Arturo believes that Jorge is under the control of the Devil and the Devil can do something through Jorge, then Arturo is allocating to Jorge such symbolic controls and powers. "All this is clearly a question of cultural potential." Moreover, "the researcher can never know whether Jorge is really possessed by the Devil (that is, we cannot know the reality potential)."

Even so, Adams does not give any special name to this kind of cultural potential. I have preferred to name it, because it is different than that which can be demonstrated by the researcher and because the conversion process entails a change in the attribution of that potential. So as not to change my terminology throughout the work, I have not called it "symbolic," for example.

4. This willingness to place the unit and belonging to it above anything else has to be understood within a level of confrontation. For example, belonging to a social unit (A) can entail belonging to a more comprehensive unit (C) (see Table A.1). If total loyalty is owed to unit (A) as opposed to unit (B), which is also encompassed by unit (C), it does not mean that the unit is willing to abandon (C) before abandoning (A), because (A) will not exist without (C); moreover, resistance to abandoning (A) could be the expression of resistance to abandoning (C), which that individual would abandon if he or she abandoned (A). In this case, (A) is a kind of adaptation of some individuals in (C) to the environment. Examples might include a guerrilla group facing an army squad, inasmuch as members of both units are Guatemalans; two churches (consider the sixteenth century), whose members owe them total loyalty, having members who claim to be Christians; or two religious groups whose members are all indigenous people. In these examples, it is clear, however, that the type of all-encompassing unit is different from that which directly demands total loyalty. One is made up of members who "recognize the community of sharing a behavior and also recognize that their orientation or interest is held in common and . . . they enjoy the feeling of identity . . ." (Adams 1973: 124). The others are made up of members who allocate powers in a centralized way, or the center (leader) wields independent power, or indeed the center delegates power (Adams 1973: 123). In my study I specify which type of unit is formed by converts.

5. Obviously, it is the researcher who characterizes this crisis as a liminal period. Nevertheless, for such an observer to be able to categorize it as such and distinguish it from any other crisis of adaptation, this crisis must be seen by the individual or part of his or her society as being made up of the three phases of initiation, even though this judgment may come after the crisis is past or at the time when it is overcome (for example, by a story or rite that recapitulates the crisis and in which these three phases may be found through the analysis of the researcher). This is the vision I have in mind here when I say that the individual regards such a crisis as liminal.

Bibliography

Adams, Richard N. 1956. La Ladinización en Guatemala. In *Integración social en Guatemala*, 213–244. Seminario de Integración Social Guatemalteca 3. Guatemala City: Seminario de Integración Social Guatemalteca.

———. 1970. *Crucifixion by Power*. Austin and London: University of Texas Press.

———. 1973. El poder: Sus condiciones, evolución y estrategia. *Estudios Sociales Centroamericanos* (Progama Centroamericano de Desarrollo en las Ciencias Sociales. San José, Costa Rica) 4: 65–141.

———, ed. 1957. *Political Changes in Guatemalan Indian Communities*. Middle American Research Institute Publication 24. New Orleans: Tulane University.

AGG (Archivo General del Gobierno). Archivo de Centroamérica, Guatemala City, Guatemala.

Aguirre Beltrán, Gustavo. 1971. Review of *Guatemala, una interpretación histórico-social*, by C. Guzmán Böckler and Jean Loup Herbert. *Estudios Sociales* (Instituto de Ciencias Político-Sociales, Universidad Rafael Landívar, Guatemala City) 4: 15–34.

Ascoli, Juan Fernando. 1973. San Pedro Jocopilas, un proceso histórico de dominación político-económico. Ms.

Baltodano, Emilio, Alfonso de la Cerda, and Ricardo Falla. 1970. Renovación cristiana de las costumbres indígenas del Quiché. *Estudios Centroamericanos* (Universidad José Simeón Cañas, El Salvador), no. 259: 213–219, 260, 286–300.

Barclay, George W. 1966. *Techniques of Population Analysis*. New York: John Wiley.

Cabarrús, Carlos Rafael. 1973. En la conquista del ser: Un estudio de identidad étnica. Master's thesis, Universidad Iberoamericana, Mexico City.

———. 1974. La cosmovisión K'ekchí en proceso de cambio. Cobán, Alta Verapaz: Centro San Benito. Mimeograph.

Carmack, Robert M. 1965. The Documentary Sources, Ecology, and Culture of the Prehispanic Quiché Maya of Guatemala. Ph.D. diss., University of California, Los Angeles. Ann Arbor, Mich.: University Microfilms.

———. 1972. Review of *Guatemala, una interpretación histórico-social*, by C. Guzmán Böckler and Jean Loup Herbert. *América Indígena* (Instituto Indigenista Interamericano, Mexico City) 32, no. 2: 529–556.

Colby, Benjamin, and Pierre van den Berghe. 1969. *Ixil Country*. Berkeley: University of California Press.

Constitución de la República de Guatemala. 1970. 3d ed. Collected and annotated by Héctor A. Cruz Quintana. Guatemala City: Imprenta Lito Arte.

Cortés y Larraz, Pedro. [1771] 1958. *Descripción geográfico-moral de la Diócesis de Guatemala*. Biblioteca "Goathemala" Vol. 20. Guatemala City: N.p.

Davis, Shelton H. 1970. Land of Our Ancestors: A Study of Land Tenure and Inheritance in the Highlands of Guatemala. Ph.D. diss., Harvard University.

"Declaración de Barbados." 1971. *Estudios Indígenas* (CENAPI, Mexico City) 1, no. 1: 17–23.

Dirección General de Estadística. 1968. Algunas características de la población de Guatemala, 1964. Results of manual tabulation. Guatemala City: Ministerio de Economía.

———. 1971. Censo de Población, 1964. Vol. 1. Guatemala City: Ministerio de Economía.

———. 1974. Resultados de tabulación por muestreo. Eighth census of the population, 1973. Guatemala City: Ministerio de Economía.

Douglas, William. 1968. Santiago Atitlán. In *Los pueblos del Lago de Atitlán*, 229–276. Seminario de Integración Social Guatemalteca 23.

Early, John D. 1970a. Demographic Profile of a Maya Community: The Atitecos of Santiago Atitlán. *Milbank Memorial Fund Quarterly* 48, no. 2: 167–177.

———. 1970b. The Structure and Change of Mortality in a Maya Community. *Milbank Memorial Fund Quarterly* 48, no. 2: 179–201.

———. 1974. Revision of Ladino and Maya Census Populations of Guatemala, 1950 and 1964. N.p.

Escribanía. Archivo de la Escribanía de Gobierno y Sección de Tierras, Guatemala City.

Falla, Ricardo. 1970. La conversión religiosa como fenómeno sociológico. *Estudios Sociales* (Instituto de Ciencias Político-Sociales, Universidad Rafael Landívar) 2: 7–32.

———. 1971a. Actitud de los indígenas de Guatemala en la época de la Independencia, 1800-1850. *Estudios Centroamericanos* (Universidad José Simeón Cañas, El Salvador) 278: 701–718.

———. 1971b. Juan el Gordo. Visión indígena de su explotación. *Estudios Centroamericanos* (Universidad José Simeón Cañas, El Salvador) 268: 98–107.

———. 1972a. Evolución político-religiosa del indígena rural en Guatemala (1945–1965). *Estudios Sociales Centroamericanos* (Programa Centroamericano de Desarrollo en las Ciencias Sociales, San José, Costa Rica) 1: 27–43.

———. 1972b. Hacia la Revolución Verde: Adopción y dependencia del fertilizante químico en un municipio del Quiché, Guatemala. *Estudios Sociales* (Instituto de Ciencias Político-Sociales, Universidad Rafael Landívar, Guatemala City) 6: 16–51.

———. 1973. Comercio y estratificación económica en una comunidad del Quiché, Guatemala. *Estudios Sociales* (Instituto de Ciencias Político-Sociales, Universidad Rafael Landívar, Guatemala City) 8: 69–95.

———. 1978. *Quiché rebelde: Estudio de un movimiento de conversión religiosa, rebelde a las creencias tradicionales, en San Antonio Ilotenango, Quiché (1948–1970)*. Guatemala City: Editorial Universitaria.

Flores Alvarado, Humberto. 1968. *Estructura social guatemalteca*. Guatemala City: Editorial Rumbos Nuevos.

Gillin, John. 1957. San Luis Jilotepeque: 1942–55. In *Political Changes in Guatema-*

lan Indian Communities, ed. Richard N. Adams, 23–27. Middle American Research Institute Publication 24. New Orleans: Tulane University.

———. 1958. *San Luis Jilotepeque*. Seminario de Integración Social Guatemalteca 7. Guatemala City: Seminario de Integración Social Guatemalteca.

Gómez de Parada, Juan. 1732. Auttos de la Visita de la Doctrina y Curato de San Pedro Jocopilas hecha por el Ilmo. Señor Doctor Don Juan Gómez de Parada, Obispo de Goathemala y Verapaz. Curia Archives, Guatemala City.

Goubaud Carrera, Antonio. 1959. Adaptación del indígena a la cultura nacional moderna. In *Cultura Indígena de Guatemala*, 253–263. Seminario de Integración Social Guatemalteca 1. Guatemala City: Seminario de Integración Social Guatemalteca.

Guzmán Böckler, Carlos, and Jean-Loup Herbert. 1970. *Guatemala: Una interpretación histórico-social*. Mexico City: Siglo XXI.

Guzmán Böckler, Carlos, Julio Quan, and Jean-Loup Herbert. 1971. Clases sociales y lucha de clases en Guatemala. *Alero* (Universidad de San Carlos de Guatemala), Suplemento 3.3: 6–23.

Hinshaw, Robert. 1968. Panajachel. In *Los pueblos del Lago de Atitlán*, 69–92. Seminario de Integración Social Guatemalteca 23. Guatemala City: Seminario de Integración Social Guatemalteca.

Hodara, Joseph. 1972. La juventud y el desempleo en Centroamérica. *Estudios Sociales* (Instituto de Ciencias Político-Sociales, Universidad Rafael Landívar) 7: 1–17.

Informes de Cortés y Larraz. 1769. Autos formados en razón de la Visita Jurídica y Canónica hecha por el Ilmo. S. Dn. Pedro Cortés y Larraz del Consejo de S. Majestad Arzobispo de Goathemala, al Curato de San Pedro Jocopilas. Curia Archives, Guatemala City.

La Farge, Oliver. [1940] 1959. Etnología maya: Secuencia de las culturas. In *Cultura indígena de Guatemala*, 25–42. Seminario de Integración Social Guatemalteca 1. Guatemala City: Seminario de Integración Social Guatemalteca.

Lessa, William A., and Evon Vogt, eds. 1965. *Reader in Comparative Religion*. New York: Harper and Row.

Ley Electoral y de Partidos Políticos. [1965] 1970. In *Constitución de la República de Guatemala*, 3d ed., collected and annotated by Héctor A. Cruz Quintana, 81–108. Guatemala City: Imprenta Lito Arte.

Libro de Actas de la Acción Católica de Santa Cruz Quiché. Held by secretary of Catholic Action, Santa Cruz del Quiché. Unpublished.

Libro de Actas de la Junta de San Antonio Ilotenango. 1954. Held by secretary of Catholic Action Center No. 1, San Antonio Ilotenango. Unpublished.

Libro de Actas de la Municipalidad de San Antonio Ilotenango. Held by Municipalidad, San Antonio Ilotenango. Unpublished.

Libro de Actas del Centro 5o. de Acción Católica de San Antonio Ilotenango. 1965. Held by secretary of Catholic Action Center No. 5, San Antonio Ilotenango. Unpublished.

Libro de Actas del Sub-Comité de Obras de la Parroquia de San Antonio Ilotenango. 1962. Sacristía de la Iglesia de San Antonio Ilotenango. Unpublished.

Libro de Asistencia a la Junta de San Antonio Ilotenango. 1952. Held by secretary of Catholic Action Center No. 1, San Antonio Ilotenango. Unpublished.

Libro de Asistencia del Centro 1o. de Acción Católica de San Antonio Ilotenango. 1964. Held by secretary of Catholic Action Center No. 1, San Antonio Ilotenango. Unpublished.

Libro de Asistencia del Centro 2o. de Acción Católica de San Antonio Ilotenango. 1969. Held by secretary of Catholic Action Center No. 2, San Antonio Ilotenango. Unpublished.

Libro de Asistencia del Centro 4o. de Acción Católica de San Antonio Ilotenango. 1969. Held by secretary of Catholic Action Center No. 4, San Antonio Ilotenango. Unpublished.

Libro de Caja del Sub-Comité de Obras de la Parroquia de San Antonio Ilotenango. 1969. Sacristía de la Iglesia de San Antonio Ilotenango. Unpublished.

Libro de Cofradía de Santa Ana. Sacristía de la Iglesia de San Antonio Ilotenango. Unpublished.

Libro de Cofradía del Santísimo Sacramento. Sacristía de la Iglesia de San Antonio Ilotenango. Unpublished.

Linton, Ralph. 1936. *The Study of Man.* New York and London: Appleton.

Mariñas Otero, Luis. 1958. *Las Constituciones de Guatemala: Recopilación y estudio preliminar de L. Mariñas O.* Madrid: Instituto de Estudios Políticos.

Martínez Peláez, Severo. 1971. *La patria del criollo.* Guatemala City: Editorial Universitaria.

Conclusiones del Primer Evento Continental de Misiones en América Latina en Melgar, Colombia. 1971. In *La pastoral en las misiones de América Latina.* Mexico City: Departamento de Misiones del CELAM.

Mendelson, E. Michael. 1965. *Los escándalos de Maximón.* Seminario de Integración Social Guatemalteca 19. Guatemala City: Seminario de Integración Social Guatemalteca.

Middleton, John, ed. 1967. *Gods and Rituals.* New York: Natural History Press.

Moore, G. Alexander. 1966. Social and Ritual Change in a Guatemalan Town. Ph.D. diss., Columbia University. Ann Arbor, Mich.: University Microfilms.

Nash, June. 1967. Death as a Way of Life: The Increasing Resort to Homicide in a Mexican Indian Town. *American Anthropologist* 60, no. 5: 455–470.

———. 1970. *In the Eyes of the Ancestors: Belief and Behavior in a Maya Community.* New Haven: Yale University Press.

Nash, Manning. 1957. Cantel: 1944–54. In *Political Changes in Guatemalan Indian Communities,* ed. Richard N. Adams, 28–32. Middle American Research Institute Publication 24. New Orleans: Tulane University.

———. 1958. *Machine Age Maya: The Industrialization of a Guatemalan Community.* American Anthropological Association, Memoir no. 87. Menasha, Wis.: American Anthropological Association.

Norbeck, Edward. 1961. *Religion in Primitive Society.* New York: Harper.

Noval, Joaquín. 1972. Comentarios a la visión de una estructura. Guatemala City: Instituto de Investigaciones Económicas y Sociales, Facultad de Ciencias Económicas, Universidad de San Carlos de Guatemala. Mimeograph.

Palerm, Angel. 1972. Crisis y crítica de la integración en América. *Estudios Indígenas* (CENAPI, Mexico City) 1, no. 3: 27–40.

Paul, Benjamin D. 1968. San Pedro La Laguna. In *Los Pueblos del Lago de Atitlán,* 93–158. Seminario de Integración Social Guatemalteca 23. Guatemala City: Seminario de Integración Social Guatemalteca.

Popol Vuh. 1968. In *Las antiguas historias del Quiché.* 6th ed. Translated into Spanish by Adrián Recinos. Mexico City and Buenos Aires: Fondo de Cultura Económica.

Recopilación de las Leyes de la República de Guatemala. Guatemala City.

Recopilación de las Leyes de los Reynos de Indias. 1791. Madrid.

Reina, Rubén E. 1960. *Chinautla, a Guatemalan Indian Community.* Middle American Research Institute. New Orleans: Tulane University.

———. 1966. *The Law of the Saints.* Indianapolis and New York: Bobbs Merrill.

Skinner-Klée, Jorge. 1954. *Legislación indigenista de Guatemala.* Instituto Indigenista Interamericano, Ediciones Especiales 18. Mexico City: Instituto Indigenista Interamericano.

Smith, Carol. 1972. Market Articulation and Economic Stratification in Western Guatemala. *Food Research Institute Studies in Agricultural Economics, Trade, and Development* (Stanford University, Stanford, Calif.) 11, no. 2: 203–233.

Spiro, Melford, ed. 1964. *Symposium on New Approaches to the Study of Religion.* Seattle: University of Washington Press.

Stavenhagen, Rodolfo. 1972. *Las clases sociales en las sociedades agrarias.* 4th ed. Mexico City: Siglo XXI.

Tax, Sol. 1964. *El capitalismo del centavo.* Seminario de Integración Social Guatemalteca 12. Guatemala City: Seminario de Integración Social Guatemalteca.

Tax, Sol, and Robert Hinshaw. 1970. Panajachel a Generation Later. In *The Social Anthropology of Latin America,* ed. Walter Goldschmidt and Harry Hoijer, 175–195. Latin American Studies vol. 14. Los Angeles: Latin American Center, University of California.

Torres Rivas, Edelberto. 1971. Reflexiones en torno a una interpretación histórico-social de Guatemala. *Alero* (Universidad de San Carlos de Guatemala), Suplemento 3.2: 48–58.

———. 1973. Notas sobre la crisis de la dominación burguesa en América Latina. San José, Costa Rica: Programa Centroamericano de Ciencias Sociales, Ciudad Universitaria "Rodrigo Facio." Mimeograph.

Turner, Victor W. 1967. *The Forest of Symbols.* Ithaca, N.Y.: Cornell University Press.

———. 1969. *The Ritual Process.* Chicago: Aldine.

Tzampop, Manuel. ca. 1850. Cartas copiadas y traducidas al Quiché por el Secretario Indígena Manuel Tzampop a mediados del Siglo 19. Microfilmed by Ricardo Falla; held by a resident in San Antonio Ilotenango, Guatemala.

Van Gennep, A. [1908] 1960. *The Rites of Passage.* London: Routledge and Kegan Paul.

Vásquez, Francisco. 1937. Crónica de la Provincia del Santísimo Nombre de Jesús de Guatemala de la Orden de Nuestro Seráfico Padre San Francisco (1714–1717). Biblioteca "Goathemala" Vols. 14–17. Guatemala City: N.p.

Velasco, Juan López de. 1952. Geografía y descripción universal de los indios y demarcación de los reyes de Castilla, años de 1571–1574. *Anales del Museo Nacional "David J. Guzmán"* (San Salvador) 3, no. 10: 33–62.

Wallace, Anthony F. C. 1966. *Religion: An Anthropological View.* New York: Random House.

Wolf, Eric. 1960. The Indian in Mexican Society. *Alpha Kappa Deltan* 30, no. 1.

———. 1966. *Peasants.* Englewood Cliffs, N.J.: Prentice-Hall.

Index